KU-419-956

MIGRACION VENEZUELA 177 D E X
27 JUL. 2000
114 STA. ELENA DE UAIREN S14
ENTRADA
PUESTO FTRZO.STA. ELENA de UAIREN

DEPARTMENT OF IMMIGRATION
PERMITTED TO ENTER AUSTRALIA.
on 24 APR 1996
For stay of 12 Month
SYDNEY AIRPORT 54

IMMIGRATION DIVISION BANGKOK THAILAND
A 72 DEPARTED
- 6 FEB 1998
SIGNED

IMMIGRATION & ETHNIC AFFAIRS
...... Person
30 OCT 1999
DEPARTED
AUSTRALIA
SYDNEY 32

TRAVELER'S
VENEZUELA
COMPANION

中华人民共和国 广东省公安厅

上陸許可
ADMITTED
15. FEB. 1996
Status: 4-1- 4
Duration: 90 days
NARITA(N)
Immigration Inspector
日本国

ADMITTED
20 OCT. 1998
Status: 4-1-16
Duration 180 days
Port: HANEDA
Signature

№ 011278

THE UNITED STATES
OF AMERICA
NONIMMIGRANT VISA
ISSUED AT
U.S. IMMIGRATION
170 HHW 1710
JUL 20 1998

...SSED Air Port

HONG KONG
(1038)
- 7 JUN 1997
IMMIGRATION
OFFICER

Venezuela
The 2001–2002 Traveler's Companions
ARGENTINA • AUSTRALIA • BALI • CALIFORNIA • CANADA • CHILI • CHINA • COSTA
RICA • CUBA • EASTERN CANADA • ECUADOR • FLORIDA • HAWAII • HONG KONG •
INDIA • INDONESIA • IRELAND • JAPAN • KENYA • MALAYSIA & SINGAPORE •
MEDITERRANEAN FRANCE • MEXICO • NEPAL • NEW ENGLAND • NEW ZEALAND •
NORTHERN ITALY • PERU • PHILIPPINES • PORTUGAL • RUSSIA • SOUTH AFRICA •
SOUTHERN ENGLAND • SPAIN • THAILAND • TURKEY • VENEZUELA • VIETNAM, LAOS
AND CAMBODIA • WESTERN CANADA

Traveler's VENEZUELA Companion

First published 2001
The Globe Pequot Press
246 Goose Lane, PO Box 480
Guilford, CT 06437 USA
www.globe-pequot.com

© 2001 by The Globe Pequot Press, Guilford CT, USA

ISBN: 0-7627-0364-4

Distributed in the European Union by
World Leisure Marketing Ltd, Unit 11
Newmarket Court, Newmarket Drive,
Derby, DE24 8NW, United Kingdom
www.map-guides.com

Created, edited and produced by
Allan Amsel Publishing, 53, rue Beaudouin
27700 Les Andelys, France.
E-mail: Allan.Amsel@wanadoo.fr
Editor in Chief: Allan Amsel
Editor: Anne Trager
Original design concept: Hon Bing-wah
Picture editor and designer: David Henry

ACKNOWLEDGMENTS

The publisher would like to thank Corpoturismo, Alpi Tour, Cacao Travel,
Bum Bum Tours, Gonzalo Boulton of Posada Caribana, and Patrizia Barsanti of Posada Kanosta
for their assistance to the author. Thanks are due on behalf of the author to Chris Sharpe
and Iokiñe Rodríguez, Willy and Tanya Harcourt-Cooze, Michael Derham, and
Karina Mellinger, who contributed invaluable help and advice, and to the many
other people and friends whose help has immeasurably enriched the book.

Printed by Samwha Printing Co. Ltd., Seoul, South Korea

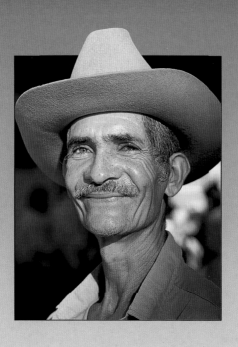

TRAVELER'S
VENEZUELA
COMPANION

by Dominic Hamilton

photographed by Anthony Cassidy

The Globe Pequot Press

GUILFORD
CONNECTICUT

Contents

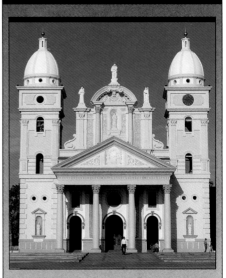

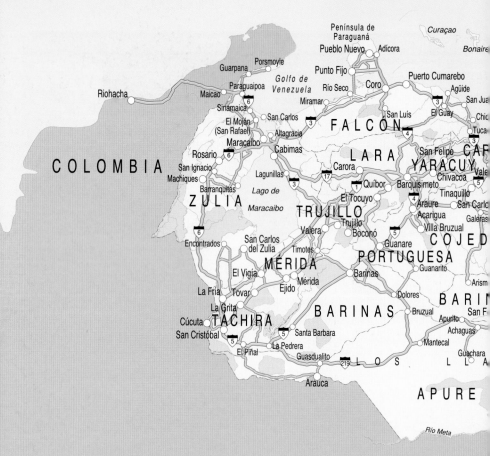
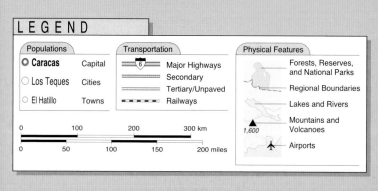

TOP SPOTS

Touch the Angel's Wings

A TOUCAN — "EEOWOOO" — STOPS US IN OUR TRACKS. It's very close. We wait for its mate to reply. "Eeowoooo, eeowoooo." The metallic cry echoes through the forest, its possible sources seeming to multiply as we listen. We stand there, peering into the forest canopy, hoping to catch sight of one of the nose-heavy birds. Then my guide Yesé grabs my arm. *"Mira,"* he says, "Look."

I turn towards the mountain, shielded by the obstinate forest. A band of ochre stretches through the trees and leaves. As the sun rises over the eastern hills, its first rays bathe the entire vertical flanks of Auyán Tepuy, the Mountain of Evil, in pure golden light.

There's no time to lose now. Like two overexcited schoolboys, we skip and scrabble up the rocks along the path through tangled roots, vines, leaves and lianas. At last we come out into the open, to a rock ledge at the foot of the mountain. There, in full view, glowing like the first gold-leaf letter of a medieval manuscript, the tallest waterfall in the world vaults from the top of the mountain. We've made it.

Angel Falls *is* the Eighth Wonder of World. It's Venezuela's most touted tourist attraction, and rightly so. The falls plunge for a near free-fall kilometer, 20 Niagaras piled atop one another. Millions of dancing droplets swirl as you gaze upon it from the lookout. After the hot walk up, it feels like an angel's wing caressing your face.

Although their name evokes some spiritual, flighty source, the falls are in fact named after a maverick bush-pilot called Jimmy Angel, who brought them to the attention of the world in 1935. Fittingly, in this land of El Dorados, he was actually searching for a "River of Gold."

In the rainy season (from early May to December), three different mouths feed its colossal serpent's plume as it chutes to the forest floor below. In the dry season, the plume becomes less distinct, forming bands of rainbows that arc at its feet. No matter what the season, bring plenty of film for your camera.

There are several ways to feast your eyes upon this wonder. The climate and your budget will decide them. For me, a boat trip is the best way to get a feel for the land of the Pemon Indians who inhabit *Tei Pun* or La Gran Sabana (The Great Savanna). Boat trips are possible only between April and December, as the river that leads to the falls, the Churún, is only navigable in the rainy season. Given the world's bizarre climate over the last years however, you might still be able to make it in January. Most trips leave from the village of Canaima and its idyllic lagoon, a five-hour boat ride away, and spend a night under a shelter close to the falls. Longer trips, which

OPPOSITE: Angel Falls vaults from the flanks of Auyán Tepuy. ABOVE: A nose-heavy toucan.

I recommend, begin in Kavak to the south of the mountain, taking you on a four-day odyssey along tea-hued rivers, visiting Pemon communities, passing the falls and ending with a cocktail in Canaima. All year round, adapted DC-3s and small planes fly tourists over the falls, from where you can snap away to your heart's content.

Beeline for the Beach

VENEZUELA CLAIMS MORE CARIBBEAN COAST THAN ANY OTHER COUNTRY IN THE REGION — 3,000 KM (1,860 MILES) OF IT. For many, the jewel in Venezuela's Caribbean crown sparkles brightest in the Los Roques Archipelago, lying just 128 km (80 miles) off its central coast. The archipelago's islands and islets, protected by a national park in 1972, bob only a short half-hour hop by plane away, but a giant leap into a marine dream world. Beneath the waves, corals and fish, sponges and anemones combine in a Technicolor dance, providing excellent snorkeling and some of the best scuba diving in the Caribbean Sea.

Since the mid-1980s, the island of Margarita, 40 km (28 miles) off the mainland and known as the "Pearl of the Caribbean," has developed into Venezuela's main international resort. Dozens of beaches to suit all tastes stretch along its coast: some long and popular such as Playa El Agua, some great for surfing like Parguito, others, Manzanillo or La Galera, perfect for paddling children.

Heading west from Caracas into Aragua State, Playa Grande by the old fishing village of Puerto Colombia arcs in a picture-perfect crescent of sand and surf. With Parque Nacional Henri Pittier's lush cloudforests, home to hundreds of species of bird, tumbling right down to its edge, you can combine beach-life with birdlife.

Deciding where to go becomes a real dilemma when you add Venezuela's two other marine national parks, Morrocoy in Falcón State and Mochima in Sucre State. Both combine corals, palms and snow-white sandy beaches, and both are easily reached from access towns on the coast: Morrocoy from the unprepossessing Tucacas or Chichiriviche; and Mochima from the lively Puerto La Cruz at its eastern extreme, or the quieter Santa Fe further west. To its already seductive attractions, Morrocoy adds the Cuare Wildlife Refuge, sanctuary to thousands of migrating flamingos, scarlet ibis and roseate spoonbills.

Playa El Agua is a long expanse of palm-fringed beach on Isla de Margarita.

As if this weren't enough, possibly the Caribbean's best kept secret, the thin fingerlike Paria Peninsula, stretches along Venezuela's extreme eastern coast, a gull's glide from the island of Trinidad. Its palm-fringed beaches are only just being discovered, with the Mediterranean-style *cabañas* of Playa Medina and Playa Pui-Puy the perfect romantic hideaway. Further east, beyond San Juan de las Galdonas, over half a dozen beaches remain utterly deserted, save for the odd fisherman. Lined by palms and backed by the steep forested hills of the Parque Nacional Península de Paria, you'll soon understand why Columbus named it the "Land of Grace."

Walk on the Wildlife Side

POISED OVER THE LUMBERING RÍO CAURA IN WESTERN BOLÍVAR STATE, binoculars in hand, I wait, in a befuddled 5 AM half-daydream. Slowly, as the sky to the east dresses in its dawn tints of pinks and mauves, the drawn-out, guttural, aspired howls, the squawks, screeches, hoots and chatter, the whoops and throaty cries of the forest prod me from my fuzzy state. And within half an hour, I've spied the howler monkey (*araguato*) hangout (the source of the guttural groans), and spotted toucans, herons, hummingbirds, two resplendent macaws and a gaggle of parakeets looking to feed on the ruffle palm, plus two blue-winged teals on their way from North America to the Amazon. I try my best to identify the species of birds from my book, but with 1,360 to choose from, it's not as easy as it sounds.

I do a better job identifying birds with expert birder Chris Sharpe in the cool, dawn mists of the Sierra de Lema in southeastern

Bolívar State. Chris translates the sounds of this giant avian auditorium. "Tepui antpitta, rose-collared piha, flutist wren," and gets very excited when we hear the loud, mechanical buzz of a scarlet-horned manakin's wings — part of its courting display.

Venezuela boasts as many species of bird as North America and Europe put together. Not only does the country play host to species found nowhere else, such as the tepui swift, the peacock coquette, the velvet-browed brilliant or the golden-tufted grackle, it also provides a haven for birds migrating across the American continent.

While birds can be impressive, for something bigger — and scarier — head to Los Llanos. Venezuela's vast network of plains, similar to Brazil's Pantanal are, without doubt, a nature-lover's dream. The waterways of the Llanos are home to families of "oversized guinea pig with webbed feet" — as one tour guide put it to me — the comic-muzzled *chigüire* or capybara, the world's largest rodent. There are turtles, occasional otters that bark from riverbanks, and scariest of all, spectacled cayman (*baba*), a smaller species of crocodile. These leathery-skinned monsters lie immobile by the water's edge, their teeth glinting, or glide along rivers like prehistoric submarines. Other mammals, which require more patience to observe, include giant anteaters, tapir and armadillos, shy ocelots and even jaguars (*tigres*). Vying with the *baba* for "most terrifying animal" status, the anaconda grows to fearful lengths of up to 12 m (36 ft).

Take to the High Wire

VENEZUELA IS A LAND OF SUPERLATIVES — SOMETIMES EVERYTHING CAN FEEL LIKE THE TALLEST THIS, THE WIDEST THAT, OR THE BIGGEST THE OTHER. The city of Mérida's *teleférico* (cable car) in the Andes boasts a double whammy: it's the longest and highest cable car in the world, carrying you to a breathtaking — and breath-inhibiting — 4,765 m (15,630 ft). To be honest, it merits a third title, since it is probably also the world's unreliablest — start praying now for all of its four stations to be open when you visit.

Even when three or sometimes only two stations function, the *teleférico* remains an absolute must for anyone venturing to the Andes. The cable car begins its 12.5-km (nearly eight-mile) high-wire act at the Barinitas station on Plaza Las Heroínas, at the eastern edge of Mérida, above the Río Chama. Cars leave every fifteen minutes. Get there

early to avoid the lines and to make the most of the clear skies, as they cloud over later in the day.

As you climb to the first station of La Montaña, at 2,400 m (7,872 ft), the verdant Chama valley, with Mérida roosting on its plateau, opens up beneath you, and you soon get used to the swing of the car. Continuing to the second stop of La Aguada at 3,452 m (11,323 ft), the car hoists you over the forest's puffy canopy to heights where hand gliders launch. Beyond this point you might begin to feel some altitude sickness (*soroche*). From La Aguada, plenty of walking or horseback riding trails lead back down the hill. But you've come this far, and the best is still to come.

The next station, Loma Redonda, nestles at 4,045 m (13,267 ft), deep in the haunting world of the *páramo* moorland, its wildflowers and unique *frailejón* (espeletia) plants in full bloom in October. Oxygen is on hand for people who begin to feel light-headed or queasy. The best thing to do is take a break between stations, go for a short walk, and take things slowly.

A short walk from Loma Redonda, cast your eyes over the obsidian-black lagoons of Los Anteojos below. To the west, a trail leads to the picture-postcard cobbled streets and whitewashed walls of Los Nevados. *Andinos* rent their mules to carry you or your luggage for the five- to six-hour journey to the village. The loop trip from Loma Redonda over to Los Nevados where you spend the night, and back to Mérida by jeep, makes for the most popular

OPPOSITE: A monkey shows off its wrestling skills in the Gran Sabana. ABOVE: Mérida's high-wire act takes to the skies above the city and the Chama valley.

excursion in the Andes. For something less strenuous, follow the trails back down from the second station, La Montaña. For more adventure, spurn the jeep from Los Nevados, and continue your hike to El Morro and the remote Pueblos del Sur.

If the *teleférico* feels generous, the station at Pico Espejo will be open, the most staggering stop of all. It seems inconceivable to travel such a great height in such a short period of time. Light-headedness from the altitude accentuates the feeling of confusion. But there you are, at 4,765 m (15,629 ft) above sea-level. As *Merideños* say: at the roof of Venezuela. Unbelievably, you're only 242 m (794 ft) short of the Pico Bolívar, Venezuela's highest (there I go again) peak. It's a three-hour hike for the equipped and fit.

Savor the Flavor

CROSS THE THRESHOLD OF MÉRIDA'S MERCADO POPULAR MARKET AND YOU ENTER VENEZUELA'S GREATEST FRUIT PALACE, surpassing any of the follies of Europe's kings and queens with one bite from a ripe, perfumed mango. The palace's courtesans include the tropical and exotic — *lechosa* (papaya), *parchita* (passion fruit), *tamarindo* (tamarind), *guayaba* (guava), *zapote* (sapodilla plum) — but also the cooler, more reserved *fresa* (strawberry), *mora* (blackberry) and *manzana* (apple).

In his travel book about Colombia, *The Fruit Palace*, Charles Nicholl crowns *guanábana* (custard apple) "the queen of fruits" — her name alone sounds majestic. If *guanábana* is the queen, then who is the king? To my mind, the answer resides in the spiky crown and prickly cloak of the *piña* (pineapple), specifically those grown in Trujillo State in the northern Andes.

If you can't make it to Mérida, don't despair. Every city and town in the country boasts a market brimming with pyramids of fruit just begging to be slit open and enjoyed on the spot. Whether you're in Cumaná, Barquisimeto, Valencia or Ciudad Bolívar, the array of produce won't fail to knock you sideways and dance a quick *gaita* on your taste buds.

If eating such lofty fruit on the hoof with a penknife offends your sensibilities, order it for breakfast at your hotel, or settle for the liquid version. On virtually every street corner, a café will sell juices, and some stores do nothing else. *Jugos*, pure fruit and sugar (Venezuelans have a sweet tooth, so ask for *"poco azúcar"*) come first, followed by *batidos* with crushed ice, and *merengadas* which add milk.

Follow El Libertador's Footsteps

IN VENEZUELA, IT DOESN'T TAKE LONG TO BECOME FAMILIAR WITH THE NAME SIMÓN BOLÍVAR. Every city, town, village and two-mule hamlet worth its salt centers on a Plaza Bolívar, with the requisite statue of the man himself — astride a steed, on foot, haranguing the masses, leading the troops, glaring stoically as if into the brilliant future, his poses only outnumbered by the myths that envelop the man who liberated half of the South American continent in the early years of the nineteenth century.

To begin at the beginning in Caracas, visit the Casa Natal where the future general, president, intellectual and Casanova was born to a wealthy landowning family on July 24, 1783. Although he never went to school, you can visit the old hacienda-cum-museum of La Cuadra Bolívar to the south of the old center. There, the young Simón received tuition from a remarkable teacher, Simón Rodríguez, and he and his friends rode horses, and no doubt played at Conquistadors 'n' Indians. Before moving on to the Quinta de Anauco, where Simón was fond of wining and dining (now the Museo de Arte Colonial replete with fantastic period furniture and furnishings), pass by the Museo Fundación John Boulton where you'll find the largest collection of Bolívar memorabilia in the country. Don't forget the Capitolio where his signed the Declaration of War to the Death against the Spanish in 1813; while in the colonial church of Santa Ana on Margarita, the now worse-for-wear chair from where he proclaimed the Third Republic in 1816 enjoys pride of place.

The dubious fame of "the town where the Liberator died of tuberculosis, exiled, penniless and disillusioned" goes to Santa Marta on the Colombian coast.

Discover Ancient Ways

EXPLORING VENEZUELA'S REMOTE RAINFOREST OR SAVANNA REGIONS, AND MEETING ITS INDIGENOUS PEOPLE, can be one of the most rewarding and fascinating experiences in the country. I fell in love with the Gran Sabana region in the southeast many years ago and continue to be spellbound not only by its natural beauty, but also by the rich and intriguing language and heritage of the Pemon who inhabit it.

Towns like Puerto Ayacucho (Amazonas State), Tucupita (Delta Amacuro State), Santa Elena de Uairén or Ciudad Bolívar (Bolívar State) now boast a number of professional operators offering a range of tours to the rivers, jungles and plains of "Orinoquia." With their help, taking a step back from the modern world to a time a million light years away from your normal life is as easy as winding the hands on a clock. Whether you're approaching Cerro Autana (the Tree of Life to the local Piaroa) south of Puerto Ayacucho, off-roading in a jeep across the savannas of Parque Nacional Canaima while mesa mountains puncture the horizon, or weaving your way through channels to the Warao Indians' houses built on stilts in the Orinoco Delta, the experience could be the highlight of your trip.

Venezuela's indigenous people make up only about one percent of the country's population. At first enslaved or murdered by the Conquistadors, then decimated by European diseases, those who survived did so by fleeing to the more remote parts of the country, or by living in areas in which even the gold-lusty Spaniards had no interest. The Guajiro of Zulia State, still fiercely independent, their territory straddling the Venezuela–Colombia border, form the largest population. The other important groups all live south of the Orinoco, either in the

most famous portraits hang, or the Iglesia San Francisco where Bolívar was declared *El Libertador* in 1813. The church also hosted his official state funeral in 1842. To complete the tour, head north to the Panteón Nacional, where around the clock guards protect his polished bronze sarcophagus, installed in 1876.

It would be impossible to follow the Liberator's life in strict chronological order. He was exiled in Jamaica and London during the early years of the wars of independence, but perhaps your enthusiasm does not stretch that far. But throughout the country you'll find his footsteps. They range from seminal events such as the Battle of Carabobo outside Valencia, which broke the back of the Royalist cause in 1821, to banal "the Liberator spent a night here" plaques in the much-forgotten town of Carora in Lara State. Bolívar, described by a Spanish general as "a little man on a mule" — he was only 1.65 m (5'6") — nevertheless dominates Venezuela's history, and overshadows its geography.

In Ciudad Bolívar on the Orinoco River, in the mansion by the cathedral, he proposed a new constitution and his project for the super-nation of Gran Colombia (comprising present-day Venezuela, Panama, Colombia and Ecuador). In the freezing, high Andes, his army marched to liberate Caracas for the first time, and the Monumento al Águila commemorates the event. In Trujillo, also in the Andes, the Museo de Historia displays a table where he

LEFT: "El Libertador" Simón Bolívar gazes into a bright future which wasn't to be. ABOVE: A Pemon Indian woman from the Gran Sabana carries wood in her *guayare* woven rucksack.

jungle lodges where you can strike out into W. H. Hudson's "Green Mansions" to be dazzled by the plants, trees, insects, birds and fauna of the forest. With a knowledgeable, preferably Indian guide by your side, the experience becomes all the more enriching as you learn about medicinal plants or the interrelationships of living things, as well as traditional beliefs, languages and societies. I believe if you imagine what *you* would feel like if Indians "dressed funny" came barging through your garden and into your living room, and proceeded to stare at you and photograph you, then you'll know how to approach the people of Venezuela's most remote regions.

Uncover Historical Heritage

ALL-BUT ABANDONED BY A SPANISH CROWN more concerned with the riches of the Inca and Aztec empires or the silver of Potosí, and ravaged by successive earthquakes, it's a miracle any historical architecture remains in Venezuela at all. But fit in a trip to Coro in Falcón State, as you travel west to the Andes perhaps, and even travelers who have wandered the streets of Cuzco in Peru, or climbed the cobbles of Salvador de Bahía in Brazil, will be pleasantly surprised. Declared a UNESCO World Heritage Site 1993, Coro's museums, shaded squares, elegant overhanging balconies and cobbled streets leave little doubt as to why it was honored.

The capital of Venezuela in the sixteenth century, the town benefited from a flourishing and mostly illegal trade with the Dutch Antilles over the centuries, and its architecture reflects the tastes of the Dutch merchants. The cathedral, big, bold and old, lies at the center of the town, but the small, unassuming yet charming churches of San Clemente and San Nicolás de Bari are the real jewels for me. Also not to be missed in Coro, the Museo Diocesano displays the finest collection of religious art and artifacts in the country. The restored Casa de las Ventanas de Hierro, which has stayed in the same family for generations, is home to the idiosyncratic Museo de Tradición Popular.

But Coro is just the beginning of a ride through the centuries from one end of Venezuela to the next. Along the central coast, villages living in constant fear tucked themselves up in the hills to escape raids by

rainforests of Amazonas, the rivers and plains of western Bolívar, amid the mesa mountains of the Gran Sabana, or in the snaking channels of the Orinoco Delta in Delta Amacuro.

In 1999, the country's new Constitution awarded its indigenous people rights to their "habitats," their ancestral lands recognized for the first time. It's still too early to know what benefits they will draw from their new legal rights. Tourism, as in other parts of the Amazon Basin, can be a double-edged sword for these remote communities. While our curiosity as travelers drives us to learn more about them, to find out how they live and think, many communities haven't been given the choice. Although they welcome the money which tourists bring — it allows them to buy medical supplies, teaching aids, outboard motors or tools — contact with tourists inevitably causes cultural erosion, and ushers in changes not always anticipated. Sadly, in a similar scenario to the Amerindian peoples of North America, the effect of strong liquor has devastated some communities. It is therefore important to choose a responsible tour operator or to stay in a lodge with an equitable relationship with the local Indians. Even better, seek out the operators or humble homes run by the Indians themselves: Iwana Meru Tours in Ciudad Bolívar, Roraima Tours in San Francisco de Yuruaní, the community of El Paují on the Brazilian border, or Mawadianojodo in the Upper Orinoco.

Venezuela hosts a number of excellent

ABOVE: A Pemon boy mends the thatch of his family's *churuata*. RIGHT: San Clemente church in Coro, Falcón, dates from the eighteenth century.

pirates and corsairs during the colonial period. The painted ceiling of the church and the dappled square of Choroní in Aragua State present two of the finest examples of these early settlements.

If you wonder why it took so long to expel the Spanish from Venezuela — over 10 years — look no further than the colossal walls of their forts. They took their investment *that* seriously. Fine examples include the most costly in the Spanish colonies, monolithic Santiago León de Araya, surveying from its heights the surreal salt-flats on the arid Península de Araya in Sucre State. Reach the fort by a bouncy motorboat ride from Cumaná, which also boasts wraparound views from its *castillo*. On Margarita, the two star-shaped forts of Castillo de San Carlos Borromeo in Pampatar and Castillo de Santa Rosa in La Asunción defended the colony's early pearl-rush from prying pirates and foreign powers, while Puerto Cabello (Carabobo State), recognized early on as a perfect harbor and port, defended its goods and mansions with two grandiose forts, San Felipe and the later Solano. The town is now enjoying some long overdue attention from restorers.

In the Andes, some villages offer not only historical sights, but also a living museum of traditional ways. Fields are still tilled by hand or oxen-drawn plough, mules provide transportation, and religious rituals and festivals are seriously observed. Although some stretches of the *Transandina* highway, which snakes its way through Venezuela's ranges, have become too touristy in my opinion, it only takes a little taste for adventure, perhaps a rental car or jeep and some imagination for you to enter a time-warp world.

The towns and villages of the Pueblos del Sur south of Mérida are among the most famous, with Pueblo Nuevo and San José the most appealing and accessible. In Táchira State, you'll find the dinky, coffee-growing Peribeca, El Topón, Rubio and Santa Ana close to the capital San Cristóbal. While in Trujillo State, San Miguel, Barbusay and Santa Ana all lie just off the highway between Boconó and Trujillo (a preferred route up to the Andes from the Llanos). All of these pockets of cobbles, whitewashed walls, colonial churches and humble locals reside in another world from the "Saudi Venezuela" image so often painted of the country.

In Oriente (eastern Venezuela), although you wouldn't have thought it today, elegant *doñas* in their finery once promenaded the avenues alongside European trams in Carúpano (Sucre State). At the now restored Casa del Cable, the first Trans-Atlantic cable connected the New World to Marseille in France in 1895, conveying the all-important prices of cacao. Further east, the square in Carúpano's poorer cousin, Río Caribe, has changed little since the Gran Cacao families of Venezuela's oligarchy as good as abandoned it when the oil boom began in the 1920s. On Sunday evenings, the whole town gathers for mass, as it has done for centuries.

Stepping further back in time, the Fundación de Etnomusicología y Folklor museum in Caracas, the ethnological and anthropological museums of Puerto Ayacucho and Maracaibo, the Museo Arqueológico of Quíbor (south of Barquisimeto in Lara State), and the Museo Etnográfico de Guayana in Ciudad Bolívar, showcase indigenous cultures, with scale models of Indian architecture and examples of ceramics, woodwork, instruments, jewelry, and handicrafts.

LEFT: The cobbles, tiles and church of the typical Andean pueblo of Jajó, Trujillo. ABOVE: The pink and white wedding-cake front to the Virgen del Valle church on Isla de Margarita.

The Great Outdoors

The scale and diversity of Venezuela's natural bounty comes as a surprise to many people. Even more surprising is how few foreign tourists visit the country. While Costa Rica receives some 15 million foreigners every year, eager to enjoy its ecotourism opportunities, barely a million reach Venezuelan shores. Incredible when you consider most of Costa Rica could fit inside Parque Nacional Canaima, Venezuela's largest park — the size of Belgium or Maryland. And all the more striking when you discover the variety of ecosystems this northern South American country harbors.

Venezuela boasts nine biogeographical regions in all: the Andes, the coastal cordillera system, the islands and archipelagos, the plains of the Llanos, the Orinoco Delta and the four subregions south of the Orinoco. These include the plateaus of the Guayana Highlands (La Gran Sabana) and the rainforest systems of the Upper Orinoco basin. Few other countries pack such a varied and diverse ecological punch.

Since establishing its first national park in 1937, Venezuela has protected over 140,000 sq km (54,600 sq miles) — an area equivalent to the state of Illinois and larger than England — some 15% of its national territory. The national parks are administered by the **Instituto Nacional de Parques** (called Inparques) ((02) 285-4106 or (02) 285-4259 FAX (02) 285-3070 WEB SITE www.marnr.gov.ve/inparques/inparque.htm, with limited, and often mismanaged funds. Some parks such as those close to Caracas (El Ávila, Guatopo and Henri Pittier) or Canaima and Sierra Nevada, boast good infrastructure, including cleared trails, cabins and organized campsites, and knowledgeable *guardaparques* (park wardens). Others, including Península de Paria, Sierra de San Luís or Sierra de La Culata, are pretty much left to their own devices. Sadly, with little means of enforcing regulations or controls, in some cases they are little more than "paper parks."

Miro Popic's *Ecotourism Guide to Venezuela* (Caracas: Miro Popic Editor, 1998) details the country's parks' main attractions, as well as access and accommodation. It also includes a useful ecological calendar produced by the Audubon; see WEB SITE www.miropopic.com (*Guía Ecoturística*).

BIRD WATCHING
Birders have long discovered Venezuela. The **Venezuela Audubon Society** ((02) 992-3268 or (02) 992-2812 FAX (02) 991-0716

LEFT: The fertile, undulating hills of Trujillo State in the Andes. ABOVE: A resplendent macaw, a common sight and always seen flying in pairs.

WEB SITE www.audubonvenezuela.org, Edificio Matisco, Pisol, Calle Veracruz, Las Mercedes, Caracas, was established as early as 1970. They work tirelessly to promote and protect not only the country's stunning birdlife, but all of its wildlife and environments. One of its most active members, Mary Lou Goodwin, published the bird-watching bible to the country, *Birding in Venezuela* (Caracas: Editorial La Brújula, 1997, fourth edition), with excellent practical information about the best spots but also details of lodging and eating possibilities. A *Guide to the Birds of Venezuela* by Rodolphe Meer de Schauensee and William H. Phelps (New Jersey: Princeton University Press, 1978) provides the definitive list of species.

Probably the king of the birding parks is Parque Nacional Henri Pittier west of Caracas, where the Portachuelo Pass, a dip in the Cordillera de la Costa mountain range, affords a migratory highway for hundreds of species. The Audubon organize regular tagging sessions where volunteers are welcome. They can also put you in touch with the best guides or tour operators.

While the forests of the Cordillera, whose spine arcs all the way round Venezuela from the Andes to the Paria Peninsula, make for wonderful opportunities, Venezuela's numerous coastal lagoons, such as Tacarigua, La Restinga (Margarita), and Cuare present ideal means to float along waterways, binoculars at the ready.

The Llanos plains also host an abundance of good birding spots, with over 300 species recorded. The dry season months make for the best multicolored displays of ibis, heron and roseate spoonbills. **Hato El Frío** (also known as Estación Biológica El Frío) ((014) 743-5329 or (047) 81223 (in Achaguas) E-MAIL elfrio@cantv.net, and the onetime ranch of the Rockefeller family, **Hato El Cedral** ((02) 781-8995 FAX (02) 793-6032 E-MAIL hatocedral@cantv.net WEB SITE www.hatocedral.com, Avenida La Salle, Edificio Pancho, Piso 5 PH, Los Caobos, Caracas, are among the popular birder haunts.

Providing access to the bird-rich forests of Imataca and the Sierra de Lema in Bolívar State, birders make a beeline for Henry Cleve's *posada*, **Barquilla y Fresa** (book through the Audubon, above), on the road to the Gran Sabana.

When the wildflowers of the moorlands (called *páramos*) of the Andes blossom in October, these otherwise bleak landscapes hum with busying birds, including high-altitude hummingbirds. Perhaps the greatest treat however is a visit to the **Mifafí Condor**

Center near Apartaderos to learn about the program to reintroduce the graceful condor to Venezuela.

HIKING

With over 40 national parks and "natural monuments" to choose from, your new boots will look decidedly worn by the end of your vacation. Hit the trails in the Andes, entering the Parque Nacional Sierra Nevada by Mérida's *teleférico*, from La Mucuy near Tabay, or from near Mucuchíes. Highlights include the glacial lagoons in the north of the park, the stone chapel of Juan Félix Sánchez in El Potrero, and the hot springs and *páramos* within the Parque Nacional Sierra de La Culata. Of Mérida's main tour operators, **Arassari Trek & Bum Bum Tours** (/FAX (074) 525879 E-MAIL info@arassari.com WEB SITE www.arassari.com and http://jvm.com/

bumbum/, Calle 24 off Plaza Las Heroínas, have some very good naturalists and experienced guides on their books.

Of the coastal parks, numerous fairly well-marked trails crisscross Henri Pittier. **Cacao Travel Group** ((02) 977-1234 FAX (02) 977-0110 E-MAIL cacaotravel@cantv.net WEB SITE www.cacaotravel.com and the **Audubon** (see above) both offer excellent hiking or trekking tours in the park, with lodges in the pretty colonial village of Choroní or in Puerto Colombia on the coast.

Península de Paria, at Venezuela's eastern extreme, retains plenty of untouched muddy cloudforest trails. Entering from the south, you emerge from the forest at paradisiacal beaches on the Caribbean. What better way to wash off the sweat of a four-hour hike? The soft sandy beaches, thankfully still Venezuela's best kept secret, provide the nesting grounds for large numbers of endangered marine turtles. For information about **turtle watching** on the coast, contact Encuentro Paria (see below).

Tours of the park are best arranged through local *posada* owners. Among the most knowledgeable guides in the area, and an intriguing man to boot, Klaus Müller runs a pioneering lodge, **Campamento Vuelta Larga** (/FAX (094) 69052 E-MAIL vueltalarga@cantv.net, near El Pilar. Also in Paria, the omnipresent **Encuentro Paria** ((094) 315241 FAX (094) 313021 E-MAIL playamed@telcel.net.ve, Avenida Independencia, Carúpano, manage a series of beach cabañas, a water buffalo ranch, thermal springs, and an old cacao hacienda. They can

The country's tallest mountains, Bolívar and Humboldt, bare their incisor peaks in the high Andes.

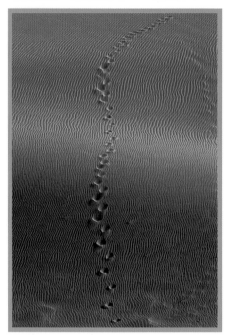

Wonken, in the heart of the savanna and seldom visited, while close to the unique frontier community of El Paují on the Brazilian border, settlers from the cities or local Pemon guide you through the forests and savanna to some wonderful sights.

Of Venezuela's numerous caves, the longest courses through the mountains of the Sierra de Perijá in Zulia State (Cueva del Samán), though the most famous cave in the country burrows into the hills of Monagas State: the Cueva del Guácharo, home to the country's largest colony of the unique *guácharo* (oilbird). **Spelunking** is best organized through the members of the Venezuelan Speleological Society ((02) 730-6436 or (02) 272-0724 E-MAIL rafaelcarreno@hotmail.com or urbani@cantv.net.

Sporting Spree

If you've hiked the trails of Henri Pittier, or trekked the paths of Sierra Nevada, but need some adrenaline to complete your vacation, Venezuela doesn't disappoint. Adventure tourism has grown in leaps and bounds over the last years. The potential is still massive, and infrastructure will doubtless increase in the next decade. For now, the capital of adventure lies in Mérida in the Andes, with an array of activities on offer, and the operators to facilitate them (see under MÉRIDA, page 155, for details on paragliding, mountaineering and whitewater rafting).

SCUBA DIVING

With the longest coastline in the Caribbean, it's no surprise to find attractive scuba diving options in Venezuela. With three marine national parks (Los Roques, Mochima and Morrocoy) protecting its reefs, not only is diving comparatively economical in Venezuela, it's among the best in the Caribbean, rivaling Belize or the Cayman Islands. Due to the variety and number of the country's reefs, beginners and experienced divers alike come away delighted. You can expect dramatic drop-offs, forests of Technicolor corals, thermal springs, gulf walls, caverns and old shipwrecks. Sharks, turtles, barracuda, rays, angelfish, parrotfish, snapper and butterflies abound.

King of the dive locales, the **Los Roques Archipelago** off the central coast rules for its variety of corals and number of fish encountered. Sesto Continente ((02) 731-1507 WEB SITE www.scdr.com, based on Gran Roque island, is the only company to provide dive services and courses. For live-aboard yachts

arrange all sorts of tours of the region. For birding and hiking, Billy Esser and his family's **Hacienda Bukare** ((094) 652003 FAX (094) 652004 E-MAIL bukare@cantv.net WEB SITE http://think-venezuela.net/bukare/, south of Río Caribe, is one of the friendliest lodges in the area.

And then there's Canaima, along with the Sierra Nevada, king of Venezuela's adventure parks. Although most people visit the park to feast their eyes on Angel Falls, reached by river in the rainy season and by small plane in the dry, more adventurous hikers can discover its hundreds of waterfalls, sylvan pools and tea-tinted rivers. A growing number of operators, including the competent **Cacao Travel Group** (see above) arrange the demanding hike up the Auyán mountain, from where Angel Falls plunges, starting from the hamlet of Kavak. The hike can also be attempted independently by bringing your own food and contracting a local Pemon Indian as a guide.

The eastern sector of Canaima, reached by the Highway 10 leading to Brazil, presents a tapestry of trails to blaze. To the southeast, fit travelers embark on the six-day trek up to the lunarscape atop Mount Roraima, the highest of the mesa mountains (called *tepuys*) of the Gran Sabana. The trek is regarded as one of South America's finest. But you can also head off into the savanna at any number of points. From San Francisco de Yuruaní, a three-day trail heads west to the mission village of

contact Alpi Tour ((02) 283-1433 FAX (02) 285-6067 FAX IN THE UNITED STATES (520) 447-7959 E-MAIL alpitour@viptel.com WEB SITE www.alpi-group.com.

Some of the sites suit more experienced divers, though Boca del Medio, only 10 m (33 ft) in depth but nonetheless teeming with fish and pristine corals, makes a great beginners' dive. Of the other sites scattered throughout the islands and islets of the archipelago, Dos Mosquises, with its turtle-breeding research center, and the shipwrecks near Nordisquí are my personal picks, but you could add the vertical cliffs off Cayo Sal or the labyrinths of Nordisquí to the list, and still not exhaust the possibilities. Add the deserted and pristine La Tortuga island, north of Los Roques, in case you run out of options.

The shallows and sandy bottoms of **Morrocoy**, west of Caracas in Falcón State, are regarded as the best venue for beginners, with good dives off Cayo Sombrero and Cayo Borracho. Contact the experienced Mike Osborn of Submatur ((042) 830082 FAX (042) 831051, Calle Ayacucho No. 6, Tucacas, or multilingual Pierre and Monika of Agua-Fun Diving ((042) 86265 E-MAIL aguafun@cantv.net WEB SITE http://ourworld.compuserve.com/homepages/pierreclaude, in Chichiriviche. Both enjoy good reputations and also offer PADI and NAUI courses.

Mochima, the marine national park stretching between Puerto La Cruz in Anzoátegui State and Cumaná in Sucre State, offers some great deep-water dives, though waters are colder than elsewhere in the country. Dolphins are numerous, and whales have also been spotted. If you want to combine sophisticated hotels, nightlife and divelife, head to Puerto La Cruz where several companies organize trips to the nearby reefs, among them the Scuba Divers Club (/FAX (081) 635401, based in the Bahía Redonda Marina, Avenida Tajamar, El Morro, east of the town. For something more relaxed, and less luxurious, two *posadas* in the traveler-friendly Santa Fe, Playa Santa Fe Resort and Dive Center (/FAX (014) 733-3777 E-MAIL santaferesort@telcel.net.ve WEB SITE www.santaferesort.com, and Siete Delfines ((016) 638-5668 E-MAIL dolphins@telcel.net.ve WEB SITE www.emergente.com.ve/sietedelfines, offer combined lodging and diving packages.

One of the best dives on **Margarita Island**, El Farallón near Pampatar, includes a religious statue among the brain corals and sea fans. However, you should head further afield for the best diving off the "Pearl of the Caribbean": Los Frailes, a cluster of islands to the northeast, and Los Testigos are only just being discovered by divers and offer sites comparable to Los Roques. Contact Centro de

OPPOSITE: Footprints march across the *médanos* dunes in Coro, Falcón State. ABOVE: Two-up among the *fralejón* and rugged terrain of the Andes.

Buceo Pablo Montoya ((095) 644746 E-MAIL cbpablom@cantv.net, which runs PADI, NAUI and CMAS courses, or Enomis' Divers (/FAX (095) 622977 E-MAIL enomis@telcel.net.ve WEB SITE http://members.xoom.com/ enomisdivers, in the Hotel Margarita Dynasty.

For all sorts of information regarding scuba diving in Venezuela, and elsewhere, see WEB SITE www.scubayellowpages.com.

SAILING

Yachts seeking a safe haven from the Caribbean hurricane season find welcome refuge along Venezuela's coast. With so much coast to explore, and ever-improving infrastructure, the country is fast becoming a popular destination with the yachting set. The greatest concentration of marinas and yachting facilities are found in Anzoátegui State's El Morro and Puerto La Cruz developments.

El Morro, a vast project initiated in the 1980s, continues to expand. With its various marinas, luxury resorts, shopping malls and classy restaurants, it's *the* place to head for on Venezuela's Caribbean. The country's largest regatta, the **South Caribbean Ocean Regatta** takes place every year, usually in August. For yachties, the Centro Marino de Oriente ((081) 677011 FAX (081) 678550 E-MAIL cmoplc2@ telcel.net.ve, Avenida Tajamar No. 8 (on the northeast side), has the most modern facilities of the three marinas in El Morro.

If you're a group of four or more, chartering a yacht to cruise the islands of **Mochima**, or to head east to **Los Roques**, can be more economical than you might think. Dockside (/FAX (081) 677344 E-MAIL dockside @telcel.net.ve, Marina Bahía Redonda, El Morro, is a very organized local tour, travel and yacht agent, within the marina. They can help you charter the right yacht for your needs. Another recommended local company for sailing charters is Nelson & Nelson ((081) 778232 or (014) 802232, run by Nelson Lozada in the Américo Vespucio Marina.

Several yacht charters on **Margarita Island** are also tempting. Day trips to the islands of Coche and Cubagua to the south, with their quieter, beautiful beaches, can be arranged through Viola Turismo ((095) 630715 or Octopus ((095) 611535, in the Margarita Hilton.

Accommodation on Los Roques can get quite expensive if you're a group of more than four. Chartering a yacht for a few days in order to explore the islands can save you money. Contact Alpi Tour (see above) who can offer a range of packages.

OTHER WATER SPORTS

Generally speaking, the major beach resorts of Margarita and Puerto La Cruz offer an abundance of water sports. Margarita especially teems with hotels and beach concessions providing jet skis, banana boats, parasailing, windsurfers and catamarans. These can be quite pricey.

If you bring your own board with you, **surfing** in Venezuela may not be Hawaii but it will keep you smiling through your vacation. On Margarita, surf dudes head for Playa Guacuco and Playa Parguito. On the mainland, Playa Cuyagua north of Maracay across Parque Nacional Henri Pittier draws plenty of surfers.

One of the top locations in the world for **windsurfing**, El Yaque on Margarita's southern coasts boasts howling winds all year-round, strongest from November to March. Its annual regatta, attracting windsurfers from all over the world, is held in May. For a windsurfer's perspective see WEB SITE www.crocker.com/~barnett/guide.html. Not only are the winds intense, the accommodation and nightlife is first-class, making it a great place to come even if you're not a windsurfer. Rivaling El Yaque on the mainland, winds at Adícora, on the east coast of the "giant's head" Península de Paraguaná in Falcón State, also howl. Accommodation and sail rental is available at Windsurf Adícora ((069) 88224 WEB SITE www.adicora.com.

FISHING

Along with birders, in the last decade anglers have begun to flock to Venezuela. Off the central coast from **La Guaira**, the deep waters make for exhilarating bill fishing. The best months for marlin are February to May and September to November, while you can fish for yellowfin tuna, wahoo, snook and tarpon year-round. The annual La Guaira Bonefish Shootout takes place in April every year. One of the operators with the most experience is Venezuela Marlin Safari ((02) 394-8868 FAX (02) 394-4078 E-MAIL marlinsafari@ cantv.net, with its offices within the Hotel Gran Caribe.

Inland, serious anglers keen on catching the weighty peacock bass or *payara* in the **Llanos** book into to the Cinaruco Bass Lodge (reservations through Alpi Tour). In the **Andes**, trout were introduced to many glacial lakes around Mérida; local tour operators can arrange for transportation and advise you on

Cardón cactus fingers its way to the sky along the roadside in the Andes.

the best spots. The trout season runs from mid-March through September.

Fishing permits must be acquired through the Ministerio de Agricultura y Cría (Agriculture and Livestock Ministry) in Caracas ((02) 576-0067. The offices occupy the tenth floor of the Torre Este in Parque Central.

MOUNTAIN BIKING

As fans of two-wheeled adventures know, a cyclist's real enemy is wind, not hills. The **Andes** aren't short on hills. Among the best routes, biking the back-roads of the Pueblos del Sur south of Mérida or the trails from Apartaderos (north down to Timotes, or south down to Mérida) have cyclists scribbling postcards home. **Bum Bum Tours** (/FAX (074) 525879 E-MAIL info@arassari.com WEB SITE www.arassari.com and http:// jvm.com/bumbum/, Calle 24 off Plaza Las Heroínas, Mérida, rents bikes in good condition and can advise you on other excellent circuits.

Elsewhere in the country, finding a bike rental company can be more problematic. In **Coro**, Posada El Gallo ((068) 529481, Calle Federación No 26, run by the Frenchman Éric and his Venezuelan wife, rents bikes and shows you routes through the colonial villages and cool hills of the delightful Sierra de San Luís, south of the town.

In **Paria**, the friendly Arlet of La Posada de Arlet (/FAX (094) 61290 E-MAIL cristjose @cantv.net WEB SITE http://think-venezuela .net/arlet/, on the corner of Calle 24 de Julio in Río Caribe, also rents bikes, an excellent move considering the lack of public transportation to the wonderful beaches nearby.

The hills around the **Cueva del Guácharo** — known as *El Jardín del Oriente* (The Garden of the Orient) — make for some great biking territory, plus they're refreshingly cool. With the numerous restaurants dotted along the roads, and some great *agriturismo posadas* in the area, a bike offers plenty of freedom. Contact Trekking Travelers Tours ((092) 51352 FAX (092) 51843, Calle Guzmán Blanco, Caripe.

HORSEBACK RIDING

Venezuela's mythical heart lies in the plains and horsemen of Los Llanos — though cynics would argue it's more in the beaches and boutiques of Miami. Ever since the *Llanero* cavalry played such a pivotal role in the War of Independence, the cowboy — rugged, resourceful and romantic — has occupied pride of place in the country's pantheon of heroes.

Look no further than the **Llanos** for great adventures on horseback. Many of the *hatos* (ranches) scattered throughout the plains states offer riding tours of their lands, making a far better alternative to the open-sided safari trucks usually employed. On horseback, you can get much closer to the abundant wildlife and feel far more in tune with the natural environment of the plains. After days spent in the saddle you'll also understand why the *Llaneros* are so tough. The dry season offers the best opportunities for both exploring and wildlife spotting. The 80,000-hectare (200,000-acre) Hato El Piñero boasts some of the best horses in the region, but you could also contact Las Churuatas de Capanaparo, which enjoys privileged access to Parque Nacional Cinaruco-Capanaparo.

In many towns throughout the **Andes**, local *Andinos* rent mules and small *criollo* horses for day-trips. Spend an afternoon exploring the hills around Jají; take a mule over the hills from the Loma Redonda *teleférico* station to the village of Los Nevados; or rent a horse to meander the trails close to Laguna Mucubají. For better quality animals, it's best to contact one of the specialized *fincas* around Mérida which offer larger horses and professional guide services. Contact the competent José Luís Troconis of Natoura

Adventure Tours ((074) 524216 FAX (074) 524075 E-MAIL natoura@telcel.net.ve WEB SITE www.natoura.com, also on Calle 24, Plaza Las Heroínas, Mérida.

Over on **Margarita**, the westerly Macanao Peninsula makes for some fantastic riding, but trails also exist throughout the inland villages of the main peninsula. The landscapes of Macanao, arid and cactus-covered, are as dramatic as the heat is unforgiving. Take a tour early in the morning or in the evening and enjoy some rides along the near-deserted beaches of the southern shores. Rancho Negro ((095) 423197 (014) 995-1103/995-1018 E-MAIL ranchonegro@veweb.com WEB SITE www .veweb.com/ranchonegro, based near La Asunción, have years of experience, while Cabatucan ((016) 681-9348 FAX (095) 617259 WEB SITE http://cabatucan.freeyellow.com/ index.html lies close to Boca de Río on Macanao.

For some wonderful riding in the cool hills of the **Sierra de San Luís** above Coro, contact the *posada* La Soledad (/FAX (014) 690-8889, which enjoys superb views. It is run by two brothers who know the area's wonders like the backs of their hands. In Paria, explore the forests, colorful villages, cacao haciendas and unsurpassed beaches with the people of **Ruta del Cacao** ((014) 994-0115, just south of Río Caribe.

SPECTATOR SPORTS

Venezuela's greatest spectator sport is *beisball* (baseball), brought over by the oil workers in the early twentieth century. Fans follow the highs and lows of the World Series and Venezuelan players with a passion, but also their home league, who play from October to February. The two biggest teams are Caracas' *Leones* and Valencia's *Magallanes*. Their rivalry is legendary, and the noise-level in the 20,000-seat Universidad Central only comparable to an Italian soccer derby.

Basketball is also big in Venezuela; the season runs from March to July. More interesting from a foreigner's point of view are the traditional **bullfights** held throughout the country. Valencia's ring is second only to Mexico city's in size, while Maracay's "Sevillan" *La Maestranza* arena makes for a wonderful show. The biggest events are held during celebration of Maracay's patron saint San José in March, and during San Cristóbal's huge *Feria de San Sebastián* in January. In Caracas, bullfights take place every Sunday afternoon at the Plaza de Toros Nuevo Circo, between November and March.

OPPOSITE: An open-top safari jeep tours the back-roads of the Llanos. BELOW: The passive crowd at San Cristóbal's annual *feria*.

The Open Road

With the largest reserves of oil in the Western Hemisphere, it comes as little surprise that gas in Venezuela is among the cheapest in the world. Although car or jeep rental prices are comparable to those in the United States, by taking advantage of the "three-for-the-price-of-two-days" specials many car rental firms promote, with unlimited mileage and air-cheap gas, it becomes altogether too tempting to spend a bit more on private transportation.

Not so tempting may be Venezuelans' driving. Although we're not talking about battling across Kashmir or negotiating the streets of Delhi perhaps, Venezuela can still be a demanding country to drive in. While many automobiles are slick and shiny four-by-fours (Cherokees, Jeeps and Toyotas), driven at high speeds by apparently important people in a hurry, the rest of the country still bumps along in clapped-out old Chevys, Mavericks and Dodges at 60 km/h (40 mph). With no rail transportation, convoys of trucks are common. This leads to a two-speed confrontation which, with mainly two-lane highways crossing the country, sometimes ends in tears.

But don't be put off. Compared to the roads of say Bolivia or Ecuador, Venezuela's asphalt is in extremely good condition, and you can't beat the feeling of satisfaction drawn from independent exploration. The signs in Venezuela may not be up to much, but with a copy of Miro Popic's *Guía Vial de Venezuela* (Caracas: Miro Popic Editor, 1998) by your side, you'll be fine (see also GETTING AROUND, page 270 in TRAVELERS' TIPS).

ITINERARIES

To my mind, the whole point of renting a vehicle is to enjoy sights and roads that public transportation renders too complicated or fleeting. One drive, west from **Caracas to the beaches of Parque Nacional Henri Pittier**, is a case in hand. To begin, head down to the coast at La Guaira, and turn west along the coast road to Chichiriviche de la Costa. From there, the road winds through the overhanging forest to the anomalous Colonia Tovar, the colony founded in the 1840s by immigrants from the Black Forest in Germany. Spend the night in one of the alpine-styled lodges.

From Tovar, you can link up with the highway heading west from Caracas to Maracay. From Maracay's northern suburb of Las Delicias, take the sinuous road built by convicts under the rule of dictator Gómez.

It's one of the most hair-raising and dramatic in the country, coursing through the wonderful cloudforests of Henri Pittier Park via hairpin bends and narrow widths, and on down to the famous Playa Grande beach and the range of lodgings in Choroní and Puerto Colombia.

The Andes beg to be explored at your own pace. The little villages with their colonial churches and portraits of rural life will reward your patience and adventurous spirit 10 times over. Several routes lead to these fabled highlands, and choosing one can be tough — they're all fantastic.

If you decide not to take one of the all-inclusive deals offered by the *hatos* (ranches) in the Llanos, then consider heading to the **Andes via Los Llanos**. Drive south from Maracay through San Juan de los Morros to San Fernando de Apure. Although neither of these towns is particularly appealing, you'll

pass through the colonial Calabozo and begin to get a feel for the unbending horizons of the plains. From San Fernando, take the westerly Highway 19 along real Llanos backcountry roads, where capybara and cayman congregate around water sources in the dry season, and birds paint the trees and skies in the evening light.

Spend the night in either Hato El Cedral or Hato Doña Bárbara, on the road to Elorza. In the morning, double back to La Ye, and work your way north up through the floodplains of the Río Apure to Bruzual, across to Ciudad de Nutrias and on to Barinas, nestled into the southern skirts of the Andean range. From Barinas, a spectacular road coils up the mountains via Santo Domingo and the Hotel Los Frailes — a must for lunch or the night — and joins the *Transandina* at Apartaderos.

The **Andes** alternative to the Llanos route is just as appealing. Beginning in Barquisimeto (where you can rent a car), an old road leads south to the hammock-making town of Tintorero, through colonial Quíbor and El Tocuyo (once capital of Venezuela) and on to the delightful Parque Nacional Yacambú and the hill town of Sanare. The next day, continue on the road which gets ever more verdant on its way to Biscucuy. Continue to Boconó, gateway to the Andes, where choices for a bed for the night are numerous.

At Boconó, two options open up. If you've rented a jeep, consider the adventurous route up through the small, whitewashed towns of Tostós and Niquitao, and over the rough road across the *páramo* to the picture-perfect Jajó.

Have boat, will paddle: Guajiro Indians on the Laguna de Sinamaica.

From there, link up with the *Transandina* for Timotes, and stay the night at the cozy Hotel Las Truchas, before hitting the serpentine road up to Apartaderos the next day.

The second route from Boconó heads west over to Trujillo, the state capital. On the way, stop off at half-forgotten San Miguel, Barbusay and Santa Ana, with their colonial churches and elaborate altarpieces. You could stay the night in Trujillo, or head south, via the teeny villages of San Lázaro and Santiago to the unique, friendly and first-class Posada Nidal de los Nubes, high up on the edge of the *páramo*. From there, proceed down the road and link up with the *Transandina* north of Timotes.

Finally, you've reached Mérida State. Even though only 56 km (35 miles) separate Apartaderos and Mérida, it's probably the most frustrating stretch of asphalt in Venezuela. Not because of the traffic, but because you could easily dedicate a week to exploring the environs and still not feel you've done them justice. You'll also encounter some of the best *posadas* in the country.

Absolute musts include admiring the stone chapel of Juan Félix Sánchez in San Rafael de Mucuchíes, lunching in the baronial splendor of the Castillo San Rafael, wandering round the plazas of Mucuchíes and Tabay, and stopping at the numerous roadside stands and stores for fruit (including strawberries in season), cured hams or homemade blackberry wine. You could also fit in a step back in time at the theme park of Los Aleros.

Roads in various conditions of repair crisscross southern Mérida. The most popular weave through the towns known as the Pueblos del Sur, detailed in the Andes chapter (see page 168). Not to be missed on the way to Táchira State, the restored Hacienda La Victoria near Estanques houses two excellent museums, with the one dedicated to coffee providing an invaluable insight into the economy of the Andes.

From Bailadores, the *Transandina* winds up again to the high *páramo* of La Negra, before descending once more to fertile hills and La Grita. A great option for the night en route to San Cristóbal is Finca La Huérfana, south of the village of El Cobre. Around San Cristóbal, a car will allow you to explore the old coffee-growing villages south of the town, Santa Ana and Rubio — close to El Tamá Park. West and north of San Cristóbal, Peribeca and San Pedro del Río benefited from loving restoration in the last years.

Focusing on **eastern Venezuela**, after enjoying the beaches of Puerto La Cruz, rent a car for the drive along the "Costa Azul" all the way to Cumaná. It's the most spectacular coast road in the country. Every other bend offers views of crescent bays, fringed by palms and backed by tumbling hills. Just out of Puerto La Cruz, take a detour up to the village of Los Altos de Santa Fe for the best views over the blue hues of Mochima National Park.

In **eastern Sucre State**, the area around Carúpano in the Península de Paria offers fine rental-car explorations. Consider looping south towards El Pilar or heading east on Highway 9 for a dip at the thermal springs at Agua Sana. Soon after Bohordal, a memorable coast road cuts east to San Juan de las Galdonas. Back on the road from Bohordal, turn east for the secluded beaches of Playa Medina and Playa Pui-Puy with their romantic beach cabins, or continue on to the other beaches close to Río Caribe, Los Cocos or Playa de Uva.

Last, but by no means least, of Venezuela's great roads is **Highway 10**, linking Ciudad Bolívar and Ciudad Guayana (Puerto Ordaz) on the Orinoco with Santa Elena de Uairén on the Brazilian border. The first stretch is fairly uneventful until you approach the Imataca forest and the mining towns of El Callao, Tumeremo, and — yes, it had to be — El Dorado. And yes, you can buy gold in the stores in any of them.

Starting the count from El Dorado at km 0, the highway ploughs south through the lush forest until the obligatory gas stop at km 88, before the climb called La Escalera (The Staircase). La Escalera winds up the Sierra de Lema range, where it nearly always rains deep in the tangled and epiphyte-draped forest. At the top, you enter the magical realm of the Gran Sabana. Along the route from Luepa to Santa Elena, on clear days you'll see the eastern *tepuy* mountains puncturing the

horizon, while dotted at intervals come an embarrassment of waterfalls — Kawi, Kamá, Quebrada de Jaspe and Yuruaní, to name but a few. Camp or stay in one of the rustic lodgings run by the Pemon close to the waterfalls and rivers, or else continue to the *campamentos* of Santa Elena.

If you've been itching to drive a jeep along the dirt roads in the outback, the **Gran Sabana** offers three exceptional drives. The first splits from Highway 10 at Luepa and heads across the savanna towards the mission village of Kavanayén, ringed by *tepuys*. On the way, detour to the 100-m (328-ft) Chinak Meru (Aponwao) falls and the village of Liwo Riwo, where you can find a meal and sling a hammock for the night.

The second forks from the highway at San Francisco de Yuruaní, carving east to the hamlet of Paraitepui. Trekkers begin their excursion to Roraima from Paraitepui, and the views of the mountain and its twin Kukenán make crossing the two rivers on the way truly worth it.

The third dirt road cuts west from Santa Elena through savannas and forests towards the frontier community of El Paují, and on to the mining town of Ikabarú. The 74-km (46-mile) drive to El Paují, if the road has been newly repaired, can take as little as two hours.

LEFT: Beasts of burden take the weight off travelers' legs in the Andes. ABOVE: Coche Island's arid, copper-colored bluffs.

Most of the time, however, it can take four or five, and sometimes longer. If you truly want to get "off the beaten track," you won't find a worse definition of the word "road" in all Venezuela. The settlement of El Paují, composed of Pemon, miners and artistic-creative types living lives in the wilderness, presents a wonderful opportunity to flee the modern world.

Backpacking

With the most economical inbound flights to South America, Venezuela offers the ideal gateway for many backpackers beginning their tour of the continent. Living on a budget of around US$20 a day is possible, but requires some planning. As the bolívar continues to devalue, Venezuela will become even cheaper.

Road transportation throughout the country is fast and economical, and you can save your cents by taking the normal buses without air-conditioning or toilets. If you're short on time, internal flights can be cheaper than you might expect (Caracas to Mérida costs US$50 one-way, for example), and become even more attractive when part of an air-pass.

Budget accommodation is plentiful and gets very cheap if you forsake private bathrooms, hot water and air-conditioning. You might have to ignore the "by the hour" rates for rooms however! The high season in

Venezuela obeys national holidays, as opposed to the Northern Hemisphere's winter; busiest are Christmas and New Year, Carnival, and Easter Week. School vacations in August are sometimes considered high-season too. At these times prices go up, so it's best to hide out in a non-touristy place. Even better, bring a tent and camp out in a national park, where park wardens usually welcome the company.

Cheap and cheerful restaurants (*comedores*, *tascas* or *luncherías*) are plentiful, and you should aim to enjoy your main meal at lunch, taking advantage of the *menú del día* or *menú ejecutivo*. Chicken or shredded meat (*pabellón criollo*) with rice, beans and plantains are the main staples, but along the coast, delicious fresh fish is always on the menu. At other times, maize-bread *arepas* and *empanadas* sold with a variety of fillings make economical stopgaps. With its bounteous fruits, regional cheeses and delicious pastries, eating well and cheaply couldn't be easier.

As many of the country's best sights are remote or inaccessible, it is hard to avoid taking a tour. In general, throughout Venezuela, and depending on the size of your group, tours begin around the US$25 mark per day. Joining other travelers will always bring the price down. Fierce competition between operators in "springboard" towns such as Mérida, Ciudad Bolívar, Santa Elena de Uairén, Tucupita and Puerto La Cruz means bargaining hard for an acceptable price will get results.

Mérida in the Andes is "Backpacker Central." The city, with its attendant large student population, offers Venezuela's cheapest accommodation and meals, plenty of lively bars and nightclubs, language schools, and the incomparable landscape of the high mountains as a backdrop. With many walks and trails close to the city, or accessible by public transportation, you won't feel pressured to take a tour.

Along the coast, among the most popular backpacker haunts are the villages by the great Playa Grande beach, Puerto Colombia and Choroní. On the weekends or during holidays Venezuelans get the party going on the beachfront *malecón*, with drumming, dancing and drinking until the early hours. Both villages offer plenty of inexpensive accommodation and seafood restaurants.

The beach at Santa Fe, with its economical *posadas*, snorkeling or diving trips, and sandy beach bar is beginning to look like a corner of Thailand. The town itself is best forgotten, but after a few days of lounging, you'll wonder where the week went.

It's harder to live cheaply in Puerto La Cruz, but for partying and flirty nightlife, it's probably the best bet outside Margarita which, with its swanky resorts and posh restaurants, could put you off. Away from Porlamar, you can find plentiful reasonably-priced accommodation and meals at beaches such as Playa El Agua or the ones close to Juangriego. The windsurf Mecca of El Yaque probably hosts the liveliest young scene on the island, with beach bars, economical restaurants and a range of places to stay. Watch out for their wind-based high season prices.

Ciudad Bolívar, despite the heat, makes a natural destination for backpackers heading to the wilds of the Delta, Canaima or the Gran Sabana. With historical sights, and an abundance of tour operators, the city teems with travelers enjoying the culture while bargain-hunting.

In the southeast, Santa Elena de Uairén, gateway to the wonders of eastern Canaima Park, also caters to travelers on tight budgets. The largely unprepossessing town makes for the best meeting place if you're looking to bring down the costs of the Roraima trek or a tour of the region's waterfalls and missions.

From Santa Elena, many backpackers find themselves drawn to the frontier community of El Pauji. Bring as much of your own food as you can carry, sling a hammock, camp out, or stay in one of the rustic *campamentos*; after a few days you may consider building your very own house in the wilds.

Living It Up

EXCEPTIONAL HOTELS

As Venezuela's tourism infrastructure continues to expand and improve, so too have the number of top-class resorts, hotels and exclusive lodges. Caracas alone witnessed the inauguration of three new five-star hotels in the last five years. Opened in 2000, the **Four Seasons** in Altamira is as luxurious as the chain's other hotels. In the meantime, the **Hotel Ávila**, tucked up in the hills overlooking the city, provides an ideal haven from the noise and chaos, replete with antiques and artwork, an excellent restaurant, a pool and lush gardens. Topping the list of the five-stars in the city, the **Caracas Hilton** enjoys the most central location, combined with first-class service and the pick of three restaurants. It is perfect to come back to after a night at the opera or ballet across the walkway in the Teresa Carreño complex.

Disastrously affected by the floods of late 1999, the luxury options near the airport at Maiquetía should be back in service by the time you read this, or soon thereafter. The **Macuto Sheraton** offers lap-of-luxury facilities and the chance of heading out to sea for some fishing or to visit Los Roques and Las Aves

OPPOSITE: Decoration first, tires later is the rule on buses. ABOVE: Beach life in Santa Fe, Mochima National Park.

islands. Further along this coast, the **Aloe Spa** combines an outstanding natural setting and creative architecture with pampering massages, therapies and superb (and healthy) cuisine. For a luxury way to explore Los Roques, charter a yacht through Alpi Tour, or book into the top-of-the-range **Bequeve Los Roques** or **Mediterraneo**, both original and very well managed.

Margarita of course presents many exclusive possibilities. Among these, the **Hotel La Samanna Resort & Sea Spa** spoils its guests silly with its luxury rooms and an array of beauty and health treatments, while the **Isla Bonita** combines indulgence and an 18-hole golf course, the only one on the island.

Back on the mainland, the El Morro development continues to grow into one of the country's most exclusive destinations. Both the **Hotel Doral Beach Villas** and **Golden Rainbow Maremares Resort** are the latest in top-class resorts, with every water sport and activity catered to in style on their vast grounds. For something smaller yet just as exclusive, check in to the **Hotel Punta Palma**, boasting unrivalled views of the bay. Further east, along the road to Cumaná, I defy you not to come away raving about **Villa Majagual** and its intimate, whitewashed cabins,

stunning location, and unsurpassed Mediterranean cusine.

If you fancy some "wilderness with knobs on," Venezuela boasts well-established jungle lodges to rival any in the Amazon. I recommend you head for **Camturama Amazonas Resort** or **Campamento Orinoquia** near Puerto Ayacucho. Both make ideal springboards for river trips up the Orinoco. Properly in the wilds of Amazonas' forests, **Camani** is the most luxurious option, with all sorts of tours and activities to keep you contented.

Close to the idyllic shores of Canaima lagoon (a boat ride from Angel Falls), the prize for top resort goes to **Campamento Ucaima** for its more personalized feel, although the **Campamento Canaima** comes a close second thanks to its unsurpassed views of the waterfalls and *tepuys* — unhealthily romantic at sunset.

In the Llanos, **Hato El Cedral**, with its swimming pool and new set of air-conditioned rooms, presents probably the most upscale option of all the lodges vying to show you the wondrous wildlife of the plains. Capybara are so common they graze right outside your window.

With years of experience as Venezuela's alpine playground, the accommodation in the

Andes rates among the best in the country. For luxury and history, head for the famous **Hotel Los Frailes** on the sight of an old monastery high in the hills. Or for the royal treatment, check in to the medieval castle of **Hotel Castillo San Ignacio** which couples baronial splendor with top-of-the-line furniture, fittings and decoration.

EXCEPTIONAL RESTAURANTS

You could spend a lifetime dining out in Caracas and still not exhaust its possibilities. My top three favorite places to blow my wages are on the rooftop terrace of **Ara**, with its stylish and delicious World cuisine; **Tambo**, mixing Peruvian and Japanese in a heady blend popular with oh-so-beautiful people; and **L'Operetta**, for thoroughly overindulgent Italian cuisine at its best, served in an opulent, exclusive ambience.

Away from the capital, finding truly outstanding cuisine presents more of a challenge. Echoing the luxury accommodation, the best restaurants often reside within the top hotels and resorts. This is certainly the case on Los Roques, where the best meal I enjoyed was at **Mediterraneo**. On Margarita, head to **Le Chateaubriand** inside the Margarita Hilton for plush surroundings and exquisite French cooking,

Nikey & Tiberio at the Samanna Resort with first-class Peruvian and Japanese, or **Cocody** for the freshest lobster in the most romantic atmosphere on the island.

Among the options in El Morro, the Maremares' Italian restaurant **Al Fresco** proves most enticing, with a great ambience and delightful setting. Down the road in Puerto La Cruz, the refined French and Caribbean menu, often with unexpected twists, of **Chic e Choc** won't disappoint. Nor will their wine list.

With its fresh trout and cornucopia of fruit and vegetables, the Andes present dozens of possibilities for fine wining and dining. Perhaps the most unique restaurant of all lies within the baronial Great Hall of the **Castillo San Ignacio**, where waiters and waitresses in medieval garb serve revived old European dishes. The restaurant at the **Hotel Los Frailes** also enjoys a great reputation for its trout. The ambience is just right, while a cozy fireplace is on hand to warm you during a postprandial nap.

Family Fun

In Venezuela, children are everywhere. And Venezuelans tend to dote, if not spoil, their children. Many hotels throughout the country — particularly the beach resorts — cater to children with various activities, and can often provide childcare or babysitting facilities.

Sure to appeal to the modern child's dinosaur obsession, in his novel, *The Lost World*, Arthur Conan Doyle envisioned prehistoric creatures and tribes running amok atop the mesa mountains of Canaima and the Gran Sabana. If you're off to view Angel Falls, consider acquiring a copy of the book (before you leave your country) to read on the way. It's a great adventure yarn, equally popular with adults who haven't grown up yet.

The walks and horseback or muleback rides around Mérida should also prove popular with children. Add some *abrillantado* sticky sweet fruits to the equation, and the result should be smiles all round. Mérida also offers theme parks for families, **Los Aleros** and **Venezuela de Antier**, and I defy any child not to get excited about the prospect of traveling the world's longest and highest cable car up the mountains from Mérida.

Zoos also make good family days out. In Caracas, the **Parque del Este** offers various displays including a snake pit, while the larger

The swooping arc of Chimana Grande, one of Mochima's many island beaches.

Caricuao does a fine job of showing off native as well as African animals amid expansive grounds. **Maracay**'s zoo is probably the next best in the country.

On the beaches, my experience of children is that you just let them get on with it. You should probably bring their own flippers and masks just in case hotels don't have children's sizes, and maybe a fishing rod. With that in hand, they can fish for the infamous piranha along the Orinoco's tributaries — sure to be a hit!

In general, children under 12 (although the cutoff age can sometimes be younger) can enjoy discounts in most hotels. Call in advance to make sure.

Cultural Kicks

Venezuela is often berated as a cultural desert, or criticized for being materially obsessed and importing wholesale North American culture. This simply isn't so. It might not be a heavyweight intellectual hotbed to contend with Brazil or Argentina, and indeed, few of its writers, painters or musicians are known worldwide, but to dismiss the country outright would be a grave injustice. Don't judge it by its Coca-Cola cover.

For **art**, a visit to the Museo de Arte Contemporáneo in Caracas will prove my point. Here you'll find Moore and Botero sculptures alongside Léger, Matisse and Chagall canvasses, as well as one of the greatest collection of Picasso engravings outside of Spain. The Museo de Bellas Artes hosts cutting-edge modern art, while a wander through the Galería de Arte Nacional leaves little doubt that Venezuela has produced some fine painters, among them Martín Tovar y Tovar and Arturo Michelena. Their foremost works can be viewed inside the Capitolio and at the Museo Fundación John Boulton.

Housing the country's finest collection of period furniture and furnishings, the Museo de Arte Colonial in the old Quinta de Anauco also hosts chamber music concerts on Sunday mornings. Even taking the metro in Caracas can become a culture vulture's dream, as each station displays sculptures and installations by dozens of Venezuela's most prominent modern artists, including Jesús Soto and Cruz Diez. Public art litters the city — like the bottle-tops squished into the asphalt. The fountain and sculptures of Plaza Venezuela or the works around the Parque Central complex are the city's most eye-catching open-air galleries.

For modern art outside the capital, first prize goes to the Museo de Arte Moderno Jesús Soto in Ciudad Bolívar, with an admirable collection focussing on the great leader of the "kinetic" art movement in Venezuela and his innovative works.

Along with art, Caracas' boasts a vibrant **performing arts** scene. With their home at the Ateneo, Rajatabla is probably the country's most famous theater group, but also a cutting-edge dance troupe. The giant Teresa Carreño complex next door hosts the national theater, national symphony and various dance groups (including folkloric Danza Venezuela and more modern Ballet Nuevo de Caracas). The auditorium also showcases world class orchestral, operatic and ballet companies from abroad. The capital's international theater festival takes place in April, while El Hatillo hosts a series of festivals throughout the year.

In eastern Caracas, the Casa de Rómulo Gallegos (CELARG) forms Altamira's cultural heart, with a varied program of concerts, art exhibitions, lectures and films. It is one of the few movie theaters that promotes Venezuelan films.

Outside Caracas, **regional historical museums** more often than not focus on the life of Bolívar or the War of Independence. The Casa Páez in Valencia, its walls painted with murals depicting the battles fought by the *Llanero* general and future president, rates among the best. In Ciudad Bolívar, the Casa de San Isidro, home to a modest but delightful museum of colonial antiques or the Casa Morales in Maracaibo both make unpredictable alternatives to the usual run-of-the-mill memorabilia.

The **architecture**, **altarpieces** and particular atmosphere of Venezuela's **churches** paint an intriguing tableau of its art and culture. The Iglesia San Francisco and the stained glass of Santa Capilla are the finest examples in Caracas. I have dozens of favorite churches, but recommend above all San Clemente and San Nicolás de Bari in Coro and the altarpieces and colonial charm of San Miguel and Barbusay churches in Trujillo State. On Margarita Island, the solemn columns of Venezuela's oldest cathedral at La Asunción, Nuestro Señora de la Asunción, echo the early Conquistadors' roots in Inquisition Spain. At the other end of the scale, the Santuario de la Virgen near Pampatar sings a symphony to "wedding cake" taste: it's pink.

La Capilla de Juan Félix Sánchez in San Rafael de Mucuchíes in Mérida State, is only

No need to ask why they're called Devil masks. A fine example from San Francisco de Yare.

most audible mark of the descendants of African slaves brought over to work the plantations. The displays are usually impromptu, springing up on weekends, holidays or for the festival of San Juan in June, and the rhythms are as addictive as the dancing is seductive.

Shop till You Drop

When they're not working, dancing, socializing or sitting in traffic jams, Venezuelans are shopping. When they do manage to reach the fabled shores of Miami, boutiques, not dolphins, are top of the list. With the economic crisis of the last decades, Miami languishes out of reach for the majority. National tourism has therefore grown, and so has the trade in souvenirs and crafts. These may not suit foreign travelers' tastes, but Venezuela does boast some first-class artisans.

One of the first purchases you should consider is a **hammock**, the best tried-and-tested means of relaxation on a beach. If you're on a tight budget, they'll also save money. Caracas' Mercado Guajiro sells millions of them. For better quality, and the chance of meeting the people who make them, head to the village of Tintorero outside Barquisimeto, or one of the inland villages of Margarita. The country's indigenous people weave the finest hammocks, akin to works of art (and therefore costly). Among the very best are those of the Warao of the Delta.

In recent years, **Indian crafts** have begun to receive the recognition they truly deserve. If you can't make it to Puerto Ayacucho's Mercado Indígena (go early), then head to the Centro CEPAI in Caracas' El Paraíso district. There you'll find the same intricate baskets, wood carvings (often depicting animals), mobiles, crafts, honey, hot sauces, nuts and palm oil from the south. Your money will also go more directly back to the original craftsperson. Many lodges in the south of the country also trade in crafts — you'll notice a price tag attached to the wooden anteater seat you're resting on.

For the highest-quality indigenous crafts in the country, seek out the Casa Caruba in Los Palos Grandes, Caracas. The largest selection of all lies within the dozen or so rooms of Hannsi, in El Hatillo. Both these stores sell the gruesome devil masks worn by the dancers in their festivals, but also works from the Andes, which include the skinny and tall naïf-style wood carvings of saints and generals.

The Llanos offers **leatherwork**, with great bargains in cowboy boots and leather bags,

surpassed by his first chapel in the isolated valley of El Potrero, a five-hour hike away. This mystical, talented man built them both, with the help of his wife, stone by stone by stone.

Music, you'll soon notice, is everywhere in Venezuela. Although much of what you hear comes from other countries in the Caribbean, and often includes the "latinified" version of techno music (called *changa* in Venezuela), the country also boasts some homegrown *salsero* talents. King of these is the by-now aging Oscar D'León, with the younger Eric Franchesqui, Pasión Juvenil and Servando y Florentino also hugely popular.

The country's traditional music hails from the Llanos, but like sweat across a dancer's back, it spread to the rest of the country. The most popular folk rhythm is still the Llanos' *joropo*, while its main challenger comes from Maracaibo's *gaita*, danced in the rest of the country only at Christmas — why, I have no idea. Different regions throughout the country also nurture their preferred rhythms, from *bambuco* in the Andes to *fulías* and *jotas* in the Oriente. All of these rhythms are accompanied by singing, fast and furious or slow and romantic, and four main instruments: the *cuatro* (a small four-stringed guitar), the *arpa llanera* harp, a double bass and maracas gourd rattles.

If you venture along the coast, particularly among the fishing communities around Puerto Colombia, or to the west along the Litoral Central, *tambores* drums dominate. They're the

while on the road near Píritu east of Caracas, dozens of stands sell all manner of **woodwork**, from children's chairs to wooden spoons. Further east in Cumaná, Señor Jaime Acosta of Tabacos Guanche makes and sells **cigars** to rival those of Cuba, and on the road east of the city, **model ships** and **rag-dolls** people the roadside stalls. In Paria, Klaus Müller of Campamento Vuelta Larga trades beautifully crafted wood-and-weave **blinds** produced by local Warao Indians. Maracaibo's Mercado de los Guajiros is very much a trading-place for Venezuela's largest Indian group, but you can also pick up their distinctive **hats** and **amulets**.

For the most original backpack you're likely to encounter — it'll definitely impress your friends back home — seek out one of the woven *guayares* made by the Yekuana or Pemon of Bolívar State. They also produce large and small **blow pipes** that will keep older children amused for hours.

Short Breaks

With the top attractions in Venezuela scattered to the four corners of the country, travelers short on time face the unenviable task of choosing but a few, and fitting as many in as possible. Taking advantage of the extensive national air networks by buying an air-pass from abroad will allow you to see many sights in a short period of time.

Caracas itself offers no end of activities to keep you occupied, and to get a feel for a tropical forest, you need look no further than the hills of the Ávila that dominate the city. Within an hour's drive of the capital, the beaches of the Litoral Central (east or west of Maiquetía airport), the idiosyncratic Colonia Tovar (with lovely cloudforest trails), the Guatopo National Park south in Miranda State, and the colorful village of restaurants and crafts shops of El Hatillo all provide excellent possibilities. Within a five-hour radius of the capital, you can take in the wonders of Henri Pittier National Park and the beach at Playa Grande, or head east to historic Barcelona and the party-town Puerto La Cruz.

With the help of a travel agent, you could organize a very tight itinerary, including a day-trip to fly past Angel Falls, a flight to Mérida for the high-wire cable car ride, and even a night at one of the Llanos lodges. For the ultimate trip, contact Bob Sonderman of Alpi Tour ((02) 283-1433 FAX (02) 285-6067 FAX IN THE UNITED STATES (520) 447-7959 E-MAIL alpitour@viptel.com WEB SITE www.alpi-group.com, with years of experience tailoring "flying safaris" in the wilds of the south, including Angel Falls, the Llanos, and Amazonas.

OPPOSITE: Figures of saints and generals are typical of Mérida. ABOVE: A rainbow floats across the falls of Salto Yuruaní.

Increasing numbers of foreign travelers fly directly to Margarita, bypassing Maiquetía. Popping over from Margarita to the mainland is straightforward enough on the ferry, but take the plane to save precious time. Lineas Turísticas Aerotuy (LTA) ((02) 761-8043 or (02) 761-6231 FAX (02) 762-5254 WEB SITE www.tuy.net offer packages direct to Angel Falls, Canaima and the Delta, while Rutaca ((02) 355-1838 FAX (02) 355-1643 fly to Carúpano where you can take a two-day tour of the forests and beaches of the Paria Peninsula.

Festive Flings

Every town in Venezuela boasts a patron saint, and fiestas spring up throughout the year, throughout the country. Even if you're only traveling for a month, you're more than likely to stumble across one. Although they often have strong religious roots and overtones, with local people making religious promises and commitments lasting a lifetime, many of them have become little more than a good excuse for some pagan partying.

The country's most famous and colorful event is the **Diablos Danzantes**, the "Dancing Devils" brought over from Spain by the Conquistadors, with Indian and Black African influences grafted on over the centuries. Held on Corpus Christi (the ninth Thursday after Maundy Tuesday), the dancers in their colorful homemade outfits wear elaborate and decidedly grotesque wood or papier mâché masks on their heads, while bells jangle from their clothes, drums beat and maracas rattle. The dance symbolizes the Devil's submission before the Eucharist, with each male dancer of his confraternity approaching the church to whisper his promise of faith into the priest's ear. Fathers often have their young sons join a confraternity to ensure a healthy, trouble-free life. The festival's most renowned home lies in San Francisco de Yare in Miranda State, but the coastal villages of Cata and Ocumare also celebrate it.

Venezuela's patron saint, **Nuestra Señora de Coromoto** is fêted throughout the country on September 11, but most impressively at her shrine outside Valencia and in the small town of Chachopo in Mérida State, where locals reenact the Indian chief Guaicapuro's vision of the Virgin. **San Isidro**, celebrated on May 15, is regarded as the protector of the Andes' oxen, and processions of the animals decorated with flowers and fruit take place throughout the region, notably at Tostós, Tabay and Trujillo.

The main drum-and-rum shindig for the coastal communities descended from African slaves is **San Juan Bautista**, on June 23 and 24. Figures of the saint are ceremonially baptized in the sea, followed by all night sensual dancing to *tambores*. Caruao and Chuspa on the Litoral Central, and Puerto Colombia in Aragua make great venues to join the party.

San Benito, the country's only black saint, enjoys widespread popularity, particularly around Lake Maracaibo and in the Andes. **Los Negros de San Benito** — around December 27 — brings the *tambores* drummers out in force in the communities of Gibraltar and El Moján on the lake's shores, while the Paraujano Indians of the Laguna de Sinamaica proudly carry effigies of the saint on the prows of their wooden canoes. In the Andes, Mucuchíes puts on a colorful and noisy celebration for San Benito, locals firing blunderbusses in the air while dancing away. Not to be outdone, Timotes in northern Mérida State goes all out with its street dances of grass-skirted blacks, war-painted Indians, and vassals in flowing white cloaks and golden crowns.

Many of the celebrations for San Benito naturally fuse with those of Christmas, especially the **Santos Inocentes** on December 28, commemorating the children killed by Herod. Probably the most famous example can be found in the tiny town of Sanare in Lara State, where parents don masks and disguises and carry their children in their arms as they dance.

Christmas Eve (*Noche Buena*) and **New Year** (*Año Nuevo*) are a time for family and fun, but also for *pesebres*, nativity scenes set up in many homes. Some spill out onto the streets, with the residents of San Pedro del Río (Táchira) and Carora (Lara) going completely over-the-top, their scenes and street lights decorating entire blocks.

In the run-up to Christmas, the **Fiesta de los Pastores** (Shepherds' Festival) recreates the shepherds' joy at finding Christ. The festival's greatest expounders are the towns of Aguas Calientes and San Joaquín in Carabobo, and El Limón in Aragua. Although the celebrations involve dancing, singing, horn blowing and merrymaking, some parts are particularly solemn, with participants approaching the image of Jesus on their knees. The dances are choreographed, with the most important group of *pastores*, men dressed in multicolored streamers topped with flower-full hats, dancing with *pastorcillas*, women in typical shepherdess garb.

Combining just about every influence and tradition in its festivities, the Trujillan hill town of San Miguel (near Boconó) hosts the **Romería de los Pastores** (Shepherds' Pilgrimage) on January 6. Here you'll see devil dancers, religious processions, *pastores* dances, *San Beniteros* and even hear *tambores*. The festival takes the best elements of the country's rich traditions and combines them in a melting pot which will leave you reeling.

Proving that Brazilians don't enjoy a monopoly on having fun, **Carnival**, in the run-up to Lent, gains momentum every year.

OPPOSITE: Al Jolson, eat your heart out. ABOVE: Maypole dancers at the Fiesta de San Benito in Mucuchache, Mérida State.

Guanare, capital of Portuguesa State and one of the last places you'd expect to host the country's largest celebrations, draws tens of thousands of people to its larger-than-life street floats and costumed dancing. The otherwise uneventful town of Carúpano in Sucre enjoys massive partying for days on end along its beaches, with a surprising Trinidadian, calypso feel to the music and decorated floats.

As the most important time in the Catholic calendar, every church in the country celebrates **Semana Santa** (Holy Week). The largest procession takes place in Caracas on Wednesday, the purple-robed lines of people ending at the Basilica de Santa Teresa to honor the city's holiest image, El Nazareño de San Pablo.

Throughout the Andean villages, processions make their way to the doors of churches, with many people carrying wooden crosses. Passion plays also attract large numbers of the faithful and curious, with the most impressive in the mountain villages of Tostós in Trujillo and La Parroquia in Mérida.

Galloping Gourmet

Reflecting its diverse ecology, Venezuela's cuisine is eclectic, with seafood and fish on the coast, slabs of steak in Zulia and the Llanos, and the indigenous staples of *casabe* bread and fried ants. Foreign influences permeate dishes, though Venezuela has its own traditional and regional cuisine.

STOPGAPS AND STAPLES

The national dish, *pabellón criollo*, combines *carne mechada* (shredded beef), *arroz blanco* (white rice), *caraotas negras* (black beans) and strips of fried *plátanos* (plantain). It's a working-class staple, with the beef usually enlivened with onions, tomato, garlic and green peppers. Some people also sprinkle sugar on their black beans, slightly *mal vu* by the middle classes, but I find it delicious. On Margarita, shredded fish usually supplants beef.

Venezuela's *arepas* are Mexico's *tortillas* or India's *chipatis*. You'll either love or hate these small, deep-fried, flattened balls of corn flour. They're sold in *areperas* and at every roadside stand, slit open with the inner dough scooped out to make way for a variety of fillings, including basic *queso amarillo* (yellow cheese) or more sophisticated *reina pepiada* (avocado and chicken salad). In the Andes, wheat flour is more common than corn, and the result is infinitely superior.

Deep-fried turnovers filled with white cheese, meat, fish or black beans, *empanadas* make a good alternative to *arepas*. Ground sweet-corn pancake *cachapas* are usually made on the spot and come folded over a slice of regional cheese, *queso a mano* or *queso guayanés*, contrasting with the pancakes' slightly sweet flavor.

MEATS

Venezuelans are great red meat eaters, although *pollos a la brasa* (spit-roast chicken) restaurants are as ubiquitous as fast-food chains and mobile roadside hot dog and hamburger stalls. The most common meat dish is the *parilla criolla*, a mixed grill of beef and sausage. Cuts include *punta trasera* (rump steak), *solomo* (chuck) and *lomito* (tenderloin). By European standards, Venezuelans tend to overcook their meats, so ask for your meat *poco cocido* if you like it pink. Also try *pernil de cochino*, a marinated ham hock served with a hot sauce, and *asados*, a round of beef fried and then boiled until tender, stuffed with raisins, capers, ham and olives.

FISH AND SEAFOOD

To the chagrin of seafood fans, much of Venezuela's lobster (*langostina*) and conch (*botuto*) is whisked abroad where it fetches higher prices. You can, however, still find them in more upscale restaurants in Caracas, Puerto La Cruz or Margarita. Along with *pulpo* (octopus), *calamare* (squid), *camarones* (shrimps), and *ostras* (oysters), you won't be short on choice. A popular consommé, *chipi-chipi* is a delightfully light clam broth. *Sancocho*, a stew with just about every vegetable thrown in, can include fish, seafood, or meat, but it's not particularly sophisticated. *Hervido* is the soup version.

With all that coast, fresh fish is plentiful, with *pargo* (red snapper), *pez espada* (swordfish), *dorado* (sea bream), *merluza* (hake), *bacalao* (cod) and *mero* (grouper) all on coastal restaurant menus. Fish is usually fried whole and served with rice and a salad. Fish dishes are often at their best in the Spanish *tasca*-style restaurants.

SAUCES
Venezuelans aren't huge on sauces, but you should try the piquant *guasacaca*, a green or red sauce made from capsicums, onions and seasonings. The red version is the spicier of the two. Strangely, the English Worcestershire sauce flavors many meat dishes, while the ultimate sauce in the country has to be top-blowing *katara* made by the Indians of the Orinoco basin from yucca, hot peppers, and the heads of the fearsome *bachaco* ant.

REGIONAL SPECIALTIES
Don't miss the distinctive *chivo en coco*, goat in spiced coconut milk, around Coro; or hearty *asados,* stuffed with whole vegetables, in the Llanos and Zulia; or delicious fresh trout in the Andes. While exploring in the south, you're sure to come across *casabe* bread, but also peccary, venison and fried *culona* ("big-bottom") ants. In the Llanos, you may well be served shredded *chigüire* (capybara), which if you've just been snapping photos of these comic creatures, may prove hard to swallow. You might see *tortuga marina* or *pastel de morrocoy* on coastal menus. Don't order them since turtles are an increasingly endangered species throughout the Caribbean.

YULETIDE SPECIAL
At Christmas, *hallacas* appear on menus. These are delicious packets of cornmeal dough filled to the brim with pork, chicken and beef and flavored with a long list of vegetables, spices and seasonings. *Hallacas* take hours, if not days to prepare, all part of the family Christmas spirit, and are tastier than turkey to be sure.

OPPOSITE: Roadside stalls sell a cornucopia of fruits and vegetables. BELOW: Venezuelans are serious consumers of meat.

DESSERTS, SWEETS AND PASTRIES

Like their Latin cousins, Venezuelans love sweets. *Panaderías* and dessert menus can put a spanner in the spokes of a well-intentioned healthy holiday. And Venezuela still produces some of the world's best cacao. The chocolate makers La Praline rival Godiva on the world stage. Boutiques in the Caracas Hilton and the Inter-Continental Tamanaco vend them.

Possibly the tastiest sponge cake this side of Ulan Bator, *bienmesabe* ("tastes good to me") comes dressed in coconut cream finery, while *suspiros* ("sighs"), with their light vanilla, cream and lime flavors will likely provoke sighs of pleasure. Danish-style pastries (*pasteles*) clog the window of *panaderías*, all too-tempting as you wait for a fresher-than-fresh *cafecito* (little coffee) hit.

COFFEE

Venezuelans' love for their coffee is justified. It's delicious. Always sticklers for things they consider important (like fashion or automobiles), Venezuelans have devised a vocabulary to define *exactly* how they want their injection of rocket fuel. Practice your ordering now: begin with gradations, from *guayoyo* (black and weak, American-style), *negro* (black and deadly), *marrón oscuro* or *marrón claro* (dark or light brown), *con leche* (with more milk), and through to *tetero* (literally a "baby's bottle" and mostly milk). Follow that with size: a *grande* for large, and *pequeño* for small (or just add -*ito*). "*¡Dáme un marrón clarito, por favor!*"

BEER, WINE AND LIQUOR

Venezuelans consume more beer than any other Latin American nation — that's a lot of *cerveza*. The ubiquitous polar bear mascot of Polar beer adorns every *licorería* (liquor store), cheap restaurant, and — somewhat worryingly — most highway signs for villages and towns (Venezuelans' record for drinking and driving is dismal). They like their *polarcitas* and *tercios* (the two sizes) served just above freezing, and at any time of day. The same company also produces the stronger *Solera*, while other beers include Zulia's *Regional*, and Brazil's *Brahma Chopp*.

Before the economic crisis, Venezuela was the world's largest importer of Scotch whisky. They still consume plenty of it, but hard times have forced this nation of *bon buveurs* to fall back on their homegrown, and excellent, rum. Pampero produce the best *ron añejo* golden rum, with their *Aniversario* being the oldest and most highly regarded. Sugarcane *aguardiente* makes for the poor-man's alternative, popular along the coast and in the

Llanos, while anise-flavored rot-guts can also be found, but aren't recommended if you cherish your liver. The Andeans beat the cold with *calentado* (or *calentaíto*), anise-flavored *miche* mixed with hot brown sugar. The Oriente is famous for its fruit-based rum and sugar cane concoctions known as *guarapitas*, often featuring *parchita* (passion fruit).

Special Interests

LANGUAGE COURSES

Venezuelan Spanish can be fast and furious, dotted with slang and colloquialisms. It might not be the first country of choice for learning the language, but if you're keen to get under the skin of its people and get a feel for their quick wit and humor, taking a course will furnish you with the skills.

Mérida is undoubtedly the best city for learning Spanish. The Andean accent is the clearest in the country to the untrained ear,

and with its large population of students keen to learn English, finding someone for reciprocal chats is easy. The courses are also the cheapest in the country. Contact the **Instituto Latino-Americano de Idiomas** (/FAX (074) 447808, Centro Comercial Mamayeya, Piso 4, Oficino 26, Avenida Las Américas, or the experienced **Iowa Institute** ((074) 526404 E-MAIL iowainst@ing.ula.ve, Avenida 4 at Calle 18. The WEB SITE www.andes.net provides a more detailed list.

VOLUNTEERING

Environmental organizations are always on the lookout for eager volunteers for their conservation programs. The **Audubon Society** is perhaps the best conduit for information about how to become involved in environmental projects. Contact them at ((02) 993-2525 FAX (02) 993-9260 WEB SITE www .audubonvenezuela.org. **Tierra Viva** (/FAX (02) 951-2601 E-MAIL tierraviva@compuserve.com, carries out primary healthcare work with

the Warao of the Delta, but also runs educational programs and activities throughout the country.

International nongovernmental organizations based in the United States with projects or interest in Venezuela include the **Nature Conservancy** ((703) 841-5300, 1815 N Lynn Street, Arlington, Virginia 22209, and **Cultural Survival** ((617) 621-3818, 215 First Street, Cambridge, Massachusetts 20142.

Earthwatch ((617) 926-8200 E-MAIL info@earthwatch.org WEB SITE www .earthwatch.org, 680 Mount Auburn Street, Box 403, Watertown, Massachusetts 02272, organize working trips on scientific and ecological projects.

In the United Kingdom, **Survival International** ((0207) 723-5535, 310 Edgware Road, London W2 1DY, works closely with many groups in the Orinoco Basin.

Meandering through the rivers of the Llanos in a dugout canoe.

Taking a Tour

You can only reach top attractions such as Angel Falls, Cerro Autana, the Delta and parts of the Andes with the help of a tour operator. Concerns about your level of spoken Spanish or negotiating travel in Venezuela might also motivate you to contract one. Certainly, the knowledge of a local guide will be invaluable when exploring rainforests or learning about Venezuela's diverse culture.

Many national and international tour operators organize trips. The travel agency **Turisol** ((02) 959-6091 or (02) 959-8147, Nivel PB of the Centro Comercial Ciudad Tamanaco (known as the CCCT) in Chuao, Caracas, is one of the best in the country. They also deal with American Express refunds.

With years of experience, particularly in yachting, **Alpi Tour** ((02) 283-1433 FAX (02) 285-6067 FAX IN THE UNITED STATES (520) 447-7959 E-MAIL alpitour@viptel.com WEB SITE www.alpi-group.com, run by United States expatriate Linda Sonderman, enjoys an excellent reputation for comfortable tours. Her husband Robert puts together first-class flying safaris.

The **Venezuela Audubon Society** ((02) 992-3268 or (02) 992-2812 FAX (02) 991-0716, Edificio Matisco, Piso 1, Calle Veracruz, Las Mercedes, Caracas (this is their office, as opposed to their store) acts as a tour organizer and can book accommodation throughout the country. All profits go toward funding their projects. They also sell books, provide information on national parks, and list recommended specialized guides — including Chris Sharpe (/FAX (02) 730-9701 E-MAIL rodsha@telcel.net.ve. They can prove invaluable for up-to-date advice and know the country intimately. Contact them well in advance if possible.

Cacao Travel Group ((02) 977-1234 FAX (02) 977-0110 E-MAIL cacaotravel@cantv.net WEB SITE www.cacaotravel.com, Calle Andromeda, Quinta Orquídea, El Peñon, Apartado 88627, Prados del Este, Caracas, offer adventurous tours (trekking, kayaking, horseback riding) throughout the country, as well as managing several *posadas* throughout the country.

With ecologically sound credentials, and established in 1950, **Grupo Turven** ((02) 952-6961 TOLL-FREE IN UNITED STATES (800) 810-5021 FAX (02) 951-1176 E-MAIL turven@ven.net WEB SITE www.venez.com, Calle Real de Sabana Grande, Edificio Unión, Piso 1, PO Box 60627, Caracas, arranges tours throughout the country, employing bilingual guides, and staying in moderate accommodation.

Of Mérida's many tour operators, **Arassari Trek & Bum Bum Tours** (/FAX (074) 525879 E-MAIL info@arassari.com WEB SITE www.arassari.com and http://jvm.com/bumbum/, Calle 24 off Plaza Las Heroínas, enjoys one of the best reputations.

Among the most well-known and reputable operators in the United States is **Eco Voyager** ((305) 665-9050 TOLL-FREE (800) 326-7088 E-MAIL ecotour@ecovoyager.com WEB SITE www.ecovoyager.com. They have years of experience in Venezuela and excel in trips to national parks with knowledgeable and often specialized guides. One of the best operators for tours of the Gran Sabana and Amazonas, **Lost World Adventures** ((404) 971-8586 TOLL-FREE (800) 999-0558 FAX (404) 977-3095 WEB SITE www.lostworldadventures.com, 1189 Mountain Ridge Drive, Marietta, Georgia 30066, also comes highly recommended.

For small-number birding tours, few guides in the United States surpass Richard Ryan of **Neo-Tropical Bird Tours** ((973) 716-0828 TOLL-FREE (800) 662-4852 FAX (973) 884-2211, 38 Brookside Avenue, Livingston, New Jersey 07039-4030. In the United Kingdom, **Footprint Adventures** ((01522) 804929 FAX (01522) 804928 E-MAIL sales@footprint-adventures.co.uk WEB SITE www.footprint-adventures.co.uk, have very knowledgeable guides.

For more information about choosing a responsible tour operator in the United States, which I would urge you to do, contact the **Ecotourism Society** ((802) 447-2121 FAX (802) 447-2122 E-MAIL ecomail@ecotourism.org WEB SITE www.ecotourism.org.

Of the operators based in the United Kingdom, two spring to mind for excellent reputations and experience. Both of them specialize in personalized, small group tours, with the emphasis on culture and ecology. They also arrange more arduous trekking trips. The first is **Geodyssey** ((0207) 281-7878 FAX (0207) 281-7878 E-MAIL enquiries@geodyssey.co.uk WEB SITE www.geodyssey.co.uk, 28 Harberton Road, London N19 3JS, while the second is **Last Frontiers** ((01296) 658650 FAX (01296) 658651 E-MAIL info@lastfrontiers.co.uk WEB SITE www.lastfrontiers.co.uk, Fleet Marston Farm, Aylesbury, Bucks HP18 0PZ.

Of the tour operators and travel agencies organizing trips all over South America that include Venezuela on their itineraries, **Journey Latin America** ((0208) 747-8315 E-MAIL tours@journeylatinamerica.co.uk WEB SITE www.journeylatinamerica.co.uk, 12–13 Heatherfield Terrace, London W4 4JE, I can recommend personally.

Playing in the waters of the Quebrada de Jaspe, Gran Sabana.

Welcome
to
Venezuela

WHEN COLUMBUS FIRST SET FOOT ON TO THE SOUTH AMERICAN CONTINENT, it was Venezuelan soil he described as a "Paradise on Earth." The country's people and its A to Z of ecosystems have been charming visitors ever since. Venezuela's population is young, dynamic and outgoing — nearly two-thirds of the country is under 30. What's more, they're beautiful, producing more Miss Worlds than any other nation. The country's gene cocktail has been mixed more times than the fruit-shakes sold on every street corner, where a myriad of different-colored faces meet.

Cultures Spanish, European, Caribbean, African and homegrown *criollo*; beliefs indigenous, esoteric and New Age; influences North American, Latin and European. All melt in a tropical cauldron of music, dance and food, making Venezuela a beguiling nation to explore. Just when you thought you had it pigeonholed and pack-

aged, you uncover another layer of color and contradiction.

It is a markedly urban society — 85% of the population live in cities — yet the peasant culture of another era strangely prevails. It is hyper modern, with muzak-wafted shopping malls and a swish Metro, yet surprisingly backward when it comes to education and literacy. Venezuela boasts some of the continent's most progressive environmental legislation and a fifth of its land falls under some protection. But you'll see people on the highways tossing trash from bus windows, and coffee is served in millions of disposable plastic cups. The family is of utmost importance, yet adultery is commonplace, and divorce increasingly common. People resent the influence of the United States, but ask a Venezuelan where they'd like to go for their next vacation, and the answer you'll get is Miami.

For the visitor, Venezuela can be perplexing. The country seems somehow ill-at-ease with its identity, pulled between conflicting extremes of modernity and tradition, appearance and reality. Its condition is caused, above all, by the breathless pace of change its citizens have experienced. The result is a nation with a structure and culture dating back to the search for El Dorado, projected into the modern world by the "black gold" economic boom of the twentieth century.

Venezuela's affluent years furnished it with extensive infrastructure, making it a straightforward country to travel — though Spanish will always be an advantage. Flights connect all the major cities and comfortable "executive" buses run all the important routes. Tourism is a growth industry, still finding its feet in some regions, while the island of Margarita, "the pearl of the Caribbean" with its exclusive resorts and lively nightlife, rivals any destination in the region.

While Venezuela is captivating, and its laidback *mañana* mentality seductive, bring patience and a sense of humor along with sun-block and insect repellent. Rent a car and explore Venezuela's hinterland, where strong regional and traditional cultures prevail. Pick up the rich, passionate and often hilarious language, and the rewards are comparable only to the first sip of a freshly made fruit-shake after a long day on the road.

Blessed with a tropical climate, immense natural riches and a youthful, effervescent cultural melting pot, the biggest problem facing the visitor to Venezuela isn't how many pairs of socks to pack, but how to pack all of its wonders into a two-week vacation.

Fishermen haul in their boats after the morning's catch at Puerto Fermín (El Tirano), Isla de Margarita.

The Country and Its People

VENEZUELA IS UNDENIABLY A LAID-BACK, HAMMOCK-SLUNG COUNTRY, where "mañana" peppers every conversation, fruit and vegetables grow as if by magic, and tomorrow is always another day. To the foreigner, Venezuelans appear friendly, carefree and fun. Although they can be brash, uncouth, superficial, and sometimes painfully non-PC, the warmth of the people you'll meet will be a constant surprise, and their *joie de vivre* infectious. And once you remove the thin veneer of modernity and homogeneity from Venezuela, you uncover a diverse country, with distinct regional traditions and heritages, and begin to taste its rich mix of peoples, creeds and color.

Venezuelan society is often called *"cafe con leche,"* describing the color of its people's skin, and its comparative lack of racism. Just as coffee served in Venezuela is graded into a half-dozen different shades, so the country is a blend of different races — from its original Indian peoples who inhabit the savannas and forests south of the Orinoco as well as important lands on the Colombian frontier, the black slaves brought from Africa to work the cacao plantations and the early Spanish and European migrants to the populations from the huge immigration from Europe, China, the Middle East and other Latin countries of the twentieth century. This last wave of immigrants featured Italians who colonized the country's coast, Portuguese who typically run bakeries in the cities, and Canary Islanders and Galicians who have integrated particularly well into all walks of Venezuelan life.

Strong regional differences exist—a *Maracucho* (someone from oil-rich Maracaibo) for instance probably has more in common with a Texan than with an Andean farmer plowing his field with an ox, while the world of a Pemon Indian from Bolívar State is a million miles from that of a black fisherman from Barlovento (the region east of Caracas dominated by ex-slave communities). Accents and vocabulary differ too: *Andinos* speak clearly and ponderously, *Caraqueños* are immediately distinguishable since they call everyone *pana* (buddy), and *Margariteños* speak so fast and furiously their language almost amounts to a dialect.

In addition to regional differences, a gaping urban-rural divide separates two Venezuelas. Its citizens — fashion-conscious, frenetic and clinging to the shirt tails of *gringo* modernity — contrast with the underpopulated countryside, where people continue their traditional agrarian ways, speak with idiosyncratic expressions and wonder what all the fuss in Caracas is about.

In a country of such diverse natural environments and unique twentieth century history — few countries in the world have changed so dramatically and so quickly as Venezuela — it may come as little surprise to find a heterogeneous people where each regional and racial piece contributes to the complex jigsaw of modern Venezuela. What will constantly surprise you however is just how many pieces come in the box, and the fun and the challenge you'll experience attempting to fit them all together.

PRE-COLUMBIAN YEARS

The first nomadic peoples arrived in Venezuela sometime around 14,000 BC. Not until the last millennia before Christ did these communities settle and begin to till the earth, bake ceramics and establish distinct cultures. The glyphs carved into rock faces around Lake Valencia in Carabobo State and near Puerto Ayacucho in Amazonas State provide traces of these early civilizations. Little is known about the people who made them, or for what reason they made them, and their exact age remains undefined. Recent finds near Barquisimeto in Lara State attest to later peoples' adept use of clay and pottery.

By the time of the Spanish conquest, three distinctive linguistic groups dominated Venezuela. The fierce Caribs, origin of the word "Caribbean," occupied the central and eastern coast and lived from fishing and agriculture, while the Arawaks, subsisting from hunting, gathering and occasional farming, took up much of the land in the Llanos and the central plains. In the Andes, the Timote-Cuica of the Chibcha linguistic group formed the most advanced of the country's pre-Hispanic peoples. Some of the ancient stone walls around Apartaderos are thought to date back to these Indians. Their irrigation systems and knowledge of astronomy impressed the early Spanish explorers.

Fundamentally, however, the pre-Hispanic peoples of Venezuela failed to reach the architectural or cultural heights of the Mayas of Mexico and Guatemala, or of the Incas of Peru. They had no knowledge of writing and the best sources of information about them come from the Spanish chroniclers of the fifteenth and sixteenth centuries.

THE CONQUEST

Despite being the only country of the South American continent upon which Christopher Columbus actually stood, the country he dubbed the Land of Grace was subsequently all but ignored by the Spanish Crown in whose name he claimed the land. On his third voyage of discovery in 1498, Columbus sailed from Trinidad to the coast of the Paria Peninsula. From there, he navigated south towards the delta of the Orinoco, soon realizing that what he had thought was just another Caribbean island was in fact the tip of a vast continent.

A typical Andean church, and local, from Timotes, Trujillo State.

Columbus was unequivocally enamored with this New World. The Indians who came to meet his caravels were friendly and welcoming, adorned with gold and pearls and inhabiting a fruit-rich land. "I'm convinced this is Paradise on Earth," he wrote to King Ferdinand and Queen Isabella. Paradise didn't last long.

A year after Columbus, Alonso de Ojeda sailed further along the Caribbean coast, entering the mouth of Lake Maracaibo. Here, one of his crew, the Italian Amerigo Vespucci, who would later give his name to the entire American continent, noted — no doubt with some sarcasm — that the Indians living in thatched houses on stilts linked by walkways reminded him of Venice. The idea caught on, and the province was thereafter known as Little Venice — Venezuela.

Soon after, the Spanish established the settlement of Nueva Cádiz, on the island of Cubagua, south of Margarita Island. With a ruthlessness that would become the hallmark of the Conquest, they exploited the pearl beds they discovered, enslaving the local Indians who dove until their eardrums burst. Cubagua became known as the "Island of Satan." Within three decades, the Spanish had picked the beds clean, exporting a staggering 11 tons of pearls before the fledgling town was wiped out by a tidal wave in 1541.

Meanwhile, in 1519, Cortés conquered the great Aztec empire in Mexico, sending boatloads of gold and jewels back to Spain. The wealth provoked renewed interest in the New World, and Venezuela, as the most accessible country of South America, was a natural target for gold-thirsty Spaniards. In 1521, settlers established Cumaná in eastern Venezuela, the first settlement on continental South America, while in 1530, a well-equipped expedition led by one of Cortés's lieutenants, Diego de Ordaz, made its way up the Orinoco. Of the 600 men who set off from Spain, only 200 were left after months of futile searching along the Orinoco and in plains of the Llanos.

Ordaz's dismal record didn't seem to discourage later desperate attempts to find El Dorado or Manoa, the myth of the Golden Man, or the Golden City, depending which version you believed. In a strange twist of European fate, the Spanish Crown literally leased the Province of Venezuela to the German banking house of Welser. Carlos V, in a fit of vanity, bought the title of Holy Roman Emperor, thus accruing a huge debt to the bankers. In return, Venezuela received some of the most bloodthirsty "explorers" of the Conquest era. The consequences of their cruelty to the Indians made colonization even harder. The Indians fought tooth and nail to defend their lands, but had no defense against the European's greatest weapon: disease. An outbreak of smallpox decimated their populations, completing the subjugation of the province by the end of the sixteenth century.

THE COLONIAL PERIOD

The muddy outposts of colonial power — Caracas, Cumaná, Mérida and Maracaibo — grew slowly. Until 1717, Santo Domingo in present-day Dominican Republic ruled eastern Venezuela, while Lima governed the Andes and the west. The pearl beds exhausted and no great civilization to ransack, and with the riches of Peru and Potosí to keep the Spanish rulers occupied, Venezuela was left to wallow as a colonial backwater.

Grid-like patterns of adobe-brick town houses still shape the centers of Caracas, Barcelona or Cumaná today. Semi-feudal *haciendas* (plantations) spread across the fertile valleys, where cacao became the most important crop. In the unending plains of the Llanos, cattle raising centered on the *hatos* (ranches), establishing Venezuelan's obsession with juicy steaks and barbecues, but also founding the country's mythical heart, peopled by the hardy, resourceful and individualistic *Llanero* cowboy.

With the lack of Spanish immigrants willing to risk a life in the Venezuela outback, and with increasing numbers of slaves brought in to work the sugar and cacao haciendas, the country's population soon became a melding of races. By 1700, only a quarter of Venezuelans were deemed *blancos* (whites). Excessively paranoid, they embedded a system of racial apartheid to separate them from the *pardos*, the people of mixed white, Indian and black descent. By the time of the cacao boom of the mid-1700s, the *blancos* were divided between the Spanish-born members of the administration and clergy (the *mantuanos*), and the Venezuelan-born Creoles. Although less-marked than 250 years ago, whites still dominate Venezuela's elite, while the poorest in the country remain dark-skinned.

The fashion for chocolate which swept continental Europe in the mid-eighteenth century elevated the country's backwater status, if only briefly. Venezuela leapt from obscurity as its haciendas, with the choicest pods in the tropics, fed the growing demand. With their new-found wealth, the landowning *Gran Cacao* as they were known, obsessed with following European fashions, hosted elaborate dinners and dances, and imported the latest lace, furniture and fashions. Alexander Freiherr von Humboldt, on his travels in 1800, remarked "in no other part of Spanish America has civilization assumed a more European character." Along with lace and chamber music however, came the new ideas of the Enlightenment that fired the revolutions in Europe in the dying years of the eighteenth century. Although the Venezuelan Creole elite were wary of separation from Spain, the chaos and uncertainty caused by Napoleon's invasion of Spain in 1808 forced their hand.

INDEPENDENCE AT A PRICE

Although they couldn't have known it at the time, Venezuela's Creoles were right to fear the consequences of independence. The irony of their reluctance to reject the power of the Crown is all the more bitter when one considers the human and economic cost of the wars that ravaged the country. When Venezuela finally emerged from the conflict in the 1820s, it lay in ruins: the white elite decimated, haciendas either pillaged or abandoned, livestock virtually wiped out, and a quarter of its citizens dead. The price of exporting the revolution to the continent, and spawning its

fortune, and recently grieving the death of his young wife, climbed the ranks of the patriot forces. Tutored by the enlightened Simón Rodríguez during his travels in Europe, and without any formal military training, Simón Bolívar swiftly rose to the rank of colonel. Exiled after Miranda's collapse, Bolívar and other generals regrouped in the Andes where they declared "War to the Death" against Spain. They ended their *Campaña Admirable* (Admirable Campaign) with the liberation of Caracas in 1814. Bolívar, with his charisma, leadership skills and military genius now fully fledged, became president of the Second Republic. His reign was short-lived. The *Llanero* plainsmen led by their ruthless commander José Tomás

greatest hero, Simón Bolívar, would set the country back a 100 years or more.

But all that was unknown when a group of Creole displaced the Captain-General of Venezuela and established the Junta Suprema de Caracas on April 19, 1810. Three months later, a National Congress convened to sign the Declaration of Independence from Spain, creating the First Republic on July 5. With growing opposition, particularly from the *pardo* classes unconvinced by this new ruling class, Francisco de Miranda assumed dictatorial powers in May 1812, but was forced to capitulate to Royalist troops two months later, betrayed by patriot conspirators. He was exiled in Spain, where he later died, the first great martyr of the revolution.

Lurking in the wings of the early years of the First Republic, a young man, heir to a Gran Cacao

Boves, descended on the capital, ousting Bolívar and the patriots.

Events in Europe conspired to aid Bolívar's next campaign. With the demobilization of troops following the end of the Napoleonic Wars in 1815, his agents in London found a willing pool of mercenaries to fight in the War of Independence. Although at first troubled by storms and bureaucracy, by 1819 as many as 5,000 mainly British soldiers had joined Bolívar on his campaigns. In addition to this influx of experienced legionaries, the new leader of the fearsome *Llanero* cavalry, José Antonio Páez, agreed to back Bolívar in return for the confiscated estates of Royalist landowners.

With renewed vigor, Bolívar set out from Angostura — present-day Ciudad Bolívar —

The bloodshed and battles of the *Guerra a la Muerte* (War to the Death) campaign.

and marched west to the Llanos, where in a bold move which cost him a quarter of his troops, he struck out over the Andes in midwinter. At the Battle of Boyacá he brilliantly defeated the Spanish and so liberated the province of Nueva Granada. Returning to Angostura in 1819, he presented his project for the new Constitution of Venezuela. He also outlined his plans for the creation of La Gran Colombia, the new South American superstate, which Congress subsequently approved on December 17. Spanish power in Venezuela was finally broken following Bolívar's decisive victory at the Battle of Carabobo (near Valencia) in June 1821, though it would take the naval victory of Lake

was too late for Bolívar. He was outlawed as a traitor in Venezuela and shunned in Colombia. He declared bitterly, "Those who serve the revolution plough the sea. The only thing to do in America is to emigrate." Portrayed vividly by Gabriel García Márquez in *The General in his Labyrinth*, Bolívar made his way to the Colombian coast in 1830, with the intention of boarding a ship to Europe. He never made it. Still only 47, but racked by tuberculosis and all-but abandoned by his friends, he died in Santa Marta "shaken by the overwhelming revelation that the headlong race between his misfortunes and his dreams was at that moment reaching the finish line. The rest was darkness."

Maracaibo, and the expulsion of the Spanish from their stronghold at Puerto Cabello on November 7, 1823, before the last remnants of the Crown were finally exiled.

Bolívar's ambitions didn't stop there. His dream of establishing the world's largest nation from the old Spanish colonies drove him ever southward to become, along with Gran Mariscal José Antonio de Sucre, the liberator of Ecuador, Peru and Bolivia by 1824. Despite his glorious victories and the creation of La Gran Colombia, which included present-day Panama, Colombia, Venezuela and Ecuador, regional interests soon began to pick El Libertador's unified dream apart.

By 1826, General Páez and the Creole elite of Venezuela demanded more autonomy, resenting the control of the new nation's capital in Bogotá. Despite assuming dictatorial powers in 1828, it

THE BIRTH OF A NATION

The *Llanero* General Páez took control of the new Republic of Venezuela in 1830. He succeeded in stamping his authority on the country until he finally lost power, after various terms in and out of office, in 1848. Despite being economically ruinous, the wars of Independence changed little of Venezuela's social structure. Although land confiscated from Royalists was divided between the victorious soldiers, the smaller plots proved unworkable, and soon enough the officer class once more regained its status at the top of the pyramid. As in the rest of Latin America, the issue of land reform remained suppressed, only surfacing in rebellions that were ruthlessly quashed. The racist elite would take until 1854 to abolish slavery. But, in reality, the slaves swapped their shackles for debt peonage, and blacks continued to live in misery. Once again the *pardos* were excluded from high office, and the vote was restricted to property-owning men.

Páez succeeded in providing some stability in the republic's early years by forging alliances among landowners in the Andes, the Llanos, and coastal areas, along with urban merchants and professionals. A recovery based mainly on coffee exportation brought new wealth, particularly to Caracas and the haciendas of the Andes. The legacy of the war years however was one of violence, the country's isolated regions ruled by *caudillos* — strong men who rose to power through patron-client relations, and who plunged the country into successive civil wars during the mid-nineteenth century. Although the appearance of a Liberal opposition contributed to some social reforms, it was not until the politician-general Antonio Guzmán Blanco emerged triumphant from the chaos in 1870 that these really came into effect.

Guzmán Blanco is remembered as *El Modernizador*. He rebuilt much of Caracas, encouraged European immigration, separated the Church from the State, made primary education free, ordered roads cleared and schools built. His reign also marked the cementing of the nation-state, following Venezuela's humiliating loss of the Essequibo territory to British Guiana (present-day Guyana) — still disputed today as the *Zona en Reclamación* — and the even more disastrous bombarding of Venezuela's coast in 1902 by European powers pressuring Venezuela to repay its foreign debt. The influence of the military on civilian life remains one of Guzmán Blanco's most lasting legacies. One hundred years later, ex-Colonel and now President Hugo Chávez is once again keen to revive this legacy.

THE BOYS FROM TÁCHIRA

Between Guzmán Blanco's tenure and the arrival of democracy in 1958, Venezuela was dominated by successive military rulers hailing from the Andean State of Táchira. The first, Cipriano Castro, was possibly the most disastrous. His irresponsible rule from 1899 resulted in foreign bombardments and growing unrest. It ended with one of Venezuela's most controversial *caudillos*, Juan Vicente Gómez, seizing power in 1908.

Despotic power and the catapulting of Venezuela into the modern world characterize the Gómez years. The general behaved like a latter-day Caesar, protected by a secret service, and holding onto power through a combination of cunning, nepotism and repression. An accountant and land owner, he stamped his authority on the nation like a branding iron, and then ran it like his own private hacienda — indeed, until his death

in 1935, Gómez's ranch outside Maracay became the de facto capital of the country. Opponents were tortured and murdered, while members of the student revolt of the "Generation of '28" were exiled en masse. Although Gomez's regime was undeniably a cruel one, even by Latin American standards, some historians are now calling for his rule to be reassessed in the political, social and economic context of his day, as opposed to by modern, Western criteria.

The Gómez era witnessed the great oil strikes around Lake Maracaibo, which brought hundreds of international companies flocking to Venezuelan shores and undreamed of revenues to the government's coffers. The boom began in earnest at the village of La Rosa near Lake Maracaibo in 1922 and changed Venezuela forever. For better or for worse, it transformed the country within two generations from a backward, rural, agrarian nation into a modern, urban and industrial powerhouse of the Latin American continent. Along with the government high-rises, roads, hospitals, schools, a middle class and riches came the abandonment of Venezuelan agriculture, urban migration and the growth of shanty towns. Manufacturing never got off the ground as everything was imported. Venezuela's economic structure, forever over-reliant on oil, was irreversibly set in place, focussed on the new black gold El Dorado.

When Gómez finally died in 1935, he was succeeded by the reforming Eleázar López Contreras, and six years later by another Táchiran general, Isaías Medina Angarita. During these years, the leaders of the Generation of '28 formed the Acción Democrática (AD) party. AD persuaded a group of young military officers to stage a coup in 1945. Angarita resigned, and by 1947, Venezuela boasted a new constitution and its first civilian president, novelist Rómulo Gallegos. In 1948, following civil unrest and resentful of being sidelined, a military junta seized power. The Táchiran colonel Marcos Pérez Jiménez assumed the presidency in 1952 having declared the election he himself had called void. The new regime reversed the reforms achieved since Gómez's death.

Although Pérez Jiménez is now vilified for his abuses of human rights and his pandering to foreign oil companies, at the time he was the darling of the United States, even receiving the Legion of Honor from President Eisenhower. He initiated the great projects of the postwar period, from highways and universities to schools and petrochemical plants, brought stability to the country and the currency, and established Venezuela's place in hemispheric affairs. Although waste and corruption characterized many schemes, some historians argue it's all been downhill since then.

Simón Bolívar's birthplace in downtown Caracas.

DEMOCRACY OR DEMAGOGUERY?

Pérez Jiménez was toppled from power following conspiracies and rivalries within the armed forces, and a crippling general strike. One of the leading lights of the Generation of '28, Rómulo Betancourt, became president in 1959, beginning an era of democracy which continues today. In an electoral pact, AD agreed to share power with the newer, more right-wing COPEI party, founded by Rafael Caldera, who would be president from 1969 to 1974.

The 1960s were boom years for Venezuela. Betancourt increased government taxation of the oil industry, and played a leading role in the creation of OPEC in 1960. Crises from right-wing conspirators, left-wing guerillas and the continuing imbroglio with Guyana were all overcome. As the price of oil continued to rise, the party seemed to have no end. Venezuelans vacationed in Europe, and were known in Miami as *"los dáme dos"* — the gimme-two's.

With the Arab oil embargo of 1973, Venezuela took advantage of its windfall to nationalize industries, including, during Carlos Andrés Pérez's administration, the holy cow of the petroleum industry. By the end of his term however, the world recession and the slump in oil prices were already making the "Saudi Venezuela" decidedly shaky. By the "Black Friday" crash of 1983, an already slowing economy completely at the mercy of the oil price and importing up to three quarters of its food, began to spiral out of control. Despite President Luís Herrera Campíns' attempts to impose exchange controls and devalue the bolívar, an inefficient economy coupled with an obese and corrupt bureaucracy spelled the beginning of the end of the "weekend in Miami" years.

Jaime Lusinchi of AD came to power in 1984 more by default than popularity. Consumer prices were controlled to harness inflation and industry given preferential exchange rates. However, the package ate into the country's foreign reserves, and Lusinchi's term of office was tarnished by his embarrassing affair with his personal secretary and wannabe Evita, Blanca Ibañez, and by growing corruption scandals. The country fared no better under Carlos Andrés Pérez's second term from 1989. Desperate for credits from the International Monetary Fund (IMF) and realizing the extent of Venezuelan industry's inefficiencies, he embarked on a privatization plan, unraveling virtually everything he had achieved during his first presidency. Price controls were removed, subsidies cut, and a floating exchange rate introduced. The consequences, arguably unnecessarily harsh, triggered a wave of protests and looting across the country.

In Caracas, the bloody riots resulted in the deaths of 300 people as the army hit the streets to restore order. The episode became known as *El Caracazo.* On February 7, 1992, mid-ranking military officers led by Colonel Hugo Chávez Frías attempted to overthrow the government, following with another coup attempt on November 27. Both were unsuccessful as the army stayed loyal to the government and popular support failed to materialize.

In the end, it wasn't the military or civilians who brought about Carlos Andrés Pérez's demise, but the judiciary. In May 1993, the Supreme Court indicted him for alleged embezzlement and suspended him from office. He later received a sentence of two years under house arrest, most of which he spend with his mistress, Cecilia Matos. After a brief interlude with Ramón Velásquez in power, the 1993 elections saw another aging ex-President elected.

This time it was Rafael Caldera's turn to bring back the good times. He ran as an independent candidate at the head of a dozen splinter parties — AD and COPEI thoroughly discredited by their years in power. Before he even had time to assume office, Venezuela plunged into its deepest financial crisis. The government took over the country's second largest bank, Banco Latino, and spent billions of dollars it could ill-afford to bolster the nation's other financial institutions. Caldera's economic plan, which failed to tackle obese bureaucracy while fixing unrealistic prices for oil, soon floundered. Despite extra revenues from the auctioning of oil concessions, the government's domestic and foreign debt mushroomed. The bolívar continued its downward slide, and Caldera was forced to renege on his pre-election promises and go cap in hand to the IMF.

The fund imposed strict conditions to its US$3 billion bailout loan in 1996. Gasoline prices rose 500% overnight, and other prices rocketed: inflation soared over the 100% mark. By 1997, Caldera's piecemeal policies, coupled with his dithering public appearance, became increasingly unpopular.

Venezuela had gone from rags to riches and back again in a mere 75 years: by 1997, over two-thirds of the country were living at a level of extreme poverty, as defined by the World Health Organization.

VENEZUELA TODAY

Much to the amusement of foreign commentators, an early front-runner in the 1998 elections was former Miss Universe and mayor of Caracas's wealthy Chacao district, Irene Sáez. In a move which cost her the election, she decided to forfeit her independent status and run as COPEI's candidate. Amidst a climate of increasing economic desperation, the rhetoric of the leader of the Movimiento de la Quinta República, none other than 1992 coupster Hugo Chávez, sounded a note with the electorate.

The red-bereted Chávez was swept to victory, while the Venezuela elite and foreign investors held their breath. He is without doubt Venezuela's most controversial and intriguing leader since Pérez Jiménez: a strident, tireless orator to equal Fidel Castro, a man whose vision matches that of his hero Bolívar, a charismatic leader from the Clinton school of charm, with a single-minded, impetuous and sometimes dogmatic character which could be his making, or his undoing.

Movimiento is engaging. Some commentators fear Venezuela will descend into dictatorship. Chávez, they say, will become intoxicated by the concentration of power the 1999 Constitution grants him, and will hand out jobs and contracts to his cronies. Once in power, and with the armed forces increasingly immersed in public life (whether as directors of state companies or as laborers on new schools), he will be impossible to displace.

His plans to overturn a system which has never coupled political democracy with economic democracy are radical and ambitious, and could easily founder on the rocks of incompetence, corruption, or foreign intervention from the powers whose investments he might threaten. His

Chávez vowed to do away with the old corrupt political system, revitalize the agrarian economy, restore law and order and bring back dignity and national pride. During his first year in power he suspended Congress and the Senate in a controversial move. Elections in May 1999 voted a new Constituent Assembly, who over a breathless 90 days drew up a new constitution, Venezuela's twenty-sixth. In December, the Constitution was approved, ushering in the fifth republic since independence, and changing the country's name to La República Bolivariana de Venezuela. Keen to legitimize his reforms and government, in early 2000 Chávez called an election which was eventually held in August. He won it comfortably, though he failed to achieve the hoped-for majority for his party in Congress.

Although it is still too early to pronounce on the Chávez regime, the phenomenon of the

reforms may prove too much for the Venezuelan people. He could also turn out to be a tyrant. My personal view is that at this critical juncture in Venezuela's history — unemployment at 20%, inflation high, investment low and growing violence in the cities — Chávez is the right man at the right time.

He commands huge popular support. With this behind him, he could see the country through the cold turkey it desperately needs to endure before truly capitalizing on its wasted natural and human resources. With this support, he can lay the foundations of a national revival, a framework which, one can only hope, will serve the interests of the majority of Venezuelans according to Simón Rodríguez's dictum: "[Latin] America should not slavishly imitate, but should seek to be original."

Striking modern architecture is the hallmark of twentieth century Venezuela.

Caracas
and
Environs

CARACAS

As you emerge from the Boquerón tunnel on the freeway from Maiquetía airport, you come face to face with one of Latin America's greatest megacities: terracotta shanties clinging to the hillsides, modern tower blocks spiking the skyline, noise, fumes, cars, buses, hawkers, grime and chaos. It's frenzied, congested, cosmopolitan, car-obsessed, cool and contradictory. Love it or hate it, flock to it or flee it; whatever the Caracas of the twenty-first century truly is, it's undeniably in-your-face. Caracas's eclectic mix of people and styles, coupled with its youthful dynamism, can win over even the most profound country mouse. There's a buzz and a *joie de vivre* about the city that many visitors find infectious, and often irresistible. Few cities in the world quicken the pulse like Venezuela's capital.

Along the city's northern flank, separating it from the coast, the verdant slopes of the Ávila mountain rise abruptly to nearly 3,000 m (9,840 ft). Like Caracas's numerous parks and open spaces, the Ávila is an escape valve for stressed-out citizens, and a haven for the city's rich birdlife.

The city's museums meanwhile, offer some of the best art collections in Latin America, from the colonial and religious to the contemporary and kinetic. Epicurean Caracas boasts variety, quality and quantity — you could dine out every night of the year and still not exhaust its possibilities. For nightlife, only Río and Buenos Aires rival Caracas.

BACKGROUND

Originally founded as San Francisco in 1560, the settlement's early years were marred by attacks by Toromaima Indians. It was not until seven years later that Indian resistance was overcome, by Captain Diego de Losada, sent from the then capital El Tocuyo. He finally founded the township of Santiago de León de Caracas on July 25, 1567.

The capital was moved to Caracas in 1577, even though it consisted, at the time, of little more than a few blocks of streets and some 60 families. The bishops weren't convinced, and it was not until 1657 that they deigned to move the archdiocese from Coro.

In the seventeenth century, pirate raids, disease and earthquakes racked the fledgling town. Only the establishment of a university, followed by the arrival of the Real Compañía Guipuzcoana in 1728 signaled a positive turn in its fortunes. The Spanish crown awarded the company of Basque merchants and sailors a trading monopoly in the colony, which contributed to develop the nascent province and its capital, not without widespread discontent and rioting.

During the nineteenth-century struggles for independence, Caracas played a leading role. In 1810, a Supreme Junta made up of wealthy *Caraqueños* and councilors rejected the authority of the Crown, and by July 5, 1811, Congress had declared the independence of Venezuela. It would take a further 10 grueling years to end Spanish power in the country. In 1812, the capital succumbed to the worst earthquake in its history, which killed over 10,000 people and devastated towns across the country. The patriot forces fared worse than the Royalists in their strongholds, and the conservative clergy were quick to claim an act of divine retribution for Venezuela's rebellion against the Spanish Crown.

Under the guidance of *El Modernizador*, General Guzmán Blanco, Caracas saw many new civic monuments erected in the 1870s, notably the Capitolio and the Panteón. But another earthquake in 1900 sent the urban planners and architects back to their drawing boards. Their plans began to see the light of day as oil revenues made even the most ambitious projects seem feasible.

Out went the old colonial buildings, shaded squares and small-town feel of the capital. In came urban freeways, shopping precincts, and government tower blocks. By the end of the 1950s, the freeway to the coast at Maiquetía, one of the costliest civil engineering projects in Latin America, was nearing completion. Raúl Villanueva's blueprints for the Parque Central housing and shopping complex, and the vast Universidad Central de Venezuela campus, were soon to become fact. Caracas's population soared to one million.

Over the next four decades, as the country's economy boomed, the city's population quadrupled. Expansion pushed its boundaries eastwards along the valley, and southwards over the *colinas* (hills), gradually carpeting its onetime country estates with *urbanizaciones* (suburbs). The new growth effectively decentralized the city, making Plaza Bolívar only one of the many *centros*, while the superrich built mansions on the northern and southern slopes. By the time the economy began to slow in the 1980s Caracas was unrecognizable. Within a generation, it had gone from backwater to megatropolis, with an ever-growing population in "greater" Caracas of nearly five million inhabitants.

From the orderly grid of streets of Caracas's old colonial center around Plaza Bolívar, the tentacles of the capital now reach into the adjacent hills and valleys of Miranda, Vargas and Aragua states. As Venezuela's wealth grew exponentially after World War II, so the exodus of peasants from the countryside and the influx of immigrants from Europe and other Latin nations overtook the city's ability to house, provide or cope. Although many

The imposing Panteón Nacional houses Simón Bolívar's sarcophagus.

ranchos (slums or shanties) have developed into well-established working-class communities, linked by buses and furnished with electricity, telephones and sewage systems, many languish in abject conditions, where crime, drug abuse and violence are part of everyday existence.

As the *ranchos* continue to grow, comprising the majority of the capital's inhabitants, the already creaking Venezuelan state can do little more than observe. As the events of late 1999 proved — when the slums on both sides of the Ávila were virtually washed away by torrential downpours and mudslides, causing the death of over 20,000 people — the plight of the urban poor all too frequently ends in tragedy.

GENERAL INFORMATION

The offices of **Corpoturismo** (the official state tourism agency) ((02) 507-8607 FAX (02) 573-8983, are on the thirty-fifth floor of the Torre Oeste (west tower) of the Parque Central complex. The nearest metro station is Bellas Artes. Confusingly, you have to take the elevator from Sótano Uno in order to get to the correct floor. Once there, you can't just pick up leaflets at will, but have to wait for an assistant to see you personally. They are usually very helpful, speak several languages, and can provide you with most of what you need to know about the capital and the rest of the country. The office is open Monday to Friday, 8:30 AM to 12:30 PM and 2 PM to 5 PM. They also have a booth at the international terminal at the airport in Maiquetía ((031) 551060, open 7 AM to 5 PM daily.

For further information about Venezuela's national parks, and for camping permits, **Inparques** (Instituto Nacional de Parques) ((02) 285-4106 or (02) 285-4259 FAX (02) 285-3070 WEB SITE www.marnr.gov.ve/inparques/inparque .htm, has administrative headquarters at the eastern exit of Parque del Este. The offices are open Monday to Friday 8:30 AM to 12:30 PM and 1:30 PM to 5 PM, east of the Parque del Este metro station.

There are plenty of banks throughout the city which will advance money from ATMs on Master-Card or Visa cards (Banco Unión or Banco de Venezuela). Banco Consolidado offers the best rates for changing American Express travelers checks. The travel agency **Turisol** ((02) 959-6091 or (02) 959-8147, Nivel PB of the Centro Comercial Ciudad Tamanaco (known as the CCCT) in Chuao, deals with refunds. If in doubt, the American Express 24-hour help-line is ((02) 206-0333.

The best place to change cash and other non-Amex checks is at the *casa de cambio* called **Italcambio** (open Monday to Friday 8:30 AM to 5 PM, Saturday 8:30 AM to noon). They have branches at Maiquetía airport; Avenida Urdaneta (Esquina Veroes, west of Santa Capilla); Avenida Casanova, three blocks east of metro Sabana

Grande; and Avenida Ávila, south of Plaza Altamira. Western Union money-mailing is also available at DHL (see below).

Emergency numbers in Caracas are: **police** (169; **traffic police** (167; **fire** (166; **ambulance**, center ((02) 545-4545, east ((02) 265-0251. For serious medical problems, consult your embassy about doctors and hospitals. If you have insurance, book into a private clinic. One of the best is **Clínica El Ávila** ((02) 208-1001, Avenida San Juan Bosco con 6a Transversal, Altamira. Clinics can also provide vaccinations.

GETTING AROUND

Caracas spreads for at least 20 km (12.5 miles) over the Río Guaire valley, now little more than a polluted watercourse hemmed by concrete banks. The city's heart lies at Plaza Bolívar, to the west, where the colonial grid layout of *cuadras* (blocks) survives. Plaza Bolívar provides the cardinal center of streets labeled *norte*, *sur*, *este* and *oeste*, with numbers ascending from this point. However, in the old center, directions are still given by *esquinas* (street corners) whose names bare no relation to street numbers. They originate in local lore or from important houses which once stood there. For instance, the central Ipostel post office lies at Carmelitas, after the Carmelite convent of the eighteenth century. An address in the La Candelaria district might be given as "Peligro a Alcabala," implying it lies between these two *esquinas*. In the more modern areas such as Altamira, *avenidas* run north–south, while *transversales* cross east–west, beginning at 1 near Avenida Francisco de Miranda and ascending as they go up the hill.

The Metro

The savior of Caracas urban traffic nightmare comes in the form of the French metro. From a tourist point of view, you need look no further than line 1, which makes getting around along the city's main east–west artery a cinch. Line 1's terminuses are Propatria to the west and Palo Verde to the east, and stations are open 5:30 AM to 11 PM. If you plan to use the metro more than half a dozen times, invest in a *Multi Abono* ticket which entitles you to 10 rides anywhere in the system.

Metrobuses and Buses

Connecting metro stops to outlying areas (for example, San Bernadino, El Cafetal or Sebucán), the metrobuses make comfortable and efficient alternatives to normal urban buses. You can buy a combined metro and metrobus ticket called a *Boleto Integral* or a *Multi Abono Integral*. The drivers are generally very helpful, with departure points and routes posted on the walls of metro stations.

Buses, as you will notice from your first hour in Caracas, are anarchic, polluting, dangerous and numerous. These *carritos*, as they are known, make a lively alternative to the metrobuses or metro lines, and their routes are either painted or posted on their windshields. You shout "la parada" above the salsa blaring from a cracked speaker when you approach your stop — and they stop and start anywhere and everywhere. You either pay the driver or his assistant when you get on or off. They cost peanuts.

Taxis

Taxis are plentiful in the capital, identified by either "Taxi" or "Libre" on their roofs or dashboards, and yellow registration plates. They are economical for getting around at night, or beyond the metro route. In recent years, modern, air-conditioned white taxis have appeared, many of which use meters rather than a fixed price. These charge slightly more than the older taxis, but are far safer.

Older taxis, usually beaten-up old Buicks, Fords and Chevrolets provide an eye-opening way to see Caracas, and though you'll be lucky to find a seat-belt — let alone an air-bag — more adventurous visitors should take one at some point. Always settle on a price before getting in, and offer the driver 20% less than what he quotes you. Tipping is not customary unless the driver carries your bags or performs an extraordinary feat — like *not* using his horn.

There are also plenty of radio taxis in Caracas, of which **Coventaxis** TOLL-FREE (800) 81111, is among the best. Other numbers are **Taxi Móvil** ((02) 577-0922, **Caracas Taxi** ((02) 793-9744, and **TeleTaxi** ((02) 752-4155.

Car Rental

Unless you really enjoy tortuous *colas* (traffic jams) — four times a day, since most people go home for lunch — or want to hone your offensive skills, renting a car to explore Caracas isn't advisable (see GETTING AROUND, page 270 in TRAVELERS' TIPS for more on car rental).

WHAT TO SEE AND DO

Centro

As you emerge from the metro at Capitolio station, vendors of everything from antiques to alarm clocks clog the streets. In downtown Caracas, an unofficial curfew sets in at about 7 PM when the stores close. As a rule, tourists shouldn't venture west of Avenida Baralt, just west of Capitolio.

First stop is the brilliant white, neoclassical **Capitolio Nacional** with its golden dome — the heart of Venezuela's colorful politics since the 1870s when Guzmán Blanco razed the convent which once stood here. The Salón Elíptico is the main attraction, the mural by Martín Tovar y Tovar of the Battle of Carabobo looming down from the cupola. The next hall displays further works by Tovar y Tovar, and Tito Salas' paintings of Bolívar, including the moving portrait of El Libertador on his deathbed. The original Act of Independence of 1811 is kept inside a chest within the pedestal supporting the bust of Bolívar.

Northeast of the Capitolio, a statue of Bolívar on his steed dominates the old Plaza Mayor, laid out by Diego de Losada when he founded Caracas. It became **Plaza Bolívar** in 1883, having served as a bullfighting ring, a marketplace and a square for public hangings. In true Spanish style, symbols of power ring the shaded, tranquil plaza: the Federal District Government House to the north,

the former royal prison and presidential residence and now Foreign Ministry (Casa Amarilla) to the west, the Consejo Municipal (Town Council) to the south, and the cathedral to the east.

The Consejo served as a seminary and a royal university for the town's elite, but now houses the enlightening **Museo de Caracas**, with scale models of the town and Raúl Santana miniatures depicting daily Caracas life down the ages. An enlarged map of 1578 Caracas hangs on a wall in the cloister. The museum opens Tuesday to Friday 9 AM to noon and 2 PM to 4:30 PM, weekends and holidays 10:30 AM to 3 PM.

The **cathedral**'s size and architecture may not impress — it was rebuilt and remodeled following various seismic calamities — but inside, its collection of paintings is superb. Arturo Michelena's unfinished *Last Supper* and Cristóbal Rojas' *Purgatorio* are both powerful canvases, only surpassed by *The Resurrection*, attributed to Rubens. In one of the side chapels, the Bolívar family were laid to rest.

Next to the cathedral, the **Museo Sacro**, located in a beautifully restored vintage mansion, houses a small collection of religious art and a network of catacombs. The house is more popular as a

Caracas's highrises punctuate the valley floor.

modest center for the arts, with recitals and exhibitions on weekends, and as a great little café serving excellent lunches.

A block north of Plaza Bolívar, **Santa Capilla** is the best example of a Venezuelan neo-Gothic church. It occupies the site of the San Mauricio chapel where it's said the first mass was celebrated after the town's foundation. Inside, one of Michelena's greatest paintings, the *Multiplication of the Bread*, hangs amid the colors cast by elaborate stained-glass.

South of the Capitolio, the **Iglesia San Francisco** lies next to the Biblioteca Central (Central Library) and the former Supreme Court. Although its façade was remodeled by Guzmán Blanco, the interior retains much of the feel of a sixteenth-century colonial church. Along both walls, elaborate baroque altarpieces rank among the best in the country. It was here that Bolívar — aged only 30 — was proclaimed El Libertador in 1813, and to here, following his death from tuberculosis in 1830, that his body was brought from Colombia for his massive funeral in 1842.

Heading east along Avenida Universidad, you'll find the **Museo Boliviariano** and the **Casa Natal**, open Monday to Friday 9 AM to noon and 2 PM to 5 PM, weekends 10 AM to 1 PM and 2 PM to 5 PM. The museum displays memorabilia pertaining to both Bolívar — uniforms, portraits, swords — and other important families of his era. Next door, the reconstructed Bolívar family home contains period furniture and paintings, but few original features. El Libertador was born here on July 24, 1783, the fourth child of Don Juan Vicente de Bolívar and María Concepción Palacios y Blanco, who both died before his tenth year.

Just up from the houses, Bolívar gave an impassioned speech following the earthquake of 1812 at Plaza El Venezolano. Also worth a side-trip for Bolívar groupies, the **Cuadra Bolívar** lies a long way south of Plaza Bolívar, at Esquina Bárcenas on Oeste 18 and Sur 2. The family's old summer home (*quinta*), where Simón and his friends would ride horses, was restored in a similar vein to the Casa Natal, with some fine examples of nineteenth-century furniture. It's open at the same times.

The **Museo Fundación John Boulton** is usually overlooked by tourists, but houses a trove of Bolívar memorabilia, period furniture, paintings by Michelena, and a world-class collection of china and pottery. The museum is on the eleventh floor of the building on Esquina El Chorro, open Monday to Friday 8:30 AM to 11:30 AM and 1:30 PM to 4:30 PM.

West of the Capitolio area lies the *barrio* (neighborhood, in the pejorative sense) of El Silencio. The irony of the name is not lost on *Caraqueños*. Here, off Avenida Urdaneta, you find the presidential palace built by General Joaquín Crespo in the 1880s, although he died before its completion.

It's known as the **Palacio de Miraflores**. Caracas's oldest park occupies a hill just south of the palace. **El Calvario** was named after the Stations of the Cross once found on its summit, where pilgrims would gather. Unfortunately only *malandros* (thieves) from nearby barrios gather there now, so stay clear unless you're keen on wealth redistribution.

Of the other attractions close to the old center, the **Panteón Nacional** is best visited around 5 PM when the guards parade through the building where a total of 138 of Venezuela's founding fathers are interred. Two empty tombs still await the return of the Independence heroes Francisco de Miranda and José Antonio de Sucre's remains. Bolívar's bronze sarcophagus takes pride of place in the chancel. Hanging from the ceiling, the chandelier commissioned for the centenary of his birth boasts no fewer than 4,000 pieces of crystal and 230 lights. The Panteón lies six blocks north of Plaza Bolívar.

Parque Central and Bellas Artes

A 25-minute walk east of Plaza Bolívar, or a short hop on the metro to Bellas Artes, two reflective glass, 56-story towers shine amid white tower blocks. An ode to modernism at the time of their conception in 1970, the Parque Central complex was designed to provide central housing and amenities for the city's growing population. The towers accommodate the city's cultural heart.

Of the five museums in the main complex, the Museo de Arte Contemporáneo and the Museo de los Niños are the most important. The others include the Museo del Teclado (Keyboard Museum), the Museo Audiovisual, and the Museo Criminológico. At the office at Sotano Uno level of the west tower, ask for permission to visit the lookout on the fifty-third floor, with stunning views of the city. Unless otherwise noted, museums are open Tuesday to Friday from 9 AM, weekends from 10 AM, until 5 PM.

To the west, the **Museo de los Niños** is a well-designed, hands-on children's museum, with displays covering all the physical sciences as well as communications and ecology. A new, equally impressive wing focuses on science and technology. Doors are closed on Tuesdays, and between noon and 2 PM. A short walk west of the museum, the new **Museo de la Estampa y del Diseño Carlos Cruz Diez** houses a varied collection of designs, prints, lithographs and works by the renowned Cruz Diez.

At the northeastern corner of the Parque Central complex, the **Museo de Arte Contemporáneo Sofía Imber** showcases one of the best modern art collections on the Latin continent. Here you'll find works by European greats such as Léger, Moore, Braque, Matisse and Chagall, as well as Latin heavyweights like Botero, Cruz Diez, and

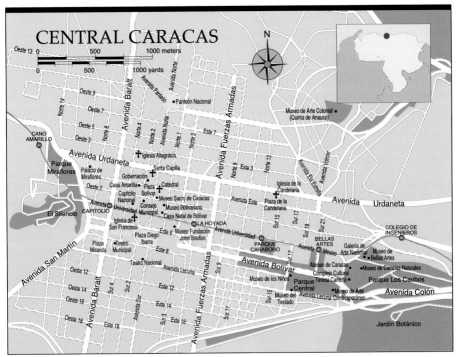

CENTRAL CARACAS

the leader of the "kinetic" movement, Jesús Soto. My favorite room contains over two dozen engravings by Picasso from the 1930s, including the Minotaur series. The museum also hosts excellent temporary exhibitions, with a café serving light lunches among sculptures in the gardens.

Near the entrance to the museum, a walkway carries you over the highway by the Hilton Hotel to the concrete-gray angles of the **Teresa Carreño cultural complex**. Soto's hanging metallic-yellow needles of rain dominate the vast atrium. The complex's two main halls are home to the national theater, national symphony and various dance groups, and play host to touring orchestral, operatic and ballet companies. The complex has great views east over the Parque Los Caobos, where Caracas's culturati chatter during intervals; guided tours are available. Next to Teresa Carreño, the **Ateneo de Caracas** adds to the area's cultural hubbub, with a further concert hall, the Rajatabla theater and dance groups, a cinema, library, café, bookshop, and two bars.

Continue round to the right from the Ateneo and wander down the short tree-lined avenue where artisans often set up their stands on the weekend. At its end, the circular Plaza Los Museos provides the gateway to the delightful Parque Los Caobos (mahogany). The **Museo de Ciencias Naturales** and the **Galería de Arte Nacional** flank the plaza. The former is a general science museum, revived recently with the addition of a robotic dinosaur display popular with children; it is closed

noon to 2 PM and from 1 PM on Thursdays. The latter features a large permanent collection of exclusively Venezuelan artists and sculptors chiefly from the nineteenth century. The galleries wreathe an inner patio where recitals are held on Sunday afternoons. The museum also houses the Cinemateca Nacional, the national film library, and projects regular art-house and foreign films.

Behind the Galería de Arte Nacional, the ultramodern **Museo de Bellas Artes** abuts the Parque Los Caobos. Although hard to imagine, the same Venezuelan architect, Carlos Raúl Villanueva, designed both the Galería and the museum, though nearly half a century separate the two. The Fine Arts Museum hosts mainly temporary modern art exhibitions, with the added bonus of a rooftop terrace giving great views of the park.

The **Museo de Arte Colonial** is best reached by taxi from around Bellas Artes metro. It's a good half-hour walk uphill to the colonial hacienda known as Quinta de Anauco, up in the San Bernadino district. The effort is very much rewarded by the lovingly restored old coffee mansion, once nestled amid the green hills of the city, and often visited by Bolívar. Guided tours describe not only the period furniture and furnishings, but also the practical aspects of the kitchens, water supply and stables in the rear. Chamber music recitals are held on the grounds, usually on Sundays at 11 AM, with *El Universal* newspaper detailing these on Saturdays.

Southwest from San Bernadino, you come to the district named after the **Iglesia de La Candelaria**, on Avenida Urdaneta. The church's fine *retablos* (altarpieces) are all but ignored by visitors. Most Venezuelans come to visit the tomb of José Gregorio Hernández. Born near Valera in the Andean state of Trujillo in 1864, Doctor Hernández is considered the founder of bacteriology and experimental science in the country. He was renowned for his work among the poor. After his death in 1919, many miracles were attributed to him and he is regarded as a saint by many Venezuelans.

Midtown

The **Boulevard de Sabana Grande** (also Avenida Abraham Lincoln) stretches for two kilometers (one and a quarter miles) east of Plaza Venezuela to Plaza Chacaíto. Young families, couples, teenagers, tourists and chess-players people its boutiques, bookstores, street stalls, and ice-cream parlors. At its western end, dominated by the Torre Previsora and its digital clock, the boulevard accommodates several outdoor cafés, ideal for a light lunch. The most famous, the Gran Café, serves the most elaborate cappuccinos in the capital, and is *the* place to meet for an after-work drink. The boulevard is most vibrant in the evenings or on weekends.

Southwest of Plaza Venezuela's large fountain and modernist sculptures (walk west from metro Plaza Venezuela), the **Jardín Botánico** at the entrance to the Universidad Central de Venezuela (UCV) complex provides a welcome haven from the crowds and traffic. The park is only partly open to the public; in all, the gardens are home to 2,200 species and include a herbarium and orchid greenhouses. Doors open from 8:30 AM until 5 PM.

The home of the **UCV** is actually a mini-city of some 60,000 students, comparable to Brasilia for its integration of form and function. Designed by the omnipresent Villanueva, it took over 12 years to build and was completed in 1957. Though worse-for-wear today, it's still striking. The complex of buildings includes murals, stained glass windows and sculptures, created by both Venezuelan greats such Otero and Soto, but also names like Kandinsky, Léger and Laurens.

South of Chacaíto, at the boulevard's eastern extreme, sophisticated *Caraqueños* diners head to the district of El Rosal, while continuing south under the freeway, a younger crowd turns the Las Mercedes district from a relatively quiet, art gallery-filled area in the day into the city's most vibrant, neon heart at night.

Eastern Caracas

Caracas's Distrito Federal ends at Chacaíto, but it's by no means the limit of the city. Above and east of Chacaíto, the Country Club boasts some of the capital's most luxurious mansions set amid lush gardens. It's now hemmed by urban development on both sides.

Chacao is a busy residential and commercial district, with a lively market every Thursday morning on Calle Cecilio Acosta. However, its biggest claim to fame in shopaholic Venezuela lies within the walls of two of the capital's newest shopping malls. The **Centro Lido**, northeast of Chacao, and the monumental **Centro Sambil**, one block south of the metro, thought to be the largest in Latin America.

East of Chacao, **Altamira**, near the Avenida Francisco de Miranda, has great restaurants, bars and cultural attractions. Climbing up to the hills

of the Ávila, its quiet residential district — along with Los Palos Grandes and Sebucán further east — is one of the most sought-after in the capital.

Above the large Plaza Altamira, on Avenida Luís Roche, the **Casa de Rómulo Gallegos** (CELARG) forms Altamira's cultural heart, with a varied program of concerts, art exhibitions, lectures and films. Also close to the plaza, within the walls of the old Hacienda La Floresta, you find the **Centro de Arte La Estancia**. The Centro features graphic design, three-dimensional art, the plastic arts, and photography. The chief attraction however is the enchanting gardens, where you can enjoy a guided tour followed by a delightful meal at their ever-popular small restaurant ((02) 208-6922; open Tuesday to Sunday 9 AM to 4 PM.

If the gardens of La Estancia whet your appetite for some open air, head east along Avenida Miranda by foot, bus or back on the metro, to

Parque del Este (also Parque Rómulo Betancourt). Encompassing 80 hectares (200 acres) of a former hacienda, Brazilian landscape architect Roberto Burle Max transformed it in the 1960s. The result is a stunning urban park, replete with paths, lawns, woods, lagoons, a monkey island, jaguar pit, snake house and even a replica of Columbus' ship the *Santa María*. For some stargazing, visit the **Planetarium** on the weekends, which puts on hourly shows between 1 PM and 4 PM. The park opens Tuesday to Sunday at 5:30 AM for joggers, and 8 AM for the general public, and closes at 5 PM.

At the park's eastern end, a walkway crosses over to the **Museo del Transporte**, which has a grand collection of vintage cars, many of them used by presidents and dictators down the years. Other exhibits include steam locomotives and earlier horse-drawn carts and carriages. The museum is only open Wednesday from 8:30 AM to 12:30 PM and Sunday 9 AM to 4:30 PM.

Beyond Parque del Este, tourist attractions include **La Casona**, the presidential residence, south of Los Dos Caminos, which houses a fine collection of Venezuelan art and antique furniture. If their guided tours have resumed, the house is very much worth visiting. For information call ((02) 286-7822, or consult Corpoturismo.

Southern Caracas

In the southwestern suburbs, Caracas's largest zoo, **Parque Zoológico de Caricuao**, is the most extensive in the country, covering 480 hectares (1,200 acres). Within its confines, you find many native species of birds, mammals and reptiles, as well as some from Africa, such as elephants and giraffes. The zoo lies at the end of the metro's line 2, a short walk from the Zoológico station, and is open Tuesday to Sunday 9 AM to 4 PM. A mini-train around the grounds runs on weekends.

Also in the south of the city, the museum at the **Fundación de Etnomusicología y Folklor** (FUNDEF) provides an excellent introduction to Venezuela's indigenous cultures. The museum showcases a large number of musical instruments, and crafts such as ceramics, weaving and woodcarving. It's the closest thing the capital has to a sorely lacking anthropological museum, and provides the most complete collection of indigenous creative production you can find in the country. The museum is open Monday to Friday 8:30 AM to noon and 2 PM to 4 PM, housed within a restored mansion called Quinta Micomicona, on Avenida Zuloaga, two blocks east of La Bandera metro stop on line 3 (change at Plaza Venezuela).

SHOPPING

The monumental shopping mall of Centro Sambil boasts plenty of boutiques and designer stores, but nothing you won't find cheaper back home.

For crafts however, one of the best stores is **Casa Caruba**, Edificio Everi, Avenida Andrés Bello, between Transversales 1 and 2, Los Palos Grandes, which stocks stunning crafts a long cut above the run-of-the-mill tourist souvenir. For a cheaper and more cheerful selection, the somewhat worse-for-wear **Mercado Guajiro**, just to the west of Plaza Chacaíto in Paseo Las Flores, includes a large selection of *hamacas* and *chinchorros* (fishnet weave hammocks), as well as every variety of crafts and T-shirts.

Far from the tourist trail, and not always stocked (so phone in advance), money spent at the **Centro CEPAI** ((02) 481-1389, Quinta Etey, Avenida Monte Elena, El Paraíso district, south of downtown, will make its way back to the original craftspeople in Amazonas State. They sell all the crafts, honey, hot sauces, nuts and palm oil that you can find in the Mercado Indígena in Puerto Ayacucho. The **Audubon Society's** shop ((02) 993-2525, in *La Cuadra*, Centro Comercial Paseo Las Mercedes, is also another small but worthy store, also good for books and maps. Call ahead. **Hannsi**, in El Hatillo, is a huge repository of crafts and souvenirs (see EL HATILLO, page 85).

From a tourist perspective, the best bookshop in Caracas is probably **Tecni-Ciencia Libros** ((02) 959-5547 or (02) 959-5035, Nivel C-2 of the CCCT, Chuao or in the Centro Sambil. It has the best selection of travel and coffee table publications on Venezuela, as well as dictionaries and maps.

WHERE TO STAY

If budget is not a problem, you will find Caracas's hotels amenable, comfortable and excellent value. The city's five- and four-star hotels rival any in Latin America. Generally speaking, with the exception of the Hilton, most luxury and five-star accommodation clusters in the east of the city, around Altamira, Chacao and Las Mercedes.

If you're looking for something more moderately priced, the range is still ample, but begins to be restricted geographically. In the midtown (Sabana Grande to Chacaíto) area there are many moderate hotels, but unfortunately the district has taken a turn for the worse over the last years. During the day it's still comparatively safe.

A few budget places are also found midtown, but the majority clump either close to the Nuevo Circo bus terminal — not recommended — or north of Avenida Méjico — better, but still curfewed late at night.

Many of the more expensive hotels that deal primarily with a business clientele offer extremely attractive weekend discounts. These can amount to up to 50% reductions.

The owner of "The Snails" sidewalk store awaits a customer.

Luxury

Of Caracas's luxury hotels, **Caracas Hilton (** (02) 505-5000 TOLL-FREE (800) 44586 FAX (02) 503-5003 WEB SITE www.hilton.com, Avenida Libertador and Sur 25, El Conde, commands the best central location, and enjoys an excellent reputation for service and comfort. The hotel's tower dominates the Parque Central area. The complex includes an appealing pool area, tennis courts, a French and a Japanese restaurant, and chic boutiques. The staff at the information desk are among the best trained in the country, and very helpful. The Hilton also has an annex called **Residencias Anauco Hilton** with less expensive rooms and apartments, most with fully equipped kitchens.

In the midtown area, the recently inaugurated and still expanding **Gran Melia Caracas (** (02) 762-8111 TOLL-FREE (800) 63542 FAX (02) 762-3737 WEB SITE www.granMelia.com, Avenida Casanova and Calle El Recreo, Sabana Grande, ranks among the very best. The ambitious modern complex comprises 432 rooms and a further block of apartment-suites, with every comfort imaginable, including a fitness center, sauna, two pools, restaurants and an important business center. The decor is opulent without being over the top; it is, primarily aimed at the business traveler, but also caters to tourists.

On the hill at the end of the chic dining and dancing district along Avenida Principal de Las Mercedes, the 1950s-built **Tamanaco Inter-Continental (** (02) 909-7111 TOLL-FREE (800) 12132 FAX (02) 208-7116 E-MAIL caracas@interconti.com WEB SITE www.interconti.com, Avenida Principal de Las Mercedes, has been renovated and refurbished of late and is still regarded as one of the capital's best luxury options. All the rooms are suitably comfortable and spacious, with the upper floors offering great views towards Ávila mountain. The large, well-maintained grounds include a stunning pool area cupped by tropical plants and palms. Perhaps its only drawback is the freeway that runs right by its door, with associated noise and fumes.

The newest choice in trendy Altamira, the **Four Seasons Hotel Caracas (** (02) 286-5264 FAX (02) 286-9020 WEB SITE www.fourseasons.com, Avenida Francisco de Miranda and Avenida Luís Roche, on the corner of Plaza Altamira, occupies a striking shiny tower, with rooms and apartment-suites boasting all the comforts of the Four Seasons chain. As the capital's newest hotel, you can expect spanking new facilities as well as service eager-to-please. It was due to open at the end of 2000.

Expensive

Combining both exclusivity and tranquility, the **Hotel Ávila (** (02) 515155 or (02) 520170 FAX (02) 523021, Avenida George Washington, San Bernardino district, offers both these qualities in abundance and adds tropical gardens, a swimming pool, top-end furnishings and an excellent restaurant to the list. Originally built by the Rockefeller family, the Ávila was one of the first luxury hotels in the capital, and thanks to extensive remodeling, it remains probably the best in its class, and by far the most gracious. The hotel's location on the San Bernardino hill means you sacrifice some ease of access to the city's sights in favor of peace and quiet. A price worth paying.

Midtown, just up from Plaza Venezuela, the **Hotel Atlántida (** (02) 793-3211 FAX (02) 781-3696, Avenida La Salle, Los Caobos, Caracas, makes a good, comfortable choice with spacious rooms. The hotel includes a restaurant, pool and tennis courts, and is not overly noisy considering its location. In the Sabana Grande area, the most sophisticated choice after the Melia is the **Hotel Lincoln Suites (** (02) 761-2727 FAX (02) 762-5503, Avenida Francisco Solano, between San Jerónimo and Los Jabillos, providing good service and commodious rooms, although the decor feels a bit dated and the hotel lacks a pool.

In the Las Mercedes district, if the Tamanaco is beyond your budget, the **Hotel Paseo Las Mercedes (** (02) 901-0033 or (02) 901-0077 FAX (02) 993-0341, Avenida Principal de Las Mercedes, within the Centro Comercial Las Mercedes, still holds four stars, and with art galleries, boutiques, restaurants and nightlife only a stone's throw away, makes an excellent choice. Like the Tamanaco however, it suffers from noise pollution from the nearby busy freeways.

In Altamira, with its pool, restaurant, landscaping and comfortable rooms, along with its prime location in this district of sophisticated dining and nightlife, the **Hotel Continental Altamira (** (02) 261-6019 or (02) 261-9091 FAX (02) 262-0243 E-MAIL hotelcontinental@cantv.net, Avenida San Juan Bosco, Altamira, surpasses its similarly priced competitors in the area.

Moderate

Downtown, you have to accept the unofficial curfew that sets in late at night. On weekends, you can still find plenty of people walking the streets, emerging from restaurants and diving into bars, but when they head home, you should follow their example.

The best choice in the old center, with plenty of character, and a very good restaurant on the top floor is the **Hotel Plaza Catedral (** (02) 564-1797, Esquina La Torre, Boulevard Plaza Bolívar. Enjoying an unrivalled position next to the cathedral, the rooms aren't luxurious but certainly comfortable, and the staff are friendly.

The midtown Sabana Grande hosts a plethora of mid-range hotels. One of the few with a pool,

Classically inspired figures crown the top of the Teatro Nacional.

though admittedly tiny, is **Hotel Las Américas** ((02) 951-3787 FAX (02) 951-1717, Calle Los Cerritos, Bello Monte, south of Boulevard de Sabana Grande. Its rooms are all acceptable and good value. The other good choice is the **Hotel Coliseo** ((02) 762-7916 through 7919 FAX (02) 761-7333, Avenida Casanova, between Calles Coromoto and Primera de Bellomonte, efficiently run and friendly.

Continuing east into Altamira, the **Hotel Residencia Montserrat** ((02) 263-3533 FAX (02) 261-1394, Avenida Ávila, Sur Plaza Altamira, offers good value for money with a range of rooms, some with self-catering kitchens—a good choice if you plan to stay a while. The hotel is understandably popular in this upscale and safe part of town, so reserve in advance. The next-door **Hotel La Floresta** ((02) 263-1955 FAX (02) 262-1243 provides an acceptable alternative.

Inexpensive

Cheap hotels in Caracas tend to double as "love hotels" or "hot-sheet hotels" with rooms often rented by the hour, or else booked solid over weekends. If you need a budget place upon arrival in Caracas, either call in advance, or else avoid the weekend. The really cheap hotels cluster around the Nuevo Circo bus terminal and are honestly not worth the risk.

Of the inexpensive hotels found downtown, the best is the **Hotel Inter** ((02) 564-0251 or (02) 564-7031, Esquina Calero, one block up from Avenida Urdaneta. The hotel is comparatively safe and quiet, and a short hop from the lively *tascas* and restaurants of La Candelaria. Also nearby, but on the noisier Avenida Fuerzas Armadas, is the **Hotel Metropol** ((02) 562-8666, Plaza López a Socorro, acceptable for the price.

The best area for budget hotel hunting is Avenida Las Acacias (Prolongación Sur), running south from metro Plaza Venezuela. Although the area transforms into a bit of a red-light district at night, and particularly on weekends, if you're not a single female it's acceptable. Leading down from the junction of Avenida Las Acacias and Avenida Casanova, perhaps a dozen hotels line up. Ask to see the rooms yourself, and avoid those that face the street for more peace and quiet. Of the choices here, the **Hotel La Mirage** ((02) 793-2733 and the **Hotel Ariston** ((02) 782-7723 (at the end), both offer tidy rooms with air-conditioning (often noisy), televisions and hot water. **Hotel Odeon** ((02) 793-1322 FAX (02) 781-9380 is also a popular backpacker choice, with a decent Colombian restaurant attached.

Near Sabana Grande, the **Hotel Cristal** ((02) 761-9131, Pasaje Asunción, off Boulevard de Sabana Grande and close to Sabana Grande metro, may not be sophisticated, but it's clean and comfortable with air-conditioned doubles,

televisions and hot water, making it good value for the area.

WHERE TO EAT

Caracas claims perhaps the greatest number of restaurants per capita of any Latin America city. Their variety is also mind-boggling, reflecting the city's immigrant heritage, and its citizens love for dining out and partying. Whether it's traditional Venezuelan, *haute cuisine* French, fresh Italian, Chinese, Japanese, Arabic or Thai, the problem in Caracas is not being starved for choice, but spoiled.

If you're serious about your gastronomy, acquire a copy of Miro Popic's annually updated *Guía Gastronómica de Caracas* (Caracas: Miro Popic Editor), published in English and Spanish. It reviews all the city's restaurants, nightspots, cinemas and museums exhaustively; available at most bookshops. The restaurants are online at WEB SITE www.miropopic.com.

Expensive

The most sophisticated restaurants are found in the Las Mercedes district and around Altamira (including La Castellana and Los Palos Grandes). *Caraqueños* love to dress up and show off their new designer outfits, and men should wear a jacket, and usually a tie, in the restaurants listed below.

The top restaurants of the capital are dominated by foreign cuisine, with the French brigade led by **Le Gourmet** ((02) 208-7242, inside the Hotel Tamanaco. Le Gourmet enjoys an enviable reputation and a loyal clientele. The menu, though dominated by the traditional, isn't afraid of striking out in new directions. Claiming none of the pretensions of Le Gourmet to haute cuisine, **Le Petit Bistro de Jacques** ((02) 263-8695 or (02) 266-0321 E-MAIL lepetitbistrot@cantv.net, Avenida San Felipe, Quinta No. 24, La Castellana, serves superb traditional French dishes, such as foie gras and confit de canard, in a setting which will send shivers down the spines of Paris-lovers. Combined with an enviable wine list and attentive service, the Bistro is hard to beat, though perhaps slightly overpriced.

Hot on the heals of these established *restos* comes the newer, more inventive **Cathay** ((02) 286-9715, Centro Comercial Las Cúpulas, Avenida 2 at Transversal 4, Los Palos Grandes, which combines Pacific Rim influences and French touches to perfection, attracting a sophisticated crowd who like to be seen while they dine in the airy and modern glass-and-wood interior.

Keeping with the Mediterranean theme, the kings of Caracas's Italian restaurants are the family-run **Vizio** ((02) 285-5675, inside the CELARG on Avenida Luís Roche, up from Plaza

An extravagant exterior announces the Galician delights of *Casa Farruco*.

Altamira, consistently excellent and friendly, and the more extravagant **L'Operetta** ((02) 265-3293, Calle El Bosque at Avenida Principal de La Castellana, La Castellana, where the opulent furnishings and antiques, the quiet murmur of diners and the traditional cooking are second-to-none.

Turning to Oriental food, **Tambo** ((02) 952-4243, Torre Europa, Avenida Francisco de Miranda, near Chacao, took Caracas by storm with its combination of Peruvian and Japanese dishes, known as "Nikkei." Still exceedingly popular, its smart, modern decor make it one of the trendiest restaurants in town, with a sushi bar upstairs, and over 140 dishes to choose from.

For pure Japanese cooking, few come close to **Hatsuhana** ((02) 264-1214, Avenida San Juan Bosco at Transversal 5, Altamira, with very stylish wood and bamboo decor and fantastic tepanyaki, knife-wielding chefs, sushi, and a new terrace-with-a-view.

The chic rooftop setting and oriental gardens of **Ara** ((02) 953-3270, on the eighth floor of the Centro Lido in El Rosal district, match its exquisitely presented Japanese and World menus, proving a popular blend among the jet-set. Aficionados of Chinese cooking claim **Chez Wong** ((02) 761-4194, Edificio Isabelita, Avenida Francisco Solano, Sabana Grande, remains king despite growing competition. It excels in creative dishes combining Sichuan and Hunan cuisine with unexpected ingredients and spices.

In Las Mercedes, arguably the best Mexican restaurant in Caracas is **El Tajín** ((02) 993-0442, Calle California at Calle Perijá, Las Mercedes, with the most exceptional presentation you're likely to find outside of Mexico. The setting is luxurious, crowded with Mexican antiques. The queen of beauty and taste in Thai food has to be **Samui** ((02) 285-4600, Multicentro Los Palos Grandes, Avenida Andrés Bello between Avenida Francisco de Miranda and Transversal 1, next to Arabica Café. *The New York Times* rated it the best Thai restaurant in South America, and it even offers a far more economical lunchtime menu.

Moderate

In Sabana Grande, the choices are numerous, but not always excellent or good value. The following all cluster along Avenida Francisco Solano, which runs parallel one block north of the boulevard. For some wonderful Basque cooking, **Urritia** ((02) 710448, Esquina Los Manguitos, Avenida Francisco Solano, is the best outside La Candelaria, with a long-standing reputation and very good service. Evening meals are more expensive. My choices among the many Italian options are **El Rugantino** ((02) 761-4411, inside the Hotel Tampa, with live music on the weekends, and **Da Guido** ((02) 710937, with friendly and attentive service, and very fresh pasta.

For excellent Venezuelan dishes in a Spanish-colonial decor complete with Venezuelan crafts, head to **El Portón** ((02) 952-0027, Avenida Pichancha No. 18, El Rosal. Sample *aguacate relleno con camarones* (avocados stuffed with shrimp) as a starter, followed by a *pabellón criollo* or a *parilla* mixed grill, and finish with a *bienmesabe* dessert.

In Las Mercedes, again you're faced with an embarrassment of choice. Of the hundreds of places, **Bar Sí** ((02) 993-2740, Calle Madrid between Veracruz and Caroní, with its fresh fish and delicious cuts of meat prepared along Asian lines with a flair for invention and innovation, elevate it beyond its competitors in the area.

For some of the best meats in this area, the **Maute Grill** ((02) 991-0892, Avenida Río de Janeiro, Las Mercedes, is hard to beat. Bypass the somewhat tasteless American-style bar (of which there are many in this district, with names like Texas and Cowboys) at the front. At the rear, enjoy a chunky, excellent value steak in a beautiful tree-covered patio.

People argue over the best Italian establishment in Las Mercedes, but my personal favorite is **Il Cielo** ((02) 993-4062, Calle La Trinidad, Las Mercedes, for its good wine list, personable service, ample menu and tasty desserts.

Among the array of restaurants in the Altamira and La Castellana districts, many provide very good lunchtime value at inexpensive prices. For something more sophisticated, **Altamar** ((02) 262-1813, Transversal 3 at Avenida Luís Roche, has long been regarded as the best seafood restaurant in its class, while for meats, **La Estancia** ((02) 261-1874, Avenida Principal de la Castellana, just south of Plaza La Castellana, brings in the best prime cuts from Zulia State.

Inexpensive

For lunch while sightseeing in the downtown district, two of the choices within museums provide more stylish alternatives to the large number of *luncherías* and *areperas*: the small **Café Sacro** inside the Museo Sacro on Plaza Bolívar, and the MACCSI's terrace restaurant, **Café del Museo** ((02) 577-5710, Parque Central. A good value, typical *criollo* lunch can be found at **Caracas Típica**, just by the Ipostel Correo de Carmelitas, north of Plaza Bolívar. On Plaza Bolívar, the Swiss restaurant, **Les Grisons**, on the top floor of the Plaza Catedral Hotel, also serves international food, with an unbeatable view.

The best area to head for hearty food is La Candelaria (about three blocks up from metro Parque Carabobo), where the mainly Spanish *tascas* and restaurants present a number of excellent choices. Most of the establishments have been family-run since the first Spanish immigrants claimed the area as theirs in the first half of the twentieth century. The majority are closed on Sunday.

Tascas are more informal than restaurants, dealing mainly with busy lunchtime crowds. They also serve *tapas* and *raciones* at the bar (small portions of squid, shrimp, spicy potatoes, fried eggplant), making excellent stopgaps. Cuisine in La Candelaria excels in fresh seafood, but also traditional northern Spanish favorites such as lamb, rabbit, spicy sausages, stuffed peppers and beef stews.

An institution in the area for generations, **Bar Basque** ((02) 576-5955, Alcabala a Peligro, La Candelaria, is very busy at lunch, closed on Sundays, and you'll need to reserve in advance since the six tables are understandably at a premium. You can always nibble at the bar while you wait. The restaurant is famous for its dishes such as sea bass in green sauce (*donostiarra*). Don't leave without trying the camembert with honey for dessert.

Other popular haunts in the district are **La Tertulia** ((02) 574-1476 and **La Cita** ((02) 572-8180, both on the southeast corner of the Plaza La Candelaria. South a block and east, between Esquinas Peligro and Puente República, **Casa Farruco** ((02) 572-9343 ranks among the best in the area for traditional Spanish fare.

The ever-popular Sabana Grande presents a wealth of acceptable restaurants where lunches are particularly good value. At the western end of Avenida Francisco Solano, try **Sorrento** for tasty Venezuelan dishes, or else **Da Vito** for home-cooking Italian style.

For one of the best lunches in the capital, **Café Estancia** ((02) 208-6922, Avenida Francisco de Miranda opposite Primera Avenida de los Palos Grandes, Altamira, inside the graphic-design

The old church of Santísima Trinidad among the brash tower blocks of downtown.

Centro La Estancia, open Tuesday to Sunday, enjoys a great reputation, with the incomparable setting of the tropical gardens of the old hacienda.

ENTERTAINMENT AND NIGHTLIFE

With such a young population, many with money to burn, Caracas nightlife hops all night, and not just on the weekend.

Nightspots change as fast as people change their socks in Caracas, with the "in" crowd constantly seeking the new place to be seen sipping an imported Scotch or trendy Vodka. Along with the loud clubs and video bars however, there are plenty of places for an older, more sophisticated crowd to enjoy a drink and some music. In Caracas, the party doesn't even start until midnight. Dress code is generally smart, so no sneakers, and sometimes no jeans.

For the latest place to *rumbear* (party) and concert listings, *Urbe* WEB SITE www.planetaurbe.com is the *pavitos'* (young rich kids) bible, a weekly newspaper-magazine available at most news stands. The English-language *Daily Journal* also publishes cinema and art gallery listings, while *Date en Caracas* is also useful. *El Nacional's* Sunday supplement *Feriado* often reviews the latest restaurants and bars, and its *Cultura* section rounds up cultural events, WEB SITE www.el-nacional.com.

Downtown places are pretty off-limits for nighttime drinking and dancing, with the exception of the Bellas Artes area around the Ateneo. On the first floor of the Ateneo, the small, semi-open air **La Terraza**, usually includes live music every night, patronized by an arty crowd. Round the side of the Ateneo, the Bohemian's favorite, **Cafe Rajatabla**, only stretches to around midnight, but makes for one of the best informal, chatty places for a drink in the capital.

Sabana Grande is dominated by salsa and merengue bars and clubs, with **El Mani es Así**, Calle El Cristo, Las Delicias (north of Avenida Francisco Solano) the cathedral of salsa, where pilgrims come to hotfoot about the dance floor to the best live Caribbean rhythms in the capital. It's small, intimate and hot, and if you didn't dance when you walked in, you will do when you leave.

For something more sedate in the Chacao area, **Juan Sebastián Bar** ((02) 951-5575, Avenida Venezuela, El Rosal, south of Avenida Francisco de Miranda, is the city's longest-standing jazz bar, though it includes a restaurant. Thursday night is usually best if you want to avoid the crowds, with the capital's best jazz musicians often gathering for impromptu sessions.

Altamira's list of nightspots grows ever-longer, with the terrace of **El León** on Plaza La Castellana a popular meeting place for early drinks and

chatter. Close by, one of the "in" clubs is **The Flower** with loud techno, merengue and salsa until dawn, but also some great ska nights. Proving popular for a while now, **Café L'Attico**, Avenida Luís Roche, just south of Primera Transversal, doubles as a restaurant, but on the weekends most people come to have a good time, something they manage to do with style.

Before getting to Las Mercedes, one other bar is worth mentioning, since it's one of the capital's most elaborate and sophisticated. **Barrock** ((02) 266-1851, Transversal 4 between Cuarta Avenida and Avenida San Felipe, Prados del Este, lies a taxi ride away, south of the Centro Comercial Concresa off the Autopista Prados del Este. Combined with its expensive drinks, it's a high-priced proposition. But if you want to feel part of *le tout* Caracas and sip cocktails amid a luxuriant and decadent eighteenth-century style decor, this is the price you have to pay. An alternative, but equally smart place is **Citron**, in the Centro Sambil.

Of the profusion of bars, restaurants and clubs in Las Mercedes, one of the quieter alternatives is **Zoe Caffe**, Avenida Río de Janeiro, between Calles Veracruz and Caroní, with a very relaxed and quiet feel, serving vegetarian food until late. For something louder, **Liverpool** is a long-established disco over several floors on Avenida Principal, with **Ozono**, Calle Madrid, and **Vertigo** nearby, also packed with young people at the weekend.

HOW TO GET THERE

Simón Bolívar International Airport lies over the mountains in Maiquetía, close to the port of La Guaira on the coast. Depending on traffic, the journey takes an hour. All international and national flights for Caracas arrive there; buses and taxis connect city and airport (see GETTING TO VENEZUELA, page 268 in TRAVELERS' TIPS).

La Bandera is now the terminal for all long-distance buses to the central and western towns — for example, Maracay, Valencia, Coro, Maracaibo, Mérida, Puerto Ayacucho — with **Nuevo Circo** (the former chaotic terminal downtown) only employed for shorter distances (for example, San Francisco de Yare, La Guaira, Higuerote, El Junquito). La Bandera is on metro line 3, connecting to line 1 at Plaza Venezuela. The terminal is close to the metro's exit, and though still confusing for the newcomer to Venezuela, is infinitely superior to the unsafe, dirty and noisy Nuevo Circo.

For buses to eastern Venezuela — Barcelona, Puerto La Cruz, Cumaná — and southeastern destinations — Ciudad Bolívar, Ciudad Guayana (Puerto Ordaz), Santa Elena de Uairén — the new **Terminal del Oriente** ((02) 243-2606 lies on the eastern outskirts of the city, on the highway to Barcelona. To get there, take a metro to Petare, and either catch a bus or a taxi from there. Avoid passing through Petare at night, when it's probably best to take a taxi from the center, or from the terminal if you're arriving. Buses also run to and from Nuevo Circo to the terminal.

Several companies providing more luxurious, air-conditioned buses with televisions, videos and toilets run their own terminals, and make for first-class transportation — albeit freezing, due to the air-conditioning: bring a sweater.

Aeroexpresos Ejecutivos ((02) 266-3601 or (02) 266-9011, Avenida Principal de Bello Campo, south from metro Altamira, travel to several cities, including Valencia, Barquisimeto, and Puerto La Cruz, while **Rodovías de Venezuela (** (02) 577-7011 or (02) 577-6622 WEB SITE www.rodovias .com.ve, on Avenida Libertador, Paseo Amador Bendayan, close to metro Colegio de Ingenieros, service similar routes.

EL ÁVILA

Many visitors to Caracas gaze longingly at the verdant hills of the Ávila mountain as they struggle through the crowds and the traffic of the city. The mountain is easily accessible from the city, protected by the 85-sq-km (33-sq-mile) Parque Nacional El Ávila, with excellent infrastructure and plenty of walking and hiking trails. Protected by the national park for 86 km (53 miles) of its length, the Cordillera de la Costa rises dramatically from the northern limits of Caracas, and tumbles down to the Caribbean on the other side. Up to its peaks, which undulate between Pico Occidental at 2,478 m (8,128 ft) and Pico Naiguatá at 2,765 m (9,069 ft), trails lead first through deciduous forest, then climb higher through more humid cloudforest, and end in windswept moors.

The trails harbor a profusion of birdlife, with over 200 species spotted, the forests providing habitats for monkeys, mammals and even large felines — with the promise of a beautiful, sylvan waterfall never far away. The Ávila's wonders are far from being secrets, with a city of some five million on its doorstep, but neither is it overrun.

GENERAL INFORMATION

Contact Señor Contreras of the **Centro de Excursionistas de Caracas (** (02) 235-3155 or (02) 985-3210, for more information about hiking in the Ávila and about their schedule of hikes. Corpoturismo's El Ávila leaflet contains informative text and a map of trails in Spanish, while Inparques also produces a more detailed *Mapa para el Excursionista*. The most extensive infrastructure in the

park is found at the Centro Recreacional Los Venados, to the west. Temperatures can drop dramatically along the top of the mountain, and water can be scarce, so bring cold-weather waterproof gear and plenty of water.

WHAT TO SEE AND DO

As you look up to the mountain from the city, you can't help but notice the tower atop one of its western peaks. The 14-story construction is in fact the Hotel Humboldt — the German explorer climbed the mountain in 1800 — built in 1956. At the time, the luxury hotel was linked to the city and the coast by the ambitious *teleférico* cable car. In 1988, the *teleférico* stopped functioning, and despite rumors that it would resume soon, and that the hotel would be remodeled, very little has materialized, unfortunately. Plans now exist to convert the hotel into Caracas's only casino and to resume the cable car service.

Without the *teleférico* to hoist you up, you're left with your legs — or nearly. For a great shortcut to admire the views from the top without the strain, take a jeep from the top of San Bernadino district area known as Cotiza, at the end of Avenida Peñalver. A paved, coiling road leads up to the *teleférico* station, with a fork to the flower-growing village of Galipán. From the top, walk across the spine of the mountain via Pico Occidental. Here you can choose to return via the Sabas Nieves route to Altamira, continue to Pico Oriental descending via the Quebrada Sebucán waterfall, or even follow the trails further east over to Pico Goering and Pico Naiguatá. If you leave very early in the morning, you can be back in town in the afternoon.

In the western sector, you can follow the old *Camino de los Españoles*, via the ruins of old haciendas and eighteenth-century forts, and on down to Maiquetía. Due to safety concerns at the hike's start (at La Pastora) and end, only attempt this route if you're part of a group.

If you just want to find some easily accessible, leisurely trails, head to the Altamira entrance. *Carritos* (buses) climb from Plaza Altamira up Avenida San Juan Bosco to Transversal 10. Walk west to the entrance. Although a bit crowded on weekends, during the week you can easily find some peace on the numerous trails, with a lovely waterfall about half an hour's walk away.

EL HATILLO

Smart suburbs and country clubs now besiege the little hamlet of El Hatillo, with its restored church and multicolored houses, cupped by the hills southeast of Caracas. On weekends, the village bustles with *Caraqueños* enjoying a day out, browsing the multitude of craft and curio shops, and

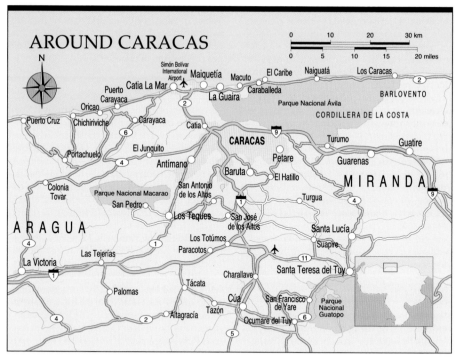

AROUND CARACAS

enjoying meals at the dozens of restaurants that have sprung up over the last decade. During the week — except Mondays when stores are closed — the old streets and shaded plaza are quiet and friendly, making for an ideal getaway in cooler climes.

WHAT TO SEE AND DO

The charming old streets of El Hatillo cluster around Plaza Bolívar with the Iglesia de Santa Rosalía de Palermo on its west side. The one-story houses, painted blues, greens and ochres, have nearly all been turned into antiquarians, art galleries, *artesanía* stores, cafés and restaurants. The largest handicraft center in Venezuela, **Hannsi**, Calle Bolívar No. 12, up from the northeast corner of Plaza Bolívar, makes for a bewildering shopping experience, with crafts and souvenirs packed floor to ceiling. Quality varies, but the choice is undeniably impressive. Calle 2 de Mayo, running parallel to the north of the square, and Calle Comercio to the south, offer the greatest concentration of interesting stores.

WHERE TO EAT

Moderate

Many sophisticated restaurants have opened of late, catering for the tastes of wealthy *Caraqueño* families. The choice of cuisine is surprising, rang-

ing from the ginger and lemongrass of the Thai **Sokuthai** ((02) 963-5698, Calle Miranda south, to the traditional Swiss cooking of **L'Arbalette** ((02) 963-7278, Calle Santa Rosalía (west), with its great terrace affording views across the hills.

For something typically Venezuelan — spit-roasted pork and beef — with live Llanos music on weekend nights, the thatched **La Romana Hatillana** ((02) 961-1816 on Calle Miranda is an old favorite. At the other extreme is the stylish terrace of **Sake** ((02) 963-5551, Calle Sucre No.8, serving excellent Japanese sushi and tepanyaki.

Inexpensive

Typical *pabellón criollo* and fried chicken are served up by Señora Ninette of **La Gorda** ((02) 963-7476, just before L'Arbalette on Calle Santa Rosalía. For pastries and cakes with a view of the square, **Das Pastelhaus** ((02) 963-5486 has been creating them in style for over a generation and is still unsurpassed. **Oker's** ((02) 963-2249, Calle Bolívar, serves all sorts of Spanish dishes from *tapas* up to fully fledged fish and meat standards, and is one of the liveliest places in the evenings for a drink.

HOW TO GET THERE

The easiest and most economical way to get to El Hatillo is on metrobus route 12, which leaves from metro Chacaíto. You could also negotiate with a taxi driver for the round trip.

LITORAL CENTRAL

Vargas State encompasses the fringe of Caribbean coast north of Caracas from Puerto Maya in the west to Chuspa in the east. The area is known as the Litoral Central.

Vargas is Venezuela's youngest state, but it is also its most tragic. In late 1999, following unprecedented rainfall along the coast, huge mudslides swept thousands of hillside dwellings into the sea, resulting in the greatest natural disaster in Venezuela's history. Over 20,000 people died, with more than 100,000 injured. Some 6,000 people are still unaccounted for in the area from Catia La Mar to Los Caracas. Already a poor state, struggling with insufficient infrastructure and ever-mushrooming shanty town *ranchos*, the rains of 1999 were a vast human calamity. As this goes to press, many roads are still impassable, and many lives only just beginning to be rebuilt.

Foreign travelers rarely ventured beyond the hotels close to Maiquetía airport, and Vargas' wild coast was a secret known to very few — a constant surprise so near to the capital. Its eastern *pueblos* form part of the area known as Barlovento, Venezuela's black African heartland, where fishing and agricultural villages sprang from their sleepy states for the festival of San Juan in June (see BARLOVENTO, page 186).

The historic port of La Guaira will take years to restore. Beyond Carabellada damage from flooding was less severe, with the old rutted road leading all the way to Chirimena and on to Higuerote. First you come to the intriguing government vacation resort of Los Caracas, built by dictator Pérez Jiménez, and then the small villages and great beaches of Osma, Todasana, La Sabana and Caruao.

SPORTS AND OUTDOOR ACTIVITIES

For enthusiasts of deep-sea fishing, several companies in the area offered various trips of a day or longer on the La Guaira Bank. They may be back in operation by the time you read this. The best times for billfish are February through to November, though tarpon, wahoo and snook are abundant all year round. Inside the Sheraton, you'll find **Yachting Tours** (/FAX (02) 394-0591, and inside the Gran Caribe, **Venezuela Marlin Safari** ((02) 394-8868 FAX (02) 394-4078 E-MAIL marlinsafari@cantv.net.

Further west from the Sheraton lies **Gigi Charters** ((02) 944689 FAX (02) 948970 E-MAIL mail@gigifish.com.ve WEB SITE www.gigifish.com.ve. All of these companies provide full-board, upscale trips with bilingual guides. Family trips of three days on a yacht can work out to cost less than one might expect.

WHERE TO STAY AND EAT

The hotels around Macuto and east to Carabellada made useful overnight stays for travelers taking early morning flights or arriving late. They provided an alternative to dealing with intimidating Caracas. At the time of writing, these were still inoperable, with the hope they would soon be fully functional once again. Hotels include the international-class resort of the **Macuto Sheraton** TOLL-FREE (800) 74372 FAX (02) 394-4317 E-MAIL sheratonmacuto@telcel.net.ve WEB SITE www.sheraton.com/Macuto, Sector Caribe, Carabellada, and in Macuto, the three-star **Hotel Quince Letras** ((02) 334-1551 FAX (02) 334-1432 E-MAIL Hqletras@att.com.ve, Avenida La Playa, Macuto.

I would urge travelers to check on their current status with the Corpoturismo office upon arrival in Maiquetía, and patronize them if possible. Tourist revenue will be all the more vital for the region since the disaster.

Of the many *posadas* along the road, the expensive yet excellent **Aloe Spa** ((02) 952-3741 IN THE UNITED STATES (718) 802-0037 WEB SITE www.aloespa.com, just west of Caruao, ranks among the best in the country. The grounds of the spa are extensive, planted with aloe and a profusion of medicinal and herbal plants used for preparing their delicious, gourmet meals. The spa package includes healthy, though not always vegetarian, breakfast and dinner, plus Hatha yoga and Tai Chi sessions in the morning and afternoon. Optional hiking, boat trips, therapies and massages (including hydro-, clay and aroma therapies, as well as exfoliation and chakra treatments) can all be arranged with prior notice. Transfers from Caracas or Maiquetía can be arranged.

In Chirimena, ask for the road to Chirere. About 10 minutes up and over the hill lies the **Hotel Playa Chirere** ((014) 934-0258 (call between 5 PM and 8 PM weekends only, reservations essential). The attractive hotel encompasses 14 double, brightly painted rooms of two sizes, the larger ones allowing space for a mattress at a push. Electricity is only available for air-conditioning from 7 PM at night, and the metal-roofed cabins tend to bake in the sun during the day. The handsome grounds (as you'd expect from a Swiss-owned enterprise) cup a pool and adjoining bar area, with a stairway down to a beautiful, nigh-on private, beach.

WESTERN BEACHES

Since the disastrous floods in eastern Vargas State in late 1999, the beaches of the western Litoral draw more of the weekend crowds to their sandy stretches and small coves. My personal favorite is Puerto Maya. You can reach them either by heading west towards Catia La Mar when you hit the coast near Maiquetía airport, or, coming the other way, by taking the turnoff eight kilometers (five miles) before the Colonia Tovar.

In the words of my schoolteacher, the roads from Tovar "could do better," but the one to Puerto Cruz is fine even in a small car. To make up for their poor condition, they lead you through dense forest swept by clouds and covered in bromeliads. Small settlements appear from nowhere, houses selling produce on their doorsteps, but apart from these, there are few people to spoil the natural surroundings.

You should fill up with gas in Tovar if you intend to investigate much of the coast, since the only other station is in Cayaraca.

PUERTO CRUZ AND PUERTO MAYA

Of the many once-isolated fishing villages that dot this part of the coast, Puerto Maya is probably my favorite. Leave your car in Puerto Cruz and contract a boatman to take you around the headland to the Puerto Maya bay. A road links the two, but requires a vehicle with high clearance.

The villagers in Puerto Maya all seem to be related one way or another, and their houses stand in the picture-perfect cove, making the most of the shade from the hosts of tall palms. The steep hills all around cup the tranquil bay, creating calm waters and soft sand, contrasting with brilliant blue skies. Ask the locals about the paths to the rivers and waterfalls nearby.

Where to Stay and Eat
The only *posada* as yet in Puerto Maya is the inexpensive **Gua-K-Maya** ((02) 993-1695/5866 FAX (02) 979-0323, operated by Eco Posadas in Caracas, who can also provide transportation. It could do with a new lick of paint, but its position right by the sea, with ample relaxing areas and good-sized rooms, still make it a good choice. Their policy towards meals has changed down the years, so you should check whether breakfast or meals are included. Fresh fish and empanadas are sold at an informal restaurant in the middle of the beach by "la Negra."

CHICHIRIVICHE DE LA COSTA

In order not to be confused with the more famous Chichiriviche in Falcón State, the "de la Costa" was appended to the name of this small fishing village. A very rough road leads over from Puerto Cruz, but it's probably best to take the turning 10 km (six miles) after the fork for Colonia Tovar on the road from El Junquito. Like the road down to Puerto Cruz, the views of mountain, forest and sea compensate for the potholes. You'll also encounter a few shallow river crossings as

the road switches back and forth across the Río Chichiriviche. The village and its church are actually set back from the crescent bay, though many of the houses nearer to the beach can be rented.

Where to Stay and Eat
The clean and friendly **Hotel El Montero** ((02) 862-0436 at the beach's eastern entrance offers 10 decent double rooms and two cabins for six with refrigerators, as well as a good-sized pool and a restaurant serving very fresh fish. Nearby is the more basic **Posada de Loli** ((02) 945-0541 with seven rooms and homestyle cooking.

WEST OF CHICHIRIVICHE

The coast road leading all the way to La Guaira and Maiquetía begins at Chichiriviche, and the easterly parts are paved. After the bay of **Oriaco**, now a private beach club (though legally you should still have access to the beach), there is a fork. Continue on for the scenic coast road towards **Tarma** and **Carayaca** to enjoy a swim at Punta Tarma or Bikini. Or else take the southwesterly route all the way back to the Colonia Tovar by taking the right fork.

WEST OF CARACAS

Heading west from Caracas, the city soon gives way to undulating hills and the forests of the Cordillera de la Costa. If you're heading to Maracay, or else looping back to Caracas, there are some great roads to bump along and take in the rural scenery, linking the old town of La Victoria, the unique Colonia Tovar and the beaches of eastern Aragua State. For colonial La Victoria, take the old *Carreterra Panamericana* off the fast Highway 1 to Maracay as you leave Caracas. You pass through Los Teques, founded in 1703, after about half an hour. From there, the old road (once a Spanish *Camino Real*) winds its way down to green valleys and through the small old towns of Las Tejerías and El Consejo to La Victoria, 24 km (15 miles) from Los Teques.

COLONIA TOVAR

Through the overhanging leaves of tall trees, triangular roofs and exposed beams, a church spire and shuttered balconies paint the impression of an alpine idyll — as seen on countless biscuit-tin boxes and out-of-date calendars. You could be forgiven for thinking you were in deepest darkest Bavaria, when in fact you're 30 km (18 miles) from the tropical chaos of Caracas.

After the beaches of the Litoral, the Colonia, fictionalized in Isabel Allende's novel *Eva Luna*, makes probably the next most popular destination for *Caraqueños* looking for a day out. On week-

ends and at vacation times it swarms with people come to enjoy the cool mountain air, traditional restaurants serving bratwurst and, of course, the beer served in steins. At other times Tovar is quiet and sleepy. The feeling of being ensnared in a tourist trap is hard to shake off in the Colonia. But its range of well-managed *posadas* and the meandering forested walks in the nearby hills still make for a great escape from the city, or an end in itself.

Background

Following the devastating wars of Independence, Venezuela amended its immigration laws to attract farmers and settlers from Europe. The people of the Colonia Tovar are the strangest product of this legislation. A wealthy *criollo* landowner, Martín Tovar, agreed to let immigrant Germans farm his land, and Agustín Codazzi traveled to Europe to make the arrangements. The land-

hungry peasants he found came from the community of Kaiserstuhl in the German Black Forest, and on January 11, 1843, 392 hopefuls set sail from Le Havre.

Disaster struck early on when smallpox broke out on-board, claiming over 70 lives. As a result, the ship was quarantined off the Venezuelan coast for a full 40 days, until it was finally permitted to land at Puerto Colombia. News of the disease had spread meanwhile, and instead of the warm welcome expected by the immigrants, they were met by cold shoulders and little help. Finally, on April 8, 1843, they arrived at their new home, having made the long, arduous climb up from the coast.

Settlers represented every skill necessary for the development of the community, from tailor,

The uniquely Alpine San Martín church in Colonia Tovar.

priest and carpenter to printer and blacksmith. The first colonists never forgave the Venezuelans their initial rejection however, and the Colonia Tovar as it was known remained an island of German language, traditions and culture for the next century.

It wasn't until World War II that contact with the outside world increased. Spanish became the official language and the community allowed marriage with Venezuelans, which had once been forbidden. By 1963 and the completion of the road from Caracas, the colony's isolation effectively ended, with curious *Caraqueños* coming to visit in ever greater numbers and the community selling its products in the markets of the capital.

Today, you can still see Aryan-looking villagers and hear German on the streets, but much of the town's authenticity has been lost in the tourist boom of the last two decades.

What to See and Do

The wood-beamed **St. Martin's Church** lies at the heart of the town, named after the colony's patron saint, and its founder Martín Tovar. The church's black timbers are unique in Venezuela, copied from the church in Emmendingen in Germany. Note the perpendicular twin naves inside, which separated men and women. During Tovar's *fiestas patronales* on and around November 11, the statue of Saint Martin, brought from Germany by the first settlers, parades around the town to much merriment.

Walk back up the hill to the *cementerio* (cemetery) for swooping views of the town and sur-

rounding countryside. Seek out the early settlers' humble wooden crosses and later, more substantial, tombstones for a history of the settlement.

Further up the hill, amid the craft shops of Calle Museo, Nestor Rojas' **Museo de Historia y Artesanía** only opens on weekends and holidays, from 9 AM to 6 PM, but provides a good history of the unique colony. The collection includes contracts penned in swirly script, farm tools and utensils, and the old printing press. Two of the oldest of the colony's houses stand in front of the church. Agustín Codazzi lived in the **Jahn House**, while Alexander Benitz occupied the other. Benitz established Venezuela's first brewery — a true national hero. Below the church lies the pioneer **Selva**

Negra hotel, Tovar's first, and the nearby mills on the Tuy river where coffee, wheat and corn were ground.

Around the third week in March, the colony plays host to an international **Festival of Chamber Music**, which grows in size and reputation every year. At **Carnival**, Tovar's German *jokili* jesters wear carved wooden masks and leap about in costumes stitched with bells.

The colony's surrounding countryside and **petroglyphs** arouse much interest. The highest peak in the area, Codazzi, tops 2,425 m (7,954 ft), with views on clear days of the cordillera and all the way down to the coast. Birds abound. The petroglyphs uncovered by the naturalist Hermann Karsten in the nineteenth century lie quite a way to the southeast of the town. It's best to ask one of the *posada* or hotel owners about the best way to reach them.

Where to Stay

Most of Colonia Tovar's *posadas* are run very much on a family basis, some with years of experience. It's hard to find budget accommodation, and most accommodation approaches the moderate bracket.

Tovar's longest established hotel is the **Hotel Selva Negra** ((044) 551415 FAX (044) 551338, reached by a drive to the south of the church. The Gutmann family have expanded over the years, and there are now over 40 rooms available in their large grounds. The best of these are the suites which come with heaters, hot water and satellite televisions, all built and decorated in the same Black Forest style.

maintained a good reputation down the years in the inexpensive range. As well as the original 15 light and airy double rooms with balconies, there are some newly remodeled *cabaña*-style units, of which the ones on their own (as opposed to in the block) are the most appealing.

Where to Eat

For hearty meals, the **El Molino** restaurant by the river is perhaps Tovar's most famous, drawing large families on weekends and holidays. Otherwise, walking around the town, **Kaiserstuhl**, **El Codazzi** and **Perolón** all serve traditional German dishes, while **Cafe Munstall**, opposite the church sells wonderful pastries on weekends. The

Following the main road towards the town, you come to the widely praised and inexpensive **Posada Don Elicio** ((044) 551254 FAX (044) 551073. Here the Cruz Delgado family have built up their lodgings into one of the best in the area. The result feels like a private house. The rooms enjoy a cozy feel, some with their own private balconies. The food is equally good. They often request a minimum stay of two nights on weekends and during holiday periods.

Approaching the town having taken the left fork at La Ballesta, watch for the signs indicating "cabañas" near the Medicatura. The **Cabañas de Pina** ((044) 551036 offers various sizes of rooms, prettily decorated and well-maintained at inexpensive rates. The larger units come with fully equipped kitchens.

On the road heading out of Tovar towards La Victoria, the **Hotel Bergland** ((044) 551229 has

Alta Bavaria, near to the Hotel Bergland, serves good hearty food in Alpine-styled surroundings.

How to Get There

As the crow flies, Colonia Tovar isn't far from Caracas. On weekends the roads slow to a painful crawl as *Caraqueños* flee the city. Leaving Caracas by car, after the large La Araña intersection (where the right lane heads to La Guaira), watch out for the signs for El Junquito close to metro La Yaguara. From El Junquito, follow the signs.

Carritos (buses) leave Nuevo Circo terminal for El Junquito. Change to a *por puesto* for the rest of the journey. An alternative, and more scenic, route is via La Victoria.

FAR LEFT: Welcome to Colonia Tovar. OPPOSITE: A devil dancer wall painting. ABOVE: The Colonia's "chocolate box" main gates.

SOUTH OF CARACAS

Although many of the towns south of Caracas are little more than dormitory towns, from where people migrate en masse morning and evening to and from the city, the landscape of Miranda State is still lush in parts, with rolling hills of forests, essential for water generation in the capital.

PARQUE NACIONAL GUATOPO

Branching off to the south from the Cordillera de la Costa, the spine of the Serranía del Interior rises to over 1,400 m (4,592 ft). Protected since 1958, the

lush rainforests of the Parque Nacional Guatopo make an ideal day out from Caracas — a mere two hours away. The road through the park winds through towering trees, overhanging vines and exuberant tropical vegetation.

The park's infrastructure ranks among the best in the country, with a *guardaparque* (park warden) information point, interpretation trails, walks, several campsites and a few basic shelters. The park is near-deserted during weekdays, but receives more visitors on the weekend. It's a favorite haunt of birdwatchers, with macaws, humming-birds and woodpeckers making regular cameo appearances. The rare and majestic harpy eagle has also been spotted here. Fauna also abounds — as do snakes, so be careful where you walk — with sightings of jaguars, peccaries, howler monkeys, armadillos, tapirs and sloths, to name but a few.

You will find information about the local wildlife at the Inparques hut at La Macanilla, or contact the Venezuela Audubon Society (see TAKING A TOUR, page 52 in YOUR CHOICE). Recreation areas close at 3 PM on weekdays and 4 PM on weekends. Due to safety concerns, Inparques discourages campers not part of relatively large groups. The park also receives a large amount of rainfall and is an important watershed for the Tuy valley (there

are several dams close by). Take waterproof clothing, even in drier March and April.

SAN FRANCISCO DE YARE

On the map, San Francisco de Yare looks innocent enough. But this town in Miranda State enjoys a devilish reputation. As you approach the town, a six-meter (20-ft) devil's head tells you something is not quite right. San Francisco is in fact "Devil Dancing Central."

Although the dances take place in many towns of central Venezuela, San Francisco's display ranks king of this bizarre cross-cultural ritual. The town buzzes in the weeks leading up to Corpus Christi, its biggest day of the year (see FESTIVE FLINGS, page 46 in YOUR CHOICE).

The costumed members of the local confraternity, donning their grizzly masks and dressed in hand-painted costumes, leave the Casa de los Diablos Danzantes on Calle Rivas in a noisy, colorful dancing procession to the front of the church. The event symbolizes the devils' submission to the Eucharist, and participants approach the town's priest on their knees, where they whisper their promises of faith into his ear. With crowds of people descending on the town to observe the ritual, the partying goes on until late at night.

At other times of year you can meet the artisans who elaborate the wooden and papier mâché masks, the festival's most famous symbol. The **Casa de los Diablos Danzantes**, by the police station, displays masks and photos, open Tuesday and Thursday from 7 AM to 11 AM, 2 PM to 4 PM, and on Sunday from 7 AM to 11 AM only. If it's closed, ask the family next door if they'll open it for you. They can also tell you more about the festival, and where to find the famous Sanoja family of artisans.

How to Get There

By car, San Francisco lies half way between Santa Teresa del Tuy and Ocumare del Tuy. From Caracas, you can take a bus to either of these towns from Nuevo Circo. A smaller bus that shuttles between the two will drop you at San Francisco. Depending on the traffic, the journey shouldn't take more than two hours.

ABOVE: A friendly face from Barlovento. RIGHT: A blue-cheeked parakeet gives tourists the eye.

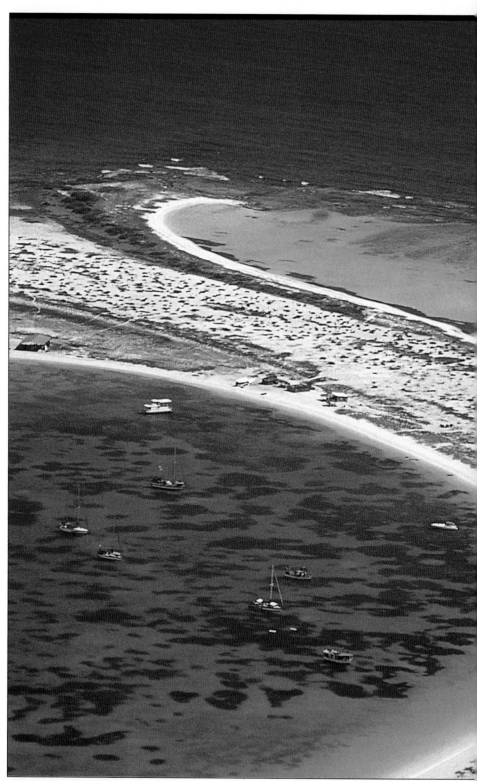

El Centro

"EL CENTRO," VENEZUELA'S CENTRAL NORTHERN REGION, is home to over half the country's population and the lion's share of its industry and agriculture, while just off the coast, due north of Maiquetía airport, the azure waters of Venezuela's greatest marine national park, Los Roques, are less than an hour's hop away.

LOS ROQUES

If God held a painter's palette as He brought light to the world, He surely perfected the color blue at the islands of Los Roques. As you fly over the hundreds of pearl-drop islands, or meander between them in a boat, every hue and shade of azure, cerulean, aquamarine, turquoise and cobalt seem to have been applied with meticulous skill and divine intention.

Beneath the waves, where walls of coral and sponge plunge, brilliant parrot and angelfish dart between a yellow, ochre and chestnut coral patchwork. On the beaches, where turtles lumber to lay their eggs, the snow-white sand blinds while the strength of the sun sends you scurrying lizard-like for shade. Frigate birds, boobies, terns and pelicans swoop and wheel on winds which at night keep the mosquitoes and midges at bay and the temperature cool. Add to all this the *posadas* on Gran Roque — among the best in Venezuela — and you begin to understand why Hollywood stars and humble travelers alike rave about Los Roques.

PARQUE NACIONAL ARCHIPIÉLAGO LOS ROQUES

The Archipiélago Los Roques lies approximately 128 km (80 miles) north of La Guaira and Maiquetía, a half-hour plane ride. A national park since 1972, it encompasses some 40 islands large enough to name and 225,000 hectares (556,000 acres), one of the largest marine reserves in the Caribbean.

The islands play host to 92 species of birds, of which 50 migrate to and from North America. Most are marine species such as boobies and terns, gulls, pelicans and herons, but one can also spy the mangrove canary. On Los Canquises island, flocks of resplendent flamingos form colonies on their travels from the mainland to the Dutch Antilles. The island's harsh environment and lack of food sources restrict fauna to reptiles, apart from one species of bat. Lizards and green iguanas scamper across the sands from refuge to hideouts in the shade.

Los Roques boasts one of the richest marine habitats in the Caribbean: a diver's paradise. Thanks to national-park protection, corals, algae, anemones and sponges carpet the sea bottom in a riot of color. Fish are everywhere, ranging from the slender trumpet fish right up to the large whipping bonefish so beloved of serious anglers.

GENERAL INFORMATION

When arriving at Los Roques, all visitors have to pay the parks fee at the Inparques office at the landing strip. Scuba divers need a permit from Inparques' headquarters (called La Autoridad Única Los Roques) at the west end of the beach, while spearfishing in the archipelago is prohibited. There are no banks on Gran Roque so bring cash, though most *posadas* will change travelers checks and accept dollars as payment. Don't count on them taking credit cards, unless you booked through a travel agent.

Flights to Los Roques are expensive in view of their short duration, and a visit to the islands is better value if you stay for at least a night or two. Nearly all travel agents throughout Venezuela can book flights and accommodation according to your budget. The airlines that fly to Gran Roque usually arrange their own tours (see HOW TO GET THERE,

page 99). Prices tend to be higher over weekends and during school vacations, and flights are often delayed, so it is wise not to book just before an international departure. If you plan on staying a few nights, the cheapest way is to find your own *posada* once in Gran Roque. Tour companies tend to use the more upmarket ones, and budget travelers can save money by doing some legwork around the tiny town, and by contracting fisherman directly for island excursions.

WHAT TO SEE AND DO

Gran Roque

Lying at the archipelago's northern edge, Gran Roque is the only island of volcanic origin in the archipelago, and the transportation hub and center for accommodation. On the southern side of the three-and-a-half-kilometer long by one-kilometer wide (two by half-a-mile) island lies the town of Gran Roque. Blue, pink and terracotta houses, nearly all *posadas*, line its six sandy streets.

There isn't a lot to see, though, inevitably, you'll find a Plaza Bolívar. Over on the island's western tip, two rocky mounds rise to over 100 m (328 ft), providing fantastic views of the town and surrounding islands, reefs and sea. There is also an old Dutch lighthouse. Be warned, the island's desalination plant and generator are far from reliable. Water is very valuable in this dry and arid climate.

Islands

In order to protect the marine habitat of the archipelago, a "recreational zone" was created within the national park. This zone encompasses a number of islands close to Gran Roque and is where tourism activity takes place. The only other island

Sand and surf on Los Roques.

that can be visited without a special permit is **Dos Mosquises**, at the archipelago's southern edge, home to the **Fundación Científica Los Roques** ((02) 263-9729 FAX (02) 261-3461. Here the Foundation uses large tanks to breed green turtles and other endangered species such as the queen conch. Over 6,000 turtles have been reared in this way. The station is open weekends and over holiday periods.

Diving and **snorkeling** in the warm waters — temperatures average 20 to 28°C (70 to 80°F) — are obviously the main activities sought by active tourists in Los Roques. Unless you rent a yacht equipped for refilling tanks, the only place on the archipelago to obtain diving services is **Sesto Continente** ((02) 731-1507 or (014) 924-1853 WEB SITE www.scdr.com, based near the Inparques headquarters on Gran Roque. They can organize all-inclusive packages, PADI courses, or simply equipment rental, and have a good reputation. Divers will need to purchase a permit, and groups are limited in number to 10, including a dive-master. One of the most popular places for diving is Cayo Sal, but given the huge number of drop-offs around the archipelago, divers won't be short of stunning dive locations.

Fishing for bonefish is becoming increasingly popular in Los Roques, where the shallows between the islands make for superb conditions. The local fish are called *pez ratón* and *macabí*, and the best times are from June to December. Permits are required by Inparques for both bone and deep-sea fishing. Many Los Roques *posadas* cater to anglers, including the **Albocora Lodge** ((014) 370-9797 and the very handsome but pricey **Pez Ratón Lodge** ((02) 975-0082 FAX (02) 975-0355 E-MAIL pezraton@ven.net WEB SITE www.gataven.net/pezraton.

WHERE TO STAY

A night on Los Roques will cost up to double what it does on the mainland for a similar standard. This said, first-class accommodation on Gran Roque is plentiful, and the standard of service, attention and language skills is often very high.

Of the more expensive hotels, many offer excursions to nearby islands as part of their package, so it's worth asking about these. As a rule, the more expensive the *posada*, the further away from Gran Roque and the crowds. Bear this in mind over peak holiday periods.

Luxury to Expensive

Mediterraneo ((02) 975-0906 or (02) 975-0082 FAX (02) 975-0355 E-MAIL elero@telcel.net.ve WEB SITE www.tarpon.com.ve/posadamediterraneo, blends elegance and style, friendly service and excellent food, making it one of the best guest-houses on the island. In addition to its bentwood

furniture and antique doors, it boasts a good reference library for brushing up on marine ecology or Venezuela in general, and a panoramic rooftop terrace with a telescope. Packages are all-inclusive with excursions to nearby keys, as well as optional fishing tours.

Posada Arrecife ((014) 373-0303 or (014) 328-5471 is another tempting offer that caters to anglers and divers, as well as tourists looking for original and luxurious accommodation: ceramic, hand-painted sinks antique chests of drawers, DirecTV with videos, safes and telephones. Their six rooms are let out on an all-inclusive basis. Close by is **La Corsaria** ((02) 993-6373 or (02) 993-5879, run by the friendly Reinaldo Calcaño. Its walls (painted deep reds and royal blues) and furniture are bold without being overwhelming. They offer eight rooms in all, cold water only, with small refrigerators, safes, televisions, and ceiling fans under an all-inclusive deal.

Over to the north of the Autoridad Única lies the well-run and beautifully designed **Bequeve Los Roques** ((02) 731-0636 or (02) 731-0863 E-MAIL caremorf484@cantv.net WEB SITE www.losroques-bequeve.com, which has an exclusive feel throughout. There are eight rooms in all. The *posada* has a shaded platform for guests on Noronquí, in the western Recreational Zone, while the meals are some of the best on the island. Their package includes reception and all meals, as well as transfers to Noronquí on a yacht as opposed to the usual *peñero* boat.

Moderate

My pick for this price range is **Piano y Papaya** ((014) 911-6467, followed by **Posada Acquamarina** ((014) 200-4882 E-MAIL posada@intercon.net.ve. Piano y Papaya is run by a young Italian couple offering five double rooms, with the option, unique on the island, of Shiatzu massages and other forms of therapy. The whole guesthouse oozes relaxation, with spacious living areas to compensate for the slightly small rooms. Acquamarina is another young operation, targeting music-lovers. They offer five rooms with rattan beds, baths and ceiling fans, as well as one of the most welcoming rooftop terraces on the island, under an all-inclusive plan only.

Inexpensive

It's hard to find anything recommendable on Los Roques below the US$50 mark, although the **Paraíso Azul** (/FAX (014) 903-2283 E-MAIL info @paraisoazul.com manages pretty well with four plain rooms with ceiling fans, three with private baths, all with cold water. The friendly owners speak English and Italian and offer breakfast and dinner in their rate. The other decent option is **Turismo Doña Carmen** ((014) 938-2284, on Plaza Bolívar, with six bare-bones rooms which come with private bathroom and fans. Breakfast and dinner are included in the rate.

Camping

Certain islands have been designated for camping. Contact Inparques for a list. Most of them are inhabited, or used by local fishermen, and you can negotiate with them for transportation, or to buy fish or drinking water.

HOW TO GET THERE

Flights for Los Roques leave from the national terminal at Maiquetía, or from Porlamar on Margarita. Some airlines may charge for baggage

on Gran Roque, and will give you more time actually exploring. The people at **Alpi Tour (** (02) 283-1433 or (02) 283-1733 FAX (02) 285-6067 WEB SITE www.alpi-group.com, have years of experience sailing and fishing off the coast and can book the right yacht for what you want.

MARACAY

Venezuela's fourth city and Aragua State's capital, the parks, wide boulevards and leafy avenues of Maracay earned it the sobriquet "La Ciudad Jardín" (The Garden City). The reality however, is somewhat different, though thanks to the grandiose plans of the dictator Juan Vicente Gómez,

over 10 kg (22 lb). If money is really tight, fishing boats leaving from Carabellada or La Guaira make the journey to the islands, and negotiating a ride is always possible.

Airline/tour companies include **Lineas Turísticas Aerotuy (LTA) (** (02) 761-8043 or (02) 761-6231 FAX (02) 762-5254 WEB SITE www.tuy.net, Edificio Gran Sabana No. 174, Boulevard de Sabana Grande, Caracas, who run a series of guesthouses at "standard" and "superior" rates on Gran Roque; **Rutaca (** (02) 355-1838 FAX (02) 355-1643, in Porlamar (095) 691346 FAX (095) 691245; **El Sol de América (** (02) 993-3703 E-MAIL elsolde america@internet.ve WEB SITE www.losroques travel.com; and **Chapi Air (** (02) 355-2786 or (02) 355-1965.

The alternative means of getting around the islands is by yacht. This often works out just as economical for small groups as spending nights

the city is pleasant enough — it might have been more pleasant still if he'd left some colonial architecture behind.

Most travelers pass through this important industrial city of around half a million people on their way to Choroní or the Cata coast. Its cultural attractions could detain you on your way to the beaches and forests.

BACKGROUND

The names Aragua and Maracay come from the local Indians and their chief whom the Spanish encountered when they first arrived. The town was officially found in 1701, though the valley had been settled some time before this. Had Juan Vicente Gómez not intervened, Maracay would

The dome and tower of Maracay's cathedral.

no doubt have continued its role as an important agricultural producer, providing indigo, tobacco, sugarcane, cotton and coffee to the colony. But the *caudillo* had other plans. Soon after he seized power in 1908, Maracay became the de facto capital of Venezuela.

With a zeal common to "modernizing" dictators, Gómez began the construction of several buildings, which include the bullring, zoo, opera house and aviation school, and of course, his own mausoleum. The opera house wasn't properly finished until the 1970s, by which time — with the highway link to Caracas — Maracay had transformed into a modern industrial city. It continues to grow today.

space in the middle of the city. The obelisk at the square's center commemorates the North American volunteers who were hung following an ill-fated landing on the Ocumare coast led by Francisco de Miranda in 1806. On the eastern side of the square, the **cathedral** with its brilliant white façade was completed in 1743. Unfortunately, almost no colonial architecture remains in the area.

On the south side of the square, the **Museo de Historia** is disappointing, while the **Instituto de Antropología e Historia** next-door makes a better effort at displaying a range of crafts and pottery made by pre-Hispanic and present-day Indian peoples, including the Warao of the Delta. The

GENERAL INFORMATION

Strangely enough, the tourist office is situated to the north of the city, in the Soledad District, and isn't really worth the schlep. For money, banks cluster southwest of Plaza Girardot, and for Amex, the Banco Consolidado is at Avenida Bolívar and Fuerzas Armadas. The **Inparques** office ((043) 413933, which you should consult if you plan to camp in Henri Pittier National Park, is found at the Parque Zoológico (zoo) in the Las Delicias District, north on the road to Choroní.

WHAT TO SEE AND DO

The city's heart, for once in Venezuela, isn't centered on the Plaza Bolívar, but on the **Plaza Girardot**. The square, along with its adjacent Parque Bicentenario, makes a large, attractive open

museums are open Tuesday to Friday 8 AM to noon and weekends 9 AM to 1 PM.

To the north of the Plaza Girardot, on Avenida 19 de Abril, the grand bullring, **Plaza de Toros La Maestranza**, designed by Venezuela's most renowned architect, Carlos Villanueva, is modeled on the famous one in Seville. If you can't find a way in, try the back door on the ring's eastern side, since the structure is well worth admiring from the inside. If you've never seen a bullfight, Maracay would be the place to change this.

Two blocks east of the bullring, the **Complejo Cultural** includes all sorts of cultural and youth activities as well as the **Museo de Arte Maracay** and the **Museo de Arte Contemporáneo**, both of which hold temporary exhibitions. The museums are open Tuesday to Sunday 8 AM to 5 PM.

At the end of the avenue, you'll find the **Museo Aeronáutico**, built by the aviation-obsessed

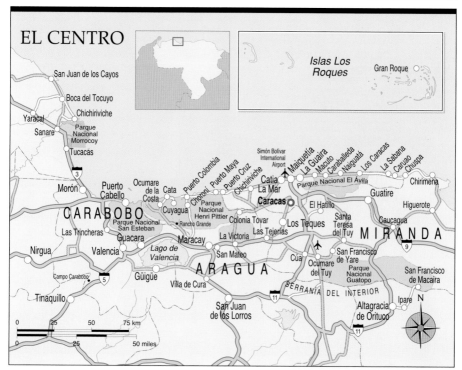

Gómez. It houses a motley collection of aircraft including the star of the show, an old French plane dating back to 1910. The museum is open on an erratic basis on weekends: try your luck any time but lunchtime.

Back on the eastern side of Plaza Girardot stands the sight most frequented by Venezuelans: the **Santuario de Madre María de San José**. Here you can admire the glass sarcophagus of Venezuela's only saint, beatified with much fanfare in 1995. Madre María grew up in Choroní and founded Maracay's first hospital. She died in 1967 at the age of 92. When her remains were disinterred for the sanctuary, they were remarkably, perhaps miraculously, intact. Doors are open Tuesday to Sunday 8:30 AM to 11:30 AM and 2:30 AM to 5 PM.

Across the Parque Bicentenario stands the colonial mansion of **La Casa de Dolores Amelía**. Though not an official sight (the house is occupied by an insurance company), it's worth persuading someone to let you in to appreciate the neo-Sevillian architecture.

Walking west along the Avenida Bolívar, you come inevitably to the **Plaza Bolívar**, the largest in Venezuela and perhaps Latin America. It was designed again by Villanueva and finished at the same time as the Hotel Jardín, now the **Palacio del Gobierno**, in 1930. The area was the linchpin of Gómez's plan to make Maracay the country's new capital. The hotel was remodeled for its new

role in the 1960s, but you can try to persuade a guard to let you inside for a look.

Top of the Gómez follies, the **Teatro de la Opera**, on the square's southwestern corner, took nearly four decades to complete. The 860-seat theater, designed to rival those of Caracas, puts on various productions including opera, theatre, ballet and folkloric shows.

WHERE TO STAY AND EAT

Maracay hosts many centrally located hotels, as well as smarter ones north of the town on the way to Choroní, in the Las Delicias district.

Top of the list in the moderate category, the renovated **Hotel Maracay (** (043) 416211 FAX (043) 410865, on Avenida Las Delicias, includes a golf course and rooftop swimming pool, as well as well-tended grounds and comfortable, breezy rooms. The restaurants in the area will probably make for more lively dining than the hotel's offer.

The modern, but inexpensive **Hotel Princesa Plaza (** (043) 332357 FAX (043) 337972, on Avenida Miranda, a block east of Plaza Bolívar, provides the best value accommodation. The hotel has 100 well-appointed rooms with air-conditioning. The next best cheaper option is the **Hotel Wladimir (** (043) 461115 on Avenida Bolívar, followed by the **Hotel Caroní (** (043) 541817, on Avenida Ayacucho

Among the pigeons of Maracay's Plaza Girardot.

Norte No 19. The **Hotel Mar de Plata** ((043) 464313, Calle Santos Michelena Este No. 23, close to the Plaza Girardot and the bullring, is the best of the lower-end hotels, with air-conditioned rooms at reasonable prices.

You'll find the best meals in Maracay along the Avenida Las Delicias, namely at **El Riacho** and **El Bodegón de Sevilla**, as well **La Terraza del Vroster**, all moderately priced. The **Brasilandia** on Avenida Bolívar near Hotel Cristal is a popular place with locals for large *parillas* (mixed grills) and chicken dishes. The restaurant at the Hotel Wladimir enjoys a good reputation. There are many cheaper eateries around Plaza Girardot, and Biergarten Park on the east side of Plaza Bolívar for German and Italian dishes.

HOW TO GET THERE

Maracay's Airport lies west of the city in the Mariscal Sucre Air Force Base. **LAI** ((031) 524746 have two daily flights from Caracas, which usually continue on to Mérida, but apart from that, there are not a lot of airborne options.

Maracay is well served by buses from its terminal to the south of the city center. It's probably easier to get a small bus than to walk from Plaza Bolívar. There are very frequent services to Caracas (two hours) and Valencia (one hour). Other cities include Barquisimeto, Maracaibo, San Cristóbal and San Fernando de Apure. If you're heading east to Puerto La Cruz or Ciudad Bolívar, **Aeroexpresos Ejecutivos** ((043) 322977, on Avenida Bolívar Este, on the east side of town, is the most comfortable line. Buses for Ocumare and Choroní leave throughout the day from the city terminal.

PARQUE NACIONAL HENRI PITTIER

Renowned as a birdwatcher's paradise, the Henri Pittier National Park encompasses over 1,000 sq km (390 sq miles) and most of northern Aragua State. Its tendrils stretch right down to Maracay. It boasts over 40% of Venezuela's 1,360 bird species and was the country's first national park.

The park brims with birdlife and bats, who fertilize the profusion of flowering trees that carpet its cloud-swept hills and lush valleys. Over six percent of the world's bird species, notably orange-winged parrots, squirrel cuckoos, jacamars, manakins and helmeted curassows, could keep your average bird-spotter busy for a lifetime and nature-lovers enchanted for days. Here you'll encounter tens of species of orchids, bromeliads, epiphytes and palms (including the "holy" and "prapa" palms), as well as the immense leaves of the *gunnera* grass, endemic to Venezuela. Large mammals such as jaguars, ocelots, tapirs and howler monkeys also find refuge within the park's boundaries.

GENERAL INFORMATION

The Rancho Grande Biological Station (see below) provides the best base from which to explore the least-intervened parts of the park, but you can also arrange tours from Choroní or Puerto Colombia (see below). For more background information on the park, contact the **Sociedad Conservacionista de Aragua** (/FAX (043) 831734 E-MAIL socaragua @tycom.com.ve WEB SITE www.tycom.com.ve/ socaragua. They also arrange bird tagging outings with volunteers. Infrastructure within the park is pretty minimal, but you can still head off along numerous trails from various starting points. **Tierra Viva** is a Venezuelan nongovernmental organization which has been working with local communities in the area on several excellent environmental projects. You can find out more about them and their work by calling Anita Reyes (/FAX (02) 951-2601 E-MAIL livearth@gn.apc.org.

RANCHO GRANDE

From Maracay, follow the signs for **El Limón** for the westerly road through Henri Pittier National Park. The road is in better condition than Choroní's and wider for the most part, and equally beautiful. Soon after the first Inparques *refugio* at Guamitas, you'll see signs announcing Rancho Grande. Beyond these is the very sharp turn on the right leading up to the Rancho Grande Biological Station ((014) 947-7330 FAX (043) 453242.

You can ask Jesús Manzanilla (at the above numbers) for permission to stay in one of the Spartan rooms with use of the kitchen and shared bathrooms. The station is housed above an old hotel built in the Gómez era, and languishes in various states of disrepair and neglect. It's a hollow and somewhat spooky place to be honest, but if you want to catch the unparalleled dawn chorus in the forest or do some camping, it's your best bet.

At the end of the parking lot, an interpretation trail takes you on a short circuit weaving between skyscraping buttressed trees. There are also two longer trails through Henri Pittier from Rancho Grande. One splits from the Andrew Field interpretation trail up to the **Guacamaya Peak** at 1,828 m (6,000 ft).

Ask the Inparques wardens about the entrance to the **Portachuelo** trail. This leads to the pass below the Guacamaya Peak which is the main thoroughfare for migrating birds, and is the best spot for birding in the park. Contact the Audu-

---

The surreal hues of a heliconia, deep in the forests of Henri Pittier.

bon Society (see TAKING A TOUR, page 52 in YOUR CHOICE) for more information.

THE CHORONÍ COAST

From Maracay, two paved roads lead through Henri Pittier down to the coast. The western one takes you to Ocumare and its beaches (see OCUMARE COAST, page 108), while the eastern one coils its way over the Cordillera to the villages of Choroní and Puerto Colombia on the coast. Both roads offer jaw-dropping views, shallow river crossings, hairpin bends, and horn-blowing buses. Venezuelans tend to refer to both Choroní and Puerto Colombia as "Choroní."

charming, pastel-painted colonial village of Choroní. The intricate painted ceiling and walls of the church of Santa Clara on the main square rank among the most delightful in the country, and are best viewed in the afternoon when light streams through the high windows. It's one of the oldest parishes in Venezuela, established in 1622.

Where to Stay

Most people opt to stay near or in Puerto Colombia for access to the beaches. However, Choroní makes a peaceful alternative from the bustle of the coast, and it's only half an hour's walk downhill to the beach.

BACKGROUND

The history of the central coast is soaked in that dark, viscous liquid, the spanner in the works of so many well-intentioned diets: chocolate. Regarded as some of the finest in the world, the cacao grown in the haciendas of Aragua finds its way to the great chocolate houses of Europe and the United States.

You'll notice that many of the older villages of the central coast, such as Choroní and Chuao, are way up in the hills. Pirates terrorized the region well into the eighteenth century, and the villages sought sanctuary away from the pillaged shores.

CHORONÍ

Coming down from the cloudforest, the foliage becomes less tangled and you enter the

MODERATE

After the village, about five minutes down the road, you'll see signs for the Hotel Hacienda El Portete on the left. It's the road to the cemetery and El Diario beach. At its start, you'll find two of the Choroní's best guesthouses in the grounds of an old hacienda split by two families.

The first, and least expensive, is **Posada La Casa de los García** ((043) 911056 or (/FAX (02) 662-2858 E-MAIL llerandi@telcel.net.ve WEB SITE www.posada-garcia.rec.ve, which boasts eight rooms along the corridor of an old whitewashed cacao mansion. The drying patio has been exquisitely landscaped with flowers and a fountain. The rooms are fairly spacious, with fans and hot water, while three new rooms with air-conditioning are planned in the garden.

Next door lies the more modern side of the hacienda, run by the English-speaking Richard

Mayerstone. The **Hotel Hacienda El Portete** ℓ/FAX (043) 911255 E-MAIL portete@telcel.net.ve is, in the words of a local friend of mine "the Choroní Hilton." This part of the hacienda includes 24 rooms, of which three are particularly spacious. Each airy room comes with a hammock, air-conditioning, hot water and artwork, though not much imagination. The Portete is undoubtedly a great place for families, with a large pool and social area, not to mention a kiddies' pool, playroom and their own television and video.

INEXPENSIVE

Just by the Plaza Bolívar, Cacao Travel's **Posada Colonial Choroní** ℓ (02) 977-1234 FAX (02) 977-0110

on a beach after some hectic traveling. Its formula of inexpensive accommodation, fish restaurants and one of the finest beaches in the country hits the mark with young travelers. When the Venezuelans arrive for the weekends and vacations, the drummers come out to play, and the parties on the beachfront continue until the early hours.

When Playa Grande gets too busy, rent a *peñero* (boat), stock up on food and drinks, and head to one of the nearby beaches, deserted and unspoiled during the week.

What to See and Do

Playa Grande, the horseshoe, palm-fringed beach the cover of many a vacation brochure, lies

E-MAIL cacaotravel@cantv.net WEB SITE www.cacao travel.com, may be small, but it's a charming *posada* with an attractive inner patio and its own bathing *pozo* pool nearby. The friendly managers speak English and German, and specialize in birding and nature trips into the hills of Henri Pittier.

PUERTO COLOMBIA

Puerto Colombia's rise from sleepy fishing village to tourist town has transformed it in little over 20 years. You'll now find a gas and a police station — a sure sign of progress — and a *posada* to suit every wallet. The village enjoys some Old World charm around the Plaza Bolívar, and personally, I've always enjoyed its laid-back Caribbean feel and friendly people.

Along with Santa Fe in Sucre State, Puerto Colombia is probably one of the best places to relax

10 minutes' walk to the east of town. Cross the river and walk up the road, or just tag along behind anyone with a cooler. It's a stunning blend of sea and surf, rivaling any of Venezuela's Caribbean gems. After busy weekends or vacations, the beaches, sadly, suffer from litter. At other times, it's still idyllic, with a host of palms from where to sling a hammock and be lulled by the breeze. The far side of the bay usually escapes the crowds — Venezuelans tend to congregate near the informal restaurants and bars at the beach's entrance. If you decide to base yourself down there, be wary of the sea's powerful undertow. The area's other beach is **El Diario**.

After a day at the beach, stroll up the road to Choroní to admire the parish church's painted

OPPOSITE: Choroní's winding, narrow colonial streets. ABOVE: The long stretch of Puerto Colombia's Playa Grande.

interior, before taking in the sunset from the beachfront *malecón*, where many artisans and souvenir hawkers set up their pitches.

Most weekends, and around the **Fiesta de San Juan Bautista** on June 23 and 24, Puerto Colombia's drummers come out in force, and the village turns into a lively party-town as people come from all over the country to join in the fun. Live bands usually perform in impromptu street concerts.

In the hamlet of El Charal, you'll see a small dirt track just before the *abasto* El Saman. Follow the track down for a great bathing spot, **El Pozo Los Colores**. On the other side lies the **Hacienda El Tesoro**. The 400-hectare (988-acre) El Tesoro was bought in 1996 by Willy and Tanya Harcourt-Cooze, an enterprising British couple who swapped their lives in West London for the jungles of Choroní. When complete, the exclusive lodge on their estate — which will rehabilitate the cacao and sugarcane machinery — will no doubt become one of the best places to stay in the area. You can contact them for information at ℂ/FAX (014) 463-0013.

Where to Stay

Please note that prices vary according to season and, in cheaper places, are often negotiable. If your group numbers four or more, ask *posada* owners about self-catering apartments, which offer good value. Most hotel owners will gladly arrange boat trips or walking tours for you.

MODERATE

Just before you enter Puerto Colombia proper, in the bend in the road you'll see an archway on your right-hand side. Down the dirt track lies the **Estancia Akelarre Choroní** ℂ (043) 911202 (advance reservations essential). Opened in 1996, the *posada* is beautifully laid out in the style of an hacienda, despite being completely new. Six rooms with tasteful artwork, wicker chairs and dark, stained-wood furniture, and air-conditioning give on to the flowering central patio, painted in bright earth tones.

Right in town on the Plaza Bolívar, the newest addition to Puerto Colombia's list, the elegant **Hostal Casa Grande** ℂ (043) 911251 has been entirely rescued by its enthusiastic owner Francisco Giuliano. He imports Mexican furniture to Venezuela and has packed his hotel with antiques, imposing doors, wood-worm mottled benches and original features. Combine these with modern art, and the effect is all the more striking. Eight rooms ring the rock pool patio, all with air-conditioning, hot water and individual touches: an excellent choice.

Finally, the long-established **Posada Humboldt** ℂ (043) 911050 or (02) 976-2222, strictly by reservation only, lies just next to the *alcabala*,

though there's no sign. It's a delightful, grand colonial-style house with a fountain and flower-choked courtyard and lots of attention to detail. The Humboldt is renowned for its cuisine, but has become pricey compared to the newer establishments.

MODERATE TO INEXPENSIVE

Between the plaza and the *malecón*, along Puerto Colombia's main street, Calle Morillo, it feels like every house is a *posada*. Here you'll find the **Xuchytlán** ℂ (043) 911114 or ℂ/FAX (02) 977-1694, designed by the amiable owner, Flavio Borquéz. The attractive entrance is modeled on the old *zaguán* stone designs of old colonial houses, now increasingly rare in Venezuela. The *posada* represents excellent value for the price, and includes breakfast and a welcoming bar.

Across the street, you'll find the reception of the ever-expanding **Hotel Club Cotopetrix** ℂ (02) 952-8617/2628 FAX (02) 951-6226. It's one of the town's most established and most successful hotels, offering package deals that include all meals and one excursion a day. They own three equipped guesthouses, ideal for families or large parties, and superior to the hotel rooms.

INEXPENSIVE

Definitely the best option in this bracket, the **Posada Cataquero** ℂ/FAX (043) 911264, Calle Morillo No. 26, renovated with care and taste by its charming owners Alejandra and Alfredo, houses eight rooms with fans on two levels. Flower arrangements, suspended birds' nests, works by Venezuela artists (including the renowned Cruz Diez), washed walls, and homelike touches such as room keys in little baskets all elevate it beyond its competitors. The only problem may be the neighbor's roosters, which get crowing early — ear plugs supplied.

The backpacker-friendly **Casa Blanca** (no phone) lies on one side of the Plaza Bolívar (look for the sign in the window), where five rooms of various sizes, with external bathrooms, fans and cold water only surround around a grass patio. You can use the kitchen facilities, and have a chat with the amiable owner, Nadjim.

Where to Eat

Most of the hotels, except the most inexpensive, have their own restaurants. Other options include the **Restaurant Araguaney** in the Avenida de los Cocos, which serves tasty fried fish, as does the **Restaurant Isla Feliz** nearby, and **El Kiki** (also known as Wili's after the German owner) just over the bridge. If you're self-catering, head down to the beachfront for some fresh fish in the afternoons.

Fishing boats moored at Puerto Colombia's rivermouth.

How to Get There

Buses leave from Maracay's bus terminal throughout the day for Puerto Colombia and Choroní. Try to pick one of the newer-looking coaches if you can. Failing that, take a good book or a decent walkman with you for the often hair-raising ride and the constant hooting around every corner. Note that on weekends, gigantic queues begin to form in front of Puerto Colombia's bus stop as early as midday on Sunday, and you will have little chance of catching a bus in the afternoon. Nor will you want to be on the road after sundown, so it's best to stay another night.

AROUND CHORONÍ

When Playa Grande gets to crowded, many people head out to one of the isolated nearby beaches for the day. These include **Chuao**, **Cepe**, **Tuja**, **Aroa**, **Uricao** and as far as **Cuyagua** (see OCUMARE COAST, below). Fares vary according to distance, but are usually negotiable, and priced for the whole boat rather than by person.

Chuao is the most interesting village, set back a mile from the beach. It is famous for its sought-after chocolate — visit the tiny museum behind the church — as well as its devil-dancing festivities for **San Juan** in June. In the next bay along lies the even tinier **Cepe**, where there's now a place to stay. All the beaches make great settings for living out a Robinson Crusoe idyll for a few days with a tent.

Day trips for bird watching and animal spotting, and to some lovely waterfalls, bathing pools and old haciendas are all easily arranged in Puerto Colombia and Choroní. Rommer is an enthusiastic young guide who works at the Pizzería Robin Hood and comes recommended.

Where to Stay

In Cepe, the **Posada Puerto Escondido** ((043) 414645 or (02) 413614 FAX (02) 730-7495 E-MAIL jfischer@telcel.net.ve WEB SITE www.puerto escondido.com.ve, includes four rooms with hot water set in well-tended gardens, just up from the beach. Packages can include snorkeling and scuba diving, as well as walks in the hills.

OCUMARE COAST

Twenty-three kilometers (14 miles) and many twisting turns beyond Rancho Grande, you'll come to a fork in the road. The right fork takes you down to the town of **Ocumare de la Costa**, 13 km (eight miles) away. The town boasts an attractive church, shaded Plaza Bolívar, and a pretty *posada* serving decent food, the **Restaurant and Posada María Luisa** ((043) 931184 FAX (043) 931073.

El Playón

Further down the road, taking the left at the round-about, you hit the coast at El Playón, an uninspiring little town set out in a grid with a popular beach. Walk west to the better beach known as **La Punta**.

Where to Stay

Along the beachfront road (Calle California), you'll find the **De la Costa Eco-Lodge** (/FAX (043) 931986 E-MAIL delacosta@etheron.net, managed by the welcoming English-speaking Fernando Nocua. The *posada* makes a good base for exploring the coast and forest. Four of the 12 no-frills renovated rooms are separate from the main house and are your best bet. The De la Costa usually offers two- to four-day packages, with food and excursions included, particularly to the La Ciénaga bay, where the corals are beautiful. They can arrange scuba gear, moped rental and transfers from Caracas.

CATA AND CUYAGUA

Cata's idyllic horseshoe bay lies a further six kilometers (three and three-quarters miles) along the coast road, which gives an unparalleled prospect of a monstrous apartment block built in the 1970s. In the words of one Venezuelan travel writer, it provokes one to acts of arson. Remember, we're still inside the national park in theory. Once you're down on Cata beach, you'll soon forget about the 30-story carbuncle.

The last beach on this stretch, Cuyagua's name is synonymous with surfing among young *Caraqueños*. Pretty much deserted during the week, the palm-lined beach enjoys good swells for surfing most of the year. A kiosk sells food and drinks at the river's mouth, but that's about it: you, the sea, and the surf.

Where to Stay

If you don't have a tent, in Cuyagua village the **Posada Cuyagua Mar** (/FAX (02) 861-1465 or (016) 620-4491 (reservations are essential) lies on the right at the end of the main street, with 26 clean and economical rooms on two floors with private bathrooms, cold water and ceiling fans. There is also a restaurant and plans for a terrace bar.

How to Get There

A regular bus service links Maracay's bus terminal to Ocumare and the coast. From there, smaller buses and *por puestos* do the run to El Playón, La Boca, Cata and Cuyagua. A good place to wait for one is the roundabout near the gas station by El Playón, where you might also hitch a ride. If you're heading for Cata, get off at the junction near to the beach, and not at the town which is further away.

VALENCIA

Some 4,000 years ago, large populations of Indians — who carved petroglyphs into the rocks, perhaps to remind the future of their existence — called the hot and humid valley around Lago de Valencia home. Today, smoke stacks and factories litter the valley.

Valencia is Venezuela's most important city for light industry. It manufactures everything from bottle tops to cars, mushrooming over the years to become the country's third largest city, with a population of over a million. As Venezuela's first capital after the breakup of Bolívar's Gran Colombia, it occupies an important place in the country's history, and includes some important sights. Often overlooked by travelers as they travel west from Caracas, Valencia deserves better — even the most fleeting glance at the restored Casa de los Celis mansion makes the delay as you rush to the Andes or hurry to Coro seem wholly insignificant.

BACKGROUND

Reading Valencia's early history makes you wonder how it survived at all. Soon after its foundation in 1555 by Alonso Arias de Villacinda (who named it after his Spanish hometown), the bloodthirsty, El Dorado-obsessed Lope de Aguirre paid a visit. He summarily sacked the town and massacred hundreds of inhabitants. The town then suffered from various calamities including a smallpox epidemic, attacks by Carib Indians, and raids by marauding French pirates. By 1800, Valencia is said to have had only around 6,000 inhabitants, and more disasters lay in wait.

In 1812, the earthquake that decimated the whole of the country left Valencia struggling once again, but it was the wars of independence that really took their toll. In all, the surrounding countryside witnessed 35 battles, while the city endured sacking by José Tomás "The Butcher" Boves, the *Llanero* general, who is said to have slaughtered even the wounded in the hospital. Fought some 32 km (20 miles) southwest of Valencia in June 1821, the decisive Battle of Carabobo broke the back of the Spanish defense of the province.

In all, Valencia has been capital three times. Once during the short-lived First Republic in 1811, then a second time in 1830 after the dissolution of Gran Colombia, and again in 1858–1859 after the fall of President José Tadeo Monagas. Following World War II, the Caracas authorities, concerned by growing industrial pollution in the capital, relocated many industries to Valencia. This coincided with the country's rapid economic growth, transforming Valencia into the powerhouse it is today, providing a quarter of Venezuela's manufacturing output. Combined with the region's strong agricultural sector, it's little wonder the city continues to grow.

GENERAL INFORMATION

Valencia's **Dirección General de Turismo** ((041) 577501 is situated in the Torre Empresarial, Piso Bajo, Avenida Cedeño at Avenida 102 Montes, but they also run an outlet in the **Parque Humboldt** on the banks of the River Cabriales — an attraction in itself. The park is home to the former train station built by Germans in the late nineteenth century, and the *modulo* is housed in an old carriage ((041) 589590. You'll find the **Inparques**

((041) 574609 office in the old station office nearby. They can give you directions for the Cerro Pintado (prehistoric petroglyphs) near Guacara, and information about the seldom-visited Parque Nacional San Esteban to the northwest of Valencia, which is also accessible from Puerto Cabello (see PUERTO CABELLO, page 111).

For money matters, banks cluster around Plaza Bolívar. On Fridays, the *El Carabobeño* local newspaper publishes a schedule of cultural events, as well as listing restaurants.

Valencia celebrates its agricultural heritage once a year during the **Semana de Valencia** in late March. The program includes an agricultural fair, cultural events, parades, and bullfights. Valencia's other *fiesta* takes place in mid-November when the Virgin is paraded through the streets in all her riches. In September, the nationally important Ateneo de Valencia (Avenida Bolívar) hosts its annual **Salón Michelena** with a wide variety of visual art shows.

WHAT TO SEE AND DO

Beginning, as ever, with the Plaza Bolívar, the **cathedral** on the east side dates from 1580, one of

A Tapara tree bares its fruit, whose hard skins make excellent bowls.

the colony's earliest. The sixteenth-century statue of the Virgen del Socorro was the first crowned by the Pope in Venezuela; its jewel-encrusted crown is regarded as so valuable it only sees the light of day on special occasions.

A block southeast of the Plaza — spot the sloths in the trees — lies the **Casa Páez**, a wonderfully restored house, formerly the residence of the War of Independence hero. The nine murals he commissioned to commemorate the battles in which he fought dominate the house, while his pet maxims adorn its outside walls. The museum opens Tuesday to Friday 9 AM to noon and 3 PM to 5:30 PM, weekends 9 AM to 2 PM.

In 1874, all religious orders were banned by President Guzmán Blanco, and their properties confiscated. Thus the **Capitolio**, west on Calle 99 Páez, fell into the hands of the state. Inside the assembly hall hangs possibly the most famous portrait of Bolívar, astride his white horse Paloma, painted by Arturo Michelena. You might have to persuade a guard to let you get a glimpse from the entrance on Plaza Sucre.

On the other side of Plaza Sucre, next to some handsome old buildings, stands the grand **Teatro Municipal**, based on the Paris Garnier Opera House and completed in 1894. The auditorium's vast ceiling mural of heroes of the Arts, painted by Antonio Herrera Toro might not be Poussin, but it's among the best in the country.

Continue west a block on Calle Colombia and south on Avenida Soublette to the **Casa de la Estrella**. Still undergoing restoration, the house occupies an important place in the history of the country and the continent. It was here that the Congress of 1812 wrote the constitution of the First Republic, and here that the Congress of 1830 withdrew Venezuela from the Republic of Gran Colombia, thus shattering Bolívar's dream of a united northern South America.

A block south lies Valencia's jewel, the **Casa de los Celis**. If you only visit one place in Valencia, make it this restored colonial mansion, one of the finest in the country. Now the **Museo de Arte e Historia**, the house's elegance is irresistible, its high ceilings giving onto a large courtyard garden. It was so large when Colonel Pedro Celis acquired it in 1837 that he sold half of it. Recently restored, the museum houses archeological finds from the Valencia Basin, colonial art, and works by nineteenth-century painters. It is open Tuesday to Friday 8 AM to 2 PM, and 9:30 AM to 12:30 PM weekends.

I'm somewhat reluctant to recommend visiting the **Plaza de Toros Monumental**, Valencia's pride and joy, and the second largest bullring in the Americas. Not because I'm against bullfighting, but because the area around the plaza is pretty unsavory. If you do come this far, probably in a taxi, do take care. The nearby **Museo de Antropología** is more interesting, with displays of fossils and prehistoric art.

AROUND VALENCIA

Carabobeños are proud of their countryside, and quite rightly so, since it includes part of the Central Cordillera. Passing tourists pay little attention to the area, despite its many historical or natural attractions, not least being the hot springs of **Las Trincheras** and the forested hills of **San Esteban**. Ask the tourist office for details of these.

Campo Carabobo

Every Venezuelan schoolchild knows where and what Campo Carabobo is. It was in these fields, on June 24, 1821, that the decisive battle of the War of Independence took place. To underline the battle's importance at the time, the troops went into battle in ceremonial dress — how they managed to fight is beyond me. Largely thanks to the bravery of Páez's lancers and the experienced British legionnaires, Bolívar, still only 36, emerged triumphant. The battlefield lies on the way to Tinaco, 32 km (20 miles) southwest of Valencia. If you're interested in history, the Campo can be fun, but otherwise you could live without visiting it.

WHERE TO STAY

Valencia has a good range of hotels, many of them geared to the business market. The more luxurious are situated in the more affluent northern part of the city.

The city's most prestigious hotel is the **Intercontinental Valencia** ((041) 211533 or (041) 211681 FAX (041) 211151, Avenida Juan Uslar, in the La Viña district, with a pool, gardens and 173 rooms. Like its brother in Caracas, the Intercontinental's restaurants are highly regarded, and the staff unfailing polite and efficient — and English-speaking. The hotel's style might not be cutting edge, but it's very comfortable. The other good option in La Viña in the expensive category is the **Apart-Hotel Ucaima** ((041) 227011/4853 FAX (041) 220461, Avenida Boyaca, near Centro Comercial La Viña, with large suites and rooms, all comfortable and with plenty of light.

The best choice in the moderate bracket is the **Hotel Stauffer Valencia** ((041) 234022/5197 FAX (041) 235044, on Avenida Bolívar in the heart of the restaurant and shopping district, yet close enough to the historic center. Probably the best of the more budget bunch around the Plaza Bolívar is the **Hotel Carabobo** ((041) 588860 or (041) 684467, Calle Libertad 100-37, since many of the others tend to be rented by the hour. The **Hotel Le Paris** ((041) 215655 or (041) 224757, Avenida Bolívar and Calle 128, is further out and more expensive, but still good value.

WHERE TO EAT

With an important business community, it's no surprise to find some excellent moderately priced restaurants in Valencia. For superb seafood amid elegant surroundings, try **Marchica** ((041) 225288, on Avenida Bolívar Norte, or seek out the city's best French food at **La Grillade** ((041) 216038, Callejón Peña Pérez, east of Avenida Bolívar, with excellent meats, generous salads and tasty desserts. The bar gets very lively at night, a good place for a sociable drink. With one of the best settings I've come across for traditional Venezuelan cuisine, the **Casa Valencia** ((041) 234823, restored and

tarted up, makes an excellent choice at the end of Avenida Bolívar Norte, near the Redoma de Guaparo traffic circle.

Inexpensive and unpretentious eateries are plentiful near Plaza Bolívar and along Avenida Bolívar, including **La Rinconada** on the square and **Fego** at No. 102-75 on the avenue. For hearty vegetarian dishes, look for **Buffet Vegetariano**, at Calle Independencia and Avenida Urdaneta, while the best sweets in town line the windows of **Pastelería Andreína**, Avenida Díaz Moreno, near the Hotel Don Pelayo.

HOW TO GET THERE

Valencia's airport is seven kilometers (over four miles) southeast of the city center. **Aserca** ((02) 953-7097 flies to Caracas three times daily, while Aserca and **Aeropostal** ((041) 345164 cover

Barcelona, Porlamar, Maturín, Puerto Ordaz, Barquisimeto and Maracaibo. **Servivensa** ((02) 561-3366 runs international flights to Aruba, Bogotá and Miami.

The bus terminal is in the large, bizarre looking Big Low shopping center, east of town center. Get there by taxi or minibus. **Aeroexpresos Ejecutivos** ((041) 715767 or (041) 715558 does the run to Caracas in fast, air-conditioned comfort nine times a day, and also links up to Puerto La Cruz four times a day.

PUERTO CABELLO

Puerto Cabello has long played an important role in Venezuelan economic life, from its early days as one of the best harbors in the New World, to its place today as one of the country's most vital ports — it often overtakes La Guaira on the Litoral for tonnage. If it weren't for the work of a foresightful mayor in the 1980s, the port would not be of interest to travelers. However, thanks to an expansive program of restoration, a growing number of tourists come to visit its old colonial architecture, shaded plazas, forts and nearby beaches.

BACKGROUND

Some debate exists as to the origin of the port's name. Whatever its source, no one doubts the harbor's location, connected to the sea and yet protected from wind and wave, was, in the words of Humboldt, "one of the finest in the world."

In the eighteenth century, the Spanish reclaimed the port from Dutch traders under the guise of the much-hated Basque Real Compañía Guipuzcoana, to whom the Crown awarded a virtual monopoly of its trade. They soon set about protecting their investment, erecting the forts of Solano and San Felipe, and improving the port's infrastructure and thereby stimulating trade.

Following their defeat at the Battle of Carabobo in 1821, the Royalist troops retreated to Puerto Cabello, where they held on by their fingernails. Finally, in 1823, the *Llanero* General Páez and his lancers forced the Spanish to surrender their last foothold on Venezuelan soil.

Puerto Cabello grew through the nineteenth century as trade in indigo, cacao, cotton and coffee from the fertile valleys of the San Esteban, Aguas Calientes and Borburata rivers mushroomed. By the latter part of the century, Puerto Cabello's docks extended over 200 hectares (nearly 500 acres), including over 30 docks and a number of shipyards.

The deep red flower of a banana tree.

Today, the presence of the navy, whose base lies over to the east, also provides an important impetus to the regional economy.

GENERAL INFORMATION

The **Dirección General de Turismo** ((042) 613921 FAX (042) 613255, open Monday to Friday 8 AM to 5 PM, is inside the Edificio Gobierno de Carabobo, Calle Ricaurte on the Plaza Bolívar. It is not particularly geared to the passing foreign traveler. To change Amex, the **Banco Consolidado** is in the newer part of town, just off the Avenida 2 Municipio, while **Banco Unión** is at Avenida 6 Valencia and Calle 12 Sucre.

colonial weapons and maps. The museum opens Monday to Friday 8 AM to noon and 3 PM to 6 PM, weekends 8 AM to noon.

Continuing up to the end of Los Lanceros (or Bolívar) stands the charming **Iglesia del Rosario**, with its funny copper dome and its wooden bell tower. The whitewashed church was built in 1780, and the bell tower is unique in Venezuela. Follow Calle Bolívar north to the **Plaza del Águila**.

Across the square, you can't help noticing the imposing **Casa Guipuzcoana**, now a public library. The building, completed around 1830, served as the company's headquarters until it lost its monopoly. However, the forts it built to protect its investment in the colony form the company's most

WHAT TO SEE AND DO

The heart of the old town, where restoration has been taking place over the last decades, beats north of **Plaza Bolívar**. On the square's east side, the **Iglesia de San José** has undergone various reforms over the centuries and seems decidedly confused about its true style. It's still worth a look inside, however. From the square, walk a block south to the **Teatro Municipal** on Calle Girardot. Built in the 1880s, it has been rescued, restored and returned to its former elegance.

The entrance to the **Museo de Historia Colonial** lies on Calle de los Lanceros No. 43, north from the theater. One of the port's oldest extant colonial mansions, dating back to 1790, houses the museum. It stretches over the second-story walkway into the building on Calle Bolívar, displaying artifacts from pre-Columbian times to

lasting monuments. Across the water from the Plaza del Águila and Parque Las Flores, the **Fortín San Felipe** (also known as the Castillo Libertador) still feels imposing today. The navy run launches over to the fort as it's situated inside the base. This service is sporadic, so consult the tourist office about how best to visit.

By the time you read this, the **Museo de la Marina** might well be open. The second important fort built by the company perches on a hillside to the south of the town, **Fortín Solano**, one of the last colonial forts erected in Venezuela. Not much is left of the fort itself, but the fantastic views of the port and bay reward an evening taxi ride up the hill.

Of the port's closest beaches, **Quizandal** is the nearest, where you can hop over to the lovely **Isla Larga**, great for snorkeling. The **Parque Nacional San Esteban** also lies close by, catch a *carrito* heading to the village of San Esteban from the corner near the main bus terminal in Puerto Cabello.

WHERE TO STAY

Unfortunately, Puerto Cabello awaits a *posada* or hotel in the colonial part of town, though you can check to see whether the **Restaurant La Fuente** has completed its remodeling of an old house ((042) 616889. The main cluster of hotels lie to the southwest of the historic center.

Moderate
Puerto Cabello's best hotel, **Hotel Suite Caribe** ((042) 643276 FAX (042) 643910, Avenida Solom 21,

WHERE TO EAT

Two favorite restaurants in Puerto Cabello are the moderately priced **Restaurant Mar y Sol** at the end of Calle Mercado, which serves great seafood including lobster and has views of the bay, and the cheaper **Briceño Ven** on the Malecón which, despite having no sign to announce it, serves tasty *criollo* dishes in pleasant surroundings. On the Plaza El Águila, **Restaurant Venezuela** comes recommended for fish and seafood and is air-conditioned, while the **Restaurant Lanceros** (with the best views upstairs) and **Lunchería La Fuente** are further good options in the colonial area.

is out to the east of airport, and offers over 60 air-conditioned uninspiring but certainly comfortable rooms with refrigerators and televisions. The hotel includes various restaurants, a decent-sized pool, a sauna and a gym.

Inexpensive
Of the hotels in this bracket, the best of the bunch is the **Hotel and Restaurant Isla Larga** ((042) 613290/741 FAX (042) 614416 on Calle Miranda, close to the bus terminal. A new pool accompanies its air-conditioned and comfortable rooms, and the overall feel, restaurant and situation make it excellent value. Next come **Hotel El Fortín** ((042) 614356, further up Calle Miranda at Avenida 9, whose rooms are basic but acceptable for the price, and the slightly simpler **Hotel Bahía** ((042) 614034. Of the budget options, check out to **Hotel Venezia** ((042) 614380 on Avenida Santa María.

HOW TO GET THERE

Puerto Cabello's airport is seven kilometers (nearly four and a half miles) west of the city center, but there aren't any scheduled passenger flights. The bus terminal is on Avenida La Paz, to the southwest of the colonial center. Buses connect regularly with Valencia (change for Caracas), San Felipe, Barquisimeto and Tucacas, while the more local *carritos* (buses) leave from a street corner nearby. The area to the north of the terminal towards Playa Blanca is notoriously dangerous for tourists, so stay away.

Tree ducks emulate Venezuelans waiting for a bus.

The Northwest

IF ONE STATE IN VENEZUELA TRULY LIVES UP TO THE PHRASE "full of contrasts," it is Falcón. Spend only a few days traveling in Falcón and you go from being Robinson Crusoe, to Beau Geste, Bolívar and Tarzan. For something different again, and often overlooked in tourist brochures, the state of Lara, and to a lesser extent Yaracuy, play important roles in Venezuelan agricultural life. The market in Barquisimeto sells over half of the country's grains, vegetables and other produce. Lake Maracaibo dominates Zulia State. The body of water holds a special place in the hearts and minds of Venezuelans. Not only is it South America's largest lake, but it is also the world's richest: the source of the country's wealth — oil. By exploiting its vast reserves, Zulia has emerged as the country's richest state, and its capital, Maracaibo, its second largest city. Zulia is one of the hottest parts of South America, with temperatures averaging 30°C (86°F), and only a little breeze in the late afternoons and nights to soothe hot brows.

But the state is not all about heat and oil, as a walk in one of its markets will reveal. It is one of the few places in Venezuela where you can still see indigenous people in traditional dress, and the Guajiros, Yupka, Bari and Paraujano rank among the most fiercely independent peoples in the country. Many Paraujano maintain their boat-bound traditional way of life, building their houses on stilts in the Laguna de Sinamaica, to the north-west of Maracaibo.

PARQUE NACIONAL MORROCOY

Morrocoy National Park was established in 1974 to protect the 320 sq km (125 sq miles) of shallow islands formed by corals and shell debris. It curves in an arc from the town of Tucacas, north around the Cerro Chichiriviche to the town of Chichiriviche. It encompasses part of the mainland as well as the offshore islands and islets, a haven for wading and water birds as much as scuba divers and sun worshippers.

There are around 30 islands or *cayos*, in all, some large enough to support mangrove ecosystems and provide shade, others little more than glorified sandbanks. In places, shallow waters — warm as a bath — provide an ideal playground for children and adults alike.

Venezuelans flock to Morrocoy in increasing numbers to enjoy its pristine waters and sandy beaches — which, sadly, they leave strewn with litter. Avoid weekends and peak vacation seasons and you'll find the keys and beaches virtually deserted. Boatmen's *unións* at both towns provide transportation to the nearest islands and can tell you about their facilities. Note the name of your boat and specify a time to be picked up; they are generally pretty reliable.

Cayo Sombrero is probably the most popular of all the keys. On its seaward side it boasts good reefs for snorkeling, while soft waves lap the mainland side. It also enjoys favorable breezes, better at keeping the biting gnats at bay than on other islands. November to February are the worst time for these infuriating creatures. Among the other islands, **Cayo Borracho** and **Cayo Peraza**, and **Playa Mero** and **Playuela** are the best for snorkeling.

On the park's western flank, to the north of the Cerro Chichiriviche, over 300 species of birds find sanctuary in the **Cuare Wildlife Refuge**. In the rainy season, flocks of flamingos, scarlet ibis and roseate spoonbills feed at the shallow salt flats,

painting the waters with their bright colors. As many as 7,000 flamingos have been spotted here. Its 11,853 hectares (29,277 acres) include mangrove swamps, essential habitat of the endangered coastal crocodile (*Crocodylus acutus*), and the semi-deciduous forests of the Cerro de Chichiriviche, home to deer, agouti and howler monkeys, among other species.

Because of the area's importance for wildlife, tourism is highly controlled. The multilingual Belgian Laurent Vaudevyère holds a permit to conduct tours of the mangroves and canals. He runs a company called **EcoMundo (** (016) 642-4985 or (042) 830131 (messages), at Playa Norte in Chichiriviche. His canoe trips leave early in the morning and guarantee one of the most rewarding wildlife experiences in Venezuela. The best months to visit are from October to February.

SPORTS AND OUTDOOR ACTIVITIES

Top of the list in Morrocoy comes **scuba diving**, although a decent snorkel and some flippers will satisfy many visitors. The outer islands seem to have been the least affected by the bleaching of a few years ago — many people blame a nearby government chemical plant for either polluting the waters or heating them up; there are still some excellent corals to be explored within the park (see SPORTING SPREE, page 28 in TOP SPOTS).

In Tucacas, Mike Osborn, with 20 years' diving experience in Venezuela, runs **Submatur** ((042) 830082 FAX (042) 831051 Calle Ayacucho 6. He

towards Chichiriviche, a right turn switches back towards the park, following the shore of the Bahía de Morrocoy and the shadow of the Cerro de Chichiriviche. There are numerous marinas along this stretch, which eventually reaches Tucacas Point and the Mayorquines beach via a path.

On the way, three handsome places to stay at moderate rates are attractive in themselves and enjoy easy access to the park. They offer package deals including meals, drinks, transfers to beaches, snorkeling gear, and sun shades and chairs. They can also arrange transportation to and from Caracas. The first is **El Paraíso Azul Posada** ((042) 850929 or (02) 952-1490 (reservations) FAX (02) 953-6677, on the left up a steep track shortly after the

organizes open water PADI courses which usually take four days, as well as catering for day dives and renting equipment. Mike can also arrange trips over to Los Roques (see LOS ROQUES, page 96) and to the islands of Las Aves, both fantastic dive spots.

Over in Chichiriviche, **Agua-Fun Diving** ((042) 86265 E-MAIL aguafun@cantv.net WEB SITE http://ourworld.compuserve.com/homepages/pierreclaude, is run by friendly multilingual Pierre and Monika, who also rent rooms for your stay at their diving school.

WHERE TO STAY AND EAT

I recommend the following places to stay within, or close to, the national park, in preference to the less appealing towns of Tucacas and Chichiriviche. At km 71 on the coastal highway, about seven kilometers (four miles) north of Tucacas heading

Guardia Nacional stop. Its most impressive feature is the sweeping view of Morrocoy Bay from the restaurant tucked into the side of the hill. The rooms are simple yet comfortable, but inferior to the other *posadas*, so perhaps just stay for a meal.

A bit further along comes the long white wall of **Villa Mangrovia** ((014) 941-5176 FAX (049) 91470, on the right-hand side. Within a spacious compound alive with the cries of birds (over 70 species have been spotted here), owner Irina Jackson offers just three double rooms in tastefully decorated cabins. Her establishment has a good culinary reputation; meals are served in the evening by candlelight in the main building. Ms. Jackson speaks several languages and attends to her guests personally. Reserve well in advance.

Visitors arriving at Cayo Sombrero in Morrocoy National Park.

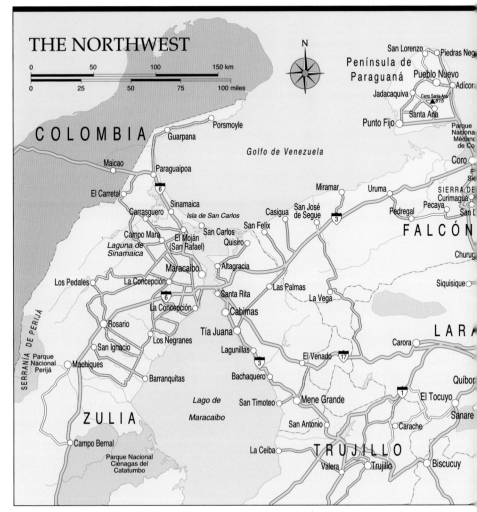

Julieta and Carlos de Valdés offer five colorful rooms with air-conditioning in the last *posada*, **La Acacia** ((014) 943-1601 or (016) 642-4534, in the hamlet of Lizardo. Around the back of the main house, a large mosaic-tiled terrace serves as the eating area, the comfortable social areas are shaded by trellising interspersed with sculptures and plants. The food is excellent and the welcome warm.

Lastly, outside the park but still well worth considering, comes **El Solar de la Luna** ((016) 647-2741, (016) 644-0915 or (02) 986-2861. It's situated in the unprepossessing village of Bella Vista, which can be reached by taking a well-marked turn off on the Tucacas–Sanare road, close to a gas station. Follow this road up to the village and take the rough road up the hill at the fork. Then take the first right and the distinctive structure of the *posada* is on your right.

Prepare to be stunned by the unparalleled view of the Morroccoy Bay from the vast terrace. Over

to one side, a Jacuzzi bubbles, while plants and antiques abound under the wonderful wooden beams and open-plan living and cooking area. The owner, Bertapaula García, is a bubbly, warm and cultured person, keen to make her guests feel at home. She serves some wonderful dishes drawn from colonial "Mantuana" cuisine. Bertapaula speaks a bit of English and can provide transfers to the islands, and offers to pick up guests at Tucacas or even further afield if necessary.

Camping on one of the islands is another alternative. Contact Inparques TOLL-FREE (800) 84847 for details of the elaborate rigmarole you'll need to go through.

HOW TO GET THERE

From the south, the town of Tucacas on the coastal highway provides access to the park. It's literally a short walk over the bridge to Punta Brava key

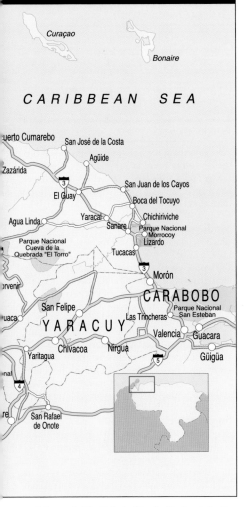

CARIBBEAN SEA

(map showing Curaçao, Bonaire, Caribbean Sea, Puerto Cumarebo, San José de la Costa, Agüide, Zazárida, San Juan de los Cayos, El Guay, Boca del Tocuyo, Agua Linda, Yaracal, Chichiriviche, Sanare, Parque Nacional Morrocoy, Lizardo, Parque Nacional Cueva de la Quebrada "El Torro", Tucacas, Morón, orvenir, CARABOBO, San Felipe, Parque Nacional San Esteban, Las Trincheras, YARACUY, Valencia, Guacara, Chivacoa, Nirgua, Güigüe, Yaritagua, San Rafael de Onote)

and the park. The ticket office for the boats is situated to the left of the vehicle entrance to the park; prices are charged per boat, not per person, so you might have to wait for one to fill up for the price to come down. Ask the local *posada* owners or divers about their favorite keys.

To the north of the park, Chichiriviche provides the other springboard. The nearest keys to the town are Borracho, Sal, Los Muertos, Peraza and Pelón, as well as the popular Sombrero. The two boatmen cooperatives at Chichiriviche (one in the center of town, the other at Playa Sur) also take tourists in to the Cuare Wildlife Refuge to visit the two caves — Cueva de los Indios with its intriguing petroglyphs, and La Piedra de la Virgen, venerated by local fishermen — and on to the mangrove swamps for bird spotting. This trip is best done in the early morning, when you'll see the greatest number of birds.

TUCACAS

I have to admit I am not fond of either Tucacas or Chichiriviche. They are an urban planner's nightmare, where the tourism boom led to development before logic, safety and health. With the increasing popularity of Morrocoy's beaches, Tucacas continues to grow very rapidly, recent developments focusing on the south of this unprepossessing town. From the coastal highway, Avenida Libertador, the town's main artery, leads all the way to the bridge over to the Cayo Punta Brava. This stretch holds most businesses and hotels.

GENERAL INFORMATION

There is no tourism information office in Tucacas, so your best bet is to consult **Varadero Tours** ((042) 834745 FAX (042) 833881, Avenida Libertador near the Hotel Esperanza, or **Inparques** ((042) 830069 which has offices close to the bridge on Avenida Libertador.

Be warned: Money-changing is frustrating in Tucacas and Chichiriviche (and most of Falcón State for that matter). For Visa and MasterCard advances you can use **Banco Unión** on Libertador, close to the highway, but it's hard to find anyone willing to change travelers' checks or cash at decent rates (try travel agents or tour operators).

WHERE TO STAY

Vacationing Venezuelans make finding rooms in Tucacas during the high season harder than usual. Prices that are already slightly higher than in other parts of the country take a further hike at peak times.

Moderate

Of the large resorts that have sprung up around Tucacas, I think the best are the **Morrocoy Coral Reef** ((042) 830301 FAX (042) 830491, off the highway, and the **Sun Way Morrocoy** ((042) 830001 FAX (042) 830005, at km 58 on the highway. Both are top-end resorts with expansive, well-tended grounds, pools, gyms and tennis courts, and their prices come down to very reasonable levels in the off-season. Both can provide water-sports facilities and tours of the park in more luxurious craft, and within both their compounds it's easier to forget about the town without.

Inexpensive

If you're into diving and on a budget, the friendly André who works at the Submatur dive shop runs the **Submar Inn** ((042) 831754, a 10-room place close to the hospital. The rooms are basic but have fans and are clean, and the garden is pleasant. Getting down to budget level, around Avenida Libertador you have **Hotel La Suerte** ((042) 831332 and **Posada Johnathan** ((042) 830325, Calle Sucre, both decent with some air-conditioned rooms.

WHERE TO EAT

A good place for seafood is the air-conditioned **Varadero** inside the Hotel Punta Brava. Also recommended are **Tito's** on Calle Sucre, east of Avenida Libertador, and **Venamar**, down by the bridge.

HOW TO GET THERE

There is frequent bus service throughout the day east to Valencia and west to Coro.

CHICHIRIVICHE

Chichiriviche is the other access town to the keys of Morrocoy. It's smaller but no more pleasant than its southerly neighbor Tucacas. Accommodation here is also slightly more expensive, though the boat fares to the islands are more affordable. You approach the town across a long causeway linking it to the Sanare–Tucacas Highway. Along both sides of the road, mangroves swamps and tidal flats extend for miles, part of the Cuare Wildlife Refuge (see PARQUE NACIONAL MORROCOY, above).

Chichiriviche's main arterial road, Avenida Zamora, carries you into the center of town right down to the waterfront and the wharf. As you approach the town, a road with a central reservation turns left, towards the growing development of Playa Norte. Further down Zamora, a right fork at the Hotel Garza takes you towards the area known either as Playa Sur or Fábrica de Cemento (the cement plant). This leads to the southern *embarcadero* (embarkation point).

GENERAL INFORMATION

As in Tucacas, there is no tourist information and your best bet for advice is **Varadero Tours** ((042) 830770 on Avenida Zamora. Nearby, the Banco Industrial de Venezuela changes cash, but not travelers' checks, and advances money on Visa cards only.

WHERE TO STAY

Prices increase for accommodation in the high season (school holidays, Christmas, New Year, Easter and Carnival), but hoteliers can often organize boat trips for you which work out cheaper than offers at the boatmen's wharf.

Moderate

Chichiriviche's newest hotel, the posh **Coral Suites** ((042) 851033, Avenida Cemento, will boast 120 rooms when completed. The complex includes tennis courts, a huge swimming pool with waterslide, and four restaurants; they have comfortable rooms as well as fully equipped suites, making it a good option for families.

Further down Avenida Cemento, the family-friendly **Apart-Hotel Villa Marina** ((042) 86759 has self-catering rooms for two to nine people set around an attractive swimming pool area. The rooms are spotless and mostly bright, with air-conditioning and hot water.

Inexpensive

Over in the Playa Sur area, the most established and popular place is **Posada Alemania** ((042) 850912 E-MAIL posadaalemania@cantv.net, run by a German man and his friendlier Venezuelan wife. In addition to providing simple but attractive rooms in a pleasant garden setting, they prepare meals and can organize tours of the area and further afield.

On Playa Norte, new places spring up all the time, of which two are worth mentioning. To get to them, take the left turn on the approach road to the town, where there is a melee of signs for hotels. Follow this road straight on until you reach the beach. Here, over to the left, a young French-Venezuelan couple offer five attractive rooms in their *posada*, **Morokkué** ((042) 86492. The house is dotted with original art and eye-catching wooden furniture, with a living room upstairs looking out on to the sea. Just south of here on the beach road, the very chatty and charming Italian Patrizia Barsanti and her husband Guido run a small guesthouse called **Kanosta** ((042) 830131 on the corner, with a small sign for the house. The two rooms are simple, with air-conditioning and private baths, but plenty of living and hammock-slinging space. Patrizia cooks all meals, and is justifiably proud of her Italian cuisine.

WHERE TO EAT

The classiest restaurant on the seafront is **Txalupa**, with some excellent fish and seafood dishes, while a bit further down, the best of the bunch is **Casa Mare** which also serves up pizza and good meat dishes. Further out on Avenida Zamora is **La Nota Azul**, which enjoys a good reputation for *parillas* (barbecues), while the **Heladería Roma** served me some wonderful ice cream. **Gelatería Italian Paradise** cooks good pasta and fast food.

HOW TO GET THERE

As with Tucacas, Chichiriviche is reached by the main highway road. However, buses coming from Coro don't stop there, and you need to get off at the Sanare crossroads and wait for the smaller *buseta* coming from Tucacas to take you the 22 km (14 miles) to town. From Caracas, take the bus to Valencia and then change to a smaller bus.

CORO

In a country that has neglected its historical heritage as badly as Venezuela, the town of Coro, capital of Falcón State, is not only beautiful, but also remarkable. The restored heart of the city, awarded UNESCO World Heritage status in 1993, is truly a gem of colonial architecture, heavily influenced by the Dutch Antilles' style of the eighteenth century.

Just to the north, always threatening to smother the town, lie the expansive *médanos* (dunes), which constantly shift and change under the sculpting hand of the coast's strong winds. In the language

OPPOSITE: With an average temperature of 28°C (82°F), refreshments are welcome in Coro. ABOVE: The eighteenth century Iglesia de San Clemente.

of the Caiquetío Indians, the original inhabitants of the land, "coro" meant wind.

Coro is a relatively peaceful town, with quite a large number of students helping to keep the arts and ambience alive. With an average temperature of 28°C (82°F), it is also hot, and lunchtime siestas are definitely the order of the day, though the winds from the sea ensure that the heat never feels suffocating.

BACKGROUND

Coro vies with Cumaná for historical "I was here first" status, although Coro wins the contest for being the first *continuously* inhabited settlement

GENERAL INFORMATION

The **Secretaría de Turismo (** (068) 511132 FAX (068) 515327 for Falcón State is found on the pedestrian Paseo Alameda, just north of Plaza Bolívar, and is open Monday to Friday 8 AM to noon and 2 PM to 5 PM. They speak English and are helpful, and provide leaflets as well as maps. On the Internet, take a look at WEB SITE www.funflc.org.ve/visita_falcon/ or www.coroweb.com/coro.htm.

Inparques ((068) 79582 has its office in the Jardín Xerófilo to the east of town, on the way to La Vela. Most banks are within a few blocks of Plaza Bolívar, and the **Budget** car rental

in Venezuela and South America. However, as with most towns in the country, its early history consists of a plethora of natural and human disasters.

Founded in 1527 by Juan de Ampiés, the town initially fared far better than Cumaná thanks to the Governor's policy of befriending the local Caiquetío Indians. When Carlos V of Spain created the Province of Venezuela in 1528, Coro assumed its place as the capital.

Until the eighteenth century, Coro's fortunes declined as it was successively sacked by pirates. The Governor and Bishop abandoned the town for Caracas in 1578 and 1659 respectively. It wasn't until illegal trade with the Dutch colonies of Curaçao, Bonaire and Aruba flourished that Coro regained some of its former glory. Its port of La Vela, just to the east, exported cacao, tobacco and horses, and the merchant families began constructing the houses which survive today.

agency is just next to the Miranda Cumberland hotel.

Coro's *fiestas patronales* take place in the last week in July. During the **Feria de los Pesebres** in early December, competitions are held for the best nativity scenes, choirs and carol singers in a pre-Christmas extravaganza.

WHAT TO SEE AND DO

Start your day as early as possible in Coro to enjoy the cool mornings. The restored heart of the city centers around the **Plaza San Clemente**, to the north of Plaza Bolívar, continuing west along Calle 14 Zamora towards the theater and San Nicolás de Bari church.

However, a walking tour should begin with the impressive yet austere **cathedral** since it and La Asunción's on Isla de Margarita are the oldest in Venezuela and among the oldest in the Americas. The structure, finally completed in 1632, is perhaps more reminiscent of a fortress than of a place of worship: during the numerous pirate attacks of the seventeenth century, it was often used as a refuge for the local population.

Turn left when exiting the cathedral to walk up the Paseo Talavera to the **Museo de Arte de Coro**, the Coro branch of the Caracas Museo de Arte Contemporáneo, housed in a beautiful mansion. Its balcony was recently restored to its full glory, and the house is known as the Balcón de Bolívar to record the Liberator's stay here in 1826. The museum holds temporary exhibitions and has a good gift shop. It is open Tuesday to Saturday

art is displayed here alongside secular works, with 22 rooms exhibiting silverware, glassware, furniture, sculpture, paintings and old colonial bells to wander through. Ask for a guided tour in Spanish. The doors open Tuesday to Saturday from 9 AM to noon and 3 PM to 6 PM, Sundays 9 AM to 1 PM only.

Crossing over the square westwards, note the old wooden cross encased within an unfortunately ugly plaster "pavilion." The cross is said to come from the *cují* tree (the mesquite tree, of the acacia family) under which the first mass was celebrated after Coro's foundation in 1527. Just across from here lies the delightful **Iglesia de San Clemente** which dates back to the eighteenth century, on

9 AM to 12:30 PM and 3 PM to 7:30 PM, and Sunday from 9 AM to 4 PM.

Just across the street, inside another old mansion, lies an extension of the **Museo de Arte Alberto Henríquez**. The main body of the small but interesting museum is on Calle Zamora, next to the Museo Diocesano. Among the temporary art exhibitions here, visit the Jewish synagogue, with its sand-covered floor and beautiful wooden furniture, restored in 1980 on its original site. It was one of the first synagogues in the New World. The museum is open at the same times as the Museo de Arte de Coro above.

Reaching the shaded Plaza Falcón, turn left and walk two blocks north until the left on Calle Zamora. Just next to the pointy-spired **Iglesia de San Francisco**, an old monastery hosts the best museum in the city, the **Museo Diocesano de Coro Lucas Guillermo Castillo**. A wealth of religious

the site of a sixteenth-century church which succumbed to pirates.

Continuing west to the next corner, the **Casa de Los Arcaya** with its fine balcony houses the unpretentious **Museo de Cerámica Histórica y Loza Popular**, which includes pre-Hispanic pottery as well as later chinaware. Opening times are the same as the Museo Diocesano. Across the street, the **Casa del Sol** and its adjacent **Casa Nazaret**, both handsome old buildings, today serve as offices.

Further along Zamora, the imposing façade of the **Casa de las Ventanas de Hierro** is unmistakable for its grand eight-meter (26-ft) elaborate plaster doorway, one of the finest examples to be

OPPOSITE LEFT: The elaborate façade of La Casa de las Ventanas de Hierro. RIGHT: A smiling *criollo* boy. ABOVE: Figure of a saint in the Museo de Cerámica.

found in the Caribbean. The house's fine wrought iron grilles were brought over from Spain via Santo Domingo in the eighteenth century. Inside, the house hoards a veritable treasure trove of family memorabilia and antiques. As the **Museo de Tradición Popular**, its doors open to the public Tuesday to Saturday from 9 AM to noon and 3 PM to 6 PM, Sundays 9 AM to 1 PM only. Guided tours in Spanish begin throughout the day, and artworks by local artists are sold in an adjoining room. They also sell copies of *Coro, Donde Empieza Venezuela*, by Carlos González Batista, a first-rate guide to the town's history and architecture, in Spanish.

Built by Andrés de Talavera in the 1770s, the **Casa del Tesoro** occupies the next corner of

xerophytic botanical gardens run by Inparques, open daily except Monday from 8:30 AM to 11:30 AM and 2 PM to 3:30 PM, where park wardens take you on a guided tour of the garden's plants. Take insect repellent to avoid being eaten alive.

WHERE TO STAY

Although there really ought to be, Coro lacks a beautifully restored old-house-turned-*posada* for weary travelers to rest their bones. This leaves the town somewhat flagging in attractive accommodation, and you might consider staying in the far more inviting places up in the cool hills of the Sierra de San Luís (see SIERRA DE SAN LUÍS, page 129).

Zamora, at Colón. A famous bishop lived in the house in the nineteenth century, so it's also known as La Casa del Obispo. The house displays contemporary art works, and ask the staff about the "tesoro" (treasure) in its name. It's open Monday to Saturday 9 AM to 6 PM and Sunday 9 AM to 3 PM.

The next left and right take you west on Calle Falcón to the small but beautiful church of **San Nicolás de Bari**, whose façade has been spared any remodeling. Have a wander around the lovely cemetery to its side.

If your feet are still up to it, head west along Zamora for about five blocks until you come to the **Cementerio Judío** (Jewish cemetery) at Calle 23 de Enero. Declared a national monument in 1970, the cemetery is the oldest still in use in South America.

Heading out east from Coro on the road toward La Vela, the **Jardín Xerófilo** is an excellent

Moderate

In front of the airport, to the north of the colonial center, the **Hotel Miranda Cumberland (** (068) 524724 FAX (02) 761-6681, Avenida Carnevalli, represents Coro's most upmarket accommodation and is a good-value option. The rooms have undergone a recent make-over and though not imaginative, they are certainly comfortable. The hotel includes a restaurant, shops, and a large pool area.

Inexpensive

The next pick down the scale is the **Hotel Intercaribe (** (068) 511811 FAX (068) 511434, Avenida Manaure at Calle Zamora, very centrally located and a favorite of traveling business people. The rooms are acceptable on the whole, but do ask to see them first. Their restaurant and *tasca* are popular for lunch, and the modest swimming pool for guests' use makes an added bonus.

Having poked my nose into the central hotels downtown, the Capri, Colonial and Roma, I can't really recommend any of them. Instead, head out to the newer, smaller establishment at Calle Comercio No. 46, **La Fonda Coriana** ((068) 526245, which is a friendly family-run place with eight spotless, simple rooms set around an inner patio.

For a backpacker haunt, consider the **Posada El Gallo** ((068) 529481, Calle Federación No. 26, run by yet another French-Venezuelan couple offering nine bare-bones rooms, acceptable if you're on a tight budget. Eric also rents mountain bikes and is a good source of local knowledge.

WHERE TO EAT

Coro is famous for its specialties made from goat's milk. These include *queso coriano*, goat's cheese; *nata*, halfway between butter and salted cream; and the children's favorite, *dulce de leche*, a soft fudge. The most typical regional dish is *chivo en coco*, kid in coconut milk.

The restaurant inside the airport, **Aero-Club** serves good-value meals, while the restaurant at the **Miranda Cumberland** is more classy and enjoys a good reputation. Just off Calle Zamora, close to the center, **El Portón de Arturo** specializes in meat *parrillas* in pleasant rustic surroundings, with live music on weekends. For something unsophisticated but friendly, try **La Colmena** on Calle Comercio, which also has a a gallery, travel agents and shops inside its shaded patio. Over on Calle Josefo Camejo, **Taco Taco** serves tasty Mexican

food. The best *panadería* (bakery) in town is the **Costa Nova**, opposite the Hotel Intercaribe.

HOW TO GET THERE

Coro's extremely central airport, opposite the Miranda Cumberland, isn't exactly a hive of activity, though Avensa does fly twice daily to Caracas via Barquisimeto, where you can change for other cities. You can also hop over to the Dutch "ABC" islands, Aruba, Bonnaire and Curaçao, with **Aero Falcón** ((068) 517884. An alternative to Coro is the airport at Las Piedras (see PUNTO FIJO, page 128), better connected to the rest of Venezuela.

The bus terminal is on Avenida Los Médanos, about 20 minutes by small bus from the old city center, and there are frequent buses throughout the day to points east, and west to Maracaibo. There are also some buses serving Mérida and the Andes. For the Península de Paraguaná, buses link Punto Fijo regularly, while Adícora is less popular. You'll find *por puesto* jeeps heading south to the Sierra de San Luís and Curimagua here also.

PARQUE NACIONAL MÉDANOS DE CORO

A complete anomaly in this tropically exuberant land, the *médanos* (dunes) of Coro present a wonderful opportunity to pretend you're in the French Foreign Legion for a day. The national park created to protect this unique environment in 1974 is in fact huge, covering some 912 sq km (356 sq miles) of towering sand dunes, dotted with the occasional lonely cactus or xerophytic plant (adapted to survival with little water).

The park stretches from Coro's northern borders up the "giant's neck" of the Isthmus of Paraguaná all the way to Adícora on the peninsula's eastern coast. In the evening or early morning light, the combination of the region's strong winds and the undulating curves of the dunes make for an unforgettable experience. Because some robbery of tourists has been reported, my advice is to stay close to the two main entry points to the park, especially if exploring alone.

HOW TO GET THERE

There are two points of access to the park. For the easterly, more popular one, take a bus marked "Carabobo" from Calle Falcón and get off just past the Monumento a la Federación. From there, walk up the wide avenue to the Monumento a la Madre traffic circle where kiosks and street vendors offer refreshments. A taxi from the city

ABOVE: The corner of the 1770s Casa del Tesoro. OVERLEAF: The haunting *médanos* (dunes) north of Coro.

center is also reasonable. The northerly entrance is off the highway to Punto Fijo, an extension of Coro's Avenida Los Médanos, just north of Plaza La Concordia. This entrance is quieter and less littered.

PENÍNSULA DE PARAGUANÁ

Seen on a map, one can't help but think of the profile of a human head when looking at this peninsula, Venezuela's largest, which juts out from the coast above Falcón's mainland. Paraguaná is essentially arid, with old white-washed churches bleached under an unforgiving sun and a metallic blue sky. It boasts not a single permanent river, and only about 40 days of rainfall a year. It is also a flat land, punctuated only by the Cerro Santa Ana mountain which looms above every inland prospect, rising 815 m (2,674 ft) above sea level. Vegetation is still largely xerophytic, dominated by the fingerlike columns of *cardón* cactus, though some rainforest species cling to the edge of the mountain's higher slopes.

Though modernity has arrived in some form with the oil refineries on the western coast, inland the old colonial towns of Santa Ana, Moruy, Jadacaquiva and Baraived still seem stuck in a sun-blanched time warp. Over on the eastern shores near Adícora, the region's strong winds have caught the attention of windsurfers from around the world. The peninsula is a barren, dramatic place. If you have time on your hands, rent a car in Coro to explore the peninsula's old towns and churches, then follow with a dip and a meal at Adícora.

PUNTO FIJO

Although Punto Fijo is the peninsula's largest town, with good amenities and transportation, it isn't a tourist town. To be honest, I can't see why you would come here at all, unless you are on your way to or from the Dutch Antilles. It's a large, dusty sort of place with few redeeming qualities.

General Information

Banco Unión is on Calle 79 close to Avenida 21. For money changing, your best bet is Casa Fukayama, Avenida Bolívar, between calles Altagracia and Girardot, and for Amex travelers checks, **Banco Consolidado** on Calle Falcón and Avenida Bolívar.

Judibana ((069) 450564 FAX (069) 456398, Calle Comercio, an English-speaking travel agent, arranges tours of the peninsula and can help with inquiries. The **Dutch Consul** can be contacted on **(** (069) 407211. The main avenues in the town are the north–south running Avenida Bolívar and Avenida Colombia.

Where to Stay

If you do happen to be en route to or from the Dutch Antilles and have to spend the night, Punto Fijo offers a range of inexpensive hotels. Book early since rooms tend to be snapped up fast regardless of the tourist season. The **Hotel El Cid (** (069) 455245 at Calle Comercio and Avenida Bolívar, with air-conditioning, televisions and decent rooms, presents the best value. Slightly cheaper is the **Hotel Presidente (** (069) 458964 at Avenida Perú and Calle Cuba.

How to Get There

Punto Fijo's airport lies around 10 km (six miles) north of the town and is known as Las Piedras. **Avensa (** (069) 461893 fly to Caracas and the ABC islands, and there are flights to Maracaibo and one planned for Mérida.

For regional destinations, buses depart from near the market, to the south of the city center. Small *busetas* to towns on the peninsula also leave from here. For longer distances, companies have their own terminals. **Expresos Occidente**, Calle Comercio near the Hotel Caribe, and **Expresos Alianza** on Avenida Colombia cover most eastern and western cities between them.

AROUND PARAGUANÁ

The three peaks of the Cerro Santa Ana dominate the peninsula. Around the mountain huddle small villages with old churches and locals lurking in the shade of a house or a storefront. Once over the thin isthmus to the peninsula, the highway forks, the easterly road leading to Adícora, the westerly to Punto Fijo. In **Santa Ana**, don't miss the Iglesia de Santa Ana whose brilliant whitewashed, fortress-like walls date back to the eighteenth century, making it the oldest church of the peninsula. Also worth exploring are the remodeled colonial church and the stores selling chairs made from *cardón* cactus in **Pueblo Nuevo**; and the churches of Moruy, Jadacaquiva and Baraived. Moruy provides the simplest access for climbing the Cerro Santa Ana. Contact **Inparques (** (069) 86185 in Santa Ana.

ADÍCORA

Of all the towns on the peninsula, Adícora is the only one with attractive accommodation. Add to this its recent efforts at restoring and revitalizing old houses, and some good swimming beaches, it's little wonder the town is increasingly popular with national tourists. Foreigners are drawn to the small fishing village for the strong winds which scour the coast all year round, where **windsurfers** revel in the excellent conditions, particularly from January to July.

The town was Paraguaná's principal port for centuries, from where salt and hardwoods were exported to the Dutch colonies. The Antillian influence pervades the architecture of the charming seafront houses in the old part of town, with their gables, finials, grilles and shutters, and of course their brightly painted walls.

Where to Stay

The most pleasant place in the center of town is run by the friendly Kitzberger family, who now own two *posadas*. The first, on the seafront, is known as la **Casa Rosada (** (069) 88004 with only two rooms set around a welcoming patio area, alongside a pretty and tasty restaurant. The second,

a range of windsurf gear to rent and can also arrange tours of the peninsula. A bit further along, **Archie's (** (014) 691-2137 has two separate houses for two or three couples, both with equipped kitchens, and both a cut above their other rooms.

Finally, quite a way out of town, but worth considering, is **Hacienda La Pancha (** (014) 969-2649 or (02) 987-0081 E-MAIL haciendapancha@ hotmail.com. The farm lies about four kilometers (two and a half miles) from Adícora, on the left of the road to Pueblo Nuevo. Perched at the top of the hill in an otherwise unpopulated area, it's easy enough to find, and your search is rewarded by the most charming *posada* on the peninsula, with meals also available — French and Catalan

Casa Carantona ((069) 88173, one block back, includes 10 recently decorated rooms, half with air-conditioning. None of these have hot water, but I'm sure you can manage.

The main base of **Hotel Moustacho Adícora (** (069) 88210 FAX (069) 88054 E-MAIL moustacho @eldish.net WEB SITE www.pfo.eldish.net/ moustacho is on Calle Charaima, well marked in the town. In addition to offering a range of different-sized rooms and self-catering apartments, they rent other rooms and apartments throughout the town, as well as beach equipment and windsurf boards. They can organize island and boat tours.

Two places on Adícora's southerly beach cater to windsurfers looking for a base. The first is the young German Alex Hausmann and his Venezuelan wife Zully's **Windsurf Adícora (** (069) 88224 WEB SITE www.adicora.com, with four basic rooms with shared bathrooms and fans. They have

cooking. Make advance reservations since the owner usually only opens the *posada* on weekends and it's pretty popular.

How to Get There

Buses shuttle back and forth to Coro (one hour) and Punto Fijo every day until the evening, and there are smaller buses to Pueblo Nuevo.

SIERRA DE SAN LUÍS

Rising up from the coastal plain south of Coro, the mountains of the Sierra de San Luís harbor an oasis of cool, wet forest dotted with old, characterful towns, walking paths, waterfalls, underground caves, birdsong and some winning places to rest weary walking legs. After the heat of the coast,

Santa Ana's blinding white church on Paraguaná.

the cool temperatures and misty dawns of the Sierra come as a breath of fresh and refreshing air. Even climbing up the mountain from Coro, you're rewarded with unparalleled views of the coast on clear days.

In view of the Sierra's importance for water generation, it is surprising that the **Parque Nacional Juan Crisóstomo Falcón** was created as recently as 1987. It harbors some 20,000 hectares (49,400 acres) of forest, home to large numbers of birds, including the *guácharo* oilbird, small parrots, and a number of iguanas, lizards and snakes, as well as some great waterfalls and a part of the old *Camino de los Españoles*.

GENERAL INFORMATION

The three largest towns in the Sierra: San Luís, Curimagua and Cabure, form a rough triangle to the southwest of the park and provide good jumping-off places for exploring. If you come independently and want to visit Cabure my advice is to approach via Curimagua and San Luís — though the road is potholed and painstaking in parts — and return to Coro on the easterly route.

All the owners and managers of the *posadas* mentioned below can organize tours of the area for you, or advise you on how to get to local sights. Although local transportation is adequate, renting a car in Coro means you'll get to see more of the sights at your own pace.

WHAT TO SEE AND DO

Of the Sierra hill towns, **San Luís** is my personal favorite. Founded in 1590 and tucked into a hillside, its old church is highly endearing, and some of the houses around the plaza have been restored. Ask locals for directions to the nearby Cueva de Peregüey and waterfalls.

Lying between Curimagua and San Luís on an old unmade road, the **Haitón de Guarataro** is thought to be one of the deepest of these peculiar geological formations. The sinkhole plunges down 305 m (1,000 ft), but, remarkably, it's only 12 m (39 ft) wide. A small path branches off the road by an Inparques hut with some didactic panels along the way.

Of the waterfalls in the mountains, most people head to the **Cataratas de Hueque**, about seven kilometers (four and a half miles) east of Cabure. The site is best avoided on weekends. An old **Spanish Road**, *El Camino de los Españoles*, runs through the Sierra de San Luís. Local *posada* owners can take you on tours, or point out the best hikes.

WHERE TO STAY AND EAT

None of the accommodation in the Sierra offers luxury, but the owners' genuine friendliness and love for this wonderful mini-mountain range compensate for the lack of frills.

In Curimagua, there are quite a few choices now available. As you approach from La Negrita and Coro, the **Finca El Monte (/FAX (068) 518271 (messages), run by the very friendly Swiss couple Ursula and Ernesto, lies on your right. They offer three very reasonably priced comfortable rooms in their house, which is surrounded by their small-holding which they farm organically. They can arrange tours of local attractions.

The most authentic looking of all the *posadas*, built by the traditional *bahareque* block method, the aptly named **La Soledad (/FAX (014) 690-8889 (reservations essential) lies further along the same

road (call for directions). The *posada* commands swooping views down to the coast and enjoys a pleasant feel, even though the decoration inside the wooden-beamed and stone-flagged house is quite Spartan. Pol Acosta and his brother have put a lot of effort into the place and know the area extremely well. In addition to pickups from Coro and tours of the sights, with advance warning they can also arrange horse riding.

In Cabure, you have two options, so ask in the town for these.

HOW TO GET THERE

Por puesto jeeps wind inland to Curimagua from Coro's bus terminal, and you can also find some for San Luís (via the westerly road) and Cabure (via the easterly road). Transportation between the towns of the Sierra is a bit hit-and-miss, but *carritos* (buses) do link all of them throughout the day. Renting a car in Coro makes the most enjoyable way to explore.

BARQUISIMETO

Founded in 1552 and one of the earliest towns in Venezuela, Barquisimeto today ranks as its fourth largest city, enjoying a reputation as one its musical capitals as well as the country's agricultural powerhouse. Because of the damage inflicted by the 1812 earthquake, little remains of the city's colonial heritage, and modern planners have wrought their own particular form of destruction on what was left. That said, the area around the

For money matters, banks cluster along the large commercial Avenida Vargas, between avenidas 23 and 20. Next to the Hotel Hevelin, the travel agents **Turisol** can organize day trips to the south of Barquisimeto, as well as changing Amex checks.

Barquisimeto's biggest bash is the **Fiesta de la Divina Pastora** celebrated around the patron saint's day on January 14, when an image of the Virgin Mary is carried from the church in the village of Santa Rosa to the city's cathedral, and on to every church in town. Locals make the most of the event, with the Parque (Complejo) Ferial hosting sports events, concerts and an agricultural fair. In the same month, Barquisimeto hosts a renowned

Plaza Lara still retains an Old World charm and, for its music and market, Barquisimeto proves worthy of its locals' pride.

GENERAL INFORMATION

The city's **tourist office** ((051) 537544 is to the northeast of the historic center, close to the Parque Ferial, Edificio Fundalara, Avenida Libertador, open Monday to Friday, 8 AM to noon and 2:30 PM to 6 PM. You take a No. 12 bus from the city center to get there, and it's worth it if you want to find out about concerts and local events. Alternatively, buy a local newspaper. The **Inparques** office ((051) 548118 is just inside the Parque del Este off the Avenida Los Leones, to the south of the Parque Ferial. They can give you more information about Lara's important national parks, Yacambú and Terepaima.

singing and choir contest. Also notable is the **Fiesta de la Zaragoza** on December 28, when people take to the streets in colorful costumes, accompanied by droves of musicians.

WHAT TO SEE AND DO

Modern buildings hem the city's shaded Plaza Bolívar, with the exception of the **Iglesia de la Concepción** on its south side. The earthquake of 1812 destroyed the original sixteenth-century edifice, the city's first cathedral, and it was later rebuilt. A block south lies the **Museo de Barquisimeto**, housed in a large building originally a hospital (hence the chapel) around 1910. Today the building hosts historical exhibits and temporary art and cultural exhibitions, as well as the

Rows of *cardón* cactus in the foothills of the Cerro Santa Ana.

impressive La Salle collection of pre-Columbian artworks and pottery. It is open Monday to Friday 9 AM to noon, 3 PM to 6 PM, 10 AM to 5 PM on weekends.

Moving east, **Plaza Lara** is the city's most pleasant square, where historic buildings have been restored and the nineteenth-century **Iglesia de San Francisco** dominates. On the plaza's east flank, the two patios of the **Centro de Historia Larense** are home to an eclectic collection of memorabilia, including weapons and furniture, while the nearby **Ateneo** is a central venue for all sorts of cultural events. Walk down the hill just east of the square for the **Concha Acústica** where regular concerts and dances take place.

The city's modernist **cathedral**, built when the Iglesia de San Francisco was damaged by yet another earthquake, is hard to miss at the corner of Avenida Venezuela (Carrera 26) and Calle 29. Its innovative parabolic design already looks worse for wear, but its interior, tinged cobalt by the blue-stained glass and haunted by a suspended Christ figure, makes a better impression. Mass is celebrated at around 6 PM during the week.

Barquisimeto offers some attractive green spaces for a read or a snooze. The smallest park, the **Bosque Macuto** lies to the south of the Río Turbio shaded by elegant veteran royal palms, while the city's zoo, **Parque Zoológico Bararida** and the **Parque del Este** are both pleasant open spaces to the northeast of the historic center. The zoo is good by Venezuelan standards; open Tuesday to Sunday 9 AM to 5 PM. An artificial lake and some playgrounds lie nearby.

To catch some of the city's agricultural richness, head to the **Mercado Terepaima**, close to the cathedral. Saturday is the best and busiest market day of the week.

WHERE TO STAY

Barquisimeto doesn't boast any particularly impressive accommodation but is generally good value and not subject to price hikes for high tourist seasons.

Expensive
The city's top hotel is the **Barquisimeto Hilton** ((051) 536022 FAX (051) 544365, Urbanización Nueva Segovia, Carrera 5 between 5 and 6, which often has deals bringing the price of a double down to moderate level. The hotel is a short ride from the places of interest, but is very pleasant with its pool, tennis courts, access to golf courses and relaxed feel. The French restaurant, Le Provençal comes recommended, while its *criollo* El Turbio overlooks the river.

Moderate
Of the central downtown hotels, my pick is the four-star **Hotel Principe** ((051) 312111 FAX (051) 311731, Calle 23 at carreras 18–19, which has nearly 100 rooms, a classic Italian restaurant and pool, making it very good value. If the Principe is booked out, try the **Hotel Bonifran** ((051) 321314, also centrally located on Carrera 19 at Calle 31.

Inexpensive
On Carrera 19 between calles 31 and 32, the **Hotel Florida** ((051) 329804 is one of the best options in this bracket, where rooms come with air-conditioning and televisions. Over on Avenida 20 at Calle 26, the **Hotel del Centro** ((051) 314525 has small, clean doubles with air-conditioning at very reasonable prices. If you're passing through and need somewhere near the bus terminal (which isn't a particularly salubrious area), the **Hotel Yaguara** ((051) 453956 is bare-bones but acceptable.

WHERE TO EAT

On Avenida Lara, over to the east of the historic center, there are several good restaurants, popular with locals on the weekend. Of these, **El Llanero** is recommended for hearty *parillas*. More central, **La Casarella**, Carrera 15 at Calle 25 serves tasty Italian dishes, while the **Villa del Mar** on Avenida 20 at Calle 19 is one the city's best seafood establishments, with live music and dancing in the evenings. Vegetarians should head to the **Centro Integral Tiempo Natural** on Carrera 15 between calles 24 and 25. For breakfasts or a sit-down coffee, **Pastelería Cafe Majestic** on Carrera 19 between calles 30 and 31 is your best bet.

A lively nightclub downtown, the **Tequila Club**, Carrera 18 between calles 31 and 32, hosts a variety of music and special nights.

HOW TO GET THERE

Barquisimeto's airport is around four kilometers (two and a half miles) southwest of the city center. There are about nine flights a day to Caracas, as well as departures with Avensa to Coro, Barcelona, Porlamar, Puerto Ordaz, Maturín and Maracaibo. You'll also find car rental offices in the airport, which include Hertz.

Barquisimeto's bus terminal lies northwest of the old city center and many *carritos* (buses) link the two (look for the *ruta 15*). Roads lead all over the country, and you'll have no trouble finding buses for the Andes (Valera, Mérida, San Cristóbal), the west (Maracaibo), north to Coro, south to the Llanos (Guanare and Barinas). Buses to the southern towns mentioned below are plentiful.

CHIVACOA

The small town of Chivacoa, 60 km (37 miles) east of Barquisimeto, on the road to Valencia, would be an unremarkable place were it not for the mysterious figure of María Lonza (see below). In the mountains to the south of the town, thousands of followers of Venezuela's strangest cult flock to the sanctuaries that have sprung up. The cult's most important day is the Día de la Raza on October 12, though believers can be found around the mountain most weekends and during holidays (especially over Holy Week).

Where to Stay
If you are thinking of staying the night here, you will find some decent, inexpensive places near Plaza Bolívar. **Hotel Leonardo** ((051) 830866, on Avenida 9 at Calle 11, and **Hotel Venezia** ((051) 830544, on Avenida 9 at Calle 12, are both acceptable.

How to Get There
You can either get off a faster Barquisimeto–Valencia bus at the highway, a few blocks north of Plaza Bolívar, or else get one of the smaller buses or *por puestos* that link Barquisimeto and Chivacoa and drop you closer to town.

CIERRO DE MARÍA LONZA

Geographically, the lush mountains that rise to the south of Chivacoa are part of the Macizo de Nirgua. But the mountain range is in fact universally known as the Cerro de María Lonza. The cult of María Lonza is an intriguing amalgam. It blends Christian practices, pre-Columbian indigenous creeds and African Voodoo, with a pinch of Eastern exotica and Cuban *santería* thrown in for good measure.

María Lonza — usually portrayed as a beautiful woman astride a tapir — is often referred to as *La Reina* (The Queen) and her court includes historical figures such as the sixteenth-century Indian chief Guaicaipuro and Negro Miguel, a slave who led a rebellion in 1552. Following this Big Three come other figures like the doctor José Gregorio Hernández; Venezuela's patron saint, the Virgen de Coromoto; and even Simón Bolívar himself—he had to get a look-in somewhere. After this follow an ever-mushrooming list of other more minor deities.

On the mountain itself, two main sites are regarded as sanctuaries to *La Reina* and her court: **Sorte** and **Quibayo**. Quibayo is the most accessible, and there is even an Inparques office. It is important to realize that the followers of the cult take their devotions very seriously and do not necessarily take kindly to curious tourists.

How to Get There
Jeeps leave Chivacoa's Plaza Bolívar for Quibayo throughout the day, though they are few-and-far-between during the week. They then wait at the entrance to the sanctuary to take passengers back. The trip takes under half an hour.

SAN FELIPE

San Felipe lies roughly halfway between Chivacoa and the coastal town of Morón, and is Yaracuy State's capital. It remains the state's commercial center, though its present importance is a far cry from its eighteenth-century glory days when it basked as the regional headquarters of the Guipuzcoana Company. Until the demise of the cacao industry, it played an essential role in the economy of central Venezuela.

The city was virtually razed by the earthquake of 1812 and a new city was founded to the north of the old site. The ruins of the old town are now part of the delightful **Parque El Fuerte**, well worth a visit if you are passing this way. The city also provides access to the southern part of the **Yurubí National Park**.

SOUTHWEST OF BARQUISIMETO

Lying southwest of Barquisimeto, the green hills — part of an Andean spur — provide the city's inhabitants with their weekend dose of fresh air, and the valleys are intensely cultivated for coffee, potatoes, avocados and flowers. History courses through the region, with many old churches still standing in small towns, and numerous remains

A reveler at Barquisimeto's Fiestas de la Divina Pastora shows off his palm-frond hat.

of indigenous settlements. Indeed, the pottery of Quíbor is inspired directly by the finds that have been uncovered since the 1960s.

TINTORERO

Tintorero (meaning "dyer"), half an hour west of Barquisimeto, is nationally renowned for its weavers and dyers, who create some of the finest hammocks, rugs and blankets in Venezuela. Many of the town's inhabitants are also craftspeople, making furniture and musical instruments such as the distinctive four-stringed *cuatro* guitar so beloved of Venezuelan musicians. An international craft fair swamps the village in late June.

de Altagracia dominating a large square. Unless you come on the patron saint's day on January 18, your only chance to get a peek inside is to turn up for morning mass.

At Quíbor, you have the choice of continuing on Highway 7 to El Tocuyo; heading southwest to Sanare; or south to Cubiro.

EL TOCUYO

Seen today, it seems highly improbable that El Tocuyo, 30 km (19 miles) southwest of Quíbor, was once the capital of the Province of Venezuela (from 1546 to 1577), and one of the first towns founded in the Americas. Yet combine the osten-

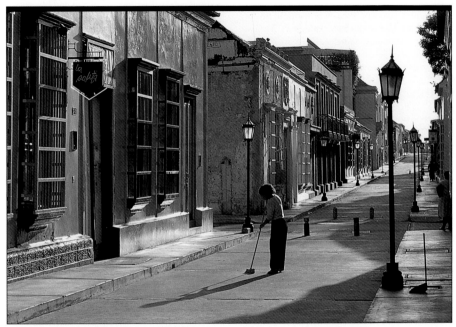

QUÍBOR

Continuing west on Highway 7, the next town is Quíbor, famous for the ceramics excavated in the town, at the site of an old Indian cemetery. On the Plaza Bolívar stands the large **Iglesia de Nuestra Señora de Altagracia** which dates from the late nineteenth century, and nearby, workshops sell modern-day examples of the peculiar ceramics.

The **Museo Arqueológico** showcases the bulk of the intriguing pottery unearthed from the cemetery, and does a good job of displaying the strange designs which include three-legged jugs and human figurines. The museum is two blocks north of Plaza Bolívar on Avenida 10, and is open Tuesday to Friday 9 AM to noon and 2:30 PM to 6 PM.

Following the Avenida north, you will eventually come to the squat yet ornate seventeenth-century chapel of **La Ermita de Nuestra Señora**

tatious full name of Nuestra Señora de la Pura y Limpia Concepción del Tocuyo with the fertile valleys surrounding the town (where the first sugarcane was planted in Venezuela) and the seven churches and various mansions that once stood in the town, and you can begin to imagine its former importance.

Tragically, an earthquake in 1950 destroyed much of El Tocuyo's colonial architecture; upon the orders of the dictator Marcos Pérez Jiménez, the damaged structures were largely bulldozed to make way for a "modern" town.

What to See and Do

The town's main church, **Iglesia de Nuestra Señora de la Concepción**, reconstructed after the earthquake, stands in a large square two blocks west of Plaza Bolívar. It presents a wonderful pink façade and an ornate bell tower outside, while inside the vast altarpiece (*retablo*) behind the high altar is one of the finest examples of the carved wooden style to be found in the country — notable for the absence of painted decoration.

On Plaza Bolívar, an old convent houses the **Casa de la Cultura**, which displays photos of the devastation wrought by the earthquake. Nearby, the **Museo Arqueológico JM Cruxent** showcases a modest collection of Indian ceramics and Spanish memorabilia from the area. The museum is open Wednesday to Friday 3 PM to 6 PM and weekends from 9 AM to 2 PM. Over on Calle 17, the **Museo Lisandro Alvarado** is another humble museum, open Tuesday to Friday 9 AM to noon and 2:30 PM to 5 PM, weekends from 10 AM to 4 PM, featuring a collection of historical objects.

El Tocuyo's main fiesta draws people from all corners. June 13 marks San Antonio de Padua's feast day, and locals celebrate by performing the *Tamunangue*, a seven-part dance, in bright garb.

Where to Stay

One of the most pleasant places to stay in the entire region, the inexpensive **Posada Colonial (** (053) 632495, Avenida Fraternidad between calles 17 and 18, occupies a beautiful old house just next to the Casa de la Cultura. The friendly owners offer 24 rooms with air-conditioning and private bathrooms, though no hot water. They serve good meals in the restaurant and provide a welcome pool in the back garden.

SANARE

Looping round first south, then east from El Tocuyo on winding roads, or else directly south from Quíbor, you come to the hillside town of Sanare. I'm very fond of the place and its small church of Santa Ana. It's undergone some renovation over the last years in the area known as El Cerrito, around Plaza Bolívar. Sanare is also the springboard-town for the Yacambú National Park.

Where to Stay and Eat

The best option in Sanare is the colonial-style **Posada Turística El Cerrito (** (053) 49016, near Plaza Bolívar, where the rooms are simple yet welcoming, with hot water and televisions. The friendly owners can arrange tours of local sights and into Yacambú National Park.

Close by, just off the plaza, is the **Restaurant Yacambú**, recommended for hearty meals, and **Cantaro de Miel**, which serves light snacks and tasty sweets, including honey (*miel*).

PARQUE NACIONAL YACAMBÚ

Yet another of Venezuela's fantastic national parks, Yacambú combines both elements of the Andean and Coastal Range ecosystems. The mountains

of the park rise to over 2,000 m (6,560 ft), part of an Andean tendril known as the Sierra de Portuguesa. Contact the Audubon Society in Caracas (see TAKING A TOUR, page 52 in YOUR CHOICE) for more details of hikes and conservation issues.

How to Get There

Transportation to and from the park is irregular. Getting there in a car or *por puesto* is straightforward from Sanare, but you should make advance arrangements for the return trip.

CUBIRO

Taking the third option from Quíbor, a lovely road leads 18 km (11 miles) to the small town of Cubiro, at the northern edge of Yacambú National Park. Although not quite as picturesque as Sanare, the town still enjoys a very pleasant mountain feel. Paths in the surrounding hills beg for exploration. Interestingly, the founder of Cubiro, a certain Diego de Losada, went on to establish the settlement of Caracas.

Where to Stay and Eat

Accommodation in Cubiro is unpretentious, but the following two places caught my attention, and their owners were friendly and helpful. **Posada Agua Viva (** (053) 48065, Calle Palermo at Calle Agua Viva, is identified by its brownish exterior wall. Although the owners only rent one comfortable room, the location, with spectacular views of the valleys and mountains, and the general feel of the *posada* is second to none.

One block below the Plaza Bolívar, on Calle Sucre, the **Hotel Diego de Losada (** (053) 48142 FAX (02) 793-2191 is set within an old restored house with an attractive restaurant and patio area, and good views of the surrounding countryside. The owner, Francisco Leitz, offers a range of double rooms and suites, all of which have hot water and good furnishings. You might also want to try the restaurant at the **Posada Turística La Flor Serrana** on Calle Consuelo.

HOW TO GET THERE

All the villages mentioned above are linked by regular bus services, and you need only ask a local for where to wait for one. Renting a car in Barquisimeto means you can explore the towns and parks of the region in your own time. It also means you can continue on Highway 7 south of El Tocuyo to Biscucuy in Portuguesa State. The road southwest of Biscucuy to Boconó is without doubt one the most beautiful gateways to the Andes (see TRUJILLO STATE, page 144, and THE OPEN ROAD, page 34 in YOUR CHOICE).

Sprucing up Maracaibo's colonial Calle Carabobo.

CARORA

Just over 100 km (62 miles) west of Barquisimeto, on Highway 17, which continues all the way to Maracaibo, Carora is Lara State's second largest town. Though the modern sector of the town is nothing to write a postcard home about, the old part, recently repainted, re-cobbled and spruced up, comes as a very pleasant surprise to most travelers. The town was founded in 1569 on the banks of the Río Morere, and farmers in the area have somehow managed to make a living from the parched land.

WHAT TO SEE AND DO

The historic part of town lies northwest of the newer districts. On Plaza Bolívar, the simple yet charming **Iglesia de San Juan Bautista** has preserved its original façade, which dates from the seventeenth century. Around the square, historic buildings bear name-plaques. The oldest surviving house, **Casa Amarilla**, today serves as a public library, while on the square's eastern side, Bolívar "once spent the night" in the colonial **Balcón de los Alvarez** house.

Following Calle 3 down to its end, you come to the tiny baroque **Capilla del Calvario**, erected in 1787, and one of the dinkiest churches you will find in the country. If the church is closed, ask for the keys in the florist shop across the road, as the altarpieces inside are pretty exceptional.

A few kilometers south of Carora, the **Bodegas Pomar** ((052) 212191 or (052) 211889 FAX (052) 217014 organize guided tours of their wine-making installations.

WHERE TO STAY AND EAT

Unfortunately, there are no hotels near the historic center, which means a short hop on bus. The best value place in town is the centrally located **Hotel Irpinia** ((052) 216362, just off the main thoroughfare of Avenida 14 de Febrero, on Carrera 9 Lara. Further out of town on the large Avenida Francisco de Miranda, the **Posada Madre Vieja** ((052) 212590 has 16 doubles set in large grounds, alongside a good restaurant.

For meals in town, try **El Casolar** on Avenida 14 de Febrero round the corner from the Hotel Irpinia, or the **D'Angelis Pizza**, three blocks down on Carrera 9 towards the old center. For a filling *parilla*, the **Hotel Bari**, also on 14 de Febrero is a good bet.

HOW TO GET THERE

Carora is just off Highway 17 connecting Barquisimeto and Maracaibo. The new bus terminal is close to the highway, and smaller buses run from the city center to the terminal all the time. From Carora, routes also connect up to the Andes.

MARACAIBO

Maracaibo is famous for both oil and music. The city mushroomed from a boondocks town at the turn of the nineteenth century to a thriving modern metropolis of around two million people. Occupying the northwestern shores of Lake Maracaibo, it's a hot, bustling city, with a "like it or leave it" attitude.

Maracaibo, like Caracas, is also a contradictory place, at once hyper-modern, with shopping malls, skyscrapers and slick freeways, yet with a deeply traditional local Indian population. The city is home to *gaita* music, only played in the rest of Venezuela at Christmas but heard pretty much year-round in Maracaibo. Although its lyrics were once pious, exalting saints and religious figures, today they are far more profane and irreverent, combining the *Maracuchos* famous quick wit, humor and machismo.

BACKGROUND

The city's early growth was linked to its trade with the Andes. Produce coming down from the mountains would be transferred to steam boats on the banks of the lake's southern rivers. From here it was transported across the lake to the city's docks. Today, Maracaibo's port is still the third most important in Venezuela.

Lake Maracaibo played an important role in the War of Independence when, on July 24, 1823, the Spanish fleet was defeated here with Colombian help. The victory, Venezuela's Trafalgar, combined with General Páez's victory in Puerto Cabello, signaled the death knell of Spanish power in Venezuela.

The discovery of oil in 1914 on the Zumaque 1 plot truly sent Maracaibo's fortunes rocketing. Following a further, and much larger, find in 1922 at Los Borrosos, foreign investors flocked to the area looking for rich pickings, dragging "Saudi Venezuela" into the twentieth century. By World War II, Venezuela was the world's second largest producer and its largest exporter of oil. It is still believed to have the largest reserves in the Western Hemisphere.

GENERAL INFORMATION

Maracaibo suffers from a split personality. The interesting old town lies to the south of the newer

skyscraper-strewn center, on the shores of the lake. Most tourists don't stray into the modern center and keep to the pleasant older area, where attractive houses have been restored and the atmosphere is more laid-back.

The downtown **Dirección de Turismo (Corpozulia)** office ((061) 921811 or (061) 921840 is on the ninth floor of the Edificio Corpozulia on Avenida Bella Vista, between calles 83 and 84, a short hop on a bus from the old town center. For more details of Zulia's national parks, **Inparques** ((061) 619298 is inside the Parque Paseo del Lago on Avenida El Milagro, to the northeast of the historic center. There are several banks just south of Plaza Bolívar, or you can change bolívares for Colombian pesos at the *casas de cambio* at the bus terminal.

OPPOSITE: The recently restored Teatro Baralt.
ABOVE: The Iglesia de San Francisco.

The city's biggest fiesta is the **Feria de la Chinita** in honor of Zulia State's patron saint, the Virgen de Chiquinquirá. It takes place on November 18, but effectively lasts for a week either side of this date, with numerous beauty contests, floats, processions, concerts and bull-fights throughout the city, with many centered on the basilica in the historic center. Maracaibo's patron saint is **San Sebastián**, whose feast day falls on January 20, when special masses are held in the cathedral and the saint's image carried around the Plaza Bolívar.

Christmas is *gaita* time par excellence, and on most street corners throughout the city, groups of musicians compose, play and rehearse — and occasionally fight. **San Benito**, Venezuela's black saint, is fêted between December 27 and 31 in towns around Zulia, including El Moján, Cabimas, Lagunillas and Gibraltar. Drums dominate the

festivities, often with several groups competing, while in Bobures and Gibraltar locals dress up in colorful costumes and maintain noisy all-night vigils.

WHAT TO SEE AND DO

A tour of Maracaibo should begin early, to take advantage of the cool air and the city's markets. The most interesting, the **Mercado de los Guajiros**, sets up at dawn on the lake side of Avenida El Milagro at Calle 96, to the west of Plaza Bolívar. Here, Guajira women in colorful caftan-like dresses sell their handmade hats, clothing and amulets from gaudy booths. They disappear by about midmorning as the day heats up. Another market you must not miss is the **Mercado de las Pulgas**, Maracaibo's flea market, a chaotic melee of colors and knickknacks, people and produce, totally bewildering to the outsider but undeniably exhilarating.

The huge seven-block-long **Paseo de las Ciencias** has the cathedral at its eastern end and the Basílica de la Chiquinquirá to the west. The Paseo was created, somewhat controversially, by bulldozing the old El Saladillo district in the early 1970s, making way for the gardens, benches, statues and band stands. The only building to escape the razing was the **Iglesia de Santa Bárbara** which stands in isolated grandeur at the heart of the Paseo.

The **cathedral**, home to one of the city's most revered images, the *Cristo Negro* or *Cristo de Gibraltar*, stands on its eastern end. Various grand buildings dominate the square's northern flank. The colonnaded **Palacio de las Aguilas** (Palace of the Eagles) was built in 1841, while next-door, the **Casa Morales** or **Casa de la Capitulación** is Maracaibo's only surviving colonial mansion. The restored house is Maracaibo's most attractive, decorated with period furniture and paintings from the War of Independence, open Monday to Friday 8 AM to 5 PM. Across the street, the grandiose **Teatro Baralt**, inaugurated in 1883, was recently reopened after years of restoration, and there should be tours of its sumptuous, somewhat over-the-top interiors by the time you read this.

Other sights to ask the tourist office about include the **Museo Arquidiocesano**, the diminutive chapel **Templo Bautismal Rafael Urdaneta** and its museum, and the **Museo Antropológico**. Besides the cathedral, Maracaibo also boasts two lovely churches: **Santa Ana**, at the eastern end of Calle 94, and the **Basílica de Chiquinquirá**. The **Feria de la Chinita**, as the Virgin here is affectionately known, is celebrated on November 18.

WHERE TO STAY

The upscale hotels are located north of the historic center, and it is hard to find anything decent downtown.

Expensive

The most centrally located of the top end hotels is the **Hotel Del Lago Inter-Continental** ((061) 924002 TOLL-FREE (800) 12132 FAX (061) 914551 on Avenida 2 El Milagro, on the shores of the lake. Rooms are all spacious with views of the lake, and facilities include a gym, night club and inviting poolside social areas.

Further out, the **Hotel El Paseo** ((061) 924422 or (061) 924114 FAX (061) 919453, at Avenida 1B and Calle 74 in the Sector Cotorrera, boasts the country's only revolving restaurant atop its tower, and unparalleled views over the city from its very comfortable suites.

Moderate

The best value option in this bracket is the **Hotel Kristoff** ((061) 972911 TOLL-FREE (800) 57478 FAX (061) 981614, Avenida 8 and Calle 67 in the Santa Rita district, which offers four-star quality at three-star prices, with a good restaurant, lively nightclub and a pool.

Inexpensive

The only hotel in the heart of Old Maracaibo is the **Hotel Victoria** ((061) 229697 on Plaza Baralt. It has suffered from neglect and abuse over the years and is only a shadow of its former self. Still, it is the only place with some character, and if you get a room with a balcony overlooking the square, it still has charm.

If you can't get a room with a view, then the next most centrally located hotel is the basic **Hotel El Milagro** ((061) 228934, close to the Templo Santa Ana, on Avenida 2.

WHERE TO EAT

Reflecting the affluence of its residents, Maracaibo has some of the best restaurants in the country, serving both regional and national dishes, as well as food from farther afield. As with the hotels, the more upscale establishments are north of the old town, and you'll find a gaggle of them around Calle 77 (Avenida 5 de Julio) and Avenida 4.

Expensive to Moderate

Top of the list has to be the **Girasol** ((061) 924422, atop the Hotel El Paseo with its unsurpassed views of the city and the lake, and excellent food at a price. For the best meat cuts in town, head to very popular **Mi Vaquita** ((061) 911990 on Calle 74 and Avenida 3H near Plaza La República, which serves up enormous steaks — the place is not called "my little cow" for nothing — in a great atmosphere often accompanied by live music and dancing.

For Zulian dishes at reasonable prices, try **El Tinajero** ((061) 915362, Avenida 3C near the hospital, and ask for the *chivo y coco*, which is kid in coconut sauce. Finally, the culture-friendly **Hotel San José** ((061) 914647, Avenida 3Y and Calle 82, is also a good bet with great ambience on weekends, and an art gallery thrown in.

Inexpensive

Between a restaurant and a café, **El Zaguán** ((061) 231183, on Calle Carabobo No. 6-15, lies in the heart of the restored street, making it ideal for a break while touring the town by day, and also a good spot to come in the evenings. They often have live music in the terrace garden, and the bar gets pretty lively. Another popular place in the old town is **Bibas** ((061) 928791, next to the Bellas

Maracaibo's nineteenth-century cathedral.

Artes center on Calle 70 and Avenida 3F, which buzzes with gossip after performances. A great place for a cocktail or three, it includes a snack menu of salads and grills.

NIGHTLIFE

Apart from the places mentioned above that have live music, *Panorama*, Maracaibo's local newspaper, lists concerts and cultural events. Of special interest would be performances in the newly restored **Teatro Baralt**, or by Maracaibo's contemporary dance group and its symphony orchestra in the **Centro de Bellas Artes** or the **Centro de Arte Maracaibo**.

On Calle 94, near El Zaguán, is another very good and relaxed bar dotted with antiques, **Lo Nuestro**. For more lively places, and a chance to hear some *gaita* music, **El Palacio de la Gaita**, Calle 77 between Avenida 13 and 13A, is a popular place with good bands.

HOW TO GET THERE

Maracaibo's busy airport is about 12 km (seven and a half miles) southwest of the city, and is only serviced by taxis. Flights connect to the entire country, as well as Servivensa's international flights to Miami, Aruba and Curaçao.

For buses, Maracaibo's Terminal de Pasajeros is centrally located, just to the southwest of Calle 100 Libertador. You can board launches over to the town of Altagracia on the eastern shores of the lake from the *embarcadero* on Avenida 100 Libertador at the end of Avenida 10.

AROUND MARACAIBO

You can enjoy several good trips close to Maracaibo, popular with *Maracuchos* escaping the city bustle. Their pride and joy is the **Puente Rafael Urdaneta**, which, at over eight kilometers (five miles) long, is the longest prestressed concrete bridge in the world, and a marvelous feat of engineering. Travelers approaching the city from the east are rewarded with fantastic San Francisco-like views of the lake and town.

ALTAGRACIA

Facing Maracaibo from across the waters, Altagracia is a small town slowly being restored by local authorities: seek out the modest **Museo de Historia** in the town's oldest house. Before the construction of the bridge, Altagracia acted as the main port for transporting goods and passengers across the lake. Fast *flecha* launches whiz back and forth to Maracaibo all day, and the town, centered around the Plaza Miranda and its painted houses, makes for a pleasant afternoon wander.

OIL TOWNS

Still on the eastern shores of the lake, but to the south of the Rafael Urdaneta bridge, the oil towns which have sprung up since the 1910s are not a tourist attraction in themselves, but the sight of hundreds of oil platforms and derricks littering the lake are remarkable — even to a Texan. The best place to observe them is from the dike built to protect the towns from encroaching waters — they are sinking from all the drilling—in **Cabimas**, **Tía Juana** or **Lagunillas**. Buses connect Cabimas to Maracaibo, and you can hop on a *por puesto* to the other smaller towns.

SAN CARLOS FORT AND SINAMAICA

Over on the western shores of the lake, and heading north to the Golfo de Venezuela, two sights make popular outings for *Maracuchos*. Visit during the week for more peace. The first, the colonial fort of **San Carlos de la Barra** lies around 30 km (19 miles) north of Maracaibo, on the Isla de San Carlos. **El Moján** (also known as San Rafael) is the jumping-off point for shuttle boats over to the island. On the way to the town, the impressive **Complejo Científico, Cultural y Turístico** (closed on Mondays) boasts an anthropological museum, planetarium and extensive grounds with lots of activities for children.

The second attraction, which still holds its special place in the hearts of Venezuelans is the **Laguna de Sinamaica**. It is the only place left in this part of the country where one can still see the *palafito* houses built on piles in the lagoon, with thatched roofs and woven walls of *estera* reed mats. The *palafitos* of the Warao Indians in the Delta of the Orinoco are far more traditional. Embarkation for boat trips is from the small *muelle* known as **Puerto Mara**, five kilometers (three miles) beyond El Moján, just before the bridge over the river Limón, or else a bit further at **Puerto Cuervito** in the village of Sinamaica.

NORTH TO THE COLOMBIAN BORDER

Continuing northward, the next town of any size is **Paraguaipoa**, 95 km (59 miles) from Maracaibo. The town lies near the Colombian border. It's the capital of Venezuela's Guajira Peninsula, inhabited by the Guajiro Indians (or Wayú or Añú in their tongue), Venezuela's largest indigenous group — numbering some 170,000 people. They hold a large market at the crack of dawn every Monday just beyond the town.

The border crossing at **Maicao** has the worst reputation in the country, but if you are heading to the Colombian Caribbean coast, you'll

have little choice. Avoid arriving at the frontier outside daylight hours and make sure your paperwork is in order. Contact the tourist office in Maracaibo for details concerning border crossings.

SOUTHWESTERN ZULIA

Traveling west from Maracaibo, Highway 6 is a lonely road that loops around Lake Maracaibo. A mountain chain rises briskly from savanna to forest-clad heights of 3,500 m (11,480 ft) to the west. Declared a national park in 1978, the **Parque Nacional Sierra de Perijá** protects 2,950 sq km (1,150 sq miles) on the Colombian border. Inparques in Maracaibo can provide more information about the park, and you should consult them about safety concerns, since the area suffers from raids from Colombia.

Further south, the **Parque Nacional Ciénagas del Catatumbo** protects a huge area of wetlands in the southwestern corner of Lake Maracaibo. The best way to see the area is on a two-day tour with a tour operator from Mérida (see TOURS, page 156 under MÉRIDA).

The Catatumbo area is also famous for the strange phenomenon known in the old days as the **Faro de Maracaibo** (Maracaibo Lighthouse), but also as the **Relámpago de Catatumbo** (Catatumbo Lightning). The cause of the stunning visual display is still debated, but the effect of hundreds of silent bolts of lightning discharging in the sky is comparable to the Northern Lights. It can be observed from as far away as the Andes around Mérida.

Colorful *palafito* houses in the Laguna de Sinamaica are built on piles.

The Andes

WIND UP THE ANDES AND YOU TURN THE CLOCKS BACK. You enter a world little altered by petrodollars, beauty queens and shopping malls of the "other" Venezuela. In the gateway state of Trujillo, seldom-visited hills announce a land of colonial towns, terracotta roofs, cobbled streets, dexterous artisans, and a cornucopia of crops harvested in the tropical climes. Further south, Mérida State is Venezuela's alpine playground *par excellence*, garnering the range's highest icy peaks. The meandering, mesmerizing *Transandina* highway traverses the state, echoing the flicks and switches of the Río Chama. In southern Mérida, the twin spines of the Sierra Nevada and the Sierra La Culata merge at the depression in Táchira State, whose hill towns, coffee-carpeted hills and strong regional pride are as stirring as the reputations of the *caudillo* dictators the state has nurtured.

The dry season from December to April offers the best weather to explore the Andes, when the peaks, flushed with occasional snow flurries, bare their full glory. In these months, cloudless, star-studded nights are as stunning as they are cold. May and June are confused months, when you can either be dazzled by sun or drenched by downpours, while a brief dry season extends from late June to late July. The *páramos* at over 3,000 m (9,840 ft) are most spectacular in September and October when the *frailejón* flower, bringing color and life to these otherwise haunting highland moors.

TRUJILLO STATE

Trujillo may be small — four times smaller than Canaima National Park in Bolívar State — but what it lacks in size, it compensates for in beauty. The singsong-sounding town of Biscucuy in Portuguesa state provides the ideal portal for exploring Trujillo. You reach Biscucuy either by climbing up the tendrils of the Andes to the southeast from Guanare, capital of Portuguesa State, or else from the north, on the *Transandina* which runs southwest of Barquisimeto through the villages of Quíbor and El Tocuyo.

From Biscucuy, the road climbs further to Campo Elías, before switching southwest, roughly following the valley of the Río Boconó. To the south of this road, the **Parque Nacional Guaramacal** is a haven for birds such as the resplendent helmeted curassow and the yellow-headed parakeet, and also home to the rare Andean spectacled bear, puma, and brocket deer. Forty-two kilometers (26 miles) from Campo Elías, you reach Boconó.

Oxen still plow the Andean hillsides too steep for tractors.

BOCONÓ

If you need a reason for choosing the westerly route into the Andes, and the countryside hasn't provided it yet, then the mountain town of Boconó surely will. Nestled into the steep valley of the Río Boconó, the town grew in splendid isolation until the highway connecting it to Trujillo and the road down to Guanare in the Llanos were completed.

Originally one of the sites of present-day Trujillo, and dubbed the "Garden of Venezuela" by Bolívar, Boconó's fertile hills and cool climate meant from its founding as early as 1563 it enjoyed virtual self-sufficiency.

GENERAL INFORMATION

Although the Alcaldía on Plaza Bolívar does run a small **Oficina Municipal de Turismo**, better information and maps can be obtained from the friendly owners of Posada Machinipé on Calle Bolívar (see WHERE TO STAY, below). Banco Unión lies on Calle 4, one block north of Plaza Bolívar.

WHAT TO SEE AND DO

Artesanía ranks high on the list when visiting Boconó. Several places in town sell crafts, of which the **Centro de Acopio Artesanal**, inside the farmers' market on Calle 5 at Avenida 5 de Julio (closed on Mondays), and the artisan cooperative **Centro de Servicios Campesinos Tiscachic**, three blocks north just before the bridge, provide the best variety and prices. On Calle Páez, the **Ateneo de Boconó** also displays and sells crafts, and includes a workshop where you can observe them being made. You can ask here for directions to the Briceño family's house, just north of town. They are the region's leading potters and welcome visitors.

Just north of Plaza Bolívar, **La Vieja Casa** houses a museum and a restaurant in a very welcoming setting packed with intriguing memorabilia and antiques (open in the mornings, closed on Tuesdays), while further along the downhill Calle Jáuregui, close to the church, the **Museo Trapiche de los Clavos** showcases botanical exhibits as well as small museums dedicated to coffee and sugar production, within a beautifully restored nineteenth-century sugar mill (*trapiche*). It's open Tuesday to Sunday 8 AM to noon and 2 PM to 5 PM.

WHERE TO STAY

There is quite a surprising range of places to stay in Boconó, with a choice of downtown or rural settings. The best are outlined below and require reservations in the high season, especially during

Easter when vast numbers of visitors descend to admire the passion play in the small town of Tostós (see SOUTH FROM BOCONÓ, below).

Moderate

Just over the bridge, on the northern outskirts of Boconó, the **Hotel Campestre La Colina** **(**/FAX (072) 522695 presents the most attractive and bucolic choice in the area. The cabins they offer can accommodate up to six people, the rooms comprising bathrooms with hot water, with small verandas giving onto the expansive grounds where birds flit around.

Inexpensive

The best *posada* of the many in Boconó, the **Posada Machinipé (** (072) 521506 lies three blocks up from Plaza Bolívar, painted pink. Owners Eduardo and Marisa Parra-Ganteaume offer a variety of rooms and apartments. They are extremely knowledgeable about all the craftspeople around Boconó and provide guests with a map of walks and villages. They also run a *finca* (country house) up in the hills, where you can rent horses to explore the surrounding countryside and the Parque Nacional Guaramacal.

WHERE TO EAT

The best place to eat in town has to be within the **Vieja Casa** (see above), while **La Alameda** on Avenida Ricaurte at Calle Bolívar also enjoys a good reputation. For the cheapest meal, head to the market, where a *comedor* serves meals for the *campesinos* (farmers). For some local snacks and drinks, such as *leche de burra* (a mixture of milk, eggs, alcohol, spices and sugar) or *torta de pán*, the crafts shop **Artesanía Antojitos Andinos** on Avenida Colombia, two blocks west of Plaza Bolívar and up a bit, makes for a delicious stop.

HOW TO GET THERE

Just to make things complicated, Boconó doesn't have a central bus terminal. Instead, stops are scattered throughout the city center. Ask the owners of Posada Machinipé for advice.

BOCONÓ TO TRUJILLO

From Boconó, several choices open-up for the traveler heading south to Mérida State and the heights of the Andes. Unless you want to try the adventurous route south via Niquitao and Jajó round to the *Transandina* north of Timotes (see SOUTH FROM BOCONÓ, below), take the stunning road through the hills west to Trujillo, described here.

The route northeast from Boconó is the continuation of Highway 7 up from Guanare in Portuguesa State. It's a spectacular sinuous route,

passing through damp cloudforest and lush hills, with several time-warp, colonial towns to distract you along the way.

SAN MIGUEL DE BOCONÓ

San Miguel lies 27 km (16.5 miles) out of Boconó, a short hop off the highway. The altarpiece in the **church** is a riot of homespun polychrome saints and archangels in tiers of niches, replete with bold motifs and carved statues. In addition to its famed church, San Miguel is renowned for the **Romerías de los Pastores y Payasos** held January 4 to 7, the best festival in the country (see FESTIVE FLINGS, page 46 in YOUR CHOICE).

BARBUSAY

The next village whose church merits a detour is the teeny Barbusay. Take the right turn north soon after the San Miguel turnoff and continue for about 10 minutes. The village, founded in 1597, is very proud of the striking *retablo* in its colonial church. Ask for the restaurant and *posada* "de la Loba" for a friendly meal and a bed for the night.

SANTA ANA

Back on the road, you come to the turn for Santa Ana, 55 km (34 miles) from Boconó or 38 km (23.5 miles) from Trujillo. On Plaza Sucre, you'll find a gem of a little colonial church among the slanted, tiled roofs.

SOUTH FROM BOCONÓ

Looping round southeastern Trujillo, the road climbs up steep verdant slopes, becomes a dirt track winding over the Páramo Tuñame at 3,750 m (12,300 ft), and continues on down to the more fertile valley of the Río Motatán, around Jajó. From there it rejoins the *Transandina* south of La Puerta, where you can either turn back to Valera, or head south to Timotes and the greater heights of Mérida State. On the way you pass yet more pockets of Andean life and history.

NIQUITAO AND TOSTÓS

Thirty-five kilometers (22 miles) south of Boconó, Niquitao boasts some lovely colonial architecture, with the **Iglesia de San Rafael de la Piedra** and the area around Plaza Bolívar well-preserved in the cool mountain air. The town was founded by two brothers in 1625 and still feels as if everyone might be related. With the great walks on offer in the area, the town makes for one of the prettiest bases you could hope for.

About halfway between Boconó and Niquitao, Tostós is another little pueblo tucked up in the

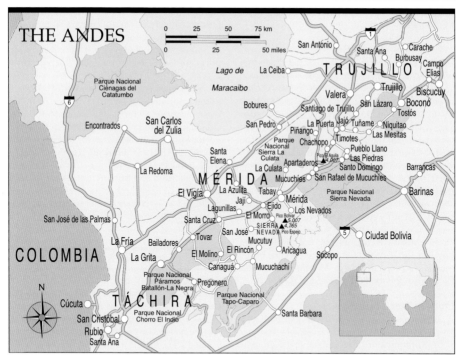

hills. Although not as picturesque as Niquitao, it's renowned for the celebrations for **San Isidro** and **Easter Week** (see FESTIVE FLINGS, page 46 in YOUR CHOICE). The hike to the **Teta de Niquitao** will keep the adventurous happy.

Where to Stay and Eat

The newest and best inexpensive *posada* in Niquitao is **La Posada Turística de Niquitao** ((9072) 523288 E-MAIL omarj@cantv.net, on the corner of Plaza Bolívar. Sixteen comfortable but not overwhelming rooms, set around the central courtyard of a vintage house with much its old character left intact, make this *posada* a welcome addition to the simpler offers in town. Their restaurant on the ground floor (open to the public) serves up some fine local dishes. The more economical alternative is the long-standing **Posada Güiriguay** ((016) 672-0773, Calle Bolívar just south of the plaza.

OVER THE PÁRAMO

The next village on this route is **Las Mesitas**, reached by a paved but damaged road which winds up to an increasingly colder, bleaker and altogether more dramatic landscape. From Las Mesitas, the road deteriorates further crossing over the stark *páramo* to **Tuñame**.

From the hamlet of Tuñame, which provides a lifeline to even more remote farming communities, you can choose the jeep track over the *páramo*

south to Pueblo Llano (only recommended if you don't mind getting lost), or else continue on a better corkscrew road down the hills to Jajó via Durí.

JAJÓ

If you've been looking for the "perfect" colonial town, hidden away in the hills far from the twenty-first century, then Jajó will make your heart leap. Of all the towns in Trujillo, it is one of the finest examples of whitewashed, cobbled-street charm, and rivals any town in the whole of the Andes — including the similar-sounding Jají, to the northwest of Mérida — without the crowds.

Founded in 1611, its streets and houses recently benefited from some care and attention as the 4,000-odd inhabitants woke up to their home's tourist potential. Apart from the odd tourist and the annual fiestas for **San Pedro** on June 29 and **San Isidro** on May 15, the town remains pretty firmly off the beaten track, sleepy yet dignified. Add to the beauty of its terraced-farm landscapes and eucalyptus trees draped in Spanish moss the small **Museo Casa Colonial** on the narrow old Calle Real — the pride and joy of Señor Sánchez — and you feel like you're the first person to have discovered this memorable little hill town. If the museum is closed, ask someone to point out his house.

Jajó also offers access to the beautiful and stark Páramo de Cabimbú and over to the village of La Quebrada to the north (see SOUTH OF TRUJILLO, page 151), and various walks to the south along the Motatán valley.

Where to Stay and Eat

A new *posada* on the square, painted turquoise, was nearing completion at the time of writing, and seemed it would outdo the other options. On the opposite side of Plaza Bolívar from the church, the architecture of the inexpensive **Hotel Turístico Jajó** ((014) 727-1593 unfortunately jars with the colonial feel of the town, but its rooms offer the best accommodation to date, though nothing to write home about. The hotel's restaurant serves good trout, but is pretty dark. A cheaper option is the **Posada Marysabel** ((071) 213007 or (014) 741-3603, on Calle Páez two blocks north of the plaza, run by a friendly couple. They offer eight simple rooms with baths and hot water, a *tasca* in the basement, and excursions into the surrounding hills. For a fine trout for lunch, you won't find better than the **Restaurant de la Abuela** on Avenida Bolívar, up the road on the right of the church.

How to Get There

Apart from the route over the *páramo* from Niquitao, Jajó is more easily accessible from the west. Running along the Motatán valley, a road heads south from Valera, with the left fork for Jajó after 39 km (24 miles). This road joins the *Transandina*, also running south from Valera, about 10 km (six miles) south of La Puerta, so you can switch back north to the Jajó turnoff. Coming from Mérida, watch for the fork in the roads soon after the turn for Mesa de Esnujaque, under 10 km (six miles) south of Timotes.

By public transportation, the easiest way to reach Jajó is from Calle 8 and Avenida 4 in Valera.

VALERA

Despite being Trujillo State's most important, and only, city, Valera has little of the charm or colonial architecture of the state's capital Trujillo. To be honest, it has none at all. It's the most important regional center for commerce and transport. With its modern infrastructure, well-connected airport and bus terminal, Valera makes a good base from which to rent a car and explore the seldom-visited villages and towns of Trujillo.

The **Centro de Información Turística** ((071) 54286, Avenida Bolívar between calles 10 and 11, is open 9 AM to noon and 2 PM to 5 PM, inside the shopping center by the spacious Plaza de los Estados. To the north along Avenida Bolívar and left on Calle 8 you come to **Plaza Bolívar** with the neo-Gothic **Iglesia de San Juan Bautista** on its southern side. Here, the Banco de Venezuela has an ATM for Visa cards. Valera hosts a large **Feria Agrícola** in the last two weeks in August, with farmers converging from all over the state. Rooms in hotels are scarce at these times.

For car rental, **Budget** can be found at the airport ((071) 442364, or on Calle Buenos Aires, downtown ((071) 211135.

A little side-trip worth considering takes you to the small town of **Isnotú**, 15 km (nine miles) west. Venezuela's most renowned doctor, José Gregorio Hernández, was born here in 1864. The doctor founded the science of bacteriology in the country, but is above all admired for his ceaseless work in the hospitals and poor areas of Caracas. He is regarded as a saint by most Venezuelans. You can visit the church and museum alongside dedicated to Hernández. Hundreds of pilgrims descend on the town for the doctor's birthday on October 26.

WHERE TO STAY AND EAT

Topping the list in Valera, the **Hotel Camino Real** ((071) 52260, Avenida Independencia, Sector La Planta, with its 60 rooms and central location, makes a good choice at moderate rates. The restaurant serves some pretty sophisticated international dishes in quite a formal atmosphere, with the piano bar on the top floor affording the best views in town.

The inexpensive **Hotel El Palacio** ((071) 56769, Calle 12 at avenidas 10 and 11, inside the Miami Center, with its 25 air-conditioned rooms, decent restaurant and parking make it popular with business people, while the **Hotel Aurora** ((071) 315675, Avenida Bolívar at calles 10 and 11, with simple yet spick and span air-conditioned rooms, is cheaper and the best budget bet.

Apart from the restaurants in the hotels above, one of the best is **Don Pedro** on Calle 9, with **Atenas** in the Miami Center and **El Guacamayo** on Avenida 11 at calles 5 and 6 also worth investigating.

HOW TO GET THERE

Valera's airport lies to the northeast of the city center on the older road to Trujillo, via La Cejita. Flights to Caracas leave twice daily, via Barquisimeto. The bus terminal is also northeast, but closer.

TRUJILLO

Trujillo's history is a tale of seven towns. That's how many times it took the state capital to eventually settle in the fertile Valle de los Cedros in 1572. Only two avenues wide, you can't help thinking the founder, Diego García de Paredes, didn't entertain high hopes for his town. But grow it did, taking advantage of the tropical mountain climate where everything the farmers sowed took

Trujillo's cathedral shines bright in the mountain air.

root and flourished. Trujillo's 56,000 inhabitants continue their provincial ways to this day, unhurried and seemingly unworried about neighboring Valera's exponential growth over the last century. The town retains much of its historical heritage in the old center, and with several colonial towns nearby, it's one of the most pleasant towns in the state.

GENERAL INFORMATION

Trujillo's official **tourist office** ((072) 34411 lies in the small, partly restored colonial town of La Plazuela, three kilometers (just under two miles) north, on the road to Valera. You'll find a booth

close to the bus terminal at the town's entrance from Valera. Both are open Monday to Friday from 8 AM to 4 PM.

WHAT TO SEE AND DO

The town's historical heart lies within the narrow confines of the two avenidas that run east (Avenida Independencia) and west (Avenida Bolívar). At the eastern end of these sits Plaza Bolívar with its cathedral and colonial houses. The **cathedral**'s iridescent white façade shines as brightly as it did in the seventeenth century. Unfortunately, little remains of the original interior.

Walking up Avenida Independencia, you come to a striking vintage mansion that played an important role in the War of Independence. It was here in 1813 that Bolívar signed the *Decreto de Guerra a Muerte* (Decree of War to the Death): all

Royalists troops captured were to be executed. The mansion was converted into Trujillo's **Museo de Historia**, where you can admire old maps, armor, colonial furniture and pre-Hispanic ceramics, as well as the table at which Bolívar signed the decree. It's open 9 AM to noon and 2 PM to 5 PM Monday to Friday. Following the avenida up, it merges with Avenida Bolívar to become Avenida Carmona. Near the Hotel Trujillo, the **Museo de Arte Popular** showcases the production of Trujillo's many talented artisans.

In Trujillo, you can't but notice the towering, blue-swathed figure of the Virgin holding a white dove on the high hill above the town. The monumental 47-m-tall (154-ft) **Virgin of Peace** statue was completed in 1983. There are unparalleled views from the various lookouts built within the structure and accessed by a staircase. On clear early mornings, you can see all the way to Lake Maracaibo and the snow caps of the Sierra Nevada. At the statue's base, a café provides refreshments, and jeeps run regularly from Avenida Carmona, by the Hotel Trujillo. Visiting times are daily 8 AM to 5 PM.

WHERE TO STAY AND EAT

At the top end of the old town, on Avenida Carmona, the inexpensive **Hotel Trujillo** ((072) 33574 provides the most comfortable central rooms, with air-conditioning, most with balconies and great views. The hotel also houses a restaurant and a pool, both open to non-guests. Not far down the Avenida Bolívar, at Calle 11, the

Posada Valle de los Mukas ℂ (072) 33148 offers eight character-full rooms within a restored old house, also for inexpensive rates. An attractive restaurant occupies the courtyard, serving tasty local dishes including fresh trout. The friendly **Hotel Los Gallegos ℂ** (072) 33193, Avenida Independencia just by the Museo de Historia, offers cheaper simple rooms, all clean and tidy with fans or air-conditioning and hot water.

On the way to the Virgen de la Paz monument, shortly after the turnoff from the main road, the **Posada Turística La Troja ℂ** (014) 971-2990 or (014) 723-1959 provides a good out-of-town alternative in the same price category. The personable owners offer six rooms with appealing beds in the lofts of the best ones, all with fans, televisions, bathrooms and hot water, and all with an individual feel. They can prepare meals for you on the terrace with a rustic style open-sided kitchen to one side.

How to Get There

The bus terminal lies to the northeast of town and is far less busy than Valera's, which is 30 km (18.5 miles) away.

SOUTH OF TRUJILLO

Coursing first west then south from Trujillo, a picturesque mountain road climbs all the way up and close to the Páramo Cabimbú, and on down to the small arty-type village of La Quebrada. From there it winds down to join the road running south of Valera along the Motatán valley, 12 km (seven and a half miles) north of the turnoff for Jajó. On the way, it passes through two of Trujillo's dinkiest old villages, **San Lázaro** and **Santiago**. Both of them are kept spotless by their proud residents.

From Santiago, the asphalt road turns into a dirt road, perfectly passable in a city car at the time of research. Climbing ever-higher up from the forests, through fields of potatoes and beans ploughed by reluctant oxen, you eventually reach around 2,000 m (6,560 ft) at Loma del Medio.

Close to the Loma, you can't miss **Nidal de los Nubes I ℂ** (014) 723-2844. It's almost worth venturing up this road for this *posada* alone, one of the friendliest and most original in the country. The Pozsoniy family's "nest in the clouds" has fantastic views, and they offer 18 rooms, all with fireplaces, baths with hot water, styled mirrors, tiles, furniture. Even if you're in a hurry, it would still be a crime not to stop for a delicious meal or a drink — call in advance, and also ask about renting horses.

From the next town of La Quebrada, you continue downhill to join the Motatán Valley road at Quebrada de Cuevas.

MÉRIDA STATE

Mérida is the Andes' number one destination. It basks in all its Andean finery, glorious from brilliant white tip to freezing blue toe, passing through the grays and browns of the *páramos*, and on down to both emerald hills and burnt-ochre mountainsides. Mérida's neighbors, Táchira and Trujillo, aren't slouches when it comes to landscapes, people, food or adventure. But somehow Mérida goes one step further. The mountain peaks are that much higher, the food that touch more varied, the traditions that much more intriguing. In Venezuela, Mérida *is* the Andes.

General Information

Although Mérida's average temperature is 19°C (66°F) — which Venezuelans regard as freezing — you'll need warm weather clothes if venturing up into the mountains. Waterproof clothing is never a bad idea, no matter what the season.

Festivals

Given the Andeans' proclivity for the traditional and the religious, you're more than likely to stumble across a festival in Mérida State. If you can, time your visit to coincide with one of these (see also FESTIVE FLINGS, page 46 in YOUR CHOICE).

OPPOSITE: The glacial Lago Mucubají and the equally icy peaks of the Sierra Nevada behind. ABOVE: The Virgin of Peace, dove in hand, gazes down over Trujillo.

Mérida boasts the Andes' largest celebrations for the **Feria del Sol**, which runs for five days preceding Ash Wednesday. They include bullfights, folklore, and music in abundance. Many of the towns around Mérida celebrate other festivals and feast days. Both the **Baile de Las Locaínas** in Pueblo Llano on January 1, and the **Día de los Reyes** in Tabay on January 6, rival any festival in the country for color and fervor.

Many towns hold **Semana Santa** (Easter) festivities, with the passion play in Lagunillas presenting the most unique event. Saint's days are also cause for celebration. Of these the most notable are those of **San Isidro** (May 15) in Lagunillas, Apartaderos, Tovar, and Jají; **Los Negros de**

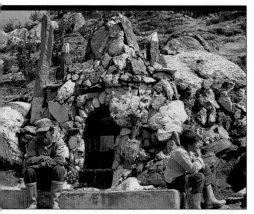

Jerónimo in Santo Domingo on September 30; and **San Rafael de Mucuchíes'** saint's day on October 24. Mucurubá's famous candlelit **Fiesta de la Inmaculada Concepción** takes place on December 7, while **Santa Lucía** is venerated in Mucuchíes and Timotes on December 13, with these towns hosting the most colorful **Giros de San Benito** — with dancers dressed as slaves, often donning masks — on December 28 and 29.

MÉRIDA

The city of Mérida, capital of the Andes, roosts on a plateau at 1,625 m (5,330 ft), in the shadow of Venezuela's highest peak — called, you guessed it, Bolívar. Although the city's population nears a quarter of a million, its character is surprisingly small-town. The mood is relaxed and informal, veering to the traditional and conservative, and yet often quite bohemian. About a fifth of *Merideños* are students, the campuses of the Universidad de los Andes, one of the country's largest, strewn throughout the city. Young people are everywhere, enlivening town squares, bars, clubs and cultural events. Mérida's

LEFT: Pious Andeans often build roadside shrines like this one. ABOVE: Venezuela's highest peak, inevitably named Bolívar.

cool climate makes for a can-do mentality, a refreshing change from the heat and *mañana* of lowland Venezuela.

The city's center — with no architectural gems, but no skyscraping carbuncles either — is compact and approachable. Its grid layout makes orientation a breeze. Within a day or two, Mérida feels familiar to many travelers; by the end of a week, it feels like home.

With so many opportunities for outdoor activities on its doorstep, Mérida rules as the country's adventure tourism capital. In high season, the city is awash with day-glo and designer outdoor gear. Countless operators offer tours, hikes and excursions, many of them with years of experience and good language skills.

BACKGROUND

Mérida's beginnings were inauspicious. The original founder of the town at nearby Las Lagunillas, Juan Rodríguez Suárez, nearly lost his head in 1558. In true Spanish style, he lacked the correct paperwork and was consequently sentenced to death by the pen-pushers. He managed to escape to Trujillo — marking the first case of political asylum in the Americas. Officially, the town wasn't recognized by the bureaucrats in Spain until Juan Maldonado y Ordóñez gave it the haughty title "La Ciudad de Santiago de los Caballeros de Mérida," moving it to its present location.

For its first two centuries, Mérida formed part of Nueva Granada and thus modern Colombia, as opposed to the Captaincy General of Venezuela. Links with its Andean neighbor remain strong, with plenty of trade between the two nations. During the Civil War the city largely escaped the ravages suffered by the rest of the country, though it couldn't avoid the devastating earthquake of 1812.

Bolívar passed through Mérida twice. The string of battles of 1813 began in the Andes, and culminated in his triumphant entry into Caracas. They became known as the Admirable Campaign. He returned to the city on his way back to fight in Colombia.

Mérida, being isolated and distant from Venezuela's economic heart, grew slowly. The completion of the roads network in the 1960s, thereby linking it to the rest of the country and fuelling trade with Colombia, injected the city with a new lease of life.

GENERAL INFORMATION

The Mérida tourism corporation is probably the best in the country and has *módulos* (booths) scattered throughout the city, open Monday to Friday, 8 AM to noon and 2 PM to 6 PM. **Cormetur's**

main office ((074) 630814 TOLL-FREE (800) 63743 FAX (074) 632782 E-MAIL cormetur@merida venezuela.com WEB SITE www.meridavenezuela .com is found on Avenida Urdaneta, near the airport. Other offices are found at the bus terminal, the *teleférico*, the Mercado Principal, the Jardín Acuario, and at the University's northern campus.

Inparques ((074) 529876 FAX (074) 528785, Calle 19 No. 5-44, is open Monday to Friday 8:30 AM to noon and 2 PM to 5 PM. The office issues permits for camping and provides information about the state's national parks. It also has an office by the *teleférico*, open Wednesday to Sunday from 7:30 AM to 2 PM.

Local tour operators and Inparques sell maps of trekking routes — particularly the *Mapa para Excursionistas*, or the MARNR map, Sheet No. 5941.

For money changing, the **Italcambio** booth at the airport is regarded as the best place to change cash and travelers checks — bring your purchase receipt. For Visa and MasterCard advances, **Banco Unión** and **Banco de Venezuela** are your best bet, on Avenida 4, just down from Plaza Bolívar. The medieval-theme café-cum-restaurant **Abadía**, Avenida 3 between calles 16 and 17, is the best option for Internet speed and ambience, followed by **Inter 2000** on Calle 21, just by CANTV.

The most comprehensive, English-language web site for Mérida is WEB SITE www.andes.net/english/index.html. It list everything you could possibly want to know in the town and the state, including the city's language schools — Mérida is Venezuela's most popular city for students wanting to learn Spanish.

Car rental companies represented at the airport are **Budget** ((074) 631768, **Davila Tours** ((074) 634510 and **Los Brothers** ((074) 630546. Note that these offices close at around 6 PM, so plan to arrive before. For motorbikes, contact **Buggys Bike & Motorcycle Rentals** (/FAX (074)

639145, Viaducto Miranda, between calles 3 and 4 (close to Parque Glorias Patria). Four-wheel-drive jeeps (usually Suzuki) are more expensive than city cars, with the Niva (Lada) jeep being the most economical.

WHAT TO SEE AND DO

Note that in high season many museums are open Monday to Sunday, whereas in the low season they are closed on Monday.

On the east side of Plaza Bolívar, Mérida's **cathedral** stands tall and handsome. Construction began in 1800 but only finished in 1958, following various earthquakes. The resulting architecture is a bit of potpourri of styles. Next door, the **Palacio Arzobispal** displays a range of religious artifacts culled from churches around the Andes, including a bell cast in Spain in 909.

On the square's northwest side, the **Casa de la Cultura Juan Félix Sánchez** sells crafts and promotes craftspeople from the region — note the distinctive thin wooden statues of saints and generals you find in many houses in the Andes. On the corner of Calle 23, within the Rectorada (Dean's Office) of the Universidad de los Andes' central campus, the modest **Museo Arqueológico**, open Tuesday to Friday 9 AM to 6 PM and weekends 3 PM to 7 PM, highlights pre-Columbian cultures (information in Spanish only). Traces of the Indian peoples encountered by the first Spanish explorers can still be found today: "*mucu*," the prefix of many towns in the region, meant "place of," while masks and maracas play integral roles in traditional festivities.

Two blocks northeast of the square on Avenida 4 you come to the **Museo de Arte Colonial**, open Tuesday to Friday 8 AM to noon and 2 PM to 6 PM, weekends from 9 AM to 4 PM. Within the **Casa Juan Antonio Parra**, a varied collection of period furniture and artworks combine to make it one the city's best museums.

Mérida is proud of its support for Bolívar. It was the first town to proclaim the general El Libertador on May 23, 1813. At the end of Avenida 4, **Plaza de las Cinco Repúblicas** claims the oldest monument erected to Venezuela's answer to George Washington. The bust was placed on its plinth in 1842.

Back by the Plaza, look for the recently finished Complejo Cultural, which hosts the **Museo de Arte Moderno**, open Tuesday to Friday, 9 AM to noon and 2:30 PM to 6 PM, weekends 10 AM to 6 PM, with a short-but-sweet collection of contemporary Venezuelan artists.

Not to be missed is the **Mercado Principal**, situated on Avenida Las Américas at Viaducto Miranda. The city's main farmers' market, it's jam-packed with stands selling regional produce on the ground floor, and arts and crafts just about everywhere else. Visit when the market is busiest in the mornings and on weekends. Here you can wander the stalls to your heart's content and grab a bite at the cheap and cheerful *comedor* found on the top floor.

Try some of the local delicacies like sugarcoated fruit candy (*dulces abrillantados*), smoked cheeses, cured hams, strawberry milkshakes, and wine made from blackberry (*mora*). Typical Andean heat-you-ups are *calentado* (or *calentaíto*), made from anise liqueur (*miche*) and brown sugar, and *ponche andino*, a warm, cinnamon-flavored milk with *miche*.

As well as enjoying the countryside in their state, *Merideños* delight in their urban parks. The

cars leave every 15 minutes or so from 7 AM until noon — sometimes earlier and later — Monday to Sunday. In the low season, they only operate Wednesday to Sunday. It's a good idea to get there as early as possible, since lines form early, and clouds close in later in the day. The last car down is around 2 PM, but there's a delightful, well-worn trail from La Aguada if you don't want to come down *just* yet.

Remember, you are about to be hoisted to over 4,000 m (13,000 ft) in little over an hour. If you wear only a T-shirt, don't wonder why you are freezing at the top; and be prepared to take things slowly if you begin to suffer from *soroche* (altitude sickness).

city boasts a coterie of these. **Los Chorros de Milla** is the locals' favorite, and makes for a welcome break from sightseeing, comprising not only lovely tended gardens and a romantic cascade, but also a good zoo. Ask the tourism office for details of others.

THE *TELEFÉRICO*

Mérida's *teleférico* (cable car) is the world's highest and longest. Even when only three — or sometimes two — stations function, the *teleférico* remains an absolute must for anyone visiting Mérida (see TAKE TO THE HIGH WIRE, page 16 in TOP SPOTS for more details).

In the high season, the cable car is understandably very popular, and **reservations** ((074) 525080 are advisable. Tour operators can also reserve tickets for you. At these times, the 36-people capacity

SPORTS AND OUTDOOR ACTIVITIES

As Venezuela's top adventure tourism city, Mérida presents an embarrassment of choice when it comes to outdoor pursuits and adrenaline rushes.

Hiking and Mountaineering

For those who love to don hiking boots and head into the mist, the **Parque Nacional Sierra Nevada** is the bees' knees. Along its spine cluster the tallest peaks of the Venezuelan Andes, known collectively after an old Indian tale as *Las Cinco Aguilas Blancas* (The Five White Eagles). The park extends over 2,760 sq km (1,076 sq miles), from the ranges of the northern Serranía de Santo Domingo, to the Sierra Nevada de Mérida in the south.

OPPOSITE: Mérida's *teleférico* rises 4,000 m (13,000 ft). ABOVE: Over hill and down vale in the Sierra Nevada.

The most popular routes with climbers are, of course, the highest. Trails lead up to **Pico Bolívar** and **Pico Humboldt**. For the latter, head to the La Mucuy entrance to the Sierra Nevada Park by bus to Tabay, and a *por puesto* from there to the Inparques station (see TABAY, page 162). For rock climbers, the most popular wall close to Pico Bolívar is **La Pared del Abanico**.

In the Upper Chama valley, near Apartaderos, more hikes beckon in **Serranía de Santo Domingo**. These include the trek up to Juan Félix Sánchez's sanctuary at El Potrero, to the south of Pico Mucuñuque (see SAN RAFAEL DE MUCUCHÍES, page 164).

Along the road from Apartaderos east to Santo Domingo, four popular glacial lakes nestle to the

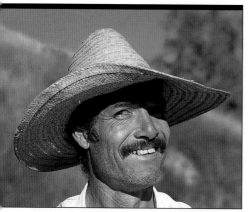

south. The largest is **Laguna de Mucubají**. From here a trail leads up to Pico Mucuñuque at 4,672 m (2,897 ft) and other peaks, some of the most dramatic in the whole region that don't require mountaineering skills. An Inparques station at the entrance to Laguna de Mucubají issues permits and provides detailed information about hiking routes (see APARTADEROS TO BARINAS, page 166).

Parque Nacional Sierra La Culata protects the western slopes of the Andes, considerably drier than their eastern cousins, typified by the Pan de Azúcar peak at 4,660 m (15,289 ft) and desert *páramo* vegetation (see AROUND MÉRIDA, page 160).

Paragliding

The flyers in Mérida claim paragliding in the area ranks among the best in the world. Not being an expert, I can't tell you if that's true, but assure you that the flights from above Las Gonzales (south of Mérida) are tremendous. They can last up to an hour or more. Unless you sign up for a course, you fly in tandem with an experienced instructor. Among the best is the friendly, English-speaking Raúl Penso. Contact him through Bum Bum Tours (see below). Hanggliders and paragliders also launch from the La Aguada or Loma Redonda substations on the *teleférico*.

Rafting and Kayaking

These white-knuckle sports are restricted to the rainy season, between May and November. During drier months, boats offer more sedate tours down rivers in the Llanos. The best rivers flow down the Barinas side of the Sierra Nevada, making a two-day minimum trip the best way to enjoy the rush of the rivers, and the beautiful natural setting.

Horseback Riding

Mérida offers some great trails for horseback riding, with local *Andinos* at both Laguna Mucubají and Pico El Águila standing by to rent small *criollo* horses for short trips around the mountains. Various haciendas and *fincas* around the area also provide larger horses for more serious and lengthy trips, and you should ask tour operators for details of these.

Mountain Biking

Several tour operators rent bikes for trips around Mérida, with the Pueblos del Sur area to the south of Mérida offering the most challenging routes for bikers. More leisurely, or downhill, trips include the ride north from Pico El Águila to Piñango and down to Timotes, or else south along the *Transandina* back to Mérida.

Fishing

The many glacial lakes in the Sierra Nevada prove very popular with anglers hoping to catch weighty trout. The season runs from mid-March to September. You need a permit from the Ministerio de Agricultura y Cría in Mérida—Inparques can give you details.

TOURS

Mérida hosts as many as 80 tour operators and travel agencies. Competition is fierce. Don't be afraid to ask for advice and information, even if you don't plan to use their services.

The operators listed below come recommended, and their specialties have been noted. All of them speak at least two foreign languages.

Arassari Trek & Bum Bum Tours (/FAX (074) 525879 E-MAIL info@arassari.com WEB SITE www .arassari.com and http://jvm.com/bumbum/, right at the end of Calle 24, is one of Mérida's top operators. The amiable Tom and Raquel Evenou run a tight operation here. They pioneered whitewater rafting in 1996 on the Río Bum Bum near Barinas, and still offer the only Grade IV (hardcore) rafting in the area. They have continued to expand, offering arduous trekking with some of the best specialized guides in Venezuela. They also rent mountain bikes in good condition. Their Llanos tours and paragliding flights are recommended.

Guamanchi Expeditions (/FAX (074) 522080 E-MAIL geca@bolivar.funmrd.gov.ve WEB SITE www

.ftech.net/~geca, on Calle 24 No. 8-39, another experienced tour operator, specialize in trekking and climbing. José Luís Troconis of **Natoura Adventure Tours** ((074) 524216 FAX (074) 524075 E-MAIL natoura@telcel.net.ve WEB SITE www .natoura.com, also on Calle 24, is a very experienced local guide and comes recommended for trekking and climbing trips, as well as for rafting.

Colibrí Expediciones ((074) 522606 FAX (074) 524961 E-MAIL colibri_merida@hotmail.com, on Calle 19 between avenidas 2 and 3, is managed by Ricardo Torres, who has some good guides working for him, while **Montaña Tours** (/FAX (074) 661448/662867 E-MAIL andes@telcel.net.ve, at Local 1, Edificio Las Américas, Avenida Las

tariffs in low and high season (all holiday periods and fiesta time). Reserve well in advance during the latter.

Expensive

The four-star **Hotel Tisure** ((074) 526072 FAX (074) 526061 WEB SITE www.andes.net/tisure/index .html, on Avenida 2, is probably the best centrally located hotel in Mérida. With only 35 comfortable rooms with phones, televisions and attractive polished steel and pinewood furniture, the hotel is intimate and suitably exclusive.

Out of town, yet still very close, **La Sevillana** ((074) 520955 FAX (074) 523051, at the end of Avenida Principal La Pedregosa, combines a tranquil

Américas, is run by the very experienced American Jerry Keaton. He specializes in mountain treks and climbs, and knows the Sierra well.

Interestingly, Mérida's tour operators cottoned on to the fact that many travelers wanted to visit the wildlife-rich plains of Los Llanos, but were scared off by the prices of these tours. To fill the gap, many now offer three- or four-day tours (see LOS LLANOS, page 175). They opt for basic accommodation owned by local people — sometimes just a hammock and a communal bathroom. These tours are consistently recommended by younger travelers.

WHERE TO STAY

To compliment its cool climate, Mérida offers a wealth of accommodation at refreshingly reasonable prices. Some establishments change their

wooded backdrop where trails lead off into the hills, with romantic, colonial-style rooms decorated with style and taste. Top-end furnishings, artwork and decor make it hard to resist.

Moderate

Your best bet downtown for the price is the **Hotel Mintoy** ((074) 520340/523545 FAX (074) 526005, Calle 25, a good business and tourist hotel, right next to the Parque Las Heroínas. This could be a problem over noisy weekends or at fiestas, but its rooms are light, clean and well-kept. At the end of Avenida 1 on the way north of Mérida, the **Hotel Prado Río** ((074) 520633 FAX (074) 525192 was recently revamped by Corpoturismo. It offers 13 rooms and 84 *cabañas*; there is a swimming

OPPOSITE: Proving not all Andeans take life too seriously. ABOVE: Dramatic landscapes of the Sierra Nevada above the Río Chama.

pool and a restaurant. The complex, despite the relaunch, feels somewhat dated, but still makes for a quiet, leafy, and more sedate option. The university hotel management school operates it, and the staff are young and enthusiastic, and keen to learn languages.

Inexpensive

There are many family-run *posadas* in Mérida. They make for better value than their similarly priced "hotel" counterparts.

One of best examples, the well-established **La Casona de Margot** (/FAX (074) 523312 E-MAIL casonamargot@hotmail.com lies on Avenida 4 between calles 15 and 16. It offers good beds,

WHERE TO EAT

Stroll through Mercado Principal, and you appreciate the cornucopia of produce flowing through the city. Restaurants echo the abundance of fresh food, with traditional, tried-and-tested Andean recipes alongside international cuisine. Though snazzy, top-class eateries are few, flavor is plentiful.

Moderate

Though it verges on the tourist cliché, **Los Tejados de Chachopo** ((074) 440430, Via Chorros de Milla, delivers authentic Andean cooking — great trout — in an antique-filled, Old World atmosphere,

furnishings and fixtures in their rooms, along with a friendly atmosphere. Next door in another vintage house, **Posada Los Bucares** (/FAX (074) 522841, has 10 simpler but still spick and span rooms in all. On the corner of the street you'll find their crafts shop and café. The newcomer is the **Posada La Montaña** ((074) 525977 FAX (074) 527055, on Calle 24 between avenidas 6 and 7, whose 16 pleasing, rustic-style rooms run off a slightly echoing central patio. Their relaxed social area has views of the mountains.

Of the cheaper hotels and guesthouses, many offering shared bathrooms and kitchen facilities, a popular option is **Luz Caraballo** ((074) 525411, on Avenida 2 on Plaza Sucre. The rooms may be simple but they're spotless, with hot water and televisions, giving on to the central patio. The *posada* and typical Andean restaurant are consistently recommended.

which, though a little overdone, still manages to pull it off. The waiters and waitresses wear traditional clothes and ensure prompt service in the restaurant's various rooms.

Downtown, the works of art on the wall, chatter of the clientele and the imaginative menu of **La Chivata** ((074) 529426, Pasaje Ayacucho, make it a firm local favorite, while **La Fonda de Tía Mila** ((074) 443308, Avenida Principal Chorros de Milla, with its informal, casual feel and huge chunks of steak weighed by the kilo will have meat-eaters raving. For some live flamenco music with a meal, in a family-friendly ambience (Thursday, Friday and Saturday), head down to **La Sevillana** ((074) 522667, Avenida Tulio Febres Cordero and Calle 29. To sample some of that famous trout, finding better than the restaurant at the **Hotel Tisure** ((074) 526072 will be hard, served in a sedate, sophisticated atmosphere.

Inexpensive

For trout at more economical prices, **Marisquería Tu y Yo**, Avenida 4 at Calle 28, enjoys one of the best reputations in town in a slightly less formal atmosphere than Hotel Chama's fine restaurant, **Miramelindo** ((074) 524851, Avenida 4 and Calle 29.

The best grilled meats (*a la brasa*) are arguably at **Cheo's** on Las Heroínas, while pizza and pasta can be found just about anywhere. The new **Abadía**, Avenida 3 between calles 16 and 17, delivers it in style, with tasty pasta and larger dishes in a monastery-theme decor, where waiting staff wear cassocks. A popular place among students and the younger crowd, and also a fast cybercafé.

Vegetarians missing their greens should head for **Rincón de Reverón**, Calle 19, which provides conducive surroundings along with very good value and tasty dishes, as does **La Fonda Vegetariana**, Calle 29 between avenidas 3 and 4, serving up great falafels, whole wheat *arepas*, and vegetable savories.

For breakfasts, the views from **Bum Bum Tours'** balcony (where you can also send e-mail) are simply peerless, with pancakes or continental breakfasts. Also good for breakfasts, and the best crepes in town, is **El Hoyo del Queque** on the corner of Calle 19 and Avenida 4. Strangely enough, it mutates into a popular bar at night.

And now for something completely different. Beer, pumpkin and whisky. Doesn't seem odd? How about spaghetti, trout and garlic? On the surface, these flavors sound perfectly straightforward. But when you're standing at the counter of an ice-cream parlor, trying to choose one of them from a cast of hundreds, you could be forgiven for thinking you were caught up in a Monty Python-esque sketch. But you're not. You're in the **Heladería Coromoto**, Avenida 3 No. 28-75, the word's most bizarre ice-cream parlor. It vends no fewer than a record-breaking 650 different flavors. Even though there may only be 60 available on the day you visit Señor Oliveira's store, you'll never look upon Chunky Monkey or Cherry García the same way again.

NIGHTLIFE

With its students — who obviously have nothing better to do than party — and its attendant population of "artistic types," it's no surprise to find numerous cafés, bars, salsa joints, booming clubs and concerts in Mérida.

Downtown, **Harrys Carmelo** ((074) 522289, on Avenida 4 and Calle 30, and **Alfredo's Bar** ((074) 521412, Avenida 4 and Calle 19, are both lively, young places, with music and cocktails.

Later on, head to **El Bodegón de Pancho** ((074) 449819, Avenida Las Américas, on the ground floor of Centro Comercial Mamayeya, where salsa

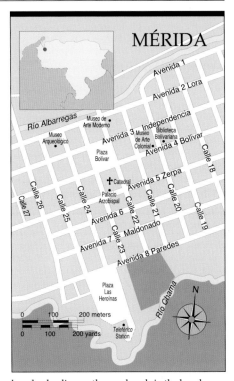

MÉRIDA

bands play live on the weekends in the bar downstairs, and the dance floor upstairs heaves later on at night. For other drinking and dancing spots, check out **El Castillo** ((074) 662984, Avenida Los Próceres, a lively discotheque, or **La Patana** ((074) 662746, Avenida Andrés Bello, Centro Comercial San Antonio, south of the airport, with live Latin tunes and people not afraid to sing along to them. For some hopping about to loud music downtown, with a big student crowd, **Birosca Carioca**, Calle 24 at Avenida 2, is an institution.

HOW TO GET THERE

About two kilometers (one and a quarter miles) southwest of the city center, and linked by small buses and economical taxis, Mérida's airport is well-served. Due to the bad weather conditions however, flights are often delayed or forced to land at El Vigía to the northwest. In this case, airlines provide transportation to Mérida. Servivensa's turboprop planes are the most likely airline to be affected by bad weather. Airlines servicing Caracas an hour away include **LAI** ((02) 263-2719 and **Santa Bárbara** ((02) 355-1813, while **Air Venezuela** also connects Mérida with Maracaibo, Porlamar, Cumaná and Puerto Ayacucho.

Mérida's bus terminal is three kilometers (two miles) southwest of the city center, from where

Color and tradition in San Rafael de Mucuchíes.

regular buses whiz into town (to Avenida 2 and Calle 25, near Plaza Bolívar); taxis are reasonably priced too.

AROUND MÉRIDA

All around Mérida roads beckon further exploration, with small towns, national parks and theme parks, *artesanía* and local color all found in abundance. Whether with a tour, in a rental car, or by *por puesto* and bus, Mérida's environs are not to be missed. For the sights along the road north to Apartaderos, see NORTH OF MÉRIDA, below, or WESTERN MÉRIDA, page 168, for the towns of the Pueblos del Sur and routes to Táchira State.

PARQUE NACIONAL SIERRA DE LA CULATA

Running parallel to the Parque Nacional Sierra Nevada, the Parque Nacional Sierra de la Culata is often overlooked by travelers, though the town of La Culata is just up from Mérida. Beyond the town, the ascent from the flowering colors of the valleys to the browns and grays of the *páramo* begins, with a camping spot near a waterfall about five hours' walk above. Ask tour operators for more details.

Just by the entrance to the national park, making it an ideal place to base yourself, the **Parador Turístico y Posada Los Pinos** ((014) 974-2864 or (074) 520682 has a crafts shop and a rustic-style restaurant with large fireplace. The three heated rooms, with baths and hot water, are decorated in the same attractive style.

LOS NEVADOS

One of the most photo-friendly villages of the Pueblos del Sur, Los Nevados is becoming an institution to Mérida visitors. Much as it is a charming, one-whitewashed-church place, in the high season it can feel more like a theme park. Either avoid these peak times, or continue on to the other pueblos that nestle on this side of the Sierra Nevada.

A six-hour hike separates the Loma Redonda *teleférico* substation and Los Nevados. It suits those who want to experience some Andean adventure, without having to invest in a new pair of limbs afterwards. If you're that concerned about your legs, you can always go by beast of burden—mules are available for rent at the station. You can also contract a jeep for Los Nevados from the *toyoteros* (literally "Toyota drivers") at Parque Las Heroínas in Mérida. They wind up a perilous dirt mountain track, where looking down on hairpin bends is not advised. You can take this route in either direction.

In the village of cobbled streets and packed-earth houses, several small *posadas* offer food and

lodging. The one managed by **Guamanchi Expeditions** (see TOURS, page 156 under MÉRIDA) is by far the best. There is also a campsite nearby. From Los Nevados, you can continue on foot to El Morro and other small villages of the pueblos, from where jeeps head back to Mérida.

JAJÍ

The village of Jají, hemmed by lush green hills and rushing rivers, was completely reconstructed in the 1960s in the style of an Andean pueblo, with a little church, cobbled streets and whitewashed walls. In the process it lost some of its true soul, and on weekends and during the high season the

souvenir shops and restaurants around the Plaza Bolívar throng with tourists. At other times, peace and quiet reign.

Lying just 38 km (24 miles) northwest of Mérida, the village makes for a popular side-trip. On the way up the winding road, you pass by a great waterfall, where paths lead up higher into the Spanish moss-draped forests. In Jají, you can rent horses through *posada* owners, or head off into the countryside by foot. The village celebrates its *fiestas patronales* on September 24 with processions.

On the way to Jají, 12 km (seven and a half miles) from Mérida, signs indicate the turnoff for **Venezuela de Antier** (Venezuela of Yesteryear). This theme park attempts to recreate various regions of Venezuela in miniature, including an Amazonian village, the bridge across Lake Maracaibo, and Caracas's Plaza Bolívar. Costumed actors play various roles. The park is fun for kids, but the high entrance fee might deter adults. It is open 9 AM to 5 PM daily.

Where to Stay and Eat

Near Jají, in the hamlet of Aldea La Playa (take the road south of the village passing by the church), the moderately priced **Hacienda El Carmen** (/FAX (074) 635852 (014) 974-0196 E-MAIL hostecar @telcel.net.ve provides a bucolic hideaway in the hills, with the added bonus of staying on a working coffee hacienda. The Monzón family very successfully converted the nineteenth-century house and offer eight double rooms and four family rooms, all with attractive furniture. Their restaurant only opens to the public during Holy Week

at Easter, but guests can enjoy their excellent meals year-round. Also included are an explanatory tour of the hacienda's coffee installations, with the option of horse-riding trips in the countryside. For children, a separate house accommodates a games room with a pool table, television and videos.

Near the plaza and well identified, the inexpensive **Posada Turística Aldea Vieja** ((074) 660072 (014) 974-6643 presents the best offer in town, with seven large rooms on the second story of the posada. The feel is rustic, with wooden plank floors and exposed beams, but the furniture is modern and the fittings and decorations eye-catching. The rooms come with bathrooms and hot water, and the restaurant below enjoys a good reputation.

The **El Bosque** restaurant serves great local dishes, probably the best establishment in town.

The Andes

LA AZULITA

Climbing higher on an adventurous road across the Andes and down to the *Panamericana* to the north, the village of La Azulita lies 62 km (38 miles) beyond Jají. It nestles at the high point of the Sierra de la Culata range and has views both down to the Chama valley, and north to Lago Maracaibo. On clear nights you can admire the awesome lightning displays at Catatumbo to the south of the lake.

Here, among the serene landscapes, artistic and "alternative" types settled back in the 1970s. There are plenty of horseback and foot paths in the area, great birdwatching (over 300 species according to the Audubon), and the chance for some very healthy eating, living, and enlightening experiences. The best *posada* is **El Tao** ((014) 960-5888 FAX (074) 97040.

LAGUNILLAS

From La Azulita, a country road switches back to the south, via small villages northwest of Mérida, emerging at Lagunillas. Near Lagunillas, the **Xamú Pueblo Indígena** is another of Mérida's theme parks, this time showcasing the lives of the Mucujún Indians. You get a good idea of how these people lived, farmed and survived before the invasion of the Spanish. Opening times have changed over the years, so check with the tourist office.

NORTH OF MÉRIDA

Running north along the valley of the Río Chama, the Trans-Andean Highway climbs ever-higher to the *páramos* of the Águila Pass at 4,007 m (13,143 ft) — "the most frustrating road in Venezuela" (see THE OPEN ROAD, page 34 in YOUR CHOICE).

Along the route north, only a few paved capillary roads fork off, leading to tiny settlements such as Gavidia and La Mucuy, while there are dozens of smaller roads and dirt tracks. Combining all of these and you get the greatest regional concentration of accommodation and restaurants in the country — literally hundreds of places to stay and eat.

Renting a car in Mérida allows you to explore at your own pace. Otherwise *por puestos* link the towns and villages of the route regularly, leaving from Calle 19 and Avenida 4 in Mérida. With the abundance of accommodation, you'll never be stuck without a bed.

OPPOSITE: Hiking the trails and rivers of Mérida. ABOVE: Mules take a well-deserved rest at Los Nevados.

TABAY

As you leave Mérida behind, and soon get a feel for the *Transandina's* sinuous nature, the first town you come to is Tabay, founded in 1689. The town retains much of its colonial character with a tree-shaded plaza where *Andinos* exchange conflicting weather predictions under the shadow of a twin-towered, weathered church.

A road off to the east of Plaza Bolívar leads to La Mucuy entrance to the Sierra Nevada park.

Tabay is renowned for its naïve wood carvings of saints and generals. Look for the signs on doorways selling *artesanía*, or ask for the *casa de la*

cultura, just off the square. Also inquire about the lovely thermal springs nearby.

Where to Stay

Shortly before Tabay, a turn on your right indicates Mucunután, leading to the moderately priced **Posada Xinia & Peter** (/FAX (074) 830214, surrounded by tall trees. The place feels exclusive right from the start: there are only three house-cabins in all, with their own kitchens and living rooms. The attention to detail is marvelous, with top quality furnishings, crafts adorning window sills, imaginative designs and faultless taste. They offer various excursions and packages to suit all needs, and there are plenty of country walks right by their doorstep.

In Tabay, the Monsalve family's inexpensive **La Casona de Tabay** ((074) 830089, and its twin **Posada Turística Tabay** (on the main square)((074)

830025 both boast Old World, wood-beamed appeal, with tiled central patios, and good restaurants. La Casona lies out of town with wonderful views. The restaurant can be reserved by prior arrangement.

About 10 minutes' drive out of Tabay, you come to the turn for the **Posada de la Mano Poderosa** ((074) 523804 or (014) 742-2862 FAX (074) 524031. This surprisingly inexpensive *posada* nestles into a lush valley, where an icy river rushes down the hills and fantastic views of the peaks to the east beg contemplation from the comfort of a hammock. Oscar and friends offer four rooms in a new, yet traditional-style tiled house, with whitewashed walls and exposed beams. The rooms share three bathrooms and living spaces. A local *señora* cooks up some delicious meals for guests.

Where to Eat

El Fogón de la Cachapa (weekends only), just north of the plaza, cooks the sweetest *cachapas* in about six different ways, and warms up some *calentaíto* to the sounds of traditional violin music, with Andean memorabilia for decoration.

LOS ALEROS TO MUCUCHÍES

Seven kilometers (just over four miles) from Tabay, the theme park Los Aleros is on the hill on your right. Los Aleros was the first of Mérida's parks and remains very popular. It faithfully recreates the typical Andean village of the early twentieth century with period furniture, arts and crafts, a cinema, a post office, and cottage industries. Actors dressed in period clothes go about their chores, and there's even the chance of catching a wedding. It's entertaining, great for children, though some adults might find it all a shade too Disneyesque. The park is open daily 9 AM to 5 PM, weekends 8 AM to 5:30 PM.

Beyond Los Aleros, the next village is **Cacute**, its colonial center off to the right of the highway recently spruced up. Soon after Cacute, lies Mucurubá, awaiting a kind, restoring hand.

Where to Stay and Eat

About thirteen kilometers (eight miles) of winding bends beyond Mucurubá, a sign on the left points to **Balcones de la Musui** ((014) 974-0712 (if you see a sign for El Vergel, you've gone too far), which is just over two kilometers (one and a quarter miles) up this steep, partly paved road. It boasts some of the most wonderful views of any *posada* in the Andes, perched on the hill at around 3,000 m (9,840 ft), with a series of six "honeymoon" cabins, all with large picture windows giving on to the mountains. Owner César Lemoine loves his food and his wine and has some good cooks in his employ. His restaurant opens its doors to the public with advance warning, and he can arrange trips to the nearby thermal springs.

Gaining institution-status just beyond Los Aleros, and before Cacute, the family-run **Catalina Delicatesses** delights all — an emporium of local produce, from homemade jams, conserves and chutneys, through smoked cheeses and on to cakes.

MUCUCHÍES

One of the Chama valley's archetypal sleepy towns, the narrow Mucuchíes dates back as far as 1596. The town only springs to life for various

winding road, only just discovered by adventurous travelers.

Above Mucuchíes, various hot springs make for some surreal bathing in these high climes, and there are trails up into the Sierra de la Culata. Local people or *posada* owners can point them out.

Where to Stay and Eat

As you leave Mucuchíes, you will come face-to-face with Mérida's greatest tourist folly to date, the expensive **Hotel Castillo San Ignacio (** (074) 820021 or (074) 820751, towering above the surrounding countryside. Much as the 30 rooms and suites amount to top-of-the-range luxury, and the craftsmanship of the stonemasons and artisans is

saints' days. On the loudest, December 29, costumed dancers with flowery hats celebrate San Benito to the firing of old blunderbusses — yes, accidents do happen... On November 24, adorned oxen from around the region are brought to the church to be blessed.

The town is famous as the home of a Saint Bernard-like, Great Pyrenees breed of dog, the *mucuchíes*, which enjoys a reputation for both its loyalty and ferocity. In the square, sharing pride of place with El Libertador, note the statue of an Indian boy called Tínajaca and his *mucuchíes* dog Nevado. They went off to fight with Bolívar and never returned. They fell together at the Battle of Boyacá.

Close to Mucuchíes, one of the few roads to branch east into the Sierra Nevada leads to **Gavidia**, a one-cobbled-street mountain village at 3,350 m (11,000 ft) reached by a spectacular

admirable, you can't help thinking "¿Qué?" Love it or hate it, it's definitely novel. The overall feel of its medieval-baronial decor, with turrets, wooden shutters, knights-in-armor, large landscape paintings on the walls, and even some stained glass, is — in the heart of the Andes — undeniably original. A meal in their grand, wood-beamed Great Hall restaurant, where waiters and waitresses don medieval garb to serve international cuisine at the trestle tables, may help you to decide whether it's for you or not.

Near Mucuchíes lies the **Piedras Blancas Ecological Refuge** (also known as Mesa Redonda) **(** /FAX (074) 638633 E-MAIL patven@telcel.net.ve (by reservation only), established by dedicated Frenchman Yves Lesenfants and run by the laudable

OPPOSITE and ABOVE: Typical scenes from the Andes' top theme park, Los Aleros.

Programa Andes Tropicales. The traditionally built *posada* enjoys a privileged position, linked by horse trails to other locally run, affordable *posadas*. Hikes and trails climb up to the stunning *páramo*, and the managers impart their wealth of information about the ecosystems and wildlife. Rates are moderate to expensive.

SAN RAFAEL DE MUCUCHÍES

Mention the town of San Rafael de Mucuchíes, a further seven kilometers (four and a half miles) up the valley, to a Venezuelan, and they'll most probably reply **La Capilla de Juan Félix Sánchez**. His original, larger chapel stands in splendid

It is open in the high season until 10:30 PM daily but, apart from Saturdays, it closes earlier in the low season. It's best to call and check. You can also reach CIDA from a turnoff after Apartaderos, via the village of Llano del Hato, high on the *páramo*. The best time to plan a visit is during the first quarter of the moon's cycle, and you can arrange a tour in English if you call in advance. There is no public transportation up to the observatory which falls within the Sierra de la Culata National Park but in Mérida, **Viajes a las Estrellas (** (074) 524771 organize tours.

For the trail to El Tisure, stop at La Mucuchaché, about five minutes by road north of San Rafael. Look for the white cross on the right-hand

isolation on the trail to El Tisure, one of the most singular sights in the Venezuelan Andes (see below). The chapel, like the terracing you see throughout the mountains, was painstakingly built stone by stone, rock by rock, an amazing achievement considering Sánchez's age—he was 83 by the time he finished it. But there's more to the chapel than meets the admittedly impressed eye. Visit it in the morning, in a mist-shrouded half-light, or in the evening as clouds gather in the valley, and you begin to understand why Sánchez was also revered as a *brujo* (mystic) — the Pope even made a point of visiting him on his tour in 1985.

Halfway to San Rafael de Mucuchíes, lies La Toma, from where a paved road heads up to the **CIDA Astronomical Observatory (** (074) 712780 or (074) 713883 WEB SITE www.cida.ve, which also doubles as the **Museo del Espacio.**

side, just by a brook. The trail from there is easy to find, and you climb slowly up to the pass of La Ventana, at around 4,000 m (13,120 ft), which is a bit of scrabble. Ask tour operators for more details.

Where to Stay and Eat

Just after the chapel coming out of town, look for the signs for the **Posada San Rafael del Páramo (** (074) 820938. The cultured owners, Omar and Mary Monsalve, have put a lot of time, effort and taste into their *posada*, employing traditional techniques with an eye for the decorative details that elevate it above the competition—niches for statues carved into of the plaster walls, colossal weathered trunks for pillars and beams, eye-catching floral designs. They have recently opened a restaurant during the high season, with an adjacent terrace for sunny days. In addition to offering all sorts of excursions, they rent tents for those who want to spend a night under the stars of the mountains.

APARTADEROS

All too soon for people only coming this far, you will come to the fork in the road two kilometers (one and a quarter miles) north of "commercial" Apartaderos — a bevy of *posadas*, hotels and souvenir shops that sell cured hams, cheeses (the white *queso del páramo*), ponchos and rugs. Driving nonstop from Mérida, the 62 km (38.5 miles) journey takes around two hours, climbing 1,850 m (6,068 ft).

About five kilometers (three miles) after Apartaderos, is the turnoff for the **Mifafí Condor Center** on the left, up a rough road. Here, you can visit the enclosures for raising the largest flying bird in the world, and learn about the program to reintroduce this creature to the Andes, whose numbers continue to decline. Contact María Rosa Cuesta ((074) 528355 FAX (074) 524084 for information. She also runs a lovely *posada* near Tabay.

On the way to Timotes, you pass through the village of **Cachopo**, famous for its celebrations honoring the Virgen de Coromoto, Venezuela's patron saint, on September 11. Groups dressed as Indians reenact the miraculous vision that appeared to Indian chief Coromoto.

At the fork in the road, where the *Transandina* continues north to Timotes, and another road splits east down to Barinas, walk down the hill through the terracotta-tiled roofs and crooked walls of the village of Apartaderos proper. In the "square," by the brick church, there's a statue of Bolívar. This being the Andes, the statue rests on a base of stones and rocks.

TO TIMOTES

Staying on the *Transandina*, from Apartaderos, the road coils higher until you reach the **Paso El Águila** at 4,007 m (13,146 ft), the highest pass in Venezuela's highway system. A statue of a condor marks the passage of Bolívar's army on his way to free Caracas. Pico El Águila is a short walk to the west, and beyond it, the tiny village of **Piñango**, 47 km (29 miles) on a jeep track — great for mountain bikes.

TIMOTES

Timotes heralds the start of the Andes for many Venezuelans beginning the climb up from the hot valleys. Lying at 2,000 m (6,560 ft) you can already feel the fresh mountain air in this busy small town. Only 52 km (32 miles) separates Timotes from Pico El Águila, but elevation-wise, the gap is a further 2,000 m (6,560 ft). It boasts more hairpins than Ivana Trump's hairdo.

I've seen people get quite emotional about Timotes, even though it offers little to retain you other than mountain charisma and a walk around the square to see the funny church. However, on December 29, all that changes for the Giros de San Benito (Venezuela's black saint). In costumes as

OPPOSITE: The Negros de San Benito in Mucuchíes perform their dances. ABOVE: Arts and crafts abound throughout the Andes.

feathered Indians, or blacked-up in grass skirts, dancers wheel and whirl around a maypole in one of the most colorful fiestas in the Andes.

If you're traveling from Mérida, a lovely little side-trip up to the mountain village of Jajó might tempt you on your drive down to Valera (see JAJÓ, page 147).

Where to Stay and Eat

A favorite of travelers for 40 years, the **Hotel Las Truchas** ((071) 89158 enjoys a tranquil hillside setting. Choose the newer set of 15 comfortable cabins with two bedrooms and bathrooms and their own kitchens. Best of all, they come with fireplaces.

APARTADEROS TO BARINAS

Taking the easterly Highway 1 at the fork just after Apartaderos, you descend from dizzying heights to the heat of the plains at Barinas via the valleys and gorges of the Río Santo Domingo. This is another of Venezuela's most beautiful roads, and a preferred route of people heading up to Mérida from the center of the country.

To Santo Domingo

Shortly after Apartaderos comes the entrance to **Laguna Mucubají** and the "lake district" of northern Parque Nacional Sierra Nevada. Buses on their way from Barinas to Mérida often stop at the restaurant and shops here.

At the Inparques office at the lake, ask for camping and fishing permits, and hiking routes to La Victoria, Los Patos (the ducks) and Lagunas Negra. The office has some excellent didactic panels on regional flora and fauna, as well as books for sale, and a small café. Horses can also be rented at the lake, though sometimes only in the high season.

Where to Stay and Eat

Halfway from Apartaderos to Santo Domingo, about 12 km (seven and a half miles), you'll spot the distinctive tower of probably Mérida's most famous inn, **Hotel Los Frailes**, which you book through Hoturvensa in Caracas ((02) 907-8130 through 8134 FAX (02) 907-8140. The hotel has expanded over the years to include cabins across the road, but I prefer the rooms in the old part of the complex with their walkways and wooden beams, set around the cobbles and fountain of the courtyard. The cuisine of the homestyle restaurant has an excellent reputation. The staff can arrange tours of the nearby *páramo* on foot or by horseback. Rates are moderate. Even if you don't plan to spend the night, or enjoy a meal, a *calentaíto* in the "English pub" bar is a must.

Santo Domingo

The 5,000-odd people of Santo Domingo huddle into a valley punctuated by the spire of the Santa Lucía church. Founded as far back as 1619, it continues its traditional Andean customs high up in the hills, with September 30 marking its one leap from tranquility for the **Fiesta de los Negros de San Jerónimo**. Locals blacken their faces, play homemade flutes, dress up, and generally have a good time on the way to a shrine to the west of town. The town survives from agriculture, trout farming and tourism, with some good stores for perusing local handicrafts, nearby lakes for fishing, and good walking country.

Where to Stay and Eat

There are two excellent choices for accommodation in Santo Domingo at moderate rates. The first, **La Sierra** ((073) 88110 or (02) 575-4835 (in Caracas)

FAX (073) 88050 on the town's main street, offers an assortment of different size suites, of which the larger ones come with great fireplaces. The grounds are lush, the views fantastic, and the feel decidedly luxurious throughout — though prices are still very reasonable. Their restaurant also enjoys a good reputation.

Coming out of town heading east on the main highway lies the second smart option, **La Trucha Azul International Resort** ((073) 88066 or (073) 88150 FAX (073) 88067, a thoroughly professionally run establishment, possibly one of the best in Mérida State. Its four stars are well-earned, and there are all the facilities you might expect, set in the high mountains. It's truly a great place to spend a few days. The staff can organize all sorts of excursions for you, and arrange transfers.

The other less expensive options include the **Complejo Turístico Las Cabañas** (/FAX (073) 88133 at the entrance to the town, with two dozen attractive cabins for up to eight people, set in grassy grounds with a reasonable restaurant; or else **El Halcon de Oro** ((073) 88044, in front of La Trucha on the main street, which offers accommodation with fireplaces that is set back from the road. The owners speak English and German.

LAS PIEDRAS AND PUEBLO LLANO

Just over five kilometers (three miles) beyond Santo Domingo, a road strikes north to Las Piedras and Pueblo Llano, two more picturesque mountain villages. Beyond Pueblo Llano you can walk up to the Páramo La Estrella, and all the way down to Timotes. Another trail heads over to Tuñame (see SOUTH FROM BOCONÓ, page 146).

Jajó's church and square bathed in ochre light.

WESTERN MÉRIDA

South of the *Transandina* between Bailadores and Mérida, the isolated villages known as Los Pueblos del Sur (The Villages of the South) lie perched and parched on mountainsides, or nestled into green valleys, with only rough roads connecting them to the outside world. Some of the hills thirst in a rain shadow, baring burnt skins in stark contrast with the woolly hills to the north of the state. Mountain bikers and paragliders revel in the dirt tracks and thermals respectively. *Por puestos* make venturing along the routes of the pueblos possible, but I suggest you rent a car or a jeep in Mérida.

other on May 22 for the Locos de Santa Rita celebrations, when the village men reenact battles in the square to much hilarity. South of Pueblo Nuevo, a rough road leads over the *páramo* and links up with Chocantá and Canaguá. Another jeep track goes east over to San José.

Further along the *Transandina*, after the surprisingly warmer colonial town of **Estanques**, you come to the *alcabala* of La Victoria. Here, ask for directions to the Hacienda La Victoria, a restored coffee hacienda which now houses a **Museo de Cafe** and the **Museo de la Inmigración**. The mansion is one of the finest examples in the state, with the interesting museums occupying the rooms that flank the huge central coffee-drying

Los Pueblos del Sur

For an adventurous route up to the neat little pueblo of **San José**, with its square, mules and church, take the turn at Las Gonzales, 20 km (12.5 miles) west of Mérida. The road is partly paved. Beyond San José, you continue to climb up to the Páramo San José, before coiling down to Mucutuy and Mucuchachí on the southern side of the range. Stop on the road and go for a wander to admire the *frailejones* on the often cloud-swept *páramo*, with many different varieties represented.

The easiest of the pueblos to reach, there is little new at all about **Pueblo Nuevo**, a colonial village of cobbles, whitewashed walls and a church. The pretty, well-paved mountain road links it to the *Transandina* at Puerto Real. The village, otherwise quiet and sleepy, bounds to life for its two main festivals: one in the run-up to Christmas, and the

patio. The hacienda is open from 9 AM to 6 PM, Wednesday to Sunday in the low season, daily at other times.

For the paved road south, take the road behind the little church in Estanques (or at Santa Cruz) and begin the fantastic climb up from the arid, rain-shadow valley, through fertile hills sown with bananas and coffee, all the way up to the freezing fog of the *páramo*. Beyond it lies the teeny, Colgate-white pueblo of **El Molino**, and then **El Rincón** where black bulls are bred for bullfights. Continuing on south, **Canaguá** is the largest of the Pueblos del Sur with around 2,500 people — but don't expect a bustling metropolis, more a Toyotapolis. The town prospers as the center of the coffee-growing hills.

From Canaguá, more country roads wind through valleys and over hills. Heading west you can loop back to Tovar on the *Transandina* — a spectacular road, particularly the last part through the **Parque Nacional Páramos Batallón y La Negra**. If you have a jeep, you can stay south, linking with Pregonero in Táchira State and crossing the Páramo Zumbador.

Where to Stay and Eat

For a bucolic setting in San José, follow the path across the stream at the end of the main street to the inexpensive **Posada Mochaba**, reservations through Natoura Tours ((074) 524216 E-MAIL natoura@telcel.net.ve. The grounds are beautiful, with its stream, trout fishing, and trails at your cabinstep. Four cabins and a separate little house set apart from the others make up the accommodation, and Natoura usually arrange all-inclusive packages.

In El Molino, a surprising offer comes in the form of the **Posada Turística El Hato** ((075) 661001. The *posada*, run by Carlos Durán and his family (ask for him on the community phone above), is simple enough, but with its flowering central courtyard, delicious meals, comfortable rooms, new furniture, and welcoming owners, it will win you over. With prior arrangement, they can arrange excursions by foot or on horseback to plenty of local sights. Rates are inexpensive.

In Canaguá, several *posadas* offer beds in town, but the superior option lies up the hill past the school. At **La Posada Turística Canaguá** ((075) 681055, you can enjoy a good, hearty meal in their *tasca*-cum-restaurant, but the friendly manageress also has four inexpensive rooms set around the central courtyard with its wide inner corridor — the pleasant rooms with hot water and baths compare favorably to the other offers in town. She can also arrange horseback riding and walking tours up in the *páramo* or to nearby rivers.

TOVAR AND BAILADORES

The last towns in Mérida State on the *Transandina* are both important agricultural centers with many fields of flowers and strawberries. Tovar is lower, the road climbing up to Bailadores at 1,750 m (5,740 ft). Both make good bases for exploring the countryside, with its many rivers, waterfalls, forests and fields.

In Bailadores, ask for directions to Parque La Cascada (also Parque Páez), to the east of town, where you encounter a delightful waterfall known poetically as the Waterfall of the Indian Maiden who Died of Love. The town hosts a large agricultural fair in the second and third weeks of August. It's very much worth attending, but either book a room ahead, or stay in a neighboring town.

Where to Stay

In Bailadores, the inexpensive **Posada La Cascada** ((075) 70289 or (/FAX (014) 755-0070 is by far the most inviting establishment in the town, with some quite refined rooms with four-poster beds, baths, hot water, and a "European" country style. Call the owners for directions, they speak English.

TÁCHIRA STATE

At first sight, when considering Mérida's promotion, popularity and attractions, the traveler may be forgiven for thinking Táchira State compares poorly. Yet the state is rich in many ways, both as the commercial center of trade with Colombia — the *Panamericana* continues down to Bogotá — but also in its variety of villages with their religious festivals and talented artisans, and the abundant landscapes of forests, rivers and tanned *páramos*. Add the region's fertile soils and diverse climate, and Táchira is far from being the poor cousin. The state is fundamentally agrarian, with one of the highest rural populations in the country, making for local people proud of their past, their traditions and their land.

BAILADORES TO SAN CRISTÓBAL

From Bailadores, the *Transandina* winds its way once again up to the moorlands. On its way back down, it passes through the busy commercial town of **La Grita**. Beyond the town, you come to El Cobre. About nine kilometers (five and a half miles) south of the village, you'll see a sign for "cabañas." These comprise the **Finca La Huérfana** (/FAX (014) 979-5350, run by the very friendly, cultured and charming Jenny Martínez and Manuel Tallafero. When I visited, I was too hurried to be able to stop for long, but the whole place left me yearning to return. From the homemade cookies, granola, cakes and juices on offer in their small handicrafts shop, up to the food in the restaurant (which I was happily able to sample) all the way to the excellent quality of the cozy cabins, the *finca* is without doubt one of the best in the country. Jenny and Manuel's land extends over 80 hectares (198 acres) with trails leading up into the *páramo*. Call in advance and arrange a package through them. You won't regret it.

SAN CRISTÓBAL

If you're coming into Venezuela from Colombia, San Cristóbal won't feel all that different. The number plates, telephones and flags change, but otherwise you could be forgiven for thinking you hadn't crossed the border at all. The comparison holds all the more true when you consider that until 1777 the city and region formed part of the Provincia de Nueva Granada, modern-day Colombia.

Emotions run high at the Feria de San Sebastián in San Cristóbal.

Founded in 1561 on the eastern banks of the Río Torbes by the man who legally founded Mérida, Juan de Maldonado y Ordóñez, San Cristóbal grew even more slowly than its eastern cousin. Though it won't waylay you for long, the city offers some striking architecture and informal squares, with several old villages and seldom-visited national parks to explore close by. Many people pass through San Cristóbal on their way to and from Colombia. The border lies 36 km (22 miles) west at San Antonio del Táchira.

GENERAL INFORMATION

The local tourist office, **Cotatur** ((076) 562805 FAX (076) 562421, Avenida España at Avenida Universidad, lies in the Pueblo Nuevo district, to the northeast of the city center; open 8 AM to noon and 2 PM to 5:30 PM, Monday to Friday only. They can provide city maps, lists of hotels, and are generally helpful. They also have unreliable *módulos* (booths) at Plaza Bolívar, at the Santo Domingo airport, and at the bus terminal.

The city is country-renowned for the **Feria de San Sebastián**, which takes place over the last two weeks in January. Visitors from all around the Andes and Venezuela come to partake in the numerous processions, fiestas, concerts and folklore shows.

For car rental, **Budget** ((076) 464741 has offices in the Centro Comercial El Parque, Avenida 19 de Abril.

WHAT TO SEE AND DO

The **cathedral** dominates the oldest of the city's squares, **Plaza Maldonado** at Carrera 3 and Calle 4. Next to the cathedral stands the fine **Palacio Episcopal**, while on the north side of the square, the imposing **Edificio Nacional**, which could do with a new lick of paint, houses the city's law courts. On the other side of it is Plaza Urdaneta.

Three blocks east, Plaza Bolívar fails to inspire anything in particular, though the handsome building which today houses the **Ateneo** has been well restored. Inside you'll find a library, an art gallery and a small theatre. Across the square, the misguided modern structure hosts the **Museo de Artes Visuales y del Espacio**. The museum is open Monday to Saturday 8 AM to noon and 2 PM to 7 PM, Sundays 8 AM to 1 PM.

Continuing east on Calle 8, you pass the Gothic spires of the Iglesia de San José, before reaching the Plaza Bicentenario one block south. On the square lies the diminutive but charming **Iglesia de San Antonio**. Southwest of the square, Plaza Sucre is the heart of the student district downtown, with the eye-catching buildings of the

Universidad Nacional Abierta and a number of old houses. Just south, the monumental **Palacio de los Leones** occupies the whole block of the plaza's east side.

On Avenida Universidad, north of the Complejo Ferial — where much of the Feria's action takes place — the **Museo del Táchira** does a fine job of displaying a collection of Andean archeology, folklore and art. The museum is housed within the restored Hacienda de Paramillo, open Tuesday to Friday 9 AM to noon and 3 PM to 5:30 PM, weekends 10 AM to 6 PM.

WHERE TO STAY

Expensive

To the northeast of the city center, the judiciously named **Castillo de la Fantasía** ((076) 530848 FAX (076) 532032, Redoma España, off Avenida España, looks much like a mock European château with its great stone walls. Inside the spacious rooms enjoy an eclectic range of decoration, from the ultramodern, through "country" style and on to medieval. Definitely the height of luxury in San Cristóbal, and worth the taxi ride for a meal at their reputable restaurant serving international dishes with a French slant.

Moderate

Once the most posh place in San Cristóbal, the **Hotel El Tamá** ((076) 558366 FAX (076) 550446, on Avenida 19 de Abril to the east of the city center, still offers plenty of comfort over its 10 floors. After visiting the Castillo de la Fantasía, the El Tamá seems decidedly sedate, but it's still a perfectly good value choice close to downtown.

Inexpensive

San Cristóbal offers a range of downtown hotels. Probably the best in this price range is the central **Hotel Dinastía** ((076) 441366 FAX (076) 448995, Avenida 7 at Calle 14, with comfortable air-conditioned rooms, followed by the more affordable, but good value **Hotel Horizonte** (430011 FAX (076) 430492, Carrera 4 at Calle 7, with 70 rooms popular with businessmen, and a restaurant serving Venezuelan fare on the ground floor.

For a central cheapy, set in an old house with simple rooms off a central patio, the **Hotel Andorra** (no phone), Carrera 4 No. 4-47, a block east of the cathedral, makes a good choice.

WHERE TO EAT

In the city center, the district around the Plaza Los Mangos known as the Barrio Obrero claims a concentration of eateries, between about Calle 10 and 14 and Carrera 23 (northeast of Plaza Sucre). Of these, the best are **Pietro Restaurant**, and

Pizzería La Cotorra, with **La Hormiga Pub** one of the best places for a lively evening drink. The Avenida Libertador, to the north of the center, is another popular wining and dining area, with **La Vaquera** ((076) 436769, a popular choice for meat and seafood dishes. For Chinese food in impressive surroundings, **Nan King** ((076) 465357, Avenida 19 de Abril, Sector La Concordia, is an institution in San Cristóbal.

How to Get There

San Cristóbal's airport is at Santo Domingo, southeast of the city. However, the airport at the border northeast of San Antonio is busier and nearer —

BOLIVAR EN SAN CRISTOBAL 1813

about an hour away. There are daily flights to Caracas, and about seven other cities (see COLOMBIAN BORDER, page 172).

The big bus terminal is south of the city center on Avenida La Concordia (formerly Avenida Libertador). There are plenty of buses to Mérida during the day, and south to the Llanos. Most buses for Caracas depart in the evening, following the Llanos Highway 5. The trip can take 13 hours. Expresos Los Llanos provides the most luxurious nonstop service. *Por puestos* to the border at San Antonio leave all the time.

AROUND SAN CRISTÓBAL

The area around San Cristóbal, usually overlooked by tour brochures and travelers alike, is rich in history, farming and wildlife. To the northwest of the city, west of the Highway 1 to La Fría,

the villages-that-time-forgot of **Peribeca** and **El Topón** (ask for directions at the *alcabala* of Copa de Oro), have both undergone restoration over the last years, and you'll find local artisans selling crafts and can enjoy a good meal in one of the typical restaurants. You can also reach the villages from a turning before Capacho Nuevo (see below) that links north to Highway 1 above Táriba.

Continuing north, a loop round to the restored village of **San Pedro del Río** (also de los Ríos), and a stop for a thermal bath at the Hotel Aguas Calientes, make for a great day-trip. In addition to visiting the church and admiring the cobbled streets, make sure to pass by the Escuela de Música (Music School). San Pedro is known for its Easter Week celebrations, which it takes very seriously with nightly processions, all-night vigils and huge nativity scenes (*pesebres*).

Heading west towards Colombia, the towns of **Capacho Viejo** and **Capacho Nuevo**, surrounded by rolling countryside, also produce some fantastic wood and ceramic crafts. Their proper names are Libertad and Independencia, respectively, but everyone continues to use their old names.

Ask the tourist office for directions to **Rubio** and **Santa Ana**, south of San Cristóbal. From there, you can wander off into the bird-rich hills of **Parque Nacional El Tamá**.

Where to Stay and Eat

In Peribeca, **La Posada de la Abuela** ((076) 880595, right on the plaza, represents an excellent example of tasteful and comfortable restoration. On the ground floor there's a coffee shop, while inside the restaurant serves some tasty meals. Upstairs, the eight rooms are all spacious and comfortable, with plenty of decorative touches, hot water, and baths. Rates are inexpensive.

In the same price category, **Posada Paseo La Chiriri** ((076) 449403 or (077) 910157 FAX (077) 915204 (ask for Marilú de Morales) offers the most typical and welcoming *posada* in San Pedro de los Ríos, with nine rooms, simple but very much acceptable, set around the courtyard of a two-story vintage house. On the approach road to San Pedro, look for the sign for the **Posada Valparaíso** ((077) 911032, the bucolic alternative to the *posadas* in town. The grounds are a delight, with a stream running through the pedicured gardens. The six rooms are all comfortable with hot water and bathrooms, and the overall feel cozy. Of the village's restaurants, **La Casona de los Abuelos** and **Río de las Casas** on Calle Real enjoy good reputations.

A stained-glass pane in San Cristóbal's cathedral depicts Bolívar's visit in 1813.

COLOMBIAN BORDER

The town of **San Antonio del Táchira** on the banks of the Río Táchira marks the border with Colombia, 36 km (22 miles) west of San Cristóbal. The town is busy and commercial, with plenty of trade flowing back and forth between the two countries, but little to interest the tourist.

GENERAL INFORMATION

When crossing to Colombia, wind your watch back one hour, and watch your back. The DIEX office, where you get an entry or an exit stamp (and pay a small tax) lies on Carrera 7, between Calle 6 and 7, open from 6 AM to 8 PM — though arrive earlier in the evening to avoid a closed office. On the Colombian side, the DAS office is just on the right over the bridge. It's best to take either a taxi or a *por puesto* over the bridge, since pedestrians have been robbed in the area.

To change money, there are numerous *casas de cambio* by the DIEX office, while Banco Consolidado on Plaza Bolívar should change travelers' checks. If not here, they will in San Cristóbal. Banco Unión is also close by.

WHERE TO STAY AND EAT

Of the limited choice in San Antonio, the inexpensive **Hotel Don Jorge** ((076) 714089 FAX (076) 791932, Calle 5 No. 9-20, offers about the best quality, with air-conditioned rooms, a small pool, games room, and its own restaurant. Cheaper is the **Hotel Colonial** ((076) 713123, Carrera 11 near Calle 3, with rooms with fans and bathrooms. It also runs an inexpensive restaurant.

HOW TO GET THERE

On Carrera 4, the main thoroughfare, by Calle 6, two travel agencies can book airline tickets for Colombia and Venezuela for you. The airport is just northeast of town, with four flights a day to Caracas, and a number of other cities. For Colombian destinations, Servivensa flies daily to both Medellín and Bogotá, at about the same price as the bus.

Halfway to the airport, San Antonio's recent bus terminal offers half a dozen buses direct to Caracas departing in the evening. *Por puestos* to San Cristóbal leave all the time, where you should change if you're en route to Mérida.

Buses and shared taxis leave from stops on Calle 6 for Cúcuta in Colombia, about 12 km (seven and a half miles) away. From there you can continue on other buses. Be very wary of your belongings on these buses, and shun help offered by "friendly" people at the terminal in Cúcuta.

Prickly cactus punctures an azure sky.

Los
Llanos

LOS LLANOS (THE PLAINS) EXTEND OVER A THIRD OF VENEZUELA'S TERRITORY: 300,000 sq km (117,000 sq miles) of sparsely populated flat grasslands that dominate the land from the Andes to the Orinoco Delta — the country's geographic, and spiritual, heart.

They are without doubt a nature-lover's dream, the wildlife in the region equaling any to be found in South America. Of the birds, perhaps the most impressive are the flocks of iridescent scarlet ibis and roseate spoonbills, but these are joined by geese, jacarandas, jabiru stork, and heron, as well as by birds of prey, the hawk, falcon and osprey. Among the animals, you'll encounter the capybara or *chigüire* — the world's largest rodent, spec-

tacled cayman (*baba*) crocodiles, small turtles, river dolphins (*tonina*), and occasionally otters that bark from riverbanks. More shy, or nocturnal, mammals include giant anteaters, tapir, armadillo (the endemic *cachicamo sabanero*), peccaries and wild cats such as ocelots and jaguars (*tigres*). Howler monkeys (*araguatos*) are often heard terrorizing forest neighborhoods. Of the Llanos' reptiles, the anaconda — the world's largest snake — is the most renowned, growing to fearful lengths of up to 12 m (36 ft). Waters are patrolled by snapping piranha (*caribes*) who, although they don't attack fauna unless bleeding, make swimming in most of the region's rivers a bad idea. Add giant electric eels and stingrays, and you can understand why tour guides actively discourage much sought-after cooling dips.

Llanero cowboys, "indomitable and long-suffering" and tough as old boots, herd thousands of head of cattle from pasture to market. Like the cowboys of *Stage Coach* or the *gauchos* of Argentina, they have assumed mythical proportions, central to the country's identity and historical heritage. Often barefooted, they break wild horses and sing laments to comfort their lonely souls. Four-string ukulele-like instruments (*cuatros*), maracas and small harps accompany their *cris de cœur*. The tunes of the *Llanero*

have become Venezuela's national music, while the song *Alma Llanera* is the country's unofficial national anthem.

The Llanos have two seasons, both extreme. In the dry months of *verano* (summer), water holes and lakes wither away to puddles, where muscular anacondas die dusty deaths in mud coffins. The heat is unrelenting. Animals throng the few remaining water sources until, finally, in May, the heavens at last open anew for *invierno* (winter). By July, swathes of grasslands are transformed into marsh and lake, flooding huge expanses, driving cattle to higher ground and the inhabitants to canoes and launches.

Whichever way you decide to see the region — whether through an *hato* ranch or with a tour operator from Mérida — the dry season offers the best opportunities for travel, with the downside of sapping heat. Venezuela's Llanos, like Brazil's Pantanal or South Africa's Kruger, are not to be missed.

ROUTES THROUGH LOS LLANOS

Corpoturismo's guide to the Llanos in English contains an informative overview of the region, plus a road map detailing five possible routes through the Llanos. Of all of them, I suggest you follow Highway 2 from San Juan de Los Morros, capital of large Guárico State, to San Fernando de Apure via the old town of Calabozo. At San Fernando, continue south towards the Orinoco and through the Parque Nacional Cinaruco-Capanaparo, or head west on Highway 19.

Traveling west on the rutted "19," you pass through the small town of Mantecal, one of the most typical "cowboy" townships of the region. West of here comes La Ye (literally "The Y"), where driving south leads to Elorza and the popular *hatos* El Cedral and Doña Bárbara. Turning north takes you up through Bruzual and Ciudad de Nutrias and into the foothills of the Andes. You emerge on the Llanos Highway 5 at Boconoíto, between Barinas and Guanare.

Here, you can either loop back to Caracas along Highway 5, which skirts the plains with various detours, or climb up to the Andes either from Guanare to Biscucuy, or from Barinas to Apartaderos, via Santo Domingo.

For where to stay or break the journey, see HATOS AND WILDLIFE LODGES, page 182.

SAN FERNANDO DE APURE

An otherwise easily forgettable town, San Fernando, capital of Apure State, with a growing population of over 100,000, is nonetheless considered by many the heart of the Llanos. Most travelers to the region will pass through it, since its position on the Río Apure at an important cross-

roads makes it the key trading hub for this part of the *bajo llanos* (low plains). Mid-April sees San Fernando's greatest event, the week-long fair and agricultural exhibition. People gather from all around for rodeo-style *toros coleados* shows and cattle auctions, but also for the much-coveted prize for the best composer and singer of the rhyming couplet *contrapunto* songs. If you can make it to the Llanos at this time, you shouldn't miss this snapshot of plains' life.

GENERAL INFORMATION

The **Corporación Apureña de Turismo** ((047) 24827 FAX (047) 28309, Edificio Julio Chávez, Mezanina B, is to the south of the Monumento a los Llaneros, on Paseo Libertador, open office hours, Monday to Friday. For information about local *hatos* and better advice than at the tourist office, head to **Agencia de Viajes y Turismo Doña**

Bárbara ((047) 413463 FAX (047) 412235, Edificio Hotel La Torraca, Paseo Libertador.

WHAT TO SEE AND DO

San Fernando's sights will not detain you, but its **Plaza Bolívar** is still a typical shaded square where locals lounge, with its cathedral on the west side. The large Paseo Libertador is the town's main artery, six blocks east. At the northern end of the Paseo, by the bridge across the Apure, a large traffic-circle with a crocodile-motif fountain is a source of civic pride. Next to it stands the bronze statue of the **Monumento a Pedro Camejo**, the *Llanero* hero known popularly as *Negro Primero*, sitting astride a steed, lance in hand — he was first black person to gain recognition in the War of

Examples of the rich wildlife in Los Llanos: An anteater OPPOSITE lumbers across the plains, and an iguana ABOVE basks on a branch.

Los Llanos

Independence. Just across from the fountain, the once-elegant **Palacio Barbarito** harks back to San Fernando's glory days at the turn of the nineteenth century.

WHERE TO STAY

All hotels in San Fernando come with much-needed air-conditioning and offer acceptable, inexpensive accommodation.

The most becoming hotel is the **Gran Hotel Plaza (** (047) 414968 on Plaza Bolívar, rated with two stars, with views over the plaza from the top floors. The modern **Hotel Trinacría (** (047) 23578, Avenida Miranda, is handy for the bus terminal,

while the **Hotel La Torraca (** (047) 22777, Paseo Libertador two blocks from the fountain, has generous-sized rooms overlooking the center of town and is well managed. For a budget option, try the **Hotel Boulevard (** (047) 23122, Paseo Libertador, close to the Monumento a Los Llaneros.

WHERE TO EAT

Chunky steaks or *carne en vara* (skewered pieces of beef roasted over a wood fire) are the order of the day in restaurants throughout the Llanos. You also might encounter *chigüire* on the menu. Some good choices along the Paseo Libertador include **Europa**, opposite Hotel La Torraca, with friendly service and fresh dishes. Close by, **Gran Imperio Romano** is cheap, cheerful and popular with locals, as is **La Taberna de Don Juan** on Avenida 1 de Mayo, west of the Monumento a Los Llaneros.

HOW TO GET THERE

San Fernando's airport, Las Flecheras, some three kilometers (under a mile) east of town, has one flight per day to Caracas, Monday to Friday. The bus terminal is between the city and the river. On the whole, buses leave for distant destinations (San Cristóbal and Caracas) in the evenings to avoid the heat, but also service Maracay and Barinas. The route south towards Puerto Ayacucho crosses over various rivers, on ferries called *chalanas*.

CENTRAL AND WESTERN PLAINS

The central and western plains (north of the Río Apure) comprise the states of Guárico, Cojedes, Portuguesa and Barinas, all fertile agricultural and farming lands feeding this great river basin. The surviving forests are home to Venezuela's national bird — the troupial, and to resplendent macaws, curassows and the cacique bird whose distinctive nests hang from tree branches.

San Juan de los Morros, capital of Guárico State, is the northern gateway to the Llanos.

SAN CARLOS

Diminutive Cojedes State's capital is San Carlos de Austria, halfway between San Juan de los Morros and Guanare on Highway 5 — more a country road than a freeway at this point. Founded in 1678 by terrified Spaniards seeking refuge from the local Indians, Bolívar planned the decisive Battle of Carabobo (see AROUND VALENCIA, page 110) in San Carlos. A peaceful little town with a several lovely colonial churches, it makes a good break on any drive.

What to See and Do

On Plaza Bolívar are the **Iglesia de la Inmaculada Concepción**, San Carlos' oldest, and the **Iglesia de San Juan Bautista** with its ornate decoration dating back to the seventeenth and eighteenth centuries. **Iglesia de Santo Domingo** on Plaza Figueredo is the newest of the bunch but still charming. Opposite the Iglesia de San Juan, the **Casa de la Blanquera** is one of the prettiest restored houses of the colonial period you can hope to chance upon. It was here that Bolívar planned his battle, and you'll find a small museum of ceramics and colonial antiques inside, open Monday to Friday 8 AM to 6 PM, weekends 8 AM to 4 PM.

GUANARE

Portuguesa State is regarded as Venezuela's breadbasket. With a growing population of over 700,000, its capital Guanare holds an enviable position between the cities of central Venezuela and the

Andes. Portuguesa is an agricultural powerhouse, producing rice, maize, sorghum, beans, sugar cane and cotton, as well as boasting large dairy and sugar-processing industries. But Man cannot live from bread alone.

Guanare is more famously known as the country's spiritual capital. Close to city, the Virgin first appeared to the Cospes Indian chief Coromoto in 1652, urging him and his people to be baptized. In order to persuade him, she left the imprint of her image on a papyrus-like parchment. In his fear and confusion, he ignored her pleading. He fled up in to the mountains where he was promptly bitten by a snake. On his death bed, the Indian chief asked to be baptized, and urged his people to follow his example.

General Information

The state **tourism office** ((057) 510324 is found on Calle 17 No. 3-14, between carreras 3 and 4, and there is also a small booth at the bus terminal. Banco Unión is on Calle 16, just south of Plaza Bolívar. The largest pilgrimage in Guanare celebrates the appearance of the Virgin on September 8, 1652. February 2 is also regarded as an important date, commemorating transfer of the Virgin's image to the city itself. Guanare is renowned for its Carnival celebrations, involving a host of gigantic floats, costumes, masks and drums. It has grown into the largest bash in the country, drawing tens of thousands of visitors.

What to See and Do

The main attraction in Guanare is the neoclassic sanctuary of the Virgin, the **Basílica Catedral de Nuestra Señora de Coromoto**, erected between 1710 and 1742, virtually destroyed in 1782, reconstructed in 1807, and thoroughly restored in 1949 — after Pope Pius XII declared the Virgin Patron Saint of Venezuela. The church stands today with the aid of the commemorative plaques plastered to its walls.

Its *pièce de résistance* is the main, three-tiered altarpiece, a wonderfully exuberant piece of baroque art. Also worthy of note are the stained glass windows from Munich, and the solid silver tabernacle. Several statues of the Virgin adorn the

A young female deer, a common sight in the plains of the Llanos.

church, one with the original piece of parchment where her image appeared to Coromoto. It has to be viewed with a magnifying glass it's so small.

Adjacent to the cathedral, the fine façade of the **Convento de San Francisco** today forms part of the local university. The convent housed the first college in Venezuela from 1825 onwards, and its interior courtyard retains much of its former elegance. Across the street, the **Museo de la Ciudad de Guanare**, showcases photographs from the old days, pre-Columbian pottery and some antiques. Also worth investigating, the **Casacoima** mansion dates back to the eighteenth century, while a block north of Plaza Bolívar, the **Parque Los Samanes** makes for a pleasant stroll under the shade of these

great, wide trees. Bolívar camped here with his troops in 1813.

Where to Stay

On the outskirts of Guanare you'll find many inexpensive motels, of which the two best are **Motel Portuguesa** ((057) 531443 FAX (057) 513516, Avenida 23 de Enero at Avenida Simón Bolívar, with its own pool, restaurant, bar and comfortable rooms with air-conditioning, televisions and telephones, or further out on Avenida Circumvalación, **Motel La Sultana** ((057) 531723, whose rooms have Jacuzzis, satellite television and a restaurant attached.

Downtown, don't expect room service, though the **Posada de Reo** ((057) 510324, Carrera 3, gets my vote since it's improbably housed in what used to be the town's jail. Its interior and patio have been thoroughly remodeled, offering 30 air-

conditioned rooms with private bathrooms, but only cold water. A comic touch: the rooms have cell numbers and their keys are linked to plastic handcuffs.

How to Get There

Guanare's terminal is well-served by buses running along the highway. It's situated about a ten-minute drive southeast of the city center. Take a *por puesto* from Carrera 5.

Santuario de la Virgen de Coromoto

Although the shrine to Venezuela's Patron Saint still remains in the Basílica, a huge church designed by Venezuelan architect Erasmo Calvani now forms the center of attention for pilgrims from all over the country. Its high altar is said to be the exact place where the Virgin appeared to Coromoto the Indian chief, and plans exist to house the faded parchment here.

Small buses whiz back and forth to Guanare throughout the day, making a visit to the undeniably impressive sanctuary very straightforward. It's 25 km (15.5 miles) south of Guanare, first on the main road to Barinas, and then 15 km (nine miles) down another road.

The huge concrete, spiky-modern structure, known as the **Templo Votivo**, dominates the surrounding countryside, and its interior stained glasswork dazzles on sunny days. In the presence of 300,000 faithful, Pope John Paul II inaugurated the Templo, which took 20 years to complete, on his papal visit to Venezuela in 1996.

Barinas

Capital of Barinas State, the eponymous city of 225,000 thrives from both its natural riches and its privileged position on main trading routes. Although you wouldn't have thought it today, Barinas in the eighteenth century was Venezuela's second city after Caracas, home to wealthy landowning families and their mansions. The wars of independence later decimated the town, its fortunes only revived by the discovery of oil in late twentieth century.

For now, it has little to waylay the traveler in search of culture or nature. However, with some wonderful, intact forests and great rivers roaring down the mountains, its potential as an ecotourism destination will undoubtedly attract more attention in the future. For now, adventure tour operators from Mérida take travelers to the Río Bum Bum (honestly) to the west for their white-knuckle whitewater rafting trips, while trekkers crossing over the Andes enjoy some pristine cloudforest paths and campsites. Contact the Audubon in Caracas for more information (see TAKING A TOUR, page 52 in YOUR CHOICE).

General Information

The **Corbatur** main tourist office ✆ (073) 27091 FAX (073) 28162 is situated on Avenida Marqués del Pumar, by Plaza Bolívar; open Monday to Friday 8 AM to noon and 2 PM to 6 PM. They also have *módulos* (booths) at the airport and bus terminal, and give out detailed city maps. Useful banks are found near Plaza Bolívar or Plaza del Estudiante, east.

What to See and Do

Barinas's Plaza Bolívar still retains some colonial charm, dominated by the only church to survive the destruction of the wars, the **cathedral**, dedicated to La Virgen del Pilar in 1780.

the poetry of Arvelo, whose use of imagery is still captivating today. The museum lies on Calle 5 de Julio at Avenida Medina Jiménez, and is open Tuesday to Saturday, 9 AM to noon and 3 AM to 6 PM, Sunday from 9 AM to noon. Also on Medina Jiménez is the **Museo San Francisco de Asís**.

Where to Stay and Eat

Barinas offers a decent selection of inexpensive hotels. The top downtown one is **Hotel Internacional** ✆ (073) 21749, Calle Arzobispo Méndez (north of Plaza Bolívar on Plaza Zamora), which, though built in the 1950s, still represents good value, with air-conditioned rooms, a good restaurant-bar and off-street parking.

Across the large plaza, the grand **Palacio del Marqués del Pumar** monopolizes the entire block. In the eighteenth century it was the most elegant mansion in Barinas. It rivaled those of Caracas and was built by the Marqués de las Riberas de Boconó y Masparro, Don José del Pumar, who today would have trouble signing credit card slips.

Two more buildings stand on the square. On one side, the old town hall and prison now acts as the center of Barinas' cultural life, the **Casa de la Cultura**. The Casa hosts temporary art exhibitions and concerts. Over on the other side of the square, the beautifully restored home of the **Escuela de Música** was once the town's Masonic lodge.

Of the city's two museums, the **Museo Alberto Arvelo Torrealba** is the most interesting for its exhibits pertaining to *Llanero* culture, but also for

Back in the center, **Hotel Residencias El Marqués** ✆ (073) 26576, Avenida Medina Jiménez No. 2-88, is the next cheapest option to the Hotel Internacional, with the **Hotel Plaza** ✆ (073) 24918 another good choice on Calle Arzobispo Méndez, south of Plaza Bolívar.

Worth a special mention is the **Posada Rosa Elena** ✆ (014) 564-3723 WEB SITE http://members .xoom.com/reposada, Calle 13, west of Parque Moromoy — ask them for directions, or for a pickup downtown — which caters for the adventurous traveler in search of thrills, as well as to people keen to explore the Llanos in general. The owners, Vivian Blanco and Víctor Sánchez, organize hikes in the foothills of the Andes, kayaking down mountain rivers, fishing for peacock bass, or mountain bike and nature trips. Both Vivian

OPPOSITE: Dead or alive, *Llaneros* love their cattle. ABOVE: A cowboy poses with his friends.

and Víctor have worked in tourism for many years and know the area intimately.

How to Get There

Barinas' airport lies a short drive out on Avenida 23 de Enero, and has two flights daily to Caracas, but to no other cities. The bus terminal is about two kilometers (just over a mile) west of the old center. There are good bus connections to many cities.

If you're considering climbing up to the Andes, the drive from Barinas to Apartaderos and on to Mérida (see APARTADEROS TO BARINAS, page 166) is one of the most spectacular in the country. Rent a car from **Budget**, at the airport (/FAX (073)

26422 or downtown (/FAX (073) 335704, Avenida Cuatricentenaria.

HATOS AND WILDLIFE LODGES

The ranches consider the dry months, from December to May (approximately), as high season, and adjust their prices accordingly. Owing to the growing international fame of the Llanos, you will need to reserve your stay well in advance during these months of the year. Wily tourists book at the very end, or at the very beginning, of the rainy season to avoid the price hikes. Booking for early May, for instance, is probably your best bet if you want to save money and still get around.

All the more sophisticated places work on a package basis, typically three days and two nights. Tour operators, hotel chains and travel agents based in Caracas own or work with many of them. Quite a few boast air strips, allowing access year-round. While flying may sound like an extravagant proposal, many guests, after a five-hour dust choked, rump-numbing ride, have wished they'd spent those few extra dollars. Most of the *hatos* I mention here offer transfers to and from their ranches, at extra cost. Many organize local *Llanero* musicians to come and play for their guests, as well as laying on traditional food from the region.

The following descriptions of recommended *hatos* are divided by state (see ROUTES THROUGH LOS LLANOS, page 176, for details of roads).

COJEDES STATE

The granddaddy of *hatos*, established as a wildlife refuge as far back as the 1960s, **Hato El Piñero**, reservations through Bio Tours ((02) 992-4413 or (02) 992-4531 FAX (02) 993-6668 E-MAIL hato pinerovzla@telcel.net.ve, lies just south of El Baúl, on one of the most picturesque roads in the Llanos. Piñero is serious about its wildlife, with a huge inventory of animal species, as well as ongoing scientific investigations. But it's also a delightful *campamento*, with oodles of rustic, whitewashed charm and artistic touches in their 11 guest rooms, all with private bathrooms and fans. Their guides are bilingual and very experienced. They have an excellent reference library and can organize horse riding with advanced notice. Rates are expensive.

APURE STATE

Expensive

Hato El Frío (also known as Estación Biológica El Frío) ((014) 743-5329 or ((047) 81223 (in Achaguas) E-MAIL elfrio@cantv.net, about halfway between El Samán and El Frío, was the pioneering ranch in this part of the Llanos, located in the heart of an 80,000-hectare (197,600-acre) farm. The *hato* is renowned for its endangered Orinoco crocodile and anacondas breeding program, while fauna and avifauna scamper close to the lodgings. Their appealing rooms come with ceiling fans, private baths with cold water only, set around a central area with plenty of space to sling hammocks.

The onetime ranch of the Rockefeller family, the **Hato El Cedral** ((02) 781-8995 FAX (02) 793-6032 E-MAIL hatocedral@cantv.net WEB SITE www.hatocedral.com, Avenida La Salle, Edificio Pancho, Piso 5 PH, Los Caobos, Caracas, is another massive private mini-empire, south of La Ye on the road to Elorza. One of the best *hatos* in the country, Cedral outlawed hunting on its lands decades ago, and the wildlife, with capybara scattered on the road outside your window, won't let your expectations down. They recently reconditioned their old cabins, with the addition of 10 slightly more luxurious newer rooms, all with air-conditioning, ceiling fans, hot water, and attractive designs.

About two hours by river from Elorza, by the Río Arauco, **Hato Doña Bárbara** ((047) 413463 FAX (047) 412235 E-MAIL barbara@sfapure.c-com.net, not only boasts an amazing array of wildlife, but also a literary heritage. Rómulo Gallegos based his *Doña Bárbara* novel on Francisca Vásquez who lived here. The Estrada family own and manage this 360-sq-km (140-sq-mile) working ranch, offering 21 no-frills rooms all under one roof, with private baths and fans. They offer horseback riding, river and land trips, and special anaconda outings in the summer months.

Moderate

The **Capanaparo Lodge (Campamento Sorocaima)** ((047) 91037, on the banks of the Río Capanaparo in western Apure, is popular with anglers, but also offers attractive and comfortable lodgings for nature-lovers. In the dry season the camp is accessible from Elorza by road, at other times by boat. Or there's always their own landing strip. The French owners' eight

Expensive

One of the newest *hatos* in the Llanos, and one of the most impressive in the region, **Hato Centenario** ((073) 22338, reservations through Alpi Tour in Caracas ((02) 283-1433 FAX (02) 285-6067 FAX IN THE UNITED STATES (520) 447-7959 E-MAIL alpitour@viptel.com WEB SITE www.alpi-group.com is northeast of Puerto de Nutrias. Cabins are spacious and come with all the trimmings, while their restaurant and social area are equally appealing. The grounds have been beautifully landscaped and include a small artificial lake, where many birds

sophisticated cabins all have hot water, bathrooms and air-conditioning, while the grounds, social areas and swimming pool are all very inviting. They can arrange horse riding and excellent river trips.

Inexpensive

With privileged access to Parque Nacional Cinaruco-Capanaparo in southern Apure State, **Las Churuatas de Capanaparo**, reservations through ((02) 235-1287 or (02) 239-2019 (Floreal Matas) provides an excellent "authentic" Llanos experience. The accommodation is managed by friendly Edgar Rivero and includes seven *churuatas* with either beds or hammock space, all with private baths. There is no electricity, bar an emergency generator, but you can ride horses and take to canoes for excursions over the *galera* hills or down the Río Capanaparo.

gather, and a very pretty swimming pool. Among their excursions, which can be on horseback or truck, they offer skeet shooting, a first in the Llanos, to be sure.

Moderate

Southeast of Barinas, near the small town of La Luz, **Hato La Madera** ((073) 330696, offers another "authentic" Llanos experience on a working ranch. The owners provide hammocks or basic beds, with shared bathrooms and cold water, as well as good horse riding in the surrounding area of savanna and forest.

OPPOSITE: The radiating beams of a large *caney*. ABOVE: A cowboy herds his cattle on to the next pasture.

El Oriente

VENEZUELA'S EASTERN CARIBBEAN COAST, KNOWN AS "EL ORIENTE," stretches from east of Caracas to the tapered finger of the Península de Paria, at the country's eastern extreme. As its name should imply, it's both exotic and rich.

BARLOVENTO

Barlovento, meaning "windward," refers to the stretch of coast between Cabo Codera and the Laguna de Unare, centered on the inland villages of Birongo and Curiepe in western Miranda State. It also includes Chirimena, Caruao and Chuspa in Vargas State. The region is synonymous with black culture and folklore, combining elements of Catholicism with African voodoo and *santería* rituals.

This strong and remarkably robust culture stems from the glory days of Venezuela's cacao plantations: glorious for the *Gran Cacao* landowners, as they became known, miserable for the slaves from Central Africa who were shipped in to work the plantations. The first cacao plantation in Venezuela flourished in the valley of Curiepe, and though slavery was officially abolished by Bolívar in 1823, it wasn't until 1854 that slaves were truly emancipated.

These communities formed relatively isolated settlements and preserved their traditions, which survive today. According to anthropologists, the main African influence come from the Bantu, Yoruba (from Nigeria) and Mandingo peoples of Africa.

At the festival for San Juan (St. John the Baptist), on June 23 and 24, the towns of Barlovento spring from their sleepy states for a veritable baptism by beat. The *tambor* drums of Barlovento are renowned, pounding relentlessly all day and all night, while the locals dance their sensual, slinky moves, fueled by firewater and rum.

WHAT TO SEE AND DO

The town of **Curiepe** probably hosts the largest celebrations for San Juan (June 23 and 24) and San Pedro (June 27 to 29). **Birongo**, also up in the hills above the coast, is known as the center of the *brujería* — magic or voodoo in Barlovento (see also LITORAL CENTRAL, page 87).

The **Monumento Natural Cueva Alfred Jahn**, reached by dirt track from Curiepe, is one of Venezuela's largest caves at over four kilometers (two and a half miles) long. From the track, there are numerous entry points to the seldom-visited, bat-festooned internal galleries. The best beaches in Barlovento are **Puerto Francés** and **Caracolito**, as well as Isla de Buche, connected by *por puestos* that leave from the Nuevo Terminal at the Carenero boat terminal, north of Higuerote.

PARQUE NACIONAL LAGUNA DE TACARIGUA

Although seldom touted by tour operators, nor particularly well-known outside Venezuela, Tacarigua Lagoon is a delight. The park, established in 1974, became one of Venezuela's Ramsar sites — noted for its exceptional wetland habitat — in 1997. It protects an important and increasingly threatened coastal mangrove ecosystem, home to the endangered coastal crocodile and thousands of migrant and resident birds.

The lagoon itself is 30 km (19 miles) long and six kilometers (just under four miles) wide,

hemmed by the rivers Cúpira and El Guapo. Its vegetation is dominated by species of mangrove, including the rarer button mangrove. But perhaps the biggest attraction of all is the avian air show performed every morning and evening. The lagoon is also rich in fish, with the communities relying on its mullet, bass, skate and shad. Fishermen can sport-fish tarpon and snook using a line with a permit from Inparques.

GENERAL INFORMATION

Boatmen organize tours around the lagoon. They typically take an hour, but can be extended by negotiation. Quite a few tour operators cluster in the part of Tacarigua de la Laguna known as Sector Belén, on the right as you approach the town from Río Chico. Remegio, of **Remegio's**

Laguna Tours ((034) 711142 FAX (034) 74579, on the second road on the right after the turn, is a toothless, cheery man whose tours include insurance, permits and many years' experience. He offers short trips, day trips and sport-fishing excursions. You can also contract a boatman at the *muelle* dock, where Inparques has its office. Officially, photography is not allowed, so stash your camera. Using a high-speed film in the evening will give the best results.

WHERE TO STAY AND EAT

Although it sounds enticing, and its location should spell "ideal hideaway," the inexpensive

HOW TO GET THERE

If you've come from Higuerote, take the turn east at Mamporal which leads round to Río Chico. From there it's 12 km (7.5 miles) to Tacarigua de la Laguna. From Highway 9, take the northern route at the misnomer-of-a-town, El Guapo (The Handsome), 24 km (15 miles) south of Río Chico. Fairly frequent buses link all these towns.

EAST TO BARCELONA

Sixty-two kilometers (38 miles) east of El Guapo on the Oriente's Highway 9, you enter

Club Miami, contact through EcoPosadas ((02) 993-5866 (in Caracas) FAX (02) 992-8984, is disappointing. Its location is superb on the never-ending beach on the coast, but the establishment has suffered neglect over the years. You can check with the operators on the current state of the rooms and restaurant, volleyball court and social area, if you're determined to stay "in" the lagoon.

In the small, rather unprepossessing town of Tacarigua de la Laguna, the best option from quite a few is the recent **Posada La Garza** (no phone), Calle Principal, with two doubles with air-conditioning and cold water, as well as two other rooms with fans. The *posada* is painted in bright and breezy colors, with many artistic touches, from wooden framed mirrors to attractive tables, chairs and bar area. Rates are inexpensive.

the Venezuelan state that foreigners have most trouble pronouncing: Anzoátegui ("anzwo-A-teguee"). It was named after General José Antonio Anzoátegui, hero of the battle of Boyacá and the War of Independence. Its capital lies further along in Barcelona, but here the coast road affords great views of the **Laguna de Unare**, another coastal lagoon famed for its birdlife, before heading inland towards **Clarines**.

If you have time, consider looping round the lagoon via El Hatillo. Catch a great meal, or spend the night at the excellent **Posada Sol, Luna y Estrellas** ((016) 610-9257 or (014) 208-5595, in the village of Marylargo, about eight kilometers (five miles) from **Boca de Uchire**.

The wetland world of Laguna de Tacarigua.

CLARINES

The **Iglesia de San Antonio de Padua**, built in 1760 and one of the prettiest restored churches in the country, is the main reason for stopping here. If you're traveling around June 14 to 15, don't miss the town's *fiesta patronal* for San Antonio, with their colorful street processions and religious services. Several old houses and buildings around the church have been restored, including the **Casa del Sol**.

PÍRITU AND PUERTO PÍRITU

Along with Clarines' church, the Franciscan **Iglesia Nuestra Señora de la Concepción** above Píritu is delightful. Built in the eighteenth century, its massive, whitewashed, sun-blanched walls cannot be missed as you approach the town from the west. The town of Píritu lies below, with the old port of Puerto Píritu by the sea. On a drive east from Caracas, the towns are ritual stopping points for Venezuelans. Along the beachfront boulevard, there are several restaurants serving delicious fresh fish, notably **Sol y Brisa**.

The islands off Píritu, **Isletas de Píritu**, are a short hop across on a boat. During the week they are wonderfully quiet, with good snorkeling on the northern shores. Also, ask in town for directions to **El Viejo Píritu**, a reconstructed nineteenth-century village similar to Venezuela de Antier and Los Aleros in Mérida State, though on a smaller scale.

How to Get There

Buses from Caracas will drop passengers off at the El Tejar gas station on the western outskirts of town, on their way to Puerto La Cruz or Cumaná, and the same applies coming the other way. They will charge you the full fare however. The other option is to hop along by *por puesto*.

BARCELONA

Poor Barcelona. You have to feel sorry for the place. Its younger upstart neighbor Puerto La Cruz virtually swallows it up whole, forever expanding westwards along the highway and the coast. It still clings on to its status as capital, but everyone knows all the smart money lies in the refineries, highrises and marinas of the El Morro development and Puerto La Cruz.

But pity it not. Barcelona stands on its own two feet, its historical heart and heritage acting as a welcome counterweight to its boisterous, culture-less neighbor. Founded by Catalans in 1671, Barcelona can be compared to its European namesake: the tropical old quarter around Plaza Boyacá is the Mediterranean city's museum-stuffed

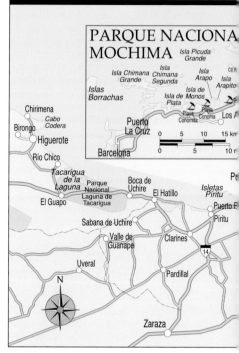

Montjuïc district, while Paseo Colón in Puerto La Cruz is without doubt the Caribbean's answer to Las Ramblas.

GENERAL INFORMATION

For tourist maps of both the city of Puerto La Cruz and for Anzoátegui State, head to the tourist office, **Coranztur (** (081) 741142 or (081) 743646, on the ground floor of the bizarre, pyramid-shaped Gobernación building, Avenida 5 de Julio (north), or the **Dirección de Cultura y Turismo (** (081) 742978, by Plaza Boyacá, who have more information on cultural events. Offices are open Monday to Friday, 8 AM to noon and 2 PM to 5 PM.

Change cash and travelers checks in Puerto La Cruz. Banco Unión advances cash on Visa and MasterCard, Avenida 5 de Julio, south of Plaza Boyacá.

WHAT TO SEE AND DO

Barcelona is a tale of four plazas — Boyacá, Miranda, Rolando and Bolívar — and two avenues — 5 de Julio and Fuerzas Armadas, both north–south. You need look no further than these. Like its Catalan counterpart, Barcelona likes to be different. Its most important square is **Plaza Boyacá**, three blocks west of the banks of the Río Neverí. The square is the city's historic heart.

On the plaza's west side stands the **cathedral**, built between 1748 and 1783 and housing an

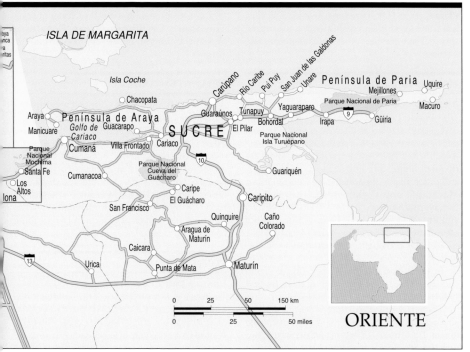

ISLA DE MARGARITA

ORIENTE

extravagant gilded altar screen. Across from the cathedral, the **Palacio Municipal** occupies an elegant building dating from 1858.

The **Museo de la Tradición** lies on the square's south side. The restored old house is said to be the fourth built in the town in 1671. It survived various incarnations as a private house, a club, and a maternity hospital. Its present incarnation is didactic, showcasing the city's history. The museum is open Tuesday to Friday, 8 AM to noon and 2 PM to 5 PM, weekends 9 AM to 3 PM.

The **Ateneo de Barcelona**, two blocks east on Calle Juncal, acts as an extension of the historical museum. This beautifully restored colonial mansion, donated by the family of the novelist Miguel Otero Silva (1908–1980), houses a collection of more contemporary paintings by Venezuelan artists.

From the Ateneo, walk north one block to the **Gunda Arte Popular**, a great crafts shop jam-packed with wares from all over the country, but also another great colonial mansion worth admiring. Walk over the old colonial bridge east to get to the ruins of the **Templo de San Felipe de Neverí**. The church, erected in 1768, was devastated, like so much of Venezuela, by the earthquake of 1812.

Back on the west side, the Plaza Rolando attests to Barcelona's wealth in the nineteenth century. It is named after the statesman who built both the **Iglesia del Carmen** and the delightful **Teatro Cajigual**. The 300-seat theater is pretty active — try to catch a concert when you visit.

The ruins of the **Casa Fuerte** occupy the western side of the royal palm-shaded **Plaza Bolívar**, with plazas Miranda and Tricentenaria nearby. In 1817, Royalist troops massacred 1,500 soldiers and civilians who had taken refuge within its walls. The ruins were left to commemorate the tragedy.

WHERE TO STAY AND EAT

If you're looking for comfort, style or modernity, head to El Morro or Puerto La Cruz (see below). Barcelona's hotels are older, and therefore less expensive, with the cheapies just about justifying their Old World charm.

Of the central hotels, the inexpensive **Hotel Oviana** ((081) 761671, Avenida Caracas near Avenida Country Club, boasts the town's best air-conditioned rooms. That's not saying a lot, but its restaurant, with Italian specials, is recommended. The other option, with slightly cheaper prices, is the **Hotel Neverí** ((081) 772376, Avenida Fuerzas Armadas at Avenida Miranda. The hotel overlooks the river and the old bridge, so if you can get one of the rooms with a view it's pleasant enough. The avenue below, however, is noisy.

The budget, charm-over-comfort option, **Hotel Plaza** ((081) 772843, looks out over Plaza Boyacá. The best basic rooms overlook the plaza — good for the price. Not all of them have private baths, so ask for those which do.

Apart from the restaurants of the hotels Neverí and Oviana, try **El Castillo de Oriente**, Avenida

Miranda, for traditional *parillas*. The **Restaurant Piazza**, next to Hotel Barcelona, Avenida 5 de Julio, has some good Italian dishes with a nice atmosphere. There are many other places along the same avenue.

HOW TO GET THERE

Barcelona shares its newish international airport with Puerto La Cruz. It lies about ten minutes' drive south of town, to the west as you approach on Highway 9. *Por puestos* run back and forth along Avenida 5 de Julio, and a taxi is cheap. There are frequent flights throughout the day to Caracas, and other major cities, including Puerto Ordaz, Maracaibo and Porlamar. Airlines include **Servivensa/Avensa (** (081) 671301 to (081) 671305 and **Rutaca (** (081) 675681. The experienced pilot Steve Patterson of **Servicios Aereos (** (081) 653371 coordinates personalized air charters to all corners of Venezuela.

In the national terminal, several car rental companies vie for custom, among them **Budget (** (081) 771325 TOLL-FREE (800) 28343.

The bus terminal is situated by the market, southeast of the city center, a short hop in a *buseta* or taxi. The terminal in Puerto La Cruz is far better served, with more long-distance buses departing from there, but you can still connect to plenty of cities from Barcelona. The fastest way to Puerto La Cruz is on a *por puesto* from the southern end of Avenida 5 de Julio, around Carrera 7. Buses also leave from the terminal for the short journey.

EL MORRO

Venezuela's most ambitious tourist development, the Complejo Turístico El Morro comprises a vast network of canals, marinas, residential homes, vacation resorts, golf courses, and shopping centers. It lies between Barcelona and Puerto La Cruz. Outside of Margarita, the resorts of El Morro offer the most luxurious accommodation and facilities you could hope to find on Venezuela's Caribbean.

GENERAL INFORMATION

For yachties, the **Centro Marino de Oriente (** (081) 677011 FAX (081) 678550 E-MAIL cmoplc2@telcel .net.ve, Avenida Tajamar No. 8 (on the north east side), offers the most modern facilities of the three marinas in El Morro. The **Marina Bahía Redonda (** (081) 677412 FAX (081) 677810 E-MAIL info @bahiaredonda.com.ve WEB SITE www.bahia redonda.com.ve, Avenida Tajamar No. 1, is more attractive, with restaurants and condominium property.

Dockside (/FAX (081) 677344 E-MAIL dockside @telcel.net.ve, Marina Bahía Redonda, are a very organized local tour, travel and yacht agents,

within the marina. They can arrange yacht charters, as well as dealing with all yachting queries. The **South Caribbean Ocean Regatta** is Venezuela's largest, held every year, usually in August.

WHAT TO SEE AND DO

Apart from living the high life in the complex's numerous bars and restaurants, El Morro and Lecherías provide the best bathing beaches for Puerto La Cruz and Barcelona. Along the northwestern coastline, **Playas Los Cocales**, **Lecherías** and **Mansa**, all enjoy cleaner waters than in Puerto La Cruz, with rows of restaurants and snack bars lining them. Head to the **Mirador**, on the eastern road which climbs the hill, for fabulous views in the evenings, with great sunsets and a refreshing cool breeze.

WHERE TO STAY

Luxury and Expensive

The touch gaudy pink villas of the **Golden Rainbow Maremares Resort (** (081) 811011 FAX (081) 813028 IN CARACAS (02) 959-0148 FAX (081) 959-0172, Avenida Américo Vespucio, announce this expansive canal-side complex set in acres of beautifully tended gardens. The resort boasts 300 rooms, the first in El Morro of its size and caliber. It encompasses a nine-hole golf course, marina, spa, tennis courts, a day-care center, and a pool the size of Iceland. It oozes five-star luxury from every tropical plant-potted pore — guests ride in golf carts it's so big.

The next mega-resort, the **Hotel Doral Beach Villas (** (081) 813252 WEB SITE www.corpl.com.ve, Avenida Amerigo Vespucio, claims to be South America's largest hotel. The complex includes over 1,000 doubles, suites, villas and apartments. It's somewhat dwarfing, with an embarrassment of pools, tennis courts, gyms, water sports and activities laid on. It took me nearly an hour to survey — just as well I had *eight* restaurants to chose from to recharge my batteries. The rooms are large, airy and comfortable, with absolutely all the trimmings of a five-star hotel *"de pimera"* (first class). I came away very impressed.

At the foot of the Morro isthmus, with 180 rooms, half of which have fantastic views of the Pozuelos bay, lies the sophisticated **Hotel Punta Palma (** (081) 811413 FAX (081) 818277. The decor is stylish yet understated, with big, bold colors predominating throughout, while the rooms are all satisfyingly comfortable. The pool, bar and restaurant area on the ground floor is all beautifully laid-out, with plenty of elegant palms and lounge chairs dotted about the place. The complex includes tennis courts, and its own marina for mooring yachts.

Further up on the Morro peninsula, you might find the **Hotel Vista Real**. I only mention it since it was the worst "luxury" hotel I visited while researching this guide. I felt sorry for the staff who had to work there.

Moderate

Above the former Gran Cacique terminal, you'll find the convenient **Hotel El Marino** ((081) 692463, which has 18 clean and decent doubles. This is a good place if you need to spend the night before catching a ferry, or if you arrive late.

WHERE TO EAT

Moderate

Within the Maremares resort, their restaurant **Al Fresco** ((081) 811011 (open evenings only) enjoys a great setting overlooking the marina and the pool, with top Italian cooking accompanied by a tinkling piano and excellent service. Close to the Plaza Mayor, the **Puerto Grill Steak House** ((081) 868069, Calle Arismendi at Calle Las Peñas, serves probably the best T-bone steaks and juicy meats in the whole area. The atmosphere is quietly classy, with eye-catching design and live music on the weekends. For seafood with a twist, head to **Sushi Chef Japanese Restaurant** ((081) 862424, Avenida Principal de Lecherías, in the main drag of shops, hotels and restaurants, which presents first-class sushi to rival any of Caracas's establishments, along with attentive and friendly service.

Inexpensive

Within the Plaza Mayor complex, the **Albatros Café** ((081) 813532 enjoys a prime position on the banks of a canal, with stylish decor, and a clientele and menu to match. Open in the evenings only, with live music Tuesday to Saturday (closed Monday), **La Churuata del Morro**, Via Principal del Morro, on Playa Cangrejo, is by far the best restaurant of the many in the area — great seafood in an even better seafront setting.

PUERTO LA CRUZ

After the old colonial quarter of historic Barcelona, Puerto La Cruz is positively brash in its modernity. It boasts probably the greatest concentration of hotels, restaurants, discotheques and bars of any other city or town in Venezuela. After Porlamar, Puerto La Cruz is Venezuela's next hottest destination for international tourism. It provides not only first-class accommodation and facilities, but also the springboard for the island wonders of Parque Nacional Mochima off the coast. Combine the growth of tourism, the huge oil refineries to the east, and Anzoátegui State's wealth in general, and it comes as little surprise that Puerto La Cruz is a-boomin'.

The town may not be a culture-vulture's first port of call, but it's certainly a night-bird's playground. If you're in search of tropical color to chase those winter blues, you need look no further than Puerto La Cruz.

GENERAL INFORMATION

You'll find the **Coranztur** tourism office ((081) 688170 in the middle of the Paseo Colón, open from 8 AM through to 9 PM. They provide maps of the town and Mochima National Park. *Boulevard* is a free newspaper with a good guide to what's happening where. All the major banks are represented in Puerto La Cruz, and the larger hotels

(Rasil, Gaeta and Riviera) have *casas de cambio*, though some charge commission on travelers' checks.

There is an cybercafé on the first floor of the Cristoforo Colombo shopping mall on Paseo Colón, next to MacDonald's. There are also several international consulates in Puerto La Cruz, so check with the tourist office if you have any problems.

WHAT TO SEE AND DO

The town's heart beats loudest along the **Paseo Colón**, the palm-fringed seafront boulevard which lies between two "poles": the Hotels Rasil and Hesperia (ex-Melia). The Paseo buzzes day and night with bars, cars, hawkers, tour-touts, karaoke choruses, cafés, restaurants, and tourists. In this part of the Caribbean, every night feels like a party, though weekends and holidays are particularly boisterous.

Though the beach may look tempting by day, the waters are unfortunately polluted. For the closest dip in the sea, head to the beaches of El Morro (see WHAT TO SEE AND DO, page 190 under EL MORRO), or make the bouncy journey on an

Pleasure boats moored at Playa Santa Cruz.

outboard-powered launch to the islands of Mochima (see PARQUE NACIONAL MOCHIMA, page 192).

The town's biggest celebrations take place on the September 8: **Virgen del Valle**. Hundreds of boats take to the water, draped in palms and festooned with balloons. Parties kick off just about anywhere, with a deafening fireworks display at around midnight. Also worth catching, the celebrations for *Cruz de Mayo* on May 3 center on the cross on Paseo Colón, with processions converging from various parishes around the area. The particular strand of *contrapunto* music called *galerón* gets the singing and dancing going, and the vigil lasts all night.

SPORTS AND OUTDOOR ACTIVITIES

Puerto La Cruz, with its marinas, access to Mochima's westerly islands, tour operators, dive shops and yacht charters make it an ideal place for some marine fun.

Yachting
Dockside (/FAX (081) 677344 E-MAIL dockside@ telcel.net.ve, Marina Bahía Redonda, are a very organized local tour, travel and yacht agents, within the marina. They can arrange a varied program of yacht charters to Mochima, but also to islands further afield such as Los Roques and Las Aves. A recommended company for sailing charters, **Nelson & Nelson** ((081) 778232 or (014) 802232, run by Nelson Lozada in the Américo Vespucio Marina, coordinate tours to Mochima, and further afield.

Boat Trips in Mochima
If you want more personalized attention than simply being dropped off on a beach by the boatmen of the cooperative, Puerto La Cruz boasts a plethora of tour operators just waiting to take you out to the Mochima islands and beyond. These trips can be molded to your desire. Whether you want to stay on one beach all day, whiz about from one island to the next, or snorkel here and scuba dive there, they offer you the flexibility, at a price. Competition between the operators is fierce, and haggling prices par for the course. Many of the operators are of Italian descent and drive a hard bargain. You can ask for a package to include food and drinks as well as rental of masks, snorkels and fins.

RasiTours ((081) 811295 FAX (081) 812863 WEB SITE www.rasitour.com, run by the amiable Max Mazzuka, is right out at the western end of El Morro, in the Marina Américo Vespucio. Max has many years' experience bringing people around Mochima, and specializes in boat trips (by yacht or powerboat) to the remote Las Aves and Las Tortugas islands.

Macite Turismo ((081) 657020 FAX (081) 656321 E-MAIL macite-turismo@eldish.net WEB SITE www.acconet.com/macite is managed by enterprising polyglot Italians on Paseo Colón. They are recommended for both local tours and trips further afield.

Many of the higher-priced hotels and resorts of Puerto La Cruz and El Morro work with their own tour operators and can often arrange tours for you directly. These can be good value, but you should still shop around.

Scuba Diving
The diving in Mochima might not attain the awesome level of Los Roques, but it still offers some first-class dives and represents a good, more economical alternative. Probably more economical — and superior — diving can be arranged in the town of Santa Fe, on the road east to Cumaná (see SANTA FE, page 196).

Possibly the most reputable company in Puerto La Cruz is the **Scuba Divers Club** (/FAX (081) 635401, which isn't a club but a tour operator, based in the Bahía Redonda Marina, Avenida Tajamar, to the east of El Morro. **Lolo's Diving Center** ((081) 673963 E-MAIL pedro@ govenezuela.com WEB SITE www.govenezuela .com, run by Pedro Rodríguez, just before the Hesperia, on your left in the Guanta marina, also claims many years' experience. Both of these offer international diving certificates; they also fill tanks and take divers to the best sites.

Explosub ((081) 653611 FAX (081) 673256 E-MAIL explosub@eldish.net, situated in the gardens of the Gran Hotel Hesperia, also enjoys a good reputation, but is more expensive than the other two.

WHERE TO STAY

Hotels in Puerto La Cruz run the whole gamut. Some change their prices according to season and often get very busy. Make reservations in advance if you can. All rooms mentioned below come with air-conditioning, and light-sleepers should avoid the noisy Paseo Colón, especially on weekends and during festival times.

Expensive
Puerto La Cruz's first five-star development is the **Hesperia Puerto La Cruz** ((081) 653611 FAX (081) 653711 E-MAIL banquetes@hotmail.com WEB SITE www.hoteles-hesperia.es. The hotel's 220 luxury rooms, all with sea views, are undergoing extensive refurbishment, and if they emerge anything like the Hesperia in Cumaná, this will be an excellent option.

Moderate
Four blocks back from the Paseo, on Calle Freites at Honduras, the good-value **Caribbean Inn** ((081)

674292 FAX (081) 672857 has 102 large and comfortable rooms, and the bonus of a relaxing terrace and pool area. The best choice for a quiet night, and professionally run.

The are two three-star hotels on the Paseo Colón, where you pay for the location. Both are about the same in standard and price, though the **Gaeta** ((081) 651211 FAX (081) 650065 is slightly newer. The other is the **Hotel Riviera** ((081) 672111 FAX (081) 651394, with 74 rooms. Ask for a room with a sea-view balcony.

Inexpensive

The best option in this class is undoubtedly the popular **Hotel Neptuno** ((081) 685413

French and Caribbean dishes, with novelties such as salmon in lemon-and-caramel sauce. The romantic, candlelit atmosphere, washed over with blues and jazz, accompanies a well-stocked wine list. By the traffic circle at the Hesperia end of the Paseo, the smart **Porto Vecchio** ((081) 652047, Paseo Colón, presents a very reasonably priced and extensive menu within a sophisticated, low-light atmosphere, matched by very attentive service. Meat-lovers should head to the **Brasero Grill** ((081) 688655, Paseo Colón. It's the most appealing restaurant of the many in town for chunky steaks, with prompt service and a piano tinkling away until the early hours.

FAX (081) 653261, on Paseo Colón at Juncal, which includes 30 plain but clean rooms on five floors, with a good restaurant on the third floor. Up the block, on Plaza Bolívar, the **Hotel Europa** ((081) 688157 has decent, no-frills doubles.

WHERE TO EAT

Seafood is abundant in Puerto La Cruz — though it isn't as cheap as perhaps it should be. You'll find a range of restaurants serving international as well as local dishes, and you can always head over to El Morro if you exhaust these (see WHERE TO EAT, page 191 under EL MORRO).

Moderate

The French-run **Chic e Choc** ((081) 622551, Paseo Colón, offers a refined menu mixing

Inexpensive

The third-floor restaurant of the **Hotel Neptuno** ((081) 650993, Paseo Colón, offers a varied menu and a terrace looking onto the sea — unpretentious but tasty. **El Rincón del Bucanero** ((081) 670765, on Plaza Bolívar, serves up excellent fish, with paella as a special, in a nautical-style interior. Also friendly, with a more lively *tasca* and bar attached, **La Barraca** ((081) 653463, Calle Bolívar, offers tasty, no-nonsense Venezuelan dishes.

For the best Arab coffee and sweets in town, visit the **Dulcería Arabe** on the Paseo. The open-all-hours **Piccolo Caffe**, also on the Paseo, will save you in an emergency. I would only recommend the beachside terrace establishments for drinking, not eating. Beware the karaoke nights.

Water sports are a popular activity in Mochima.

El Oriente

NIGHTLIFE

Puerto La Cruz rivals Porlamar for vibrant night-life. You can choose between casinos, piano bars, salsa clubs or techno discotheques.

Of the quieter places, just right for an evening cocktail, **La Boite de Brasero** ((081) 688655, Paseo Colón, west of the Hesperia, makes a good choice, while the best place to hear some Cuban son, and local salsa — or even show off the moves you learned at salsa classes — has to be **Club 12&23** ((081) 668803, Avenida 5 de Julio, between Calles Carabobo and Flores. For a vibrant, younger scene with louder music, **Harry's Bar** ((081) 653605, Calle Bolívar, gets very lively on weekends.

If you want to enjoy some blackjack, roulette, or simply throw your money away, two casinos in Puerto La Cruz provide the means. The better of the two is **Star 33** ((081) 652222, Avenida Alberto Ravel, between Calles Carabobo and Flores, with complimentary drinks for players and live music.

HOW TO GET THERE

Puerto La Cruz shares its airport with Barcelona (see HOW TO GET THERE, page 190 in BARCELONA).

The **Conferry** ((081) 677221 terminal lies beyond the Paseo Colón towards El Morro. Ferries take passengers across to Margarita in four and a half hours. Buy your ticket in advance on weekends and during peak holiday times — the lines are often enormous.

The bus terminal is situated three blocks back from Plaza Bolívar on Calle Juncal. Apart from major city connections, **Línea Caribe** ((086) 519248 or (086) 518669 travels all the way down to Boa Vista in Brazil, via Puerto Ordaz and Santa Elena de Uairén. **Aeroexpresos Ejecutivos** ((081) 67885 or (081) 67955 is the most comfortable, direct service to Caracas. Note that their buses leave from the Conferry terminal, not the city terminal.

PARQUE NACIONAL MOCHIMA

Mochima extends over 950 sq km (370 sq miles), straddling Anzoátegui and Sucre states between the towns of Puerto La Cruz and Cumaná. In addition to dozens of islands, it also encompasses part of the coast, its turquoise and azure waters earning the sobriquet *La Costa Azul* (The Blue Coast).

Along the coast, mountains covered in cactus and broom tumble down to bays where palms sway and waves lap the shores. Out to sea, the islands' barren, dust-gray hills contrast with deep blues and aquamarines. Even the beaches differ: some brilliant, Colgate-white like Isla de Plata, others red-tinted like the famous Playa Colorada. With nearly two dozen of them to choose from, finding a secluded spot under a palm tree to be lulled by the sound of the sea couldn't be easier. Bring a hammock, sit back, and admire frigate birds fishing for their dinners before you head to a beachfront restaurant for yours.

Snorkeling and scuba diving opportunities are plentiful. Several shipwrecks, bubbling underwater thermal springs, caves, and healthy reefs await exploration. The waters are colder than you might expect, and visibility clearest between July and November.

For the islands and beaches near Puerto La Cruz, see below. For locations further east, along the coastal Highway 9, see PUERTO LA CRUZ TO SANTA FE, below, and SANTA FE, page 196, and subsequent sections.

WHAT TO SEE AND DO

The island groups of Borrachas and Chimanas lie closest to Puerto La Cruz. These encompass **Playa de Guaro**, on the west side of La Borracha, and **Puinare** and **El Saco** — the latter with a good restaurant — on Chimana Grande. **El Faro**, on Chimana Segunda, is less crowded than El Saco.

Further east, near the coast, **Isla de Plata** boasts whiter-than-white sand and crystal waters. Continuing east, come the less-visited, smaller beaches of **Conomita** and **Conoma**, and **Isla de Monos** and **La Cleta**. All of these are quieter than their westerly counterparts, with more opportunity for peace and shade.

HOW TO GET THERE

Shuttle boats to the western islands of Mochima depart from the Paseo Colón, next to El Rancho del Tío restaurant (opposite Hotel Gaeta). The cooperative is called **Transporte Transtupaco** ((081) 679093, and boats leave regularly from around 8 AM until 2 PM, returning in the afternoon at 4 or 5 PM. The boats usually carry up to 12 passengers, and prices are determined by the distance to the islands you want to visit. At peak times, the lines at the pier can get long, so the earlier you're in line, the better.

For the swiftest and most economical access to Isla de Plata and the easterly beaches, take a *por puesto* from the Puerto La Cruz's Plaza Bolívar to the hamlet of **Pamatacualito** along the coast. If you don't have your own transportation, it's probably worth paying more at Puerto La Cruz than going through the hassle of catching *por puestos*.

PUERTO LA CRUZ TO SANTA FE

Highway 9 to Cumaná is the best coastal road in the country. Along its sinuous route, steep hills slink down to the sea, with each curve affording glimpses of idyllic horseshoe bays, turquoise waters and distant olive-green islands. Rent a car and stop to snap photos.

On a cautionary note, this highway is as treacherous as it is beautiful. Don't take any bend for granted, particularly during or after heavy rain, and avoid driving at night. Venezuelans drink and drive conspicuously — particularly if they've been at the beach all day. Regular *por puestos* also run this route — ask them to stop wherever you want.

LOS ALTOS DE SANTA FE

Seventeen kilometers (10 miles) east of Puerto La Cruz you come to the turnoff to Los Altos de Santa Fe, a small village at 900 m (2,952 ft) above sea

metal railings: this is **Mochima Lodge** ((014) 800-4298 (014) 236-0809 FAX (014) 804-5010 E-MAIL eljurih@telcel.net.ve WEB SITE www.lrs.com.ve/campamento, the newest moderately priced *posada* on this coast, and stunning to say the least.

The owner, Hely Eljuri, has built six rooms with sea views slap-bang in front of the Arapito islands. The rooms are large and spacious, with wooden beams, cane roofs and plenty of artwork on the walls. Each has kitchen facilities and sliding French windows giving on to small balconies. A large living and eating area completes the rustic yet sophisticated atmosphere. Hely is reluctant to take in passing trade and would rather guests opted for his two-night package, which includes all

level. It marks the division between Anzoátegui and Sucre states.

The road to the village switches back and forth up steep gradients, but your efforts will be rewarded with sweeping views of the western islands of Mochima. The best *mirador* (viewpoint) lies on the left just before the village, announced by a sign for a "Complejo Turístico" and some arches. On the first curve of this paved road, by a blue house, you'll see the Arapo and Arapito islands, with the impossibly turquoise La Piscina between them.

PLAYA EL HORNO

Back down on the coastal Highway 9, before you get to Playa Arapito, note the Coca Cola sign for Playa El Horno. Although the beach is tiny, just before this sign you'll see a house with black

meals and soft drinks and trips to nearby islands in his boat. Calling in advance is essential.

PLAYA COLORADA

One of Venezuela's most famous beaches, Colorada arcs in a beautiful horseshoe bay, cupped by tumbling hills. Its sand, from whence the name, is tinted pinky-red. Palms provide shade all along its beach, while small stalls and a restaurant keep the beach-goers from starvation.

During vacations this beach positively heaves: it lies right on the highway. At these times, look for a boat to take you across to the Arapito islands, or anywhere away from the crowds, stereos, barbecues and hawkers. During the week, the beach is relatively quiet, though still busier than most.

The swooping arc of colored sand at Playa Colorada.

PLAYA SANTA CRUZ

Winding your way along the road, you'll come to Playa Santa Cruz in its bay. Although the beach is thin and narrow it's often very quiet, with a few fishing boats nodding in the bay.

Just after the bay, on the next bend, a sign announces the inexpensive **Villa La Encantada** (ex-Chez Frédérique y María) ((014) 818-2330 WEB SITE http://members.tripod.com/villa _la_encantada.com, acquired in 1999 by Diane Wilson, an expatriate from the United States. She gave up her job accounting in Caracas to pursue her dream on the Costa Azul. The very good value

posada commands fine views of the Santa Cruz bay. Above a large pool area, 12 simple and charming rooms with hot water and fans nestle into the hillside gardens, painted lizard motifs adding an imaginative touch to the decorations. Diane's restaurant serves two meals or more a day, and she can organize boat trips.

SANTA FE

Around the last bend coming from Santa Cruz, the wide horizons of the Golfo de Santa Fe open up before you, wreathed by the mountains of the Cerro Aceite Castillo. You come down the hill to the next town on Highway 9, the unprepossessing town of Santa Fe. Appearances, however, can be deceptive.

I agree with the backpacker who described the town as "a dump" — but the beach is another

matter. It's not large or particularly beautiful, but somehow the adage "came for two days, stayed for a week" applies to Santa Fe. Old and new *posadas* have joined forces to clean the beach every day, making it one of the most impeccable in Venezuela. You'll find good value restaurants and a range of small, personalized establishments. After some time watching the dolphins dance in the bay, snorkeling along the kaleidoscope corals, and sipping cocktails at sunset, the days will mysteriously begin to merge.

The beach scene has proved a popular formula with the backpacker set. Santa Fe provides an excellent gateway to the easterly islands in Mochima Park — Las Caracas and Picuda Grande, with Arapito only 20 minutes away by boat — plus two competent dive centers. Short treks, mountain biking, horse riding and waterfall- and wildlife-spotting up in the hills can all be arranged (in advance) through *posadas*.

Please note that there are no ATMs in the town. Most *posadas* will change cash and travelers checks. Also, please pay attention to your belongings and personal security while in Santa Fe, since the town is poor and opportunistic theft is common. The *posada* owners employ a security guard.

WHERE TO STAY

All of the following *posadas* line the beachfront or lie one street back. If arriving by car, take the second turn on your left — the one after the sign for the Hotel Cardasil — as the sleeping policemen humps begin, to reach their parking lots down a very rutted road.

Moderate to Inexpensive
The **Playa Santa Fe Resort and Dive Center** (/FAX (014) 733-3777 E-MAIL santaferesort@ telcel.net.ve WEBSITE www.santaferesort.com, run by Jerry Canaday and his young Venezuelan wife, opened in Easter 1999, and its whitewashed walls, exposed beams and attractive gardens can only improve Santa Fe's reputation. A terrace area for slinging hammocks gives onto the beach, perfect for sunset moments, and there are plans to establish a small French and Italian restaurant in their front garden. Jerry has teamed up with the very experienced Rodolfo Plaza to provide the most modern diving equipment on the beach, offering CMAS and PADI certification, day dives and adventures tours in the mountains by foot or by bike.

Inexpensive
Approaching the beach from town, the first *posada* is the **Cafe del Mar** ((093) 210009, run by German Matthias and his Venezuelan wife Maggi. They offer 14 simple rooms, with expansive sliding

windows giving on to the sea and a large terrace area on the top floor with deckchairs and hammock space. Though I would definitely recommend the place, and their café/restaurant, I'm not so sure about the small green river of waste water which unfortunately passes by their land "only in the rainy season."

A few doors down on the beach you come to the amiable English-speaking José Vivas' **Sierra Inn** ((014) 993-3116. His rooms aren't up to much, but he knows the coast well and rents a separate house which can accommodate a family comfortably. Ask José about the *La Encantada* house, even better for families, and about boat excursions.

Next up, the **Siete Delfines** ((016) 638-5668 E-MAIL dolphins@telcel.net.ve WEB SITE www.emergente.com.ve/sietedelfines, owned by the friendly Ricardo and Carolina, includes 11 Spartan rooms, with fans and cold water. They're aimed primarily at young divers and snorkelers. The couple run PADI courses and recommended diving trips.

WHERE TO EAT

Just as you reach the beach, you'll see the attractive **Club Nautico** restaurant and bar. The establishment, recently revamped, offers great fish dishes for good prices, "try-hard" friendly service and wonderful views of the bay.

On the beach in front of the Siete Delfines, next to the cocktail bar, is a friendly sandy restaurant with excellent pancake and fruit breakfasts and good evening fish dishes — although the service isn't always up to scratch. Valter and his Italian friends at the **Posada los Angeles**, the last *posada* on the beach, serve great "home-cooking" pasta and pizza, and aren't averse to on-the-house glasses of Sambuca.

HOW TO GET THERE

The town of Santa Fe lies on Highway 9, about halfway between Puerto La Cruz and Cumaná. Take a *por puesto* from either town, since larger buses don't stop. Buses drop you off by the road, from where it's a 20-minute walk through the town to the beach. Avoid arriving at night.

SANTA FE TO CUMANÁ

The sights continue along Highway 9 to Cumaná, with the town of Mochima providing the best access to the easterly beaches of the national park. All along the road, stands sell local handicrafts. Ragdolls hang from wooden poles swinging in the wind next to intricate wooden bird cages and replica models of Spanish galleons.

MAJAGUAL

It's not a town, or a village, or even a beach, but this establishment warrants special mention. I believe it's the finest *posada* along the whole of Venezuela's coast. Six kilometers (just under four miles) on from Santa Fe, a discrete stylized bird logo points to the left. Follow the steep road down and you'll emerge in shaded peace, quiet, and taste.

Villa Majagual ((093) 221120 or (014) 773-0023 was the brainchild of Michel Dresso, and the houses and grounds exude a distinctively Aegean flavor. No Mediterranean blue, just mottled whitewash plasterwork, rustic tile flags, porches, and

privacy. It feels luxurious, but its beauty lies in its simplicity and attention to detail. In the morning, they bring you a thermos of coffee and some cookies, and every day new flower arrangements appear as if by magic in your room.

Nestled into a hill with 360-degree views, grassy paths crisscross Majagual's lush, tropical gardens leading to their six handsome cottages. Further trails wind down to their private deck, where below the jetty, fish swim over the colorful corals. Back in the restaurant and social area, the rattan furniture simply invites you to relax, read and snooze. The food is also first class, combining Caribbean and French cuisine. The *posada* is managed by friendly, not to mention efficient, Karina Martinengo and her assistant Lorena. They ask you to opt for their expensive-bracket two-night package, including transfers and many drinks. They can also arrange yacht and fishing trips.

MOCHIMA

The small fishing village of Mochima provides the springboard for the most-easterly and least-visited islands in the national park. It lies four

OPPOSITE: Boats in Mochima take passengers to snorkeling beaches. ABOVE: Pelicans await their dinner.

kilometers (two and a half miles) down a steep road from Highway 9. To get there, take a *por puesto* from Cumaná (from near the Redoma del Indio) or from Santa Fe; haggle for a price. The hills around Mochima also offer alternatives to the beach, with many rivers, waterfalls, and caves to be explored. Ask Rodolfo Plaza (see below) about these.

What to See and Do

Boatmen moor up off the main square and business is swift, particularly on weekends. You pay by boat, and fares vary according to distance. The least-visited beaches, backed by stark, arid hills, are all recommended for snorkeling. They cluster around the Manare Peninsula to the west, and include **Manare** and **La Garrapata**. **Catauro** is another nearer option, close to the busier beaches: playas **Las Maritas** and **Blanca**, both with restaurants.

Where to Stay and Eat

Many locals rent out rooms and you'll see signs in windows all around the town. All of them are inexpensive.

The unambitious but brightly colored **Posada de Gaby (** (014) 773-1104 sits at the end of the two-street town, run by friendly Roberto Hernández. Along with offering 21 rooms, some with air-conditioning, others with ventilators, all without hot water, he takes guests on very reasonably priced boat trips. He knows the area and tourists' needs and wants, perfectly.

The other good choice, a must for dive enthusiasts and the adventurous, is the tile-roofed **Posada de los Buzos (** (014) 929-6020 or (02) 961-2531 E-MAIL faverola@cantv.net, close to the embarkation point. Run by marine biologist Rodolfo Plaza, it has four basic rooms. Plaza is the finest adventure guide in the area, as well as a patient dive instructor. Call him to arrange details. Open on weekends and in the high season only.

The best place for a fish dish is the well-known **El Mochimero**, the baby of Hilda and José Rafael, who cook a variety of fresh fish and some tasty desserts as well as having a great jazz collection.

CUMANÁ

Cumaná, capital of Sucre State, is a bustling port town, arguably the capital of "El Oriente" proper. *Cumanenses* argue endlessly with *Corenses* about whose city "woz here" first. Cumaná — but don't tell them I told you — loses. Its early settlement was abandoned, if only briefly, following attacks by enraged Indians.

The city clings to its older architecture stoically. Not a lot remains — or has been restored — after the successive earthquakes that have plagued the town since its founding in 1521. It

makes a handy springboard to several compelling parts of the country, however: the arid Península de Araya across the Golfo de Cariaco; the wonders of Paria to the east; and the Cueva del Guácharo to the south, with the Delta and the Orinoco beyond. Cumaná isn't a tourist Mecca by any stretch but, having wandered along its colonial quarter's narrow streets, dipped into its museums, admired the churches and taken in the views from the castillo, you'll wonder why it's so often overlooked. Add the superb expanse of beach on the approach to the town, and its comparative anonymity seems even more puzzling.

GENERAL INFORMATION

You'll find the Sucre State **Tourism Office (** (093) 312232 on Calle Sucre No. 49, at the Santa Inés end. They are helpful, speak some English, and provide you with town, regional and state maps. **Banco Unión** is on Calle Mariño and Carabobo. **Oficambio**, on Calle Mariño, changes money at official rates Monday to Saturday (half day). For e-mail, head to the small computer shop, **Bios Service**, next to Pizza Pucheff, just off Calle Sucre. January 22 marks **Santa Inés** festival time, celebrated throughout Sucre State.

WHAT TO SEE AND DO

Note that museums, stores and business all close for at least two hours at lunch.

For majestic views of the city and the Araya Peninsula, walk up the hill from the Plaza Bolívar to the **Castillo de San Antonio de la Eminencia**. The castle was restored in the 1970s, following several disastrous earthquakes, the last in 1929. The fort, built in 1686, defended the town from marauding pirates, and tunnels are believed to burrow right down to the Santa Inés church at the bottom of the hill. Most of the fort lies in the imagination, since displays and reconstructions are yet to appear. The odd rusty cannon makes do in the meantime.

Just down from here, the **Contemporary Art Museum** showcases cutting-edge temporary and permanent collections — and provides some welcome air-conditioning. Off to the left of the fort as you face the sea, follow the steps down (Calle La Luneta). You emerge at the **Iglesia de Santa Inés**, begun in 1637 as the base for Franciscan missionaries. It was rebuilt after various seismic calamities, and the latest structure dates from the 1930s. Its two tall bell-towers and austere interior are impressive enough, though somewhat bulky. In the garden, spot a tiny statue to the Virgen de la Candelaria. Nearby, the ruins of Cumaná's second fort, **Castillo de Santa María de la Cabeza** (completed in 1637) await further restoration. The fort acted as a closer bolt-hole than La Eminencia during raids.

Back on shaded and busy Plaza Bolívar stands the ex-**Gobernación**, once a handsome building, until its interior was gutted during civil protests in early 1999. Further along, a restored turn-of-the-century edifice houses the **Museo Andrés Eloy Blanco**, complete with period furniture — note the lovely pianoforte. The museum exhibits works and family memorabilia from this nationally important poet and politician. He said of Venezuela *"para quererla bien hay que empezar por creerla un poco"* (to love her well, start by believing in her a little). The **Ateneo de Cumaná** is just next-door. Have a look to see what's on, as there's usually a concert or play worth catching.

Cumaná boasts another famous homegrown poet, **Antonio Ramos Sucre** (1890–1930). Stop by his modest museum on the dinky Calle Sucre, open Monday to Friday with a break for lunch. A few doors down, the once-home of Doctor Daniel Beauperthuy, who discovered the mosquito that acts as the carrier for yellow fever, serves as the modest **Museo de Arqueología e Historia**.

Over on the banks of the Río Manzanares, the imposing columns of the **Museo Gran Mariscal de Ayacucho** take pride of place in the handsome tree-lined **Parque Ayacucho**. The museum is open Tuesday to Friday 9 AM to noon and 3 PM to 6 PM, plus weekend afternoons. It houses an extensive collection of exhibits pertaining to Sucre and Bolívar's lives. Antonio José de Sucre was Bolívar's most trusted friend and lieutenant, the Liberator's most likely successor before his assassination at the age of 35. His life was nothing short of spectacular. At 16, the young José Antonio, son of a governor of the Province of Nueva Andalucía and Guayana, joined Francisco de Miranda's patriot army. He shot through the ranks, defeating the Spanish at Pichincha in 1822, thereby liberating Ecuador, and routing them again at Ayacucho, freeing Peru in 1824. A year later, he was at it once more, thrashing the Royalists in Alto Perú. Soon after, he assumed the presidency of Bolivia.

Be wary of walking beyond the street lamps along the banks of the river at night, since this area isn't safe. The **Museo del Mar**, unfortunately, is now defunct.

On Calle Rendón No. 48, on the west side of the Río Manzanares, you'll find the cigar *fábrica* of Señor Jaime Acosta, **Tabacos Guanche**. Depending on his mood, and your level of Spanish, he'll take you round on a short tour of his premises. His hand-rolled cigars are reputed to be the best in Oriente.

The bustling **Mercado Municipal** on Avenida El Islote, the largest in the northeast, is a lot of fun — a riot of colors, commerce and chickens. Visit the *artesanía* section, handy for some souvenir shopping, and catch a very cheap lunch.

WHERE TO STAY

Along the approach road (Avenida Universidad) from the west, several highrise hotels make good choices if you want to combine sunbathing with a short look around Cumaná's old quarter. Otherwise, there are many hotels near the old town.

Luxury

For a touch of luxury, check in to the five-star **Cumanagoto Hesperia** ((093) 513232 FAX (093) 521877 E-MAIL banquetes@hotmail.com WEB SITE www.hoteles-hesperia.es. Impressive and indulgent, the relaunched Cumanagoto boasts all the

luxuries of a hotel of its caliber, including a nine-hole golf course, gym, sauna, tennis courts, two restaurants, a vast swimming pool, and chi-chi boutiques. Half the stylish and modern rooms enjoy sea views, particularly good value during one of their numerous promotional offers. On ground level you'll find the offices of the competent international travel agents **IberIsla** (/FAX (093) 301502 E-MAIL iberislacum@cantv.net.

Moderate

The other hotel worthy of note on this stretch is the old stalwart four-star **Hotel Bordones** ((093) 513111 FAX (093) 515377. Situated plum on the beach, it has seen better days, but still claims a pleasant pool and restaurant area, making it decent value.

Sunset moments are a dime a dozen on the Costa Azul.

Moderate to Inexpensive

In Cumaná itself, I recommend you head straight for **Hostal Bubulina's** ((093) 314025 FAX (093) 334137, on Callejón Santa Inés, just off Calle Sucre, by the church. María Margarita de Melo's establishment provides a wonderful base for exploring Cumaná, in the heart of the old town. The 12 spacious, but by no means extravagant, rooms all have an individual feel, complemented by forged-iron furniture, remote-control air-conditioning units, and eye-catching floral motifs. The restaurant in the knocked-through adjacent house has been downsized to a very appealing bar with small appetizers. It can get quite lively on weekends.

On Avenida Universidad and set back from the beach, the **Gran Hotel Cumaná** ((093) 510218 FAX (093) 512677 offers a restaurant, a family-friendly pool, and air-conditioned clean rooms — some with views. A good choice out on this stretch.

Inexpensive

The other hotels near the old town on Calle Sucre are all budget options, of which the **Hotel Astoria** ((093) 662708 is your best bet, though the **Hotel Italia** ((093) 333678 a few doors down has some more expensive air-conditioned rooms (the others are really pretty poor). Further afield, just across the river you'll find the slightly more expensive **Hotel Regina** ((093) 322581, which offers a range of air-conditioned rooms, including some on the top floor with good views, facing east.

WHERE TO EAT

Moderate

La Casa Abierta ((093) 312332, stands on Calle Sucre at No. 8, the creation of an artistic, cultured and charming Frenchwoman, Nicole Chevalier. The space was formerly an art gallery, but Nicole expanded it recently to include a "salón de thé" and a restaurant. "The Open House" serves delicious French dishes — including a "Dish of Indecision," a selection of everything on the menu — and I fell in love with the place at once. Everything is wonderful, from the wine, the hallmarked silver cutlery, the bone-china plates and the antiques dotted about the rooms, to the lighting, service and ambience. Satchmo, Ella Fitzgerald and jazz greats romance the winers and diners. Before you know it, you'll be on to your third *digestif*. The Casa only opens from 5 PM Wednesdays to Sundays.

Just off Plaza Bolívar on Plaza Pichincha, **El Colmao** ((083) 316796 offers a varied menu with attentive service and air-conditioned surroundings. Head there for lunch.

Inexpensive

Near the Hotel Caribe, **Sandhills** and **Los Montones** serve very fresh fish on the beach. **Don**

Pietro's, next to Parque Ayacucho, cooks good pizzas. Further down from La Casa Abierta, on Plaza Rivero, you'll find several excellent value street *parilla* stalls. For the best ice cream in town, beeline to **Helados La Barquilla** on Avenida Gran Mariscal by the Banco Mercantil. The fruits are fresher than fresh. For a late afternoon drink, the open-air **Bar Jardín Sport** on Plaza Bolívar is perfect.

HOW TO GET THERE

The airport has regular flights to Caracas and Margarita. It's about a 10-minute taxi ride from the city center. Cumaná's buses can get very busy, particularly on weekends, so buy your ticket in advance (on arrival). Buses to Caracas go through Puerto La Cruz. For the Cueva del Guácharo, take a Caripe bus or you can also haggle with *por puestos* for a ride (see CARIPE, page 212, for different routes up to the hills).

Book car ferries to Araya through **Conferry** ((095) 311462. They also run two trips a day to Margarita at 7 AM and 5 PM, as does the faster **Naviarca** ((093) 315577 FAX (093) 334312 ferry at 7 AM and 2 PM. It's best to check with them for times. For passenger-only ferries to Araya, see below.

PENÍNSULA DE ARAYA

The arid Araya Peninsula stretches across the Gulf of Cariaco from Cumaná, forming the knobby western horn of northern Sucre State. Araya, in the Venezuelan popular imagination, is synonymous with salt — and heat. A famous 1950s black-and-white documentary depicted the hard lives of the men and women who harvested the valuable salt and fished in the deep blue seas. The film ingrained the peninsula forever in the hearts and minds of Venezuelans.

Only one road traverses the peninsula, hugging the northern windswept and sun-blanched shores. Araya, along with the Paraguaná Peninsula, is possibly one of the loneliest places in the country. Yet its harsh landscapes are often more intriguing and captivating than "yet another palm-fringed beach," although perhaps not everyone would agree. The trip over from Cumaná on one of the fast launches is an experience in itself.

For those coming without private transportation, Araya doesn't offer much beyond the town, and getting around is hard. In a private car, the peninsula's roads provide some adventure. To the south of Araya village lies the somnolent fishing village of **Punta de Arenas**, with the **Laguna de Chacopata** to the east, where flocks of scarlet ibis and pink flamingos alight.

Heading east along the peninsula's only road, a good *posada*, **Campamento Ecológico Churuatas San Judas Tadeo** ((014) 787-5225 E-MAIL sava@

enlared.net, has sprung up near Taguapire. **Chacopata** is the next-biggest town after Araya, from where bumpy and unreliable boats leave throughout the day for the hop over to Porlamar on Margarita. The road then veers south and links up with Highway 9 at **Cariaco**, and *por puestos* run along this route.

FORTALEZA DE SANTIAGO DE LEÓN DE ARAYÆA

Araya's salt flats were once the world's richest. In order to protect them, the Spanish began the construction of the monolithic Santiago de León de Araya fort in 1622. Today, it commands panoramic views of the salt-flats and surrounding sea. The walls of the fort undeniably impress but, as in Cumaná, the structure's original grandeur and historical significance have to be imagined. Not requiring any imagination, however, is the peculiar smell: its position right next to a popular and beautiful beach means beach-goers invariably nip up to the fort to relieve themselves.

Background

The Castillo de Santiago, the most costly construction of the colonial era, took nearly 50 arduous years to complete. Due to the incessant heat and marauding pirates, workers labored at night. All supplies — including water — had to be shipped over from Cumaná. To top that, the salt ate through the workers' shoes.

During the sixteenth century, the Spanish neglected the salt flats, concentrating instead on the pearl beds of Coche and Cubagua, off Margarita. When these were picked clean, they turned their attention back — at a time when salt was much sought-after in Europe — to the salt pans. Meanwhile, the Dutch and English had been happily exploiting Araya's riches. A series of battles ensued, with the Spanish emerging victorious. They set about protecting their investment once and for all. Once complete, the fort was the most impressive in the New World, commanding 45 cannon and a garrison of over 250 men.

In 1726, after a hurricane ruined the salt lagoons, the Spanish resolved to blow up the fort, rather than let it fall to foreign hands. They poured all the available gunpowder into the enterprise, but the structure stood firm. Somewhat worse-for-wear, and far from its glory days, the fort on its commanding hilltop remains a singular sight in this barren land.

SALINAS DE ARAYA

The surreal pink and mauve hues of the *salinas* salt-flats number among the stranger sights in Venezuela. If you have never seen these lunar-looking lakes before, this is your chance. They spread over the land like a Daliesque vision of chessboard squares, evaporating under an unforgiving sun and strong winds.

Ask the state company Ensal offices to the north of the ferry landing to show you around in the morning. They're not particularly tourist-friendly, unfortunately. You can always walk around the nearest lake and onto the beds to get a closer look.

ARAYA

The peninsula's largest town, Araya is increasingly popular with windsurfers who enjoy the offshore winds that blow most of the year, though these are not for beginners. The beach near the fort is long and inviting, though shadeless. Bring plenty of water and lather yourself in suntan lotion.

Where to Stay

The inexpensive **Araya Wind** ((093) 714442, near the fort, is run by Orlando Figueroa and makes a popular base for windsurfers, who park their sails and boards in a hangar next-door. Figueroa offers a total of 11 simple rooms with some nice cane and bamboo touches. There is also a restaurant, which isn't up to much. Nearby is the **Posada Helen** ((093) 71101, which is clean and friendly.

HOW TO GET THERE

Boats called *tapaítos* (little-roofed) take passengers across the Gulf from the Punta de Piedras docks in Cumaná. They leave about every hour or so until around 4 PM. Some of these go to **Manicaure**, where a minivan takes you on to Araya in half an hour. The crossing is rougher in the afternoon. Be wary of your belongings around the docks.

If you're coming by car, the Naviarca ferry from Cumaná leaves on an erratic basis from the docks at Punta de Piedras. You buy a ticket and wait to board what is more a barge than a ferry. Be sure to check return times from Araya when you get off, and get there early.

PENÍNSULA DE PARIA

When Columbus wrote to Ferdinand and Isabella in 1498 of his experiences on the coast of Paria, he enthused "I found a land, the most beautiful in all the world… I'm convinced this is Paradise on Earth." He named it *Tierra de Gracia*, and goodness gracious me is it beautiful.

If you're looking for vacation-brochure beaches, look no further. Literally dozens of palm-lined, white-sand expanses await the curious traveler. Paria's lush northern coast, untouched by large-scale tourism, beats any other region hands down. Not only that, when the rest of the country is heaving at Easter or over Christmas, Paria is a haven of peace.

But Paria offers much more than picture post-cards — from untamed natural beauty, over 300 species of birds, cloudforests, savannas, thermal springs, cacao haciendas, to a taste of rural Venezuelan life. The peninsula harbors some wonderful *posadas*, two national parks, off-the-beaten-track adventures, exemplary development projects, and sincere, friendly people. It's rare when reality exceeds your wildest expectations. But sometimes, it just does.

To counterbalance the superlatives, Paria's infrastructure is still, shall we say, wobbly. Power cuts are common and some public telephones frustrating. Paria isn't the easiest region to discover by public transportation, unless you have time and pack patience. Tour operators and most *posada* owners arrange varied excursions around the region, which could be by car, foot, boat or even horseback. The other option is to rent a car in Carúpano, and let the adventure begin.

CARÚPANO

Founded in 1647, Carúpano's early wealth was based on cacao. Today it still exports 80% of Venezuela's crop to Europe and Asia. Although you wouldn't have thought it today, Carúpano once basked as one of the richest towns in Venezuela. It boasted a tramway and an opera house, and avenues where sophisticated *doñas* donned their white gloves for their evening stroll.

Little remains of these halcyon days. The restored quarter of colorful façades around the Plaza de Santa Rosa de Lima is the exception. The city's chief source of income today is the fishing industry, though the city of 100,000 also provides an important hub for regional produce, with a surprisingly large Mercado Municipal.

Carupeños claim their Carnival is the largest and most colorful celebration in the country, awash with Trinidadian influence. Those who have witnessed the floats, masquerades and all-night partying tend to agree. With its airport linked to major cities, and several banks and good hotels, Carúpano makes a good base from which to explore the peninsula.

GENERAL INFORMATION

Major banks cluster around the Plaza Colón. The local tourist office is on Avenida 3 Independencia, on the first floor of Edificio FundaBermúdez, though they aren't much help. For superior local information, head to the travel agents and tour operators **Venezuela Evasión (** (094) 312157, or **Paria Intertur (** (094) 320542, both on Avenida Independencia.

Seek out the offices of **CorpoMedina**, also now known as **Encuentro Paria (** (094) 315241 FAX (094) 313021 E-MAIL playamed@telcel.net.ve, on Avenida Independencia by the Santa Rosa square. The company runs the Playa Medina and Pui-Puy beach resorts, as well as the Hato Río de Agua and Agua Sana campamentos, and the Hacienda Agua Santa. These are described later in this chapter, but it's worth asking them for a leaflet with a map.

Their lodgings are sold as an all-inclusive package, including all meals. They regard transfers and tours as extra, but as a whole, their packages offer an excellent way to get a feel for the region in relative comfort. They consider Friday and Saturday, as well as traditional holidays "high season," so book during the week.

WHAT TO SEE AND DO

A novelty in Venezuela, Carúpano's heart beats around the central Plaza Colón and up to the Plaza Santa Rosa near the sea. Plaza Bolívar, for once, is a relatively unimportant square to the south.

The name Wilfried Merle will keep popping up in Paria. In addition to being involved in the company CorpoMedina and owning the Río de Agua ranch and the Posada La Colina (see WHERE TO STAY, below), he is a driving force behind the laudable Fundación Proyecto Paria (see RÍO CARIBE, page 204), and the director of the Fundación Thomas Merle. The latter actvely promotes environmental awareness and education throughout the region.

You can find out more about the foundations, and possibly meet this remarkable man, in the **Casa del Cable** on the south side of Plaza Santa Rosa. It also happens to be a beautifully restored house. In 1895, the first cable to link South America and Europe (at Marseille) terminated here — thus the name. A century later, the house witnessed Carúpano's first Internet link. Inside, you can find out more about the various foundations and purchase T-shirts and books on Paria. Bruno Manara's *Paria, en el tiempo y en el corazón* provides an excellent ecological guide to the peninsula in Spanish.

On the corner of the square is the modest **Museo Histórico** built by English trader, J.M. Imery around 1883, which once housed a library. It displays a motley collection of exhibits and some enlarged photos of turn-of-the-century Carúpano.

On the approach to Carúpano, watch for the signs to **Playa Copey**, a lovely beach, ideal for a break from the city. The best *posada* of the few is **Posada Nena (** (094) 317624 FAX (094) 317297 E-MAIL posadanena@bigfoot.de, which can also arrange regional tours.

WHERE TO STAY

Carúpano doesn't really have a high season, but rooms around Carnival time are reserved months in advance.

Moderate

The first of the two recommended options in this bracket is the **Posada La Colina** ((094) 320527 FAX (094) 312067, which has incomparable views from its breezy, open-sided restaurant and pool area, as well as 17 beautifully finished rooms. The bentwood furniture and wooden beams give the *posada* a rustic feel, yet its rooms are very comfortable, all with air-conditioning, televisions and hot water. To get to the *posada*, take the first right after the Hotel Victoria, then right again up the hill. It's very popular, so reserve the moment you read this.

The second is **El Colibrí** ((094) 323583, the baby of Polly and Gunter Hoffman. The charming

Other choices in the center include the **Hotel Lilma** ((094) 311341, on Avenida Independencia at Calle 12, and the **Hotel San Francisco** ((094) 311074, on Avenida Juncal at Calle 11.

WHERE TO EAT

In addition to its great views, the restaurant of **Posada La Colina** enjoys a very favorable reputation and serves buffalo steaks from the Río de Agua ranch. Their breakfasts are also delicious. On Avenida Independencia, near Plaza Santa Rosa, **Trattoria La Madriguera**, an Italian place with plenty of character, serves up fine fare. **El Kiosko** ((093) 310330, on the Perimetral, specializes in very

couple built three two-story houses around a wonderful pool area, as well as a thatched-roof restaurant. Everything from the furnishings to the glasses to the kitchenware is first class. They speak Dutch, German and English. Call to ask them for directions.

Inexpensive

What seems at first to be an unprepossessing place, turns out to be a lovely small *posada* run by Erasmo Maya and José García. **Aves de Paraíso** ((094) 322001, Avenida Independencia No. 251, lies two blocks south of Plaza Bolívar and the Banco Provincial. They offer four endearing and clean rooms with ventilators and hot water. The house has been tastefully restored: antiques and knickknacks clog glass windows, and plants adorn the central patio. Erasmo cooks delicious meals served in the garden at the rear.

fresh seafood, as does the restaurant of the **Hotel Lilma**. You can also ask Erasmo at **Aves del Paraíso** to cook you up something while you sip a beer.

HOW TO GET THERE

The airport is just to the west of the town. **Air-LAI** ((094) 322186 and **AVIAR** ((094) 312867 both fly to Caracas in the morning and afternoon, as well as to Porlamar and Ciudad Bolívar. You'll find two car rental firms, **Budget** ((094) 314390 and **Saladino** ((094) 322495, and a tourism information module — staffed irregularly.

Companies in the bus terminal on Avenida Perimetral run regular services to Caracas, via Cumaná and Puerto La Cruz; east to Güiria; and south to Caripe and Ciudad Bolívar. The *por puestos*

The Iglesia de Santa Rosa dominates Carúpano's skyline.

for Río Caribe leave further east on the Avenida Perimetral, by the El Kiosko restaurant.

RÍO CARIBE

Río Caribe doesn't have a museum, useful banks, telephones that work properly, or a particularly pleasant beach. It doesn't even possess a tourist office worthy of the name. Yet it is one of the towns I'm fondest of in Venezuela. The town is Carúpano's poorer neighbor, which somehow got left behind when the *Gran Cacao* hacienda owners turned their attention from plantations to black gold. However, Río Caribe's rich landowning families — many of them Corsican immigrants; note the policemen wearing berets — have begun to rediscover their roots, and along with the burgeoning tourism industry, a "renaissance" of sorts is underway in this long-forgotten part of the country.

This sleepy fishing village might not detain you for long, but its charm and friendliness is enduring. The town is the natural springboard for venturing further east. You'll find a host of beaches nearby, and some great places to relax in comfort.

GENERAL INFORMATION

The friendly and cultured Juan Sara and Tamara Rodríguez run **Pariana Café (** (094) 61702 or (016) 694-0242 E-MAIL pariana@cantv.net, on Avenida Bermúdez, just by the Posada Caribana. They have the best tourist and general information. Between them, they speak several languages. For more information on Paria, see WEB SITE www.venezuelavoyage.com.

WHAT TO SEE AND DO

In the evening, the town's **Plaza Bolívar** dominated by the Iglesia de San Miguel, built soon after the town's founding in 1713, buzzes with the day's gossip and events. Mass on Sunday evening is an event in itself. Many of the houses around the square have been lovingly restored by their owners, and most don't mind inquisitive tourists peeping in to admire the plant-festooned inner patios.

Fundación Proyecto Paria ((094) 61883 FAX (094) 61223 E-MAIL fpprio@telcel.net.ve, has its base on Calle Rivero No. 50, by the Casa Municipal. Pick up a leaflet and learn more about the work of the remarkable foundation — an engine for sustainable development in the region — from the information boards (in Spanish) they have inside the restored old house.

Several *artesano* craftspeople live in Río Caribe, most notably José Gregorio Valencia on Calle 14 Febrero. Without meaning to sound morbid, the **cemetery** is a fascinating place if you're interested in history, and even if you're not. Ask for

directions to visit the grandiose family tombs and mausolea of Río Caribe's great Corsican families.

In Río Caribe, you can't help but spot the **Monumento a Cristo Rey**, a miniature version of Río de Janeiro's towering Christ the Redeemer. The statue commands great views of the town from its hill, perfect for an evening stroll.

WHERE TO STAY

Expensive to Moderate

Top of anyone's list in Río Caribe is the **Posada Caribana (** (094) 61162 or (02) 263-3649 FAX (094) 61242 E-MAIL caribanapos@cantv.net, owned by the amiable architect Gonzalo Denis Boulton. Within a restored old house, the smart, well-appointed rooms with imposing doors, white shutters and cool interiors open on to a central patio where a fountain burbles. Day or night, the *posada* oozes sophistication and relaxation. Gonzalo and French manageress Géraldine offer packages for two nights including all meals, tours of the local area in boats and jeeps, and airport transfers.

You should also ask about their partners at **Playa de Uva**. The romance of this location overwhelms, nestled into tumbling hills, with winding paths, ornate gardens, palms, and a tiny cove beach. Request the more inviting separate structures with their own enclosed porches. The rooms are bright and breezy, with quality furnishings, hot water, and, above all, peace, quiet and privacy.

Inexpensive

Probably the best in this class, **Villa Antillana (**/FAX (094) 61413 E-MAIL pariana@cantv.net, on Calle Rivero No. 32, is another architect-rescued house. Rigoberto Aponte and his wife offer a selection of rooms with fans and hot water, some great for families. The walls are blue-washed, attention to detail faultless — with many carved wood fixtures — and a friendly and informal feel pervades.

The friendly, polyglot Artlet runs **La Posada de Arlet (**/FAX (094) 61290 E-MAIL cristjose@cantv.net WEB SITE http://think-venezuela.net/arlet/, on the corner of Calle 24 de Julio. Rooms are spick and span with baths, cold water and fans, and are popular with younger travelers. Arlet knows Paria well, and rents mountain bikes and organizes tours.

WHERE TO EAT

The restaurant in the **Posada Caribana** serves first-class meals, with fresh fish and seafood topping the menu. Friendly, and good for lunch is **Fior Daliza**, Calle Libertad.

The best *típico* place is the quirky **Mi Cocina**, one block towards the sea from the Caribana, first left then left again. It looks like a garage from the outside. The food inside however represents extremely good value — the fish is fresh, the decor very Venezuelan and the Carúpano carnival music totally infernal. Ask for the local specialties of *tarkari* (mildly spicy stew of duck or goat), or else *chipi-chipi*, a clam chowder. Río Caribe is also renowned for its sausages (*salchichas* and *chorizos*).

Not to be missed is **La Dulce Mirna**, who holds court in her shop on the corner of Avenida Bermúdez, up by Plaza Bolívar. Mirna is one of the beneficiaries of the Fundación, baking cakes and making sandwiches. Her forté however, lies in blending the Oriente's most delicious alcoholic fruit drinks: *guarapitas*. You'll have to ask this

cheeky, smiley woman what the bottles of varying colors that line her glass cabinet contain and, most importantly, what their names mean. Mirna gives away free sample shots of each — but buy a bottle anyway — which I don't recommend on an empty stomach, so purchase a cake. She had me in hysterics.

HOW TO GET THERE

Buses leave from Plaza Bolívar, with Cruceros Oriente Sur's direct to Caracas. *Por puestos* for Carúpano also leave from here. For jeeps towards Medina, Pui-Puy and San Juan de las Galdonas, walk up to the gas station to the south of town in the morning. See below for more details. In view of the lack of local transportation, it's often wise to talk to local *posada* owners about what they can offer you.

El Oriente

AROUND RÍO CARIBE

This is where a rental car will really come in handy. The road south, which links up with Highway 9 at Bohordal (see HIGHWAY 9 EAST, page 208), boasts some delightful places to stay, colorful villages, cacao haciendas, forests, friendly locals, and — of course — fabulous beaches. **Playa Los Cocos** impressed me so much I had to have a nap in my hammock under a palm tree to recover. All along the road, local farmers lay out their cacao to dry on the side of the road, or on patios next to their houses.

This road might be one of the most picturesque in the country, but it's in a bad state of repair. All this means is that you'll have more time to savor and appreciate it. In the words of the actress Helen Hayes "Why endeavor to straighten the roads of life? The faster we travel, the less there is to see."

WHERE TO STAY AND EAT

Moderate to Inexpensive
Since opening in 1997, Billy Esser and his family have made **Hacienda Bukare** ((094) 652003 FAX (094) 652004 E-MAIL bukare@cantv.net WEB SITE http://think-venezuela.net/bukare/(by reservation only) into one of the most attractive in the area, with the added bonus of their active cacao hacienda. Just four rooms run off a central garden replete with modest swimming pool. The hacienda is very popular with bird-watchers. The Esser family offers all-inclusive meals, well-guided excursions, transfers, and they speak English. You might also want to stop just to purchase some of their cacao, sold in little painted ceramic pods. Bukare lies 14 km (nine miles) from Río Caribe, just before the colorfully painted village of San Francisco de Chacaracual.

Inexpensive
About 10 minutes' drive from Río Caribe, in the village of Guayaberos, a coral-colored wall on the left and a sign announce the great **Ruta del Cacao** ((014) 994-0115 E-MAIL rutacacao@oem.es. Apart from being charming, Oti Campos runs a very tight operation here, renting 10 comfortable rooms with bentwood furniture, cane ceilings and tiled floors, all with fans but no hot water. Well-tended gardens surround a thatched-roof restaurant and living area serving tasty meals. Their big selling point is the horses they rent, presenting an enviable means of exploring the surrounding countryside and cacao haciendas. Prices are very reasonable, and include breakfast and dinner.

Spanish moss drapes the trees on the road south of Río Caribe.

PLAYA MEDINA

Playa Medina is famous. Along with Choroní's Playa Grande and Margarita's Playa El Agua, it is Venezuela's most renowned beach. Given its history — *Club Mediterranée* planned to make it the base of their South American empire — the beach is also infamous. Fame, however, hasn't blighted its spectacular location, tucked into the green-hued hills of the Paria coast, with elegant avenues of palms giving way to wave-lapped, pristine shores. Even if you have no intention of staying in the excellent accommodation here, the beach's wondrous location make it a must-see in Paria.

WHERE TO STAY

Expensive to Moderate
Hidden away under the palms of the beach's western end, a stone's throw from the water, lie the eight exclusive cabins offered by Encuentro Paria (see GENERAL INFORMATION, CARÚPANO, page 202, for booking). Divided by frangipani, hibiscus and grassy paths, six of the cabins each house two bedrooms, living room, kitchen, and two bathrooms with hot water. Two smaller cabins — ideal for couples — have just one bedroom with bath. Their terracotta tile roofs give them a very Mediterranean feel, while the interiors are simple yet sophisticated.

Inexpensive
At the split in the road for playas Medina and Pui-Puy, on the right-hand side, the humble **Posada El Milagro(** (01) 782-1127 or (02) 545-7237 is worth considering. Owned by the friendly Nuñez family who only speak Spanish, they offer five basic, but not bare-bones rooms, with cold water showers. They also prepare breakfast and evening meals for guests, rent mountain bikes at reasonable rates, and can shuttle guests back and forth to Medina at no extra cost. Transfers from Río Caribe or Carúpano are extra.

WHERE TO EAT

A restaurant-cum-bar in the middle of the beach has an adequate menu, but perhaps more fun is the fresh food prepared by local people who have controlled concessions on the beach, under neat little thatched shades.

HOW TO GET THERE

Eighteen kilometers (11 miles) south of Río Caribe on the way to Bohordal, watch for the unmarked turn on the left, by an *abasto* (store) and a soccer pitch. Six kilometers (under four miles) down this road, after the village of Medina, comes a very evident split in the road. To the left, the dirt track winds down to Playa Medina.

Public transportation to the beaches is nonexistent, or else very costly. The closest you can get is on a truck going to the villages of Medina and Pui-Puy. From there you walk, or try your luck hitching. The trucks generally leave in the early morning from the gas station at the southern entrance to Río Caribe. Check on return times with the drivers.

PLAYA PUI-PUY

Pui-Puy's beach is larger than Medina's, arching in a grand swoop, cupped between two verdant hills, with shallow waters washed over by rolling waves. On the occasions I've visited, the beach has been virtually deserted.

Storming, or perhaps more exactly, plodding, out of the sea at Pui-Puy every April and September come another sort of visitor altogether: marine turtles. Encuentro Paria and biologists from Caracas have run several programs here, tagging and releasing this endangered species, as well as making sure the beach is clear for them to lay their eggs. Guests are encouraged to get involved.

WHERE TO STAY AND EAT

Adding to the original nine cabins under the shade of an row of palms — similar to Medina's without the kitchens — nine newer ones, with thatched roofs have been added by Encuentro Paria (for booking, see GENERAL INFORMATION, CARÚPANO, page 202). All of them include bathrooms and hot water, with porches on their front doorsteps from where you can sling a hammock or laze in a deckchair. Again the rustic feel prevails, and charms. Unlike Medina, you can ask to camp and use the bathroom facilities at Pui-Puy, in return for a small fee. At the end of the line of cabins, a restaurant serves meals and drinks, including fresh fish of the day. It's also open to the public.

HOW TO GET THERE

For Pui-Puy, take the right-hand track at the split six kilometers (under four miles) off the Río Caribe–Bohordal road. The potholed and damaged dirt road passes through the village of Chaguarrama and into the valley of Pui-Puy, seven kilometers (just over four miles) later. Follow the road, keeping left, down to the palms and the beach.

SAN JUAN DE LAS GALDONAS

If you thought Río Caribe was in the boondocks, then wait till you see San Juan de las Galdonas. If you think San Juan is a one-donkey town, wait till you see Uquire…

The small fishing village of San Juan boasts more than four beaches, three good *posadas*, two roads, one food stall, but no public telephones. It's great. When I last visited, the settlement, planted at the foot of a large bluff and backed by forested hills, was basking in the glory of the newly paved road linking it to the outside world.

GENERAL INFORMATION

The only phone in town is the portable-phone-for-rent at "Mi Rancho" on Calle Bolívar, which is in fact the local video shop. There is an *abasto* store, which stocks foodstuffs, but don't rely on it.

ranging from a quick day-tour, to longer four-day expeditions along the coast east, to include walks up into the national park, visiting remote cacao-producing farms.

WHERE TO STAY AND EAT

All lodgings in San Juan can arrange transfers from the larger towns in the area for a fee, and they all offer boat trips east, or walks in the national park.

Moderate

Inaugurated in 1998, the four-story, three-star **Hotel Las Pioneras (** (094) 761003 FAX (094) 761002 IN FRANCE 01 30 85 03 31 IN SPAIN 07 47 75 99 is an

WHAT TO SEE AND DO

The beaches around San Juan are gorgeous. The ones that stretch west — Sotavento, Tocuchire, Querepare, Treinta Pies, all the way to Cangua — provide hours of walking along solitary shores, secluded spots, and great swimming. Barlovento, to the east side of town, extends over two kilometers (one and a quarter miles). For some unparalleled sunset moments and views, walk over to the hill of the bluff.

Though San Juan doesn't have a museum, the closest you can get to a *casa de la cultura* is the shop run by ceramist and all-around lovely person, Susana. Ask in town for her house. I highly recommend her partner, fisherman **Bototu (** (014) 779-8398, as a knowledgeable and experienced guide, albeit with limited English. His trips, used by many *posadas* (e.g. Hacienda Bukare), are delightful,

ambitious project in such a back-end place as San Juan. From its prime position at the entrance to the village it offers comfortable accommodation in its 31 rooms, most with great sea views, along with appealing wicker furniture, baths, hot water, and fans. On the ground level, a large swimming pool gives on to the beach below. Their company, **Aventura Turismo Descanso** (same numbers), organizes all sorts of trips around the region, off the coast, over to Los Roques, and across Venezuela. The excursions are among the most comfortable and professional you could hope to find in Paria and Venezuela, with multilingual guides.

Inexpensive

Further into the village on Calle Comercio, also looking out on the sea, **Posada Las Tres Carabelas**

Tumbling forests and groves of coconuts at Playa Medina.

((016) 894-1052 FAX (094) 322668 E-MAIL carabelas3 @hotmail.com, has 15 simple but appealing rooms, with baths, cold water and fans. The three on the top floor are the best, with the restaurant, terraces and well-tended pockets of gardens all very attractively laid out, adorned with local crafts, driftwood sculptures, and handsome artwork. Their restaurant, with lots of local specialties, is open to the public and has wonderful sunset views.

The newest addition to San Juan's lodgings, the welcoming **Habitat Paria** ((014) 779-7955 or (081) 654592 tucks in behind Barlovento beach, east of the town. The *posada*, owned by friendly Italian, Nicole Vegetti, and her Venezuelan husband Angel José, includes 12 rooms on two stories, all with fans, baths and cold water. The *posada* is bright and breezy, painted a vivid blue and earthbrown tones, and their restaurant, *por supuesto*, proudly serves Italian pasta.

HOW TO GET THERE

Unlike Rome, only one road leads to San Juan de las Galdonas. To make up for this, it's positively spectacular, gleaming in the bright sun after its recent asphalt-surgery — it used to be a tortuous jeep-only track. It splits from the Río Caribe–Bohordal road 25 km (16 miles) south of Río Caribe, about five kilometers (three miles) north of the Bohordal crossroads. It has fantastic views of the coast and its beaches and passes through little villages where locals spread out their cacao or plod along with their donkeys. A road to savor and remember.

About five kilometers (three miles) out of San Juan, an equally memorable road forks up the hill to the left. This road, which used to be in better condition than the coastal one, emerges at Río Seco on Highway 9.

PARQUE NACIONAL PENÍNSULA DE PARIA

The mountains of Paria, the Serranía de Paria, form part of a "forest island" which once embraced Trinidad, harboring a great variety of endemic species. Its mountains rise spectacularly from the northern coast to over 1,000 m (3,280 ft), remarkable for their drenched cloudforest which thrives as low as 800 m (2,624 ft), and the huge number of birds that inhabit it. The park covers 375 sq km (146 sq miles) of the mountain's northerly spine. Its highest peak is Cerro Humo at 1,356 m (4,448 ft) to the west. Elevations gradually decrease across the Serranía to the highest crest of the east, Cerro Patao at 1,048 m (3,437 ft). Along these upper reaches, bromeliads and epiphytes cloak the cloudforest, alive with the raucous chorus of hundreds of birds, or the howls of boisterous troupes of red howler monkeys, at dawn or dusk.

Despite its wonders, the park is seldom visited and poorly protected due to limited resources. It continues to suffer forest-clearing incursions, particularly on its southern borders. Much of its lower forest is slowly recovering from the intense cacao cultivation which has powered the region's development since the seventeenth century. Isolated though it may seem, the modern world is catching up with Paria. Not only are many of the villages affected by the drug-trafficking trade, but under the auspices of the "Christopher Columbus Project" plans to exploit the liquified natural gas reserves off the Caribbean coast are being discussed. You wonder what the Admiral would think of it all.

GENERAL INFORMATION

At the Casa del Cable in Carúpano (see page 202), in addition to Bruno Manara's book, look out for a guide to the hummingbirds of the peninsula, *Los Tucusitos de Paria*, and August Braun's *Las Utilidades de las Palmas en Venezuela*, a fascinating insight into how palms have been exploited by Indians for generations. These are all in Spanish for now. A highly recommended guide for the peninsula is the English biologist, ecologist and birder, **Chris Sharpe** (/FAX (02) 730-9701 E-MAIL rodsha@telcel.net.ve.

HOW TO GET THERE

Most people opt for a boat trip along the coast, with a short hike up in to hills from one of the villages which dot the northern coast. You motor, snorkel and swim in the day, set up camp on a beach in the evening, and enjoy the day's catch at night. The trips are not for the creature-comfort-lover, but then, the Garden of Eden never did come with an en-suite…

For the more adventurous, there are several trails over Cerro El Humo from either of the hamlets of Manacal or Las Melenas at the western end of the park, off Highway 9. Other treks in the east can be organized from Patao or Macuro on the southern coast, emerging at Uquire or San Pedro to the north.

HIGHWAY 9 EAST

From Carúpano, the coast road carries on to Río Caribe, while Highway 9 (a country road) veers inland towards El Pilar. From there it switches east, joined after 36 km (22 miles) by the road south from Río Caribe (see AROUND RÍO CARIBE, page 205) at the Guardia Nacional stop of Bohordal.

The agricultural town of **El Pilar** is pretty nondescript, though there are numerous hot springs and rivers nearby. More impressive is the fledgling **Jardín Botánico**, just east of town, on the right-hand side of the road to Güiria. The botanical garden encompasses 44 hectares (109 acres) and, though still in its infancy, Proyecto Paria holds great hopes for its future. You can ask the manager, Jesús Hernández, to give you a tour pointing out the varied flora of the area.

Over five kilometers (three miles) on from El Pilar, past the village of Los Arroyos, a right turn points to Guaraúnos. The sign might have disappeared (it wasn't there when I last visited), but it's the only paved road on the right in the area. Shortly after the turn, on the left-hand side, lies the main part of Klaus Müller's **Campamento Vuelta Larga** (see WHERE TO STAY AND EAT, below).

WHERE TO STAY AND EAT

Close to El Pilar, **Campamento Vuelta Larga** ℓ/FAX (094) 69052 E-MAIL vueltalarga@cantv.net, is one of the pioneering and most renowned lodges in Venezuela. It's the baby of a German man, Klaus Müller, and his now grown-up family. Klaus arrived in the 1960s, and though raising water buffalo has been his main economic staple, he has turned conservation, innovation and aesthetics into a way of life. At the *campamento*, you can admire the beautiful thatched houses he built with local Warao Indians. One of them serves as a restaurant, open to the public on weekends, where

Back on Highway 9, Tunapuy is the next village. Five kilometers (three miles) beyond it, spot the thatched huts and the sign for **Hacienda Agua Sana** (also called Ño Carlos), where you can enjoy an invigorating bath in one of the hot mineral springs open to the public as well as to hacienda guests.

Nine kilometers (five and a half miles) further east, a large white tank on the right-hand side announces the excellent 1,000-hectare (2,470-acre) **Campamento Agro Ecológico Río de Agua**. They escort welcome visitors on a short tour of the grounds. Shortly after this, the road from Río Caribe meets the Highway at Bohordal.

On the way to Güiria, you pass the entrance to **Irapa**, once an important port for shipping cacao. Forty-two kilometers (26 miles) on from Irapa, and 737 km (457 miles) east of Caracas, you reach the end of the "highway" 9 (see GÜIRIA, page 210).

the house special is, not surprisingly, buffalo steak. The other *churuata* includes four appealing rooms, recently renovated, with their own bathrooms, while in the garden two further houses make ideal hideouts for couples. Klaus takes guests on a tour of his 2,500-hectare (6,175-acre) buffalo ranch, where some 230 bird species have been recorded. Rates are moderate.

The second water buffalo ranch belongs to Wilfried Merle and the Corporación Bufalina de Paria. Just off the highway, the 1,000-hectare (2,470-acre) **Campamento Agro Ecológico Río de Agua** (see GENERAL INFORMATION, page 202 under CARÚPANO, for booking) is the result of many years' work. Surrounded by munching water buffalo, in beautifully tended gardens crisscrossed by shallow canals, the ranch hosts five

Península de Paria offers numerous secluded — and empty — beaches.

comfortable two-single-bed cabins built in the *churuata* style. This being a highly ecological camp, their lights and ceiling fans are powered by solar panels, the water is pumped to the baths by windmills, and the kitchens make use of the biogas from buffalo manure. Guests explore the ranch in a bizarre tractor whose tires tower three meters (10 ft) high, and meet the ranch's mascot, Napolitana: a sizeable boa constrictor. Visitors are welcome and pay a small fee for a guided tour. Rates are moderate.

GÜIRIA

If Güiria were a "dotcom" company, I wouldn't buy shares in it. But as towns go, it wouldn't fare *too* badly on the stock exchange. Güiria's *raison d'être* is its port, which every Wednesday receives an injection of life when the Windward Lines ferries call in. The other five days of the week, Güiria's 25,000 inhabitants sulk. On Sundays, they aestivate — the opposite of hibernating.

Like San Juan de las Galdonas, but without the small-world charm, Güiria is of interest to the traveler only as a springboard to further adventures. It's the last place you can get to by car on Paria's southern coast before swapping four wheels for one propeller.

GENERAL INFORMATION

The town has three plazas: Sucre as you approach, Bolívar in the center, and Miranda down by the docks and fishermen's jetties. Everything you need is located among these. Güiria is yet to merit a tourist office, but does host useful banks.

WHERE TO STAY

Accommodation recommendations in Güira are inexpensive. The classiest hotel — a possibly more luxurious offer was nearly finished on Avenida Paria by the docks at the time of research — is the **Hotel El Digno (** (094) 81982 FAX (094) 820759 Avenida Miranda, on the way out of town to the north. It's comfortable and well-managed with a passable restaurant. The hotel can arrange excursions around Paria and south to the Delta, as can the similar-priced **Hotel Paraíso (** (094) 820350 FAX (094) 820451, further out on the same road.

Downtown, the best option is **La Posada de Chuchú (** (094) 81266 or (094) 820251, Calle Bideau No. 35, northwest of Plaza Bolívar, with 14 generous but simple rooms, some with balconies.

WHERE TO EAT

The restaurant owned by La Posada de Chuchú, **El Timón de Máximo**, delivers tasty fresh fish at healthy prices. **El Rincón Güireño** by Plaza Sucre is also a recommended choice, fish predominating, but also with appetizing *criollo* dishes.

HOW TO GET THERE

Güiria's airport has been closed to scheduled flights for some time, but you can ask Acosta Asociados (see below) about its current status. The bus station amounts to a cluster of companies around Plaza Sucre, servicing all points west. Note that there are also irregular boats to Pedernales across the Golfo de Paria, at the mouth of Caño Manamo in Delta Amacuro State. This route could be used as a back-door way to explore the delta (see THE ORINOCO DELTA, page 257).

TO TRINIDAD OR MARGARITA

The agents for the Windward Lines ferry are **Acosta Asociados (**/FAX (094) 81679, Calle Bolívar No. 31. Every other week a ferry leaves on Wednesdays, passes through Port of Spain (Trinidad), and loops via St. Vincent and Barbados to St. Lucia. It takes seven days all-told, before returning to Venezuela. The alternate week, the ferry goes via Pampatar in Margarita. To travel to Trinidad you must have either a return or an onward ticket. Passport formalities take place on the ferry, which doesn't usually obey its schedule (departure at 11 PM), so it is best to call and confirm. Acosta accept United States dollars and travelers' checks, but not credit cards, and tickets are valid for six months.

FAR EASTERN PARIA

Beaches, accessible by boat, dot the coast east of Güiria: Uriquito, Güinimita, and Yacua, small settlements such as Patao, and the larger and more famous Macuro (Puerto Colón). From these hamlets you can contract a guide for a trek across the Serranía de Paria to the northern coast's isolated hamlets: Don Pedro, Uquire, Pargo and Mejillones, or continue by boat. The north coast's beaches are far more spectacular than their southern counterparts; snorkeling in crystal waters in hidden coves is the order of the day. Mejillones is my personal favorite.

Macuro is thought to be the only place where Christopher Columbus actually stepped onto South American soil. It even became the capital of Venezuela for a day in 1998, to celebrate the quincentenary of the Admiral's landing. You'll find basic lodging and eateries there, as well as a tiny museum, and guides willing to take you into the hills.

MONAGAS STATE

If Zulia State is the new Texas, then Monagas State is the new Zulia. It is positively booming, pumping out millions of barrels of black gold from the vast underground oilfields which were discovered as recently as 1970. Its capital, Maturín, with its shopping malls and leafy suburbs, still lacks the tower-blocks of Maracaibo, but is fast catching up.

Monagas offers little to the tourist in search of adventure, culture, or nature. The exception, and it's an important one, is the Parque Nacional Cueva del Guácharo (see below), in the mountains of the north, whose tallest peak touches 2,400 m (7,872 ft). Monagas also includes two other routes to the delta environment, along the Río Morichal Largo, or from the small town of San Juan de Buja.

HOW TO GET THERE

Highway 10 travels south from Carúpano, through Maturín, and on down to Puerto Ordaz, across the Orinoco. From Maturín, Highway 13 cuts west, looping north to the coast at Barcelona–Puerto La Cruz. From Cumaná, a picturesque country road winds up into the hills via colonial Cumanacoa, passes by the national park and continues on to Maturín. The other smaller country road, equally striking, splits south from Highway 9 at Villa Frontado (west of Cariaco), passing close to the Embalse Clavellina, before ending at Caripe, near the national park.

PARQUE NACIONAL CUEVA DEL GUÁCHARO

Parque Nacional Cueva del Guácharo easily makes it into Venezuela's top 10 parks. The immense cave, stretching over 10 km (six miles) of galleries, rivers, lakes and tunnels, is regarded as one of the world's most complete cave ecosystems. Guácharo is Venezuela's second longest cave, thought to have been inhabited as early as 3,000 BC.

The cave's most famous resident is the *guácharo* (oilbird or *Steatonis caripensis*), a unique nocturnal, fruit-eating species, which navigates using radar. But it is also home to a variety of wildlife, including bats, pink-fish, mice, spiders, rats, crabs and centipedes. Add to this the fantastical echoing halls of pools reflecting stalactites and stalagmites and you begin to understand what all the fuss is about.

GENERAL INFORMATION

At the impressive reception building you'll find a small **speleological museum** and a cafeteria. The cave is open 8 AM to 4 PM, but you can camp nearby for a small fee, and use the bathroom facilities. For further information, contact **Inparques** ((091) 417553. Cueva del Guácharo gets busy on the weekends, as Venezuelans head to the hills to escape the heat.

If you want to penetrate further than the usual guided tour deep into the magical underground realm, permits are required. These can be obtained from Inparques in Caracas ((02) 285-5056 FAX (02) 285-3070, with about two months' notice. Contact Rafael Carreño of the **Venezuelan Speleological Society** for more advice about the cave at ((02) 730-6436 or (02) 272-0724 E-MAIL rafaelcarreno@hotmail.com or urbani@cantv.net.

WHAT TO SEE AND DO

The best time to visit the cave, without doubt, is just before dawn, or soon after dusk, when flocks of literally thousands of *guácharos* enter or leave

in a deafening avian cavalcade. The colony is Venezuela's largest, numbering some 15,000 members from August to December, declining to around 8,000 between March and April.

The **Museo Espeleológico** opens at the same times as the cave. It showcases the archeological finds recovered from the cave's galleries, as well as some impossibly large crystals. Documents, writings, maps, and drawings about Humboldt are displayed upstairs.

Elsewhere in the park — a refuge for many species of fauna, as well as being essential for water generation—several trails have been cut through the forest. The easiest leads to the great waterfall of **Chorreón**, while another hikes up to the Caripe Massif's highest crest, Cerro Negro.

The entrance to the wonders of the Cueva del Guácharo.

HOW TO GET THERE

The cave lies just over the border from Sucre State, making it an ideal detour from the coast road. The closest town with accommodation is Caripe (see below), 10 km (six miles) southeast of the cave. From Caripe, signs indicate the park's entrance above the town of **El Guácharo**. Buses or *por puestos* can stop on their route north to Cumaná. Taxis can also be contracted from Caripe, and will wait for their passengers.

CARIPE

If you've been traveling in Venezuela a while, or been frazzling on the beach somewhere, the town of Caripe comes as a breath of cool, mountain air. It's a charming little place, popular with tourists from home and abroad, nestled in rolling hills planted with coffee and oranges. It has earned the epithet *Jardín del Oriente* — Garden of the Orient. There isn't a whole lot to see in town, bar the altar in the modern church, but it's clean, tidy and friendly.

GENERAL INFORMATION

Banco Unión and Banco de Venezuela give cash advances, while the Banco del Orinoco changes travelers' checks.

All the *posada* owners mentioned below run tours of local sights and excursions, some on horseback. For further information on the area, or to compare prices, **Trekking Travelers Tours** ((092) 51352 FAX (092) 51843, Calle Guzmán Blanco, are helpful. They offer the usual tours, but also horseback riding and bike guides, and they rent mountain bikes — a great way to see the countryside. Another company, **Ecoturismo Struppek** ((092) 51364, also on Guzmán, offer interesting tours to local *fincas* and farms, with local people and cuisine an integral part of the day.

WHERE TO STAY

In Caripe, an alternative to downtown *posadas* and hotels are haciendas (*fincas*) in the surrounding area, where guests learn about rural life and get to taste the produce fresh off the farm.

Moderate

The most comfortable and inviting out-of-town option, attractive if you have your own vehicle, is **Cabañas Niebla Azul** ((092) 51501, Sector Las Delicias. It lies just off the road that loops north and east of Caripe, where there's a great *mirador* for admiring the surrounding rolling hills. The cabins for up to six people command fantastic views from their small terraces, and come with cozy fireplaces and equipped kitchens — so bring your own food.

Inexpensive

In Caripe proper, the **Hotel El Samán** ((092) 51183, lies at Avenida Enrique Chaumer No. 29, the town's main road. The 34 rooms are all comfortable, with the bonus of a solar-heated pool and a good restaurant. Similar is the **El Guácharo Hotel** ((092) 51218, on Avenida Guzmán Blanco, west of the center, with its own restaurant and pool. Just by the gas station, **Hotel Venezia** ((092) 51875 offers one of the better restaurants in town, and its 16 rooms are good value for the price, though nothing special.

Out of town, a place repeatedly recommended, and which I found first-class, is the family-run **Cabañas Bellerman** ((092) 51326, on the San Agustín-Teresén road. It includes six very pleasing, spick and span bungalow-type cabins, with one or two bedrooms. The location is superb on a wooded hill, and their shop renowned for its homemade jams, cakes and liqueurs. Worth stopping just for a bite to eat.

The other bucolic option, **Hacienda Campo Claro** ((092) 55013 lies just up from the church in Teresén, west of Caripe. The Betancourts run their 70-hectare (173-acre) farm along ecological lines and offer lodging in either rooms or more comfortable cabins with their own kitchens, baths and hot water. They take guests round the farm's coffee and orange plantations and can also rent horses for excursions, or take you on hikes by foot.

WHERE TO EAT

One of the best places for local dishes is the restaurant of the Hotel Venezia, while other possibilities include **Río Colorado**, popular with the locals, and **Tratorria Da Antonio** for some Italian and Venezuelan staples. Many of the *fincas* and haciendas in the area have restaurants open to the public, sometimes only for breakfast, and it's worth looking out for them.

HOW TO GET THERE

Caripe's bus station is by the market, at the southeastern end of town. There are two buses a day to Cumaná, departing in the morning, while there are plenty of buses south to Maturín. One night-bus leaves for Caracas, via Maturín.

MATURÍN

The booming Maturín grew as a port when nearby Río Guarapiche was still navigable all the way to the Golfo de Paria. Trinidad remained the town's main trading partner for centuries. Since the 1990s'

Apertura Petrolera ("Oil Opening"), Maturín lies at the heart of the brave new world of oil drilling in the east of the country.

For the traveler though, Maturín holds little appeal beyond its wide avenues and family-friendly parks. It's not the kind of place you would want to stay more than a night — unless you are particularly keen on shopping malls. As the regional transportation hub, with links to both the Oriente coast, the Delta at Tucupita, and Puerto Ordaz and Ciudad Bolívar, you might have to.

GENERAL INFORMATION

The **tourist office** (/FAX (091) 430798 is next to the large IPAN building, in Hacienda Sarripal, on the arterial Avenida Alirio Ugarte Pelayo. Banco Unión is by the corner of Calle Juncal and Carrera Monagas. Banco Mercantil, on Carrera Monagas, near the market, changes travelers' checks.

WHAT TO SEE AND DO

Maturín's best park, **Parque Municipal La Guaricha**, boasts a lovely lagoon, a small zoo, and a mini-train for children (and adults who haven't grown up). **Plaza Bolívar** and **Plaza Sucre** are pleasant enough.

Contact **Sergio Córdoba** ((091) 414122 FAX (091) 426647, oficina 3A, Edificio Banco Unión, Avenida Juncal, for trips to the Río Morichal Largo, a wetlands river, similar to those of the delta. Or you can contract a boatman yourself at the bridge 82 km (51 miles) south of Maturín on Highway 10.

WHERE TO STAY AND EAT

Luxury

With a prime location, the **Hotel Stauffer Maturín** ((091) 430884, Avenida Alirio Ugarte Pelayo, next to Maturín's newest mall and part of the Stauffer chain, is not only the best downtown hotel, it is also well designed. Its pool area and surrounding gardens are first class, as is the service. The restaurant serves top international fare.

Moderate

A good value downtown hotel, the **Hotel Colonial** ((091) 421183 includes 42 ample rooms and better suites, all with air-conditioning and televisions, as well as a welcoming restaurant. The best in its class and very central.

Inexpensive

The most pleasant and friendly of the central hotels in this bracket is the **Hotel Perla Princesa** ((091) 432579 FAX (091) 414008, Avenida Juncal at Ave-

nida Bolívar. The rooms come with hot water, air-conditioning and televisions, though their restaurant seems somewhat overpriced.

WHERE TO EAT

Moderate

Apart from the hotels listed, an establishment with a fine reputation is **Yarua Internacional** ((091) 413898, Carrera 7 No. 64, while live music and *carne en vara* are offered at the pretty stylish **El Portón** ((091) 418073, Avenida Raúl Leoni. The restaurant in the **Hotel Morichal Largo** ((091) 516222, out on the road to La Cruz also enjoys a good reputation.

Inexpensive

Mister Pasta ((091) 429289, Carrera 6 Juncal, has a varied menu and represents good value, with **El Brasero** nearby. In the Centro Comercial Portofino, Avenida Bolívar, try **Valerio's**.

HOW TO GET THERE

Maturín's airport lies two kilometers (under a mile) east of the city center, on Avenida Raúl Leoni. Being a booming business town, it's well-connected to the entire country, including plenty of flights to Caracas, and fewer to Maracaibo, Barquisimeto and Porlamar. **Rutaca** ((091) 421635 flies to Trinidad three times a week.

The terminal for buses is on the other side of town on Avenida Libertador, southwest of the city center. Most Caracas-bound buses leave in the evening, while there are regular connections to other regional cities. For the Cueva del Guácharo, take the northbound bus for Caripe and ask to be dropped off at the village of El Guácharo from where it's a half-an-hour walk.

The fisherman Botuto's daughter, Perla, from San Juan de las Galdonas.

Isla de Margarita

IF YOU'RE LOOKING FOR BEACH RESORTS, GOOD FOOD, NATURAL BEAUTY AND CARIBBEAN COLOR, you need look no further than "the pearl of the Caribbean" as Margarita Island, lying some 40 km (28 miles) off Venezuela's mainland, is known.

People flock to Margarita for two reasons: the shopping and the beaches. But one could quite easily add the nightlife, inland villages, mountains, mangrove wetlands, and spectacular sunsets to this list.

In the 1970s, the state of Nueva Esparta, encompassing the islands of Margarita, Coche and Cubagua, became a duty-free zone. Shopaholic Venezuelans have been boarding the ferry ever since to make the most of the bargains. All round the island stretch dozens of beaches to suit all tastes. Whether it's deserted coves, rollers for surfing, winds for windsurfing, or unending expanses of sand, Margarita's cocktail of beaches rivals any in the Caribbean.

BACKGROUND

Before the arrival of Europeans, fierce Carib Indians, as well as the more peaceful Guaiquerís and Arawaks, occupied the islands of Margarita, Coche and Cubagua. The islands were known as *Paraguachoa* or "abundance of fish." Although it's commonly believed Margarita was named after the Portuguese word for "pearl," Margaret of Austria — Princess of Castille at the time Columbus first visited — makes a more convincing candidate. However, the pearl connection holds some sway.

Columbus, in his reports to the Spanish Crown, described Indians adorned with pearls. Following a shipment of 36 kg (80 lb) of pearls in 1499, it wasn't long before a veritable "pearl rush" gripped the island of Cubagua. As with most rushes, it didn't last. A combination of greed which exhausted the pearl beds, natural calamities such as

SPORTS AND OUTDOOR ACTIVITIES

Margarita offers an array of watersports and activities to keep you from your deckchair.

Windsurfing

Ask any windsurfer where he's heading in Venezuela — and probably South America — and the answer you'll get is **El Yaque**. The beach, on the southern side of the island east of the airport, has become synonymous with the sport, famed for its strong winds and flat sea. There, you'll find a range of hotels geared to the pilgrims, some good restaurants, lively beach bars, and at least four companies renting equipment (see EL YAQUE, page 232).

Snorkeling and Scuba Diving

Following windsurfing, the island's next pull is snorkeling and scuba diving, and its reputation grows. For something close-by, **El Farallón** off Pampatar, plugs a large underwater statue as well as healthy corals and abundant large fish, including barracudas. The dive isn't spectacular, but it's the most economical choice. The ferry wreck off the island of **Cubagua** includes cars, though no cadavers, you'll be glad to hear. It's a good dive and visibility is often excellent.

For the best dives in the area however, head to the small archipelago of **Los Frailes**, northeast of Margarita. The corals and clear waters rival those of Los Roques—you won't want to leave the water. The shallows also provide plenty of sights for snorkelers. You can also ask operators about the more distant virgin dive territory of the **La Blanquilla** and **Los Testigos** islands.

Reputable dive operators include the **Centro de Buceo Pablo Montoya** ((095) 644746 E-MAIL cbpablom@cantv.net, which runs PADI, NAUI and CMAS courses, and **Enomis' Divers** (/FAX (095) 622977 E-MAIL enomis@telcel.net.ve WEB SITE members.xoom.com/enomisdivers, based inside the Hotel Margarita Dynasty (see WHERE TO STAY, page 220 under PORLAMAR). They also double as a tour operator and travel agent.

Surfing and Sailing

On Margarita, surfing is a popular, not to mention fashionable, pastime. The main beaches for dudes to hang out are **Playa Guacuco** and **Playa Parguito**. The luxury catamaran, **Catatumbo**, crosses over to Coche island in an all-inclusive package which includes transfers from your hotel and snorkeling gear. For departure days (which vary according to season) call ((095) 631072/ 643279. The Hilton rents small dinghies, while the

the tidal wave and earthquake of 1541, and attacks by mainland Indian tribes enraged by slave raiding led to the abandonment of Nueva Cádiz, the town founded on Cubagua in 1528.

The indigenous divers were worked mercilessly by the Europeans, who drove them to early deaths from water pressure, exhaustion, malnutrition or sharks. By the mid-1500s, the main focus of pearl fishing had already moved to Coche and Margarita, and little by little the pearl beds were picked clean. Today, pearling is permitted between January and April every other year, having been banned altogether in the early 1960s.

The seven forts built in the colonial era to protect the Spanish profits from marauding pirates and buccaneers comprise the most enduring testaments to the industry's importance. Only two of these, San Carlos Borromeo in Pampatar and Santa Rosa in La Asunción, have been restored.

A windsurfer satisfies his need for speed at El Yaque.

yacht **Antares I** ((016) 695-3496 E-MAIL antares@ enlared.net organizes charters year-round to any number of coastal destinations.

Ultralights

If you fancy getting a bird's-eye view of the island, and some stunning photos, there are two bases for ultralights, one at Porlamar's Aeropuerto Viejo for flights Monday to Thursday, and the other at Playa El Agua from Friday to Sunday. Contact Luís Gerardo of **SAP Flights** ((095) 637097 or (095) 636339 for more information. For more extreme flights, **hanggliders** launch from Cerro Copey, where average flight times range between 45 minutes and two hours. Contact Omar Contreras

ranchonegro, based near La Asunción, is an established stable. Over on Macanao, contact **Cabatucan** ((016) 681-9348 FAX (095) 617259 WEB SITE margaweb.conk.com, run by enthusiastic French riders near Boca de Río, and **Hato San Francisco** ((016) 695-0408.

Family Fun

Diverland, on the road from Pampatar to Porlamar, opens the strange hours of Wednesday to Friday 7 PM to 1 AM, and weekends 11 AM to 1 AM, and encompasses every aquatic activity under the sun — from waterslides to wave machines — in a massive complex. In the Centro Comercial Rattan Plaza in Pampatar, **Play Aventura** will keep

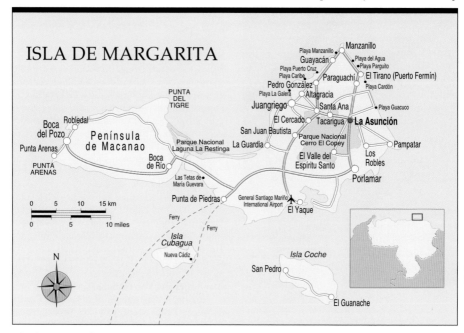

ISLA DE MARGARITA

((016) 695-0060. If you want to go all the way, he can organize **skydiving** too.

Golf

For golfers, the 18-hole golf course at the **Isla Bonita** resort (see THE NORTH COAST, page 228) is said to be one of the best in the Caribbean region, though the winds are strong. A further golf course in the Costa Azul area was under construction at the time of writing.

Horseback riding

Horseback riding makes for a great way to explore the island. It's proving increasingly popular, particularly on the wilder Macanao Peninsula. You can enjoy a two-hour or a full week excursion, depending on your tastes. **Rancho Negro** ((095) 423197 (014) 995-1103/995-1018 E-MAIL rancho negro@veweb.com WEB SITE www.veweb.com/

small children and teenagers amused with a range of slides and games, arcades and pool tables.

PORLAMAR

The original name of the fishing village founded in 1526 was Pueblo del Mar, but, in typical Venezuelan fashion, the truncated version was soon adopted. Porlamar long ruled as the island's most important port, though it enjoyed nothing of the influence it now exerts over the island's economy. It seems odd today that La Asunción with its 15,000 inhabitants remains the capital, while Porlamar has mushroomed to a city of over 300,000.

Along the avenues of 4 de Mayo and Santiago Mariño, flash boutiques are everywhere — but bargains aren't quite what they used to be since the addition of a purchase tax on many goods.

Recently, under the governorship of Irene Saez, Nueva Esparta has run a series of offers including half-price flights and prices. At these times, shopping is definitely good value. As a destination with top luxury resorts, Porlamar is awash with excellent seafood restaurants, while lively nightspots coupled with a vacation spirit keep the party going until dawn.

GENERAL INFORMATION

Strangely enough, Margarita's **Corporación de Turismo (Corpotur)** isn't in Porlamar but in the small town of **Los Robles**, north of Porlamar. It's located in the Centro Artesanal Los Robles, open

Mondays. Head to Banco Unión for ATM cash advances, at the top end of Santiago Mariño, on Avenida 4 de Mayo. Cambio La Precisa, on Calle Maneiro between Calles Guevara and Mariño, offers probably the best rates for changing cash and non-Amex travelers' checks, or else try Cambio Cafyca, on the corner of Santiago Mariño and Calle Patiño.

Many of the larger hotels in Porlamar (e.g. Bella Vista, Hilton, Dynasty) organize guided day tours of the island, which could typically include a boat ride around La Restinga Lagoon, and visits to La Asunción, Juangriego, Playa El Agua, Virgen del Valle, and Pampatar. Other agencies include **Supertours (** (095) 618781 FAX (095) 617061 on Calle

weekdays from 8:30 AM to noon and 1:30 PM to 5:30 PM **(** (095) 622514 or (095) 623638. However, you'll also find tourism information booths in the main hall of the airport's national terminal and on Avenida 4 de Mayo where you can pick up a map, and the tourist magazine *La Vista*. Look out for coupon booklets for sizeable discounts on restaurants, bars, shopping, and even car rental.

Another option, the **Cámara de Turismo** on Santiago Mariño, opens weekdays from 8 AM to noon and 2 PM to 6 PM. You might also want to find the free English-language newspaper *Mira!* from kiosks, and *Margarita La Guía* (published quarterly in English, Spanish and German), with the best map of the island.

Money changing is straightforward in Margarita. The Amex office lies opposite the Hotel Bella Vista, open business hours, though closed on

Larez, Quinta Thaid, or in Playa El Agua, **Taco Tours (** (014) 995-7893.

Lineas Turísticas Aerotuy (LTA) organize trips around the island and to Los Roques and Isla Blanquilla, as well as running charter flights to their camps in Canaima, and catamarans to Coche and Cubagua. Their offices are at the bottom of Santiago Mariño, west of the Hotel Bella Vista **(** (095) 632211 or (095) 630367 FAX (095) 617746 WEB SITE www.tuy.com.

To get to know the island or to explore inland, rent a car. Competition among companies is high, making Margarita the cheapest place to rent a car in Venezuela. Prices start at around US$50 a day for small city cars, but you can also rent open-top Suzuki jeeps, a lot more fun. Scooters are a breezier alternative to cars, though you should check the

Handcrafts abound on Margarita.

brakes thoroughly before setting off, and ask for a crash helmet. To cruise in style, rent a Harley Davidson from **Centro Comercial Buena Ventura** ((095) 618178, Avenida 4 de Mayo, opposite Tropi Burger.

The roads around the island are generally in good shape, and drivers, thankfully, tend to be less crazed than in other parts of the country, although driving at night presents additional hazards. A profusion of car rental companies clusters at the airport and in front of the Hotel Bella Vista: **Ramcar II** ((095) 614019, **Excellency** ((095) 626503 FAX (095) 622955, and **Warriors** ((095) 627076 (the latter two with branches near the Hotel Dynasty and at Playa El Agua). **Budget** TOLL-FREE (800) 28343 has offices at the airport and in Porlamar.

Useful **web sites** for browsing-up on Margarita before you get there are www.margarita-travel.com, http://think-venezuela.net, and www.veweb.com. The most pleasant cybercafé is the new **Utopia** in the Costa Azul development, just off Avenida Bolívar. Further details of those hotels with e-mails ending "@enlared.net" can be found at www.enlared.net/margarita.

WHAT TO SEE AND DO

Porlamar has few cultural or historical attractions to detain you. However, the **Museo de Arte Contemporáneo Francisco Narváez**, on the corner of Calles Igualdad and Díaz, open Tuesday to Friday 9 AM to 5 PM, weekends 10 AM to 4 PM, features works from the painter and sculptor who gave his name to the museum — note his fountain *La Ronda* by the Bella Vista Hotel — as well as temporary exhibitions of modern art. Free cultural events such as concerts and recitals take place on Friday evenings.

To the south of the old part of town, the promenade **Paseo Rómulo Gallegos** leads to the lighthouse erected in 1896. Nearby, folklore shows are often held on weekends, and you can admire the old *aduana* customs house. The boats to Chacopata on the Araya Peninsula leave from here. The **Mercado Viejo**, to the west of the pier, might be extinct by the time you read this. Large cruise ships will dock here, placing the island firmly on the luxury Caribbean cruise map.

WHERE TO STAY

Margarita boasts the most varied and extensive accommodation in the country. At the last count, there were over 100 hotels in Porlamar alone. Prices vary greatly according to season, regarded as "high" from August to September, December to January, and during Easter.

Many of the large resorts and hotels you'll find listed in this chapter offer special all-inclusive packages. The resulting deals can be very attractive and worth pursuing if you plan to stay on the island for a week or so. Contact them before you leave. On Margarita, you might want to contact **Holiday Tours** ((095) 611311 or (095) 641311 FAX (095) 642992 for the best deals on offer.

Luxury and Expensive

The clutch of five- and four-star resort-style hotels rise to the east of Porlamar, around the area known as Costa Azul near Playa Moreno, a short ride from the city center.

The most established of these is the five-star **Margarita Hilton** ((095) 624111 FAX (095) 623941 WEB SITE www.hilton.com, with 280 luxury rooms and all the facilities of a top hotel, as well as possibly the best service on the island. They offer guests parasailing flights and jetskis on their beach; classes for scuba diving, windsurfing and water skiing can also be organized.

The unique, "pampering par excellence" **Hotel La Samanna Resort & Sea Spa** ((095) 622662 FAX (095) 620989 E-MAIL info@samanna.com WEB SITE www.samanna.com, Avenida Bolívar and Avenida Gómez, Costa Azul, specializes in saltwater health treatments — with a wonderful setting to relax and recuperate. Their luxury rooms all boast balconies and sea views, while lush greenery hems their own Jacuzzis and small private pools in the suites. I came away very impressed.

Moderate

Of the many choices, I found the **Hotel Marbella Mar** ((095) 624022 or (095) 621662 FAX (095) 621389 E-MAIL info@hotel-marbellamar.com WEB SITE www.hotel-marbellamar.com, Playa El Angel, Avenida Principal and Calle Chipichipi, with 110 rooms of different types, a pool, and friendly service, an excellent choice. It's not central, but they offer free transfers to the beaches, and taxis are cheap.

The old stalwart **Hotel Bella Vista Cumberland** ((095) 617222 FAX (095) 612557, at the southern end of Avenida Santiago Mariño, includes 314 revamped rooms, perfectly acceptable for the price. Make sure you ask for a room with a sea view. Just west of here, and also with good views, you will find the much newer **Margabella Suites** ((095) 639960 FAX (095) 619246, with a combination of 90 comfortable rooms and suites, and a pool. The biggest plus of the hotel is its rooftop restaurant where the food is delicious and the breeze refreshing.

Inexpensive

The **Hotel Imperial** ((095) 614823 FAX (095) 615056 on Calle Marcano to the west of Santiago Mariño on Playa Guaraguao, gets my vote (Calle Marcano

Porlamar's bustling Avenida Santiago Mariño.

becomes the Avenida Raúl Leoni). Rooms have televisions, telephones, and balconies with sea views from the third floor up: excellent value. The area is quiet and the beach nearby.

Back nearer Santiago Mariño, the best of the bunch is probably the **Hotel Nueva Scandinavia** ((095) 642662 FAX (095) 635121, on Calle Maracano near Narváez, whose 22 rooms are spotless and comfortable, with the bonus of a Jacuzzi and a decent restaurant.

Getting to budget level, consider the **Hotel Tamaca** ((095) 611602, Calle Marcano, whose bar and restaurant area are far more appealing than its rooms, although there are some decent ones (with either fan or air-conditioning) with cold water. Its location by Playa Guaraguao makes it a good choice.

WHERE TO EAT

Margarita's numerous seafood restaurants serve everything from *chipi-chipi* (clam chowder) to *langostinas* (lobster), but you can also find international dishes throughout the town.

Expensive

The Margarita Hilton claims possibly the island's most exclusive dining at its two restaurants: the plush French restaurant **Le Chateaubriand**, with an excellent wine list, or **Los Uveros**, indoors, with an extensive à la carte menu for dinner, including such local fish as *pargo* (red snapper) and *carite* (kingfish). The Japanese-cum-Peruvian restaurant **Nikey & Tiberio** at the Samanna Resort also comes highly recommended.

Moderate

The seafront **Bahía**, located on Avenida Raúl Leoni, opposite the Hotel Imperial, serves up some wonderful lobster and paella dishes in a tropical, attractive setting with live music (only open in the evenings). A few doors down, lies the **Rancho de Pablo**, even closer to the beach and with equally good seafood. Further along from here, **Cocody** offers a romantic terrace setting from which to enjoy their French-influenced cuisine.

On Calle Cedeño at Santiago Mariño, the kitchen of **El Chipi** ((095) 636101 is well-known for its succulent lobster. The two upscale restaurants for pizza are **Rigoletto** on Calle Malavé at Patiño, with homemade pasta and wood oven for pizza, and the attractively styled **Positano**, on Calle Fermín at Tubores.

Inexpensive

Opposite the good value **Dino's Grill** on Calle Igualdad, the *tasca* **La Cueva de la Rioja** offers a more intimate atmosphere and some excellent, no-nonsense Spanish dishes. **La Gran Pirámide** on Calle Mallave at Patiño has a good range of dishes from fish to meat, while **Los Tres Delfines** on Calle Cedeño specializes in seafood at good prices.

In the large, new mall, Jumbo, on Avenida 4 de Mayo, you'll find **Dady's** whose restaurant is decent, though you'll come more for the bar and the dancing which gets very lively later at night. **Ana's Café**, atop the Avensa building on Avenida 4 de Mayo is about the most chic place to sip your cappuccino and grab a bite.

NIGHTLIFE

Porlamar is a great town to party in, and you'll find plenty of night spots around. Watch out for the happy hours, around 7 to 8 PM.

An old favorite which has withstood the sands of fashion, **Mosquito Coast**, by the Hotel Bella Vista, gives on to the sea, with some great cocktails and a good mix of music. The "place to be" while researching was **Señor Frogs** out in the Costa Azul development, which has a restaurant, grill and a massive bar area — as well as tacky merchandise. Other lively bars and nightspots include **Dugout**, **Subsuelo** and **Buccaneers** all on Avenida 4 de Mayo, and **Eye**, on Calle Marcano just east of Santiago Mariño.

On Calle Malavé, you will find two more laid-back bars, **Gator's** and **Brandy's**, while **Piano Blanco** on Calle JM Patiño and **Flamboyant** at the Hilton cater to a more sophisticated, slightly older clientele.

If you feel like blowing some of your hard-earned money at a casino, Margarita's establishments are the best in the country. You'll find the most exclusive at the **Hilton** and the **Marina Bay**, followed by the **Flamingo Beach** and the **Stauffer Hotel** on Santiago Mariño.

HOW TO GET THERE

Margarita can get very busy in peak season, and at these times book your air ticket well in advance. Expect long lines at the ferry terminals if you're coming by boat.

Most travelers on buses head straight to Porlamar, and continue to other beaches from there. Coming from Porlamar, buses for the airport leave from Plaza Bolívar. If you're debating whether to save money on the ferry, spend the extra dollars on a plane, honestly.

By Air

The Santiago Mariño airport is 20 km (just over 12 miles) from Porlamar and has both an international and national terminal. Taxis from the airport to Porlamar shouldn't cost more than US$12, and the information booth found in the national

Spindly palms sway their crowns down by the sea.

terminal (when open) provides a list of tariffs for other parts of the island. A cheaper alternative is the airbus which links the airport to Porlamar. Car rental agencies cluster in the international terminal, as do several *casas de cambio*. Flights from Europe and North America now go direct to Margarita, bypassing Maiquetía.

The island is well-served by national airlines, where the eastern part of the country is covered by Oriental, Avior, LAI and Rutaca, the center and west by Aeropostal, Air Venezuela, Aserca and Laser. There are more than two dozen flights to Caracas a day; carriers include Servivensa, Laser, Air Venezuela and Aserca. Flights to Caracas cost between US$50 and US$70 one-way. Margarita is a good place to jump to another part of Venezuela, with Aerotuy flying regularly to La Gran Sabana, Canaima, Los Roques and the Delta.

By Sea
Punta de Piedras ferry terminal lies 29 km (18 miles) due west of Porlamar. Regular bus and *por puesto* services run the route. You should confirm all ferry times with the companies listed below, and be in line for tickets at least two hours before the departure time (four if you have a car). Be warned, queues during peak times can be horrendous. Discounts are available for children aged two to seven, and for adults over 65.

From **Puerto La Cruz**, the *Gran Cacique III* hydrofoil takes two and a half hours to do the crossing, with two journeys a day, more in high season. Go first class. Contact in Puerto La Cruz ((081) 630935 and Punta de Piedras ((095) 98072 or (095) 98399 for information. The *Gran Cacique II* does the run from **Cumaná** in two hours at 7 AM and 2 PM, returning at 11 AM and 6 PM, call ((093) 320011 or (093) 312589 for information.

The other option for a faster and more comfortable crossing is Conferry's *Margarita Express*, which takes around two hours for the journey from Puerto La Cruz. There are two departures a day in low season, one more in high season. Tickets cost more than the *Gran Cacique*, but the boat is superior to the hydrofoils.

The cheapest way of getting to and from Margarita is aboard Conferry's older vessels, with four to six sailings to Puerto La Cruz depending on the season, taking around four hours — often more. Cumaná is only served twice a day. There is no first-class and the crossing, though slightly shorter, verges on a diesel-fume nightmare. Call Conferry TOLL-FREE (800) 33779. Naviarca is the other company connecting Margarita and Cumaná, but avoid it if you possibly can.

For the smaller *lanchas* (outboard engine, open boats with an awning for shade) to Chacopata on the Araya Peninsula, Sucre State, head for the Paseo Rómulo Gallegos, near the old lighthouse in Porlamar, where the *Empresa Naviera Turismo*

Chacopata do the run. The trip takes between one and two hours, costs only US$4, but it's not for the faint-stomached. However, if you want to head towards Paria, this is by far your best option. Boats leave all day from early morning to around 3 PM, and work on the same basis as *por puestos* (i.e. when they're full, they leave).

For travel to Trinidad and other Caribbean islands with Windward Islands, ferries leave at 6 PM every other Wednesday from the pier at Pampatar. Contact the English-speaking travel agents **Unitravel** ((095) 617491 or (095) 630278, Calle Cedeño at Santiago Mariño in Porlamar, for bookings, or the company's agent in Pampatar, David Hart ((095) 623527.

NORTH OF PORLAMAR

Heading out from Porlamar, the highway runs north towards La Asunción. You can take the easterly route via Los Robles and Pampatar, or keep west and pass the Valle del Espíritu Santo (El Valle). Either way, you soon get a feel for the island's green hues and the imposing mountain of Cerro El Copey. From La Asunción, follow the road north for the beaches of the eastern coast, or west to the craft villages and Juangriego.

PAMPATAR

On Margarita, it isn't long before you're stepping back in time. On route to Pampatar, stop by at **Los Robles**, a small village north of Porlamar with a brilliant white colonial church, El Pilar. From here, on October 12, the reputedly solid-gold statue of "La Pilarica" is carried around the square and the village to much fanfare and merriment. As you come off the highway, note the large — and good — crafts center where **Corpotur** has its offices.

East of Los Robles, you come to Pampatar, founded in 1535 at the island's deepest harbor, and one of the oldest towns in the Americas. It didn't take long for pirates to discover the town, razing its first fort of La Caranta. The fort's ruins over on the eastern bluff provide the best views of Pampatar's bay. The water here isn't particularly clean unfortunately, and swimming is not advised.

What to See and Do
The Spanish didn't take the pirates' raids lightly. In the seventeenth century, they embarked on a fort-building project, in the bay this time. Despite being burned early on by Dutch marauders, the **Castillo de San Carlos Borromeo** represents one of Spain's great military engineering projects. Its colossal star-shape is similar to that of Cumaná's fort, and one can still see the remains of the moat which ringed it. Inside, amid somewhat

crumbling masonry awaiting a caring hand, a small exhibition displays architects' drafts, period weapons, and paintings. Opening times are from 8 AM to 5 PM.

Over the road lies the small, unpretentious **Iglesia de Santísimo Cristo del Buen Viaje**, built in the eighteenth century, whose crucifix holds a special place in the hearts of local fishermen. The ship carrying the cross from Spain to Santo Domingo stopped en route in Pampatar. Every time the vessel attempted to leave the port, it was driven back by storms, until the statue was finally left behind, where it has stayed ever since.

Across the shaded square, the imposing neo-classical building painted a garish shade of yellow

Several fish restaurants line the bay, of which **La Luna Marina** and **Trimar** are probably the best, while **El Farallón**, by the fort, is another option.

EL VALLE DEL ESPÍRITU SANTO

Taking the western highway from Porlamar, you reach El Valle del Espíritu Santo and the entrance to the **Cerro El Copey National Park**.

The Virgin of the Valley's shrine is the most cherished in Eastern Venezuela. As patroness of the island, fishermen and the Navy, her fiesta on the September 8 makes a great excuse for a statewide holiday. Celebrations and events last the entire week.

houses the **Casa de la Aduana**. Here, in 1817, the islands of Margarita, Coche and Cubagua were named "Nueva Esparta" for the first time. Today the customs house holds the offices of Fundene, the Foundation for Development of Nueva Esparta ((095) 622494, open weekdays 8 AM to noon and 1 PM to 4:30 PM. They provide maps and tourist information. Its cool central courtyard also hosts temporary art exhibitions.

Where to Stay and Eat

The most exclusive place to stay in Pampatar is the resort-style **Flamingo Beach** ((095) 628422 FAX (095) 620271 E-MAIL flamingo@enlared.net, which lies beyond the Caranta fort, east of the town center. Set around a great beach, 170 comfortable and attractive rooms, and a swimming pool, gym, sauna and tennis courts add up to one of the island's finest resorts.

What to See and Do

The **Santuario de la Virgen** was built in the 1900s to house the image of the Virgin, on the site of previous churches. A twin-towered edifice, painted bright pink and white, it would be hard to miss. Inside, the Madonna's dresses take pride of place. Pearls adorn one, diamonds another. You should dress respectfully before entering the church.

To the side of the edifice, the **Museo Diocesano** evolved as the depository for all the gifts grateful pilgrims left behind for the Virgin. The collection is a sight to behold, displaying gold miniatures of everything from cars and houses, to legs and hands.

Cerro El Copey, the island's highest point at 920 m (3,018 ft), lies to the west and north of El

Coconuts cluster, waiting to drop: a serious health hazard...

Valle. The national park embraces 7,000 hectares (17,290 acres), including swathes of cloudforest and the wax-leaf copey tree from which it acquired its name. If you're lucky, you can spot the elusive *mono mandarín*, the capuchin monkey that inhabits the bromeliad-clad forest. To get to the park, take the La Sierra road north towards Asunción, where signs indicate the Inparques hut and lookout. From there, the hike to the top takes about two hours. As you might expect, the views in the evening, looking northwest toward Juangriego, are the best on the island.

LA ASUNCIÓN

While Porlamar buzzes away, La Asunción seems quite content to snooze, thank you very much. The small town, centered around its shaded square, feels a million miles from the hustle and bustle of the brash pretender. Nestled in the shadow of Cerro El Copey, La Asunción's valley is Margarita's most fertile and tilled. The soil might be fecund, but the town was founded here in 1565 with pirates in mind, not sugarcane or bananas. On the feast day of August 14, the town springs to life with processions and masses, but otherwise, it's a picture of somnolent health.

What to See and Do

The **cathedral**, Nuestro Señora de La Asunción, is Venezuela's oldest, dating back to 1570. It acted as a blueprint for the burgeoning colony's churches for the next 100 years. Its exterior lines, austere and sober, reflect the early Spaniard's roots in Inquisition Spain. Inside, take a minute to savor its beguiling tranquility. The two rows of colossal columns process in solemn rows along the nave, a long way from the wedding-cake frivolity of later churches on the island. The church only opens for morning or evening masses.

The **Casa de la Cultura**, situated in a modern building across the square from the cathedral on Calle Fermín, displays a collection of replica pre-Columbian pottery, alongside temporary exhibitions, open 8 AM to 8 PM weekdays, and weekends until noon. On the corner of the square, the **Museo Nueva Cádiz** houses a library and historical collection pertaining to the colony's early history. The graceful building dates from the eighteenth century, formerly the local government's seat. The first town established on Cubagua Island south of Margarita, Nueva Cádiz was founded officially in 1528, though the pearl industry had been picking the beds clean well before that. The museum also displays works by local artists, open daily, 9 AM to 6 PM, except on Mondays.

The restored and converted **Casa Juan Bautista Arismendi** lies to the west of the square along Calle Independencia. General Arismendi, the husband

of the famous island heroine, Luisa Cáceres de Arismendi, fought bravely for the liberation of the island. You'll find a modest but intriguing collection of family portraits and heirlooms. The Casa is open 9 AM to 5 PM weekdays.

Up on the hill overlooking the town — look for the signposts with a castle symbol — is the **Castillo de Santa Rosa**. From its imposing perch, the fort surveys the surrounding rolling countryside and the Cerro Matasiete — where the decisive battle to free Margarita took place. The fort includes the cell where Luisa de Arismendi was held hostage for her husband the general. A bottleneck dungeon, the grim cell is all the more macabre when you consider she gave birth to a child while incarcerated there. The child later died. Period weapons, iron balls with chains and explanatory panels complete the displays in the fort. It's open daily from 8 AM to 6 PM, except on Mondays when they close at 3 PM.

Where to Eat

You're best off catching a fresh fish meal at one of Pampatar's beachfront restaurants, or **La Trattoría al Porto** in Puerto Fermín, or else head to **La Casona** in San Juan Bautista for an excellent lunch inland.

THE EAST COAST

Turquoise waters, coconut palms, fresh fish and seafood, stretches of snow-white beaches, lively bars and the all-important ingredient of sun by the bucket explain why Margarita attracts so many foreign travelers. You'll find it all on its eastern coastline.

NORTH FROM PAMPATAR

One of the largest resorts on this side of the island, the **Lagunamar Allegro Hotel** ((095) 620711 boasts over 300 rooms and about every activity you can think of on its expansive grounds. The hotel has a nearby saltwater lagoon guests can sail and windsurf, a large beach, and if that's not enough, it also has no less than nine swimming pools, including one especially for children. The Lagunamar also claims the island's top health spa.

Further north of Pampatar, a turn takes you down to **Playa Guacuco**, popular with locals, with a series of small restaurants, as well as chairs and parasols for rent. Surfers head for Guacuco's waves, though they're not as good as Parguito.

Nearby, another luxury resort, the **Tamarindo Guacuco** ((095) 422727 includes 33 tropical-style *cabañas* with wonderful sea views, as well 25 rooms in its main building, and two swimming pools. All-inclusive deals are the norm here. North of Guacuco, the very exclusive development of Ranchos de Chana hugs the coast, while the road heads back inland around the sloping hills of **Cerro Guayamurí**.

PLAYA CARDÓN TO EL AGUA

Heading north, stop to visit the partly restored Iglesia de San José in the next village of **Paraguachí**. Coming out of Paraguachí, take the easterly road for Playa Cardón, a wide bay with a thin stretch of bleached beach with limited shade, but plenty of charm. The road runs alongside it to **Puerto Fermín**.

Puerto Fermín is actually known as El Tirano, a rather somber reminder of the bloodthirsty tyrant Lope de Aguirre's sojourn on Margarita in

Where to Stay

As you go through the village of **El Salado**, en route for Playa Cardón, watch for the signs on the right for the rustic **La Posada de Iris (Rancho Río Salado)** ((095) 619191 or (014) 789-4051. About five minutes along a bumpy earth road, the *posada* is on your left-hand side. It's a far cry from the luxury resorts, and charmingly decorated by the owner Iris with tropical colors and varied antiques and knickknacks. She rents 14 rooms in all, some with balconies. The complex includes a restaurant and small pool. The adjoining farm boasts a menagerie of animals, sure to be a hit with children.

Along Playa Cardón, the small-scale **Hostería Marymonte** ((095) 48066 FAX (095) 48557 E-MAIL

the mid-1500s. He terrorized the locals and killed the governor, nice man that he was. Werner Herzog's film, starring Klaus Kinski, *Aguirre, Wrath of God*, recreates his journey down the Amazon in vivid, gory detail. Today El Tirano is one of the most picturesque coastal villages on the island, where nearly all the houses radiate vivid oranges and vermilions, ochres and aquamarines. Try to catch the morning haul of fish brought in by the local fishing fleet in their painted boats. The fishermen are usually willing to take you out in their boats in the afternoon. You'll find two modest *posadas* in the town on Calle Picaflor.

Beyond El Tirano, the road follows the crescent and turns to earth, but follow it round to reach **Playa Parguito**, the number one beach for surfing, or just having fun in the waves. Modest fresh-fish restaurants and shade-renters people the shore. The road then turns back to the main coastal "highway."

paul@compucen.com WEB SITE www.marymonte .compucen.com, run by Paul Poinçot has six neat cabins with small terraces, and a swimming pool-cum-lounging area in the front garden. Further along, Confortel's towering **Pueblo Caribe** ((095) 657354 FAX (095) 48657 E-MAIL pueblocaribe@ telcel.net.ve, represents good value for three-star comforts. The rooms are large and breezy, the swimming pool spacious, and the 15 cabins on the ground floor ideal for families.

Where to Eat

For dining, the best option is the locally renowned **La Trattoría al Porto** ((095) 48208, run by Peruvians with some excellent fresh fish and typical Peruvian dishes such as spicy potatoes. People come from Porlamar just for the fish here.

Margarita's fishermen are regarded as the hardiest in the country.

PLAYA EL AGUA

Back on the main highway (Route 4) heading north, you come to Margarita's most famous beach, Playa El Agua, an endless four-kilometer (two-and-a-half-mile) stretch of white sand, blue sea and pink bodies. If you enjoy long walks along sea shores, you've come to the right place.

The beach is slowly being built up, though hotels still don't exceed about four stories. On weekends and during holiday times it teems with local and foreign sun-seekers, keen to make the most of the sun, surf and their precious vacations. Restaurants and beach bars line the seafront, getting livelier at night and during the holidays, while nightspots keep the party animals happy until dawn.

GENERAL INFORMATION

At El Agua, you'll find small, generally overpriced supermarkets, souvenir shops, and even Internet access (at **Baywatchers** on the seafront, best in the afternoons). The main seafront road is called Boulevard Playa El Agua, and the other main street, Calle Miragua, links it to the main highway (Avenida 4 de Mayo). Getting there by bus is straightforward from Porlamar, and there are plenty of taxis lurking.

WHERE TO STAY

Playa El Agua's lodging ranges from all-inclusive package deals through to small self-catering apartments, though budget options are few. Prices change according to season, and, except where mentioned, all rooms come with hot water and air-conditioning.

Expensive to Moderate

Set back from the beach, with access from the main road, the **Playa El Agua Beach Hotel** ((095) 616701 is probably the largest resort at El Agua, within a leafy, verdant compound, complemented by tennis courts, landscaped gardens, and swimming pools. Some rooms have great sea views, reserve these when you book.

North of the Calle Miragua turn, the **Hotel Cocoparaíso** ((095) 490117 or (095) 490274 includes 18 rooms, all well-equipped and furnished, and more colorful and eye-catching than the beachfront Le Flamboyant's. They offer breakfast on-site by their pool, but can arrange meals at their restaurant on the beach called **Merlín**.

On Calle Miragua, the best of the bunch to my mind is the new **Costa Linda** ((095) 491303 FAX (095) 491229 E-MAIL hcosta@enlared.net. Twenty-four comfortable and pleasing rooms,

combined with a small pool and good restaurant, all set in a colonial-style house painted in aquamarine and earth tones, convinced me.

Of the self-catering apartments along this road, **Casa Karlito** ((095) 490716 offers four very attractive apartments with large equipped kitchens; there is a Jacuzzi and sociable bar area in the rear.

Inexpensive

Two places on Calle Miragua offer self-catering apartments without hot water or air-conditioning: **Chalets Belén** ((095) 491707 where the owner offers two simple cabins with room for six, and **Residencia Vacacional El Agua** ((095) 491975, next door, also with two virtually identical cabins for six and eight people.

WHERE TO EAT

Recommended eating places on the boulevard and Calle Miragua include **La Cucaracha**, **Hardy's**, **Tai-Chi** and **Merlín**. The hottest nightspot in Playa El Agua is **Panare**.

THE NORTH COAST

Stretching along the coast all the way west to Juangriego, the bays, coves and beaches of Margarita's north coast bask under the sun, and comparative anonymity. Their turquoise waters and gold sand can be deserted, even at peak times. If you want to find the hidden beaches, a bit of scrambling is required, and bring your own shade, water and food.

Soon after El Agua, **Playa Manzanillo**'s wide sandy bay, cupped by hills where fishing boats nod and bob on the waves, is much quieter and far more picturesque. You'll find modest seafront restaurants, and sun shades for rent. Further on a road leads down to **Playa Puerto Cruz**, whose calm waters and white sand many rate as the best on the island.

The next turn along leads down to the village of Pedro González and **Playa Zaragoza**. A local-born Governor gave the beach a new lease of life in the early 1980s. The houses were painted blue, yellow and pink and the seafront *paseo* landscaped. The waters are warm, calm and clear here, and you can rent sun shades.

WHERE TO STAY AND EAT

Expensive

The five-star **Isla Bonita Golf & Beach Hotel** ((095) 657111 FAX (095) 639068 resort occupies nearly three square kilometers (over one square mile) boasting a total of 312 luxury rooms of which 17 are suites. At the time of writing it was the only large golf course on the island.

It's a huge complex, somewhat dwarfing, but nonetheless very impressive — despite the gaudy pink paint-work in places. Its plan comprises a European-style spa, massages, Jacuzzis, aerobic rooms, a gym and beauty salon. Water sports on offer include windsurfing, diving, sailing, and jet skis. All the facilities are state-of-the-art.

Inexpensive

At No. 11 on the Paseo at Playa Zaragoza, the charming French woman **Marie Noëlle Bourdais** (/FAX (016) 681-8119 rents two delightfully cozy apartments at the back of her house, for four upstairs and two downstairs. Kitchens are fully equipped and fittings and furniture tasteful throughout. Several restaurants vie for trade on the Paseo, of which **Los Tinajones** is the best.

PLAYAS CARIBE, BOQUITA AND LA GALERA

Of the last beaches before arriving at Juangriego, Caribe and Boquita rank among Margarita's finest. Caribe's entrance is marked and lies a short drive from the main road. Its rocky landscape lacks trees, but its two horseshoe crescents are nonetheless spectacular. **Mosquito Beach** is the best of the seafront restaurants. It moves into party mode in the high season in the evenings. A great place for a bit of vacation hedonism on the beach.

To get to Boquita, take a turn to the left along a dirt track about half way to Playa Caribe. Bring a sunshade and water, since refreshment stalls are erratic. Playa La Galera lacks the drama of the other two, but it's still pretty. You can rent water sports equipment there, and the best of

Fishermen exchange conflicting weather predictions at Puerto Fermín (El Tirano).

three modest places to stay, the cabins of **Posada del Sol** ((095) 530354, have equipped kitchens and air-conditioning.

JUANGRIEGO

The north coast's main town, and Margarita's second town to-be, Juangriego's Technicolor, picture-postcard sunsets, its fishermen and its wide, curving bay draw many travelers — even just for an evening meal at one of the seaside restaurants. With its more modest range of accommodations, if you're on a tight budget Juangriego makes an attractive alternative to the pricier El Agua or Porlamar. Unfortunately,

Royalists and Patriots in 1817. It awaits restoration. Stroll along the *paseo* in the morning and you can observe fishermen bringing in their catch and working on their wooden boats under the shade of grape-seed trees.

WHERE TO STAY

In Juangriego, you have a choice of the modest hotels near the beach, or larger and more costly establishments (often apart-hotels) on the outskirts of town. All fall into the inexpensive bracket.

Of the more expensive offers, the well-managed **Villa El Griego Hotel** ((095) 531507 FAX (095)

the town's bay is increasingly polluted by its growing population and large fishing fleet. Head down to its southern end or over to La Galera to avoid complications.

GENERAL INFORMATION

Banco de Venezuela and Banco del Orinoco lie on the Avenida Principal. Most shops and hotels will change dollars, at varying rates. Regular small buses run to and from Porlamar, via La Asunción, and the journey takes around 40 minutes.

WHAT TO SEE AND DO

A breezy walk to the north of the town, the **Fortín La Galera** provides great views of the bay and is the best spot for sunsets. The fort, built in the sixteenth century, witnessed a bloody battle between

530258, Calle Pica Quinta, also caters to package deals. Its 165 apartments for two and 16 townhouses for six, all with air-conditioning, refrigerators and televisions, represent the best value in the area. Each room comes with a hammock on its balcony or terrace and there are pools for adults and children.

Along Calle El Fuerte, a good option with views of the bay from the top floor is **Hotel Patrick's** ((095) 536218 FAX (095) 534089 run by a friendly French couple. Rooms come with air-conditioning and hot water. Right on the beach in the center of town, the Dutch-managed **Nuevo Juan Griego** ((095) 532409 has four simple and spotless rooms, some with sea views, with fans and cold water. On Calle La Marina nearby, there are two acceptable but budget options, the **Hotel Coral** ((095) 532463 and the **Hotel Gran Sol** ((095) 533216.

WHERE TO EAT

Four restaurants cluster at the foot of Calle Fuerte, on the seafront, all claiming pole position for the evening sunsets. **El Viejo Muelle** is an old favorite with occasional live music and perfectly fresh fish dishes and some pasta specials. **El Fortín** and the Arabic **Viña El Mar** are its main competitors. On the next road along, Calle Los Mártires, **Da Aldo's** serves the town's best Italian dishes. Back on Calle El Fuerte, **El Gitano**, run by the chatty Carlos, who speaks about five languages, serves tasty tapas and Spanish wines in a cozy ambience.

INLAND VILLAGES

If you want to discover Margarita's rich craft production, its source lies in the villages and small towns northwest of La Asunción. Even if you're not desperate to find souvenirs to take back home, the villages, dotted around rolling green hills, provide unexpected and thoroughly enchanting glimpses of rural Venezuelan life and Margarita's history.

Not to be missed on the coast road southwest of Juangriego at Tacuantar, the crafts center called **Así con las Manos**, **Tierra**, **Agua y Fuego** is the labor of love of Pepe García. More than just a store, it's a unique insight into traditional Venezuelan crafts and life. Fascinating vignettes and creative details pack the houses he built in the traditional *bahareque* (mud-walled) style in the back garden. Some displays are purely for show, while many others were created by artisans working on the premises.

From Juangriego, take the **Santa Ana** road east to this small village rich in history. From the lovely eighteenth-century church, Bolívar proclaimed the Third Republic on May 4, 1816, and the chair he used for the ceremony — one can tell — stands in all its dog-eared glory.

From Santa Ana, several roads take you to more villages. Heading southeast towards La Asunción, you pass through the neat **Tacarigua**, where stores hang their *chinchorros* (open-net hammocks) out on the street. **Altagracia**, known for its leatherwork, particularly leather-soled *alpargatas* (sandals), lies on the road northwest, back towards the coast.

Taking the southern road, you pass through **El Cercado**, where pottery is the local specialty. Further along, look for signs in **El Maco** for *calzados*, since the locals make great shoes. The turn for **Los Millanes** will take you back to Juangriego, but stop in the center of the village to admire the dainty blue-washed church. Just before it, near the bridge, you can find people rolling cigars from tobacco brought over from Sucre State.

San Juan Bautista lies south of Juangriego and the other villages, in the shadow of the Cerro El Copey. Around the sixteenth-century square and colonial church, stores sell palm hats made from date and coconut leaves, as well as ornate jewelry and wooden furniture. Above San Juan, the tiny village of **Fuentidueño** is famous for the sweets produced by its women, particularly *piñonate* made from papaya.

Where to Stay and Eat

At the southern edge of San Juan, look for the signs for the moderately priced **La Casona (** (095) 59333 FAX (095) 59133 E-MAIL casona@enlared.net, on Calle Miranda. This place, owned by an Austrian expatriate, is truly an oasis in the middle of the island — some might say "nowhere." He has converted an old village house into one of the most spectacular hotel/*posadas* on Margarita, 24 roomy and rustic rooms with their beds in the eaves, an intimate pool surrounded by lush green palms, and a restaurant area on the side of the stone-flagged patio. Even if you don't intend to stay, the restaurant's excellent varied menu, open in the day and romantically lit at night, won't disappoint.

PARQUE NACIONAL LA RESTINGA

Tenuously linking Margarita's two islands, a narrow sandbar (*restinga*) cups the Restinga Lagoon, providing rich fishing for flocks of migrating birds. The sandbar creates the longest beach on the island, stretching an awesome 23 km (14 miles) and carpeted with small shells and clams.

Margarita's largest tourist attraction, La Restinga National Park embraces over 100 sq km (38 sq miles), of which the most interesting part is without doubt the maze of mangroves. Depending on the season, flamingos, scarlet ibis and heron, as well as frigate birds, cormorants and pelicans descend on its shallow waters. Weaving through canals and channels in boats with small outboard engines, spotting birds and taking in the wetlands makes an ideal break from the beach. Look out for the first-class Corpoturismo leaflet to the park.

HOW TO GET THERE

Make your way to the embarkation pier, **Embarcadero El Indio**, as early as possible — the first boat leaves at 7 AM — or else late in the afternoon. These are the best times to observe the abundant birdlife. The pier lies just off the highway, and prices are fixed per boat. You can ask the boatmen to drop you off on the beach for about an hour or so.

Guests enjoying the pool at the luxurious Isla Bonita hotel.

PENÍNSULA DE MACANAO

Under an unforgiving sun and ultramarine skies, cacti such as the prickly pear — which bursts into bloom with bright yellow flowers in July — dominate the dusty, windswept landscape of the westerly Macanao Peninsula, known locally as "the other island." The peninsula, a red-earth semi-desert, is home to hardy creatures: snakes, foxes and feral goats.

On the peninsula you'll find only two modest *posadas*, and will pass small seafaring villages where some houses are made of nothing more than sheets of tin. In their shade, weather-burnished fisherman repair wooden boats employing techniques handed down from father to son.

Horseback riding on Macanao is growing increasingly popular and makes for an adventurous way to explore its cactus vegetation and hills — which reach some 740 m (2,427 ft). If you're not on a horse, or in a rental car, it's perhaps best to take a tour with a local company. A decent paved road loops 68 km (42 miles) around the peninsula.

WHAT TO SEE AND DO

Soon after you cross the bridge and leave the isthmus on the main road, watch out for some arches on your right. Follow the road down to the beach, where it then parallels it for its entire length: a lovely drive.

The only town of significance on Macanao is **Boca de Río**, lying to the south at the mouth of the lagoon. The town's pride is the **Museo Marino** on the waterfront, and rightly so. Over two stories, displays include miniature models of every type of seafaring vessel, as well as collections of shells, corals, nets and knots, and maritime memorabilia. The museum opens every day from 9 AM to 5 PM, except Mondays. The town's well-known restaurant is the **Fríomar**, easily spotted as you head west. The chef prepares all sorts of inventive dishes, including sea-urchins and rays.

The next beach worth noting is **Punta Arenas**, 27 km (17 miles) to the west, just off the main highway. It's a lovely sun-bleached stretch of sand, surrounded by a smattering of fishermen's houses and huts, their boats beached like small painted whales along the shore. You can rent sunshades, and several restaurants serve lunch. **Playa Salvaje**, decorated with palm fronds, is the most friendly and appealingly.

WHERE TO STAY

Continuing round the headland from Boca de Río, **Robledal** is the next settlement. Here you'll find a welcoming, inexpensive *posada* run on a family basis by French Canadians. **Auberge L'Oasis**

((095) 915339 has six rooms and a restaurant. You should call ahead to make sure they're home. Take the dirt road where you see the sign and follow it round the large water tank.

Not far north of Robledal, on Macanao's north coast, **Playa La Pared** is another wonderful expanse of sand and sea. It's been made all the more attractive by the quirky *campamento* **Makatao** ((095) 630578 (016) 796-7180 FAX (095) 636647, on the left-hand side of the highway, overlooking the beach. It styles itself as a place for retreat and relaxation, offering all sorts of therapies and treatments, from mud baths, crystals and massages through to meditation, yoga and tai chi. Of the four types of imaginative accommodation, the separate thatched hut is delightfully dinky and offers the greatest privacy. This is definitely an alternative to your five-star resort.

EL YAQUE

Ten years ago, El Yaque's wide bay was known as the "taxi-driver" beach, where chauffeurs from the airport would catch forty winks in the breeze. Today, El Yaque's name is synonymous with windsurfing, and the beach is totally geared to the sport — though you'll still see the odd taxi-driver having a snooze.

El Yaque rates as one of the best locations in the world for windsurfing. It boasts year-round strong winds — the greatest from November to March—gusting up to 35 knots, beginner-friendly shallows, excellent facilities and great après-surf entertainment. Its annual regatta, which attracts windsurfers from all over the world, is held in May. For a windsurfer's perspective, see WEB SITE www.crocker.com/~barnett/guide.html.

Even if you are not a wind addict, you can easily spend a day watching the hundreds of multi-colored sails whiz in and out at El Yaque, followed by some Caribbean partying at night.

GENERAL INFORMATION

There is no public transportation to the beach, although some hotels offer transfers to Porlamar or the airport. At the time of writing, El Yaque was yet to be connected to landlines, and all establishments were, unbelievably, using portable phones. As soon as the land line is connected, many places will offer Internet access and there will doubtless be a public telephone.

WHERE TO STAY

Accommodation in El Yaque is pretty expensive, hotels taking advantage of their beachfront locations and windsurfers' "need for speed." Prices vary greatly according to season, which is complicated by the high-wind season: "high season" is considered July and August, and November through to April, with Christmas as "very high." Just to confuse you further, many of the hotels' names sound the same.

All rooms come with breakfast included, and have air-conditioning and hot water, unless otherwise indicated. Note that the portable telephone numbers might well be redundant once landline phone connections are installed. E-mail is probably the most efficient way of reserving from abroad. Seasons can change a hotel's price bracket.

Moderate to Expensive

My two choices in this bracket are the more individual of the lodgings on offer: **Jump 'n' Jibe**

wonderful views of the sea, the design of the three structures is what impresses most. The bright and spacious whitewashed rooms with louvered wooden windows are angled to capture the sea breeze, thereby making air-conditioning unnecessary. The rooms include a refrigerator, safe and ventilators. Guests of Casa Viento also enjoy the bonus of using the neighboring Hotel Atti's swimming pool.

If you can't live without the beach on your doorstep, of the string of beachfront hotels **El Yaque Paradise** ((014) 995-2182 E-MAIL paradise team@cantv.net is the best. Its tropical-theme rooms of varying sizes include telephones and televisions, while the restaurant enjoys a decent

(/FAX (016) 695-2068 or (016) 695-0013 E-MAIL winsurf@cantv.net, and **Casa Viento** ((016) 695-6858 TOLL-FREE IN THE UNITED STATES (800) 660-9463 E-MAIL windsurf@casaviento.com WEB SITE www.casaviento.com.

Jump 'n' Jibe nestles between Windsurfers' Oasis and El Yaque Beach hotels and is run by the very friendly Dario, who is Swiss, and his Venezuelan wife. They offer 14 colorful and well-appointed double rooms, including some with balcony-terraces which are worth reserving. The rooms surround a pleasant shaded eating and drinking area, and down by the sail-store and beach, a grassy patch provides the perfect spot for relaxing under the shade of some palms after a hard day on the waves.

Rocky Rockwell, a native of Colorado, USA, established Casa Viento in 1995, and its excellent value has proved popular. Located on the hill with

reputation. There's also a small pool. The hotel is the brother of the **Coche Speed Paradise** hotel over on Coche island, and they provide free transfers to it.

Inexpensive

If you're with a group of windsurfing friends, renting a self-catering apartment for a week makes a lot of sense. The priciest of these in El Yaque are the very attractive **Killer Loop Condos** (no phone) WEB SITE www.windsurfingmargarita.com. At the extreme end of the beach, a series of two-story apartments line the road up the hill. The man who rents most of them, Hector Hung ((014) 995-6504 E-MAIL hectorwindsurfin@hotmail.com, works at the Hotel California.

Margarita's resorts rank among the best in Venezuela.

Away from the main avenue of hotels, on the approach to the village, two small places offer more budget accommodation, without hot water or air-conditioning. **El Yaque Motion** (no phone) has seven basic rooms with private bathrooms, and **Sail Fast Shop** ((016) 796-8352 offers three decent rooms in the back of their store, two with private bathrooms and one without.

WHERE TO EAT

Several restaurants have sprung up in El Yaque to cater to the hungry windsurfers, and most represent better value than the hotels. All fall into the inexpensive bracket, and they tend to offer special, alcohol-inclusive deals in rotation with each other. Ask around for which is hosting a fiesta. In the high season, things get very lively in El Yaque, with live bands, shows and competitions keeping the party going all night.

The restaurants group together at the entrance of the village, where **Gaby's**, an atmospheric, Blues-washed, friendly eatery is known for its good Mexican food and barbecued meats. Just before it, the rustic **Los Surf Piratas** offers a varied menu. In the bend just before the hotels, **Fuerza 6** has an unpretentious menu at competitive prices, as well as friendly management. Of the beach bars, **Mike's**, in front of El Yaque Beach Hotel is the liveliest (happy hour from 5 PM to 7 PM) and boasts the longest list of cocktails. It's also conveniently positioned for a stagger home.

COCHE AND CUBAGUA

The two islands south of Margarita have yet to be developed seriously, though it won't be long until sharp-eyed investors discover their sandy beaches and turquoise waters. For the time being, windsurfers are proving the main impetus, since Coche's winds rival those of El Yaque for year-round strength.

Local tour operators promote the islands as day trips from the mainland. Tours visit archeological and historical sites and continue on to wonderful stretches of iridescent beaches. If you've already explored the rest of Margarita and feel the need for a day's jaunt in a boat, Coche and Cubagua will add another paragraph to that effusive postcard home.

COCHE

Coche, the larger of the two islands, is a mere 11 km (seven miles) long by six kilometers (three-and-three-quarter miles) wide. The only town of significance is the sleepy **San Pedro**, from where two roads link the island's small settlements. The most attractive beaches are **La Uva** and **El Coco** on the north coast.

Where to Stay and Eat

On the island's northwestern point, Punta La Playa, the recent **Hotel Coche Speed Paradise** ((014) 995-2183 FAX (014) 996-5988 E-MAIL paradise team@cantv.net is primarily sold to windsurfers, but it's nonetheless a very handsome hotel, with 70 air-conditioned *cabaña*-style rooms with terraces, a pool and landscaped gardens. As well as windsurfing courses and equipment rental, they offer tennis, mountain biking, fishing, and scuba diving. Rates here range from moderate to expensive.

In San Pedro head to **El Bohío de Doña Carmen**, Calle Marino, which has a great seafood menu, while in **El Bichar**, on the south coast, people go straight to **El Pescador de la Isla** for its seafront location and excellent value.

CUBAGUA

Lying to the west of Coche, Cubagua is teeny — only 22 sq km (eight and a half sq miles). Yet its place in South America history is important. The island shipped vast harvests of pearls in the early sixteenth century, thus fanning the flames of the New World myths. The myth soon turned sour however, particularly for the local Indians forced to work to exhaustion diving on the pearl beds. By the mid-sixteenth century, Cubagua had been all but abandoned by settlers.

On the whole, people make the trip from the mainland for the deserted stretches of beaches, perfect for reenacting scenes from the *Blue Lagoon* or *The Beach*. Join a yacht charter for the hopover, but check whether the tour includes the ruins of **Nueva Cádiz**, which are worth exploring.

HOW TO GET THERE

If you're not booked in to one of the hotels (which provide transfers), contact the sailing boat or yachts that organize tours. These are usually all-inclusive deals including an open bar. **Viola Turismo** ((095) 630715 and **Octopus** ((095) 611535, based in the Margarita Hilton, are both recommended. For something cheaper, haggle out a price with a fisherman in Punta de Piedras — in choppy waters, the open *peñeros* might not agree with landlubbers.

Sweet dreams are made of this: sunset moments at Playa El Agua.

Orinoquia

THE REGION SOUTH OF THE ORINOCO has long mes-
merized foreign travelers to the tropics. The fabulous El Dorado, those mysterious men without
heads, tribes of fiery Amazonian women… Myths
and fantasies about this remote, inaccessible region have fired the imaginations of adventurers
and fortune-seekers since Columbus first sighted
the brown waters of the Orinoco. Explorers from
Walter Raleigh to the indefatigable Alexander von
Humboldt have fallen under the spell of its fra-
grant, tangled forests and bewitching landscapes,
alive with exotic creatures — real and imaginary.
Today, the region's spell is just as binding.

Only about five percent of the population
live in this region which extends across nearly
half of Venezuela's territory. Orinoquia is home
to Venezuela's largest concentration of Indian
peoples, the most important groups being the
Yanomami, Warao, Pemon, Yekuana and
Piaroa. They make up about 10% of the region's
population.

Orinoquia embraces the huge states of
Amazonas and Bolívar and the smaller Delta
Amacuro. Its rivers feed the mighty Orinoco River
on its fishhook arc to the Atlantic Ocean. It is a
land of savannas, forests, waterfalls, rivers and
ancient mesa mountains; of Indian peoples living
lives little-changed for centuries; of missionaries
and miners and settlers hoping for a better life. Its
natural riches defy belief, harboring not only bio-
logically diverse rain and montane forests, but also
endemic species atop its mountains.

Its mineral riches are also myriad. Reserves of
iron ore, manganese and bauxite rank among the
largest in the world, while the planned city of
Ciudad Guayana on the Orinoco boasts the
country's fastest growing industrial zone. The land
is also rich in "saint-seducing" gold, and diamonds. Since the late nineteenth century,
goldrushes have swept through Bolívar State,
attracting independent miners (*garimpeiros*) and
large multinational companies alike in search of
a latter-day El Dorado. Its greatest treasure, however, is water — pure and simple. The Guri Dam
complex, the third largest in the world, generates
around 70% of Venezuela's electricity.

Large swathes of the region benefit from various levels of protective legislation. These include
the fifth largest national park in the world —
Parque Nacional Canaima, one of UNESCO's
exclusive World Heritage Sites — and the world's
largest tropical biosphere in the Alto Orinoco-
Casiquiare Reserve of Amazonas State (see WEB
SITE www.rainforestfoundationuk.org/outof6
.html). Yet damage inflicted on the fragile and
invaluable ecosystems by mining, logging and
industry, particularly over the last decade, would
bring tears to Raleigh and Humboldt's eyes.

"Orinoquia" encompasses all the land south
of the Orinoco. It's not a term frequently used

as yet, but it defines the region better than any
other. You will also find it called "Guayana."
The distances involved and the nascent nature of
the states make it a challenging region to travel
independently. Joining an organized group is an
option many visitors short on time — or language
skills — choose to take.

BOLÍVAR STATE

Bolívar covers over a quarter of Venezuela's territory, the country's largest state. Epitomizing the
country itself, it's a strange mix of ultramodern
and industrial and the traditional and wild. The
state's mineral riches have transformed Ciudad
Guayana into the fastest growing industrial area
in the country in little over a generation, where
shiny-metal complexes and towering chimney
stacks dominate the landscape and local economy.
Away from the city however, roads are few and

far between and, bar pockets of pioneer communities of miners and missionaries, Nature rules.

In southeastern Bolívar, the Río Caroní wreathes the unrelenting savannas and forests of the Gran Sabana (Great Savanna): an adventurer's playground. Powerful rivers and plunging waterfalls quicken the pulse, while its ancient formations carry you back to the dawn of time. At the heart of the Gran Sabana, Venezuela's most touted tourist attraction, Angel Falls — the tallest waterfall in the world — thunders from the vertical flanks of one of the region's numerous mesa mountains.

Orinoquia's quartzite and sandstone massifs are known as *tepuys* by the Pemon Indians of Bolívar. A stone's throw from the Brazilian border, the trek to the moonscape summit of Roraima Tepuy is increasingly a "must" for South American travelers. In western Bolívar, another potent tributary of the Orinoco, the Caura, courses through the

home of Yekuana Indians, a haven for wildlife only just beginning to be opened up to tourism.

The old town of Ciudad Bolívar on the banks of the mighty Orinoco provides the ideal springboard to the region's attractions, while maintaining much of its colonial charm. Despite its hot and humid climate, its color, sights and museums charm most passing travelers. Ciudad Guayana (also known as Puerto Ordaz), however, is better bypassed.

CIUDAD BOLÍVAR

Though officially a city of 100,000 inhabitants, Ciudad Bolívar is more reminiscent of an easy-going town. Shoppers bump along under balconied buildings; young and old stroll along the riverfront *paseo* and Plaza Bolívar; travelers dive

A *tepuy*'s angular shoulders rise up above the savanna.

in and out of hotels and gold shops in search of bargains. Its old houses, with their tall narrow windows and wrought iron balconies, reflect an affluent trading past. In practical terms, they allow their occupants to take advantage of the precious breeze. The city can be stiflingly hot during the day, with average temperatures around 28°C (82°F), alleviated only by cool evening breezes. Do as the locals do: start your days early and indulge in a siesta.

BACKGROUND

Ciudad Bolívar is "the town formerly known as" Angostura (literally "Narrows"), lying at the nar-

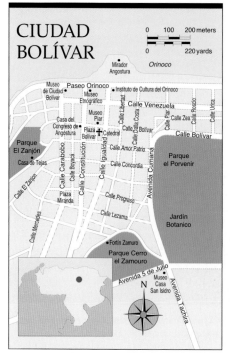

CIUDAD BOLÍVAR

rowest point of the Orinoco. Its original name was Santo Tomás de la Guayana de Angostura, founded in 1762 — perhaps it's just as well they changed it. The settlement moved from its original location to the west at the present site of the Castillos de Guayana (see CIUDAD GUAYANA, page 244). It still boasts the only bridge to span the Orinoco along its 2,140-km (1,327-mile) rush for the sea.

Angostura played a key trading role during its formative years. Ships sailed up the 450 km (279 miles) from the Atlantic, bringing goods from Spain. The merchants traded produce from the colony's forests and plains: beans, cacao, rubber, and hides. Until the nineteenth century, its greatest claim to fame came from the medicinal bark (*cortex angosturae*) the town's missionaries used

to combat fevers. The bark's fame grew after it saved explorer and botanist Alexander von Humboldt's life in the early 1800s. The bark also provides the base ingredient for the famous Angostura Bitters, now manufactured in Trinidad.

The arrival of Simón Bolívar and the War of Independence brought fame of a different kind to Angostura. As the patriot capital of Venezuela from 1817 until 1821, European soldiers arrived here en masse to fight alongside Bolívar on his campaigns. In 1819, the town hosted the Angostura Congress, convened to declare the Republic of Gran Colombia — one of the most important events in Latin American history. The supernation embraced modern-day Colombia and Panama, Venezuela and Ecuador, bringing the Liberator's long-fought dream to fruition. In 1846, the city was renamed to honor its most revered temporary citizen.

GENERAL INFORMATION

The Bolívar State **Tourist Office** ((085) 22771 FAX (085) 24803 is situated on the Avenida Táchira, between avenidas Briceño and Maracay, next to the Hotel Florida on the way to the airport, and is open 8 AM to noon, 2 PM to 5:30 PM. Information booths can also be found at the airport, while a tourism "police" is on hand to help travelers.

The major banks of Banco Unión and Banco de Venezuela will give cash advances. The Banco Consolidado offers the best rates for changing Amex travelers checks, while the Hotel Laja Real (see WHERE TO STAY, below) is probably the safer option for changing cash than the street dealers along the *paseo*.

The **Inparques** office (/FAX (085) 29908 is located on the first floor of the CVG building on Avenida Germania. It provides information about regional parks, and camping permits.

WHAT TO SEE AND DO

In 1992, for the anniversary of America's discovery, Ciudad Bolívar was awarded UNESCO World Heritage status, underlining both its historic architecture and heritage. Many of its buildings were restored, and museums inaugurated. Except where noted, museums and sights tend to close at noon for a wise three-hour siesta, and most are closed on Mondays.

The city's heart beats loudest along the **Paseo Orinoco** — and that's just the car stereos — and around the restored **Plaza Bolívar**, two blocks up the hill. On the bank-side of the *paseo*, families, couples and teenagers emerge for their evening promenade, making it an ideal place to observe Venezuelan life, stroll or grab a bite to eat from a stall.

At about the middle of the *paseo*, the **Mirador Angostura** juts out, marking the narrowest point

along the river and providing fine views of the Angostura Bridge to the west. A block west of the Mirador, one of the best anthropological museums in the country, the **Museo Etnográfico de Guayana** showcases indigenous cultures from the Guayana region, including the Pemon, Yekuana (Makiritare), Kariña and Warao people. A block further west, the **Museo de Ciudad Bolívar** is a modest museum notable for its original printing press. The eighteenth-century house produced the *Correo del Orinoco* from 1818 to 1822, the mouthpiece of the fledgling new government.

Walk up the hill to colorful Plaza Bolívar. Along with the prerequisite statue of El Libertador, five allegorical statues represent the nations he freed.

The square is dominated by the yellow-washed **cathedral**. The structure, started in 1765, took 70 years to complete, and was restored in 1979.

The young General Manuel Piar was shot by a firing squad in 1817 in front of the wall facing the square. The small **Museo Piar** on the downhill side marks the house where he was imprisoned. Piar fought for eight months to liberate Ciudad Bolívar from the Spanish, but fell foul of the Liberator when he refused to accept Bolívar's authority. He was tried, controversially, as a "conspirator and deserter," accused of stirring up the *pardos* (people of mixed blood, like himself) and slaves.

From the square's southeastern corner, on Calle Igualdad, you can't miss the anomalous aerial walkway linking the two facing houses of the **Alcadía de Heres**. Walk uphill from here to Calle Progreso and turn right until you come to the shaded **Plaza Miranda**. The large building on the

square's eastern side stages temporary art exhibitions under the auspices of the **Centro de las Artes**. Ask permission to climb up to the *mirador* view from the rooftop. From there you can see the **Fortín Zamuro** dominating the city. The fort can be visited from a path leading up from the Paseo Heres: walk up south along Calle Carabobo from Plaza Miranda.

Not to be missed in the area around Plaza Bolívar is **Parque El Zanjón**. The city's early residents simply built around, or on top of, the enormous boulders (*lajas*) strewn across the hillside above the Orinoco. A wonderful example of this phenomenon, the restored, brick-built **Casa de las Tejas** stands to the east. The house has a small art gallery and good views, particularly in the evening.

At the Paseo's eastern end stands the new **Sapoara Market**, also called La Carioca, which makes for a lively wander in the morning. Look out for the regional specialties of *queso guayanés* cheese and the cashew-praline *mazapán de merey*. Many informal restaurants within the market serve filling lunches.

TOURS

You'll find a covey of tour companies in Bolívar just waiting for you to part with your cash, and you should be aware that there are mixed reports of their services. Below is a list of recommended and reputable operators. If in doubt, contact the Tourist Office, and report any bad experiences there.

Soana Travel (/FAX (085) 22030, at Calle Bolívar 50, is run by the friendly Martin Haars, who speaks fluent English. This long-established tour operator specializes in trips up the Caura River to the Pará Falls. Inside the Hotel Caracas, **Expediciones Dearuna (** /FAX (085) 26089 is another reputable operator for Canaima, with English, Dutch, German and French-speaking guides on their books. In the Edificio Rioque on Calle Bolívar, you'll find **Agencia de Viajes Auyántepuy (** (085) 20748, who come recommended for flight bookings for Canaima. At the airport, **Turi Express (** (085) 29764 or (016) 685-0405 has the best reputation, while the only Pemon-run operator is **Iwana Meru (** (014) 853-2296, run by Nasario Rosi and his wife Luisa.

Tours to Angel Falls are best booked in Ciudad Bolívar (or Ciudad Guayana), whereas tours of the Gran Sabana and treks to Roraima are cheaper in Santa Elena de Uairén or San Francisco de Yuruaní respectively (see EASTERN CANAIMA NATIONAL PARK, page 251).

Angel Falls Tours

There are a couple ways to feast your eyes on the highest waterfall in the world: by boat and by air.

Either way, the view is spectacular and the memory lasting. Both, however, are determined by weather conditions, which don't always obey even the most well-prepared travel plans.

Car and Jeep Rental

An alternative to taking an organized tour southeast to the Gran Sabana is to rent a car or a jeep. Rental companies in Ciudad Guayana have a wider range of vehicles than those in Bolívar, on the whole. If you're planning simply to drive south to Santa Elena de Uairén, visiting the sights along the way, a city car will suffice. The highway from Kilometro 88 to Santa Elena is one of the best, and certainly most spectacular, in the country.

If, however, you want to get off the road to visit the Kavanayén mission or the community of El Paují for example, you will need a jeep. Jeeps cost about US$100 per day, and you should reserve in advance. **Budget ℂ** (085) 27413 has an office at Ciudad Bolívar airport, also in Puerto Ordaz ℂ (086) 227170 or (086) 235094. For a more comprehensive list, see WEB SITE http://think-venezuela.net.

The Gran Sabana by Plane

The Gran Sabana is dotted with airstrips, built for the missions, mines and newer settlements. You can hop from one to the other very easily. Small planes, which act somewhat like radio taxis, appear where and when there's a fare to be nabbed, and the traffic is pretty constant year-round. If you are a group of four, I can't recommend this means of transportation more. If you're fewer than that, you run the risk of some higher fares, but, in my opinion, the risk is still worth taking.

The biggest factors to bare in mind are the weather, and the *mañana* factor. For the former, I would recommend traveling in the dry season from December to April to avoid disappointment, and for the latter, some flexibility and leeway in your plans. You will need to bring your own food if you plan to stay the night in Kavak. Also, you should be aware that Monday is "engine maintenance day," and that weight restrictions on luggage apply. See WEB SITE www.thelostworld.org for more information.

RÍO CAURA

The Caura is a tributary of the Orinoco, lying further west of the Paragua and Caroní which feed the Guri Dam. The Caura flows for much of its course through rainforest, with islands and rounded mega-boulders dotted along its route and a series of rapids and falls cutting across it.

The round trip up to the **Pará Falls**, a crescent auditorium of five stunning waterfalls, takes four or five days. The trip presents a fantastic opportunity to spot wildlife and enter the Yekuana Indians' riverine world. The trip begins at **Las Trincheras**, a village about three hours southwest of Ciudad Bolívar. From there, motorized canoes carry you up-river for the best part of a day, via a Yekuana community, before reaching a beautiful beach known as El Playón. At El Playón, you sleep in hammocks where facilities are basic, and walk the hour or so up through the forest, often encountering whole Yekuana families on the move, to the Pará Falls. **Soana Travel** (see TOURS, above) in Ciudad Bolívar, **Cacao Travel Group** ℂ (02) 977-1234 FAX (02) 977-0110 E-MAIL cacaotravel@cantv .net WEBSITE www.cacaotravel.com in Caracas, and **Keyla Tours** ℂ (086) 231867 FAX (086) 231201 in Ciudad Guayana, are among the recommended tour operators for this trip.

WHERE TO STAY

The most popular place for travelers to mingle is along the Paseo Orinoco, with several hotels nearby. They tend to be at the budget end of the scale, while the more expensive options lie further out, a short taxi-ride away along Avenida Táchira.

Inexpensive US$35 to US$20

The **Hotel Laja Real** ℂ (085) 27944 or (085) 27955 FAX (085) 28778 is the best option for ease of access to the airport, though it's a taxi ride into town. The rooms are airy and comfortable, and decent for the price; the staff is friendly. Ever-popular with travelers, the **Hotel Valentina** ℂ (085) 27253 FAX (085) 27919, on the Avenida Maracay, is a recommended option with a reputable restaurant. The rooms are spacious and commodious, nothing special, but perfectly acceptable.

Inexpensive US$20 to US$10

The best choice along the Paseo (and possibly overall) is the **Hotel Colonial** ℂ (085) 24402 FAX (085) 23080, which has seen better days, but makes up for it with its good balcony-restaurant, views of the river (more expensive) and convenience. Be wary of the blaring disco on the first floor, however, and book in advance during high season.

Getting to budget level, along the Paseo, the **Hotel Italia** ℂ (085) 27810, long a mainstay with travelers exchanging stories and tips, buzzes with tour touts at all hours. It's battered and worn, but retains a certain charm, and some of the rooms on the first floor have views over the Paseo, though they're all very basic, some without baths. The nearby **Hotel Caracas** ℂ (085) 26089 is another budget-traveler haunt, with the advantage of a terrace-bar area, where you can sip a cool beer and watch the world bustle by. The rooms are very basic however. Around the corner, on Calle

The Capuchin church at Kavanayén, in the heart of the Gran Sabana.

Urica 11, the bland **Hotel Unión** ((085) 23374, includes clean and tidy doubles with air-conditioning and private bathroom for similar prices, making it better value.

WHERE TO EAT

Apart from the restaurants at the hotels Valentina and Laja Real, and the ones at the market, a popular place serving decent Italian food is on the first floor of the **Hotel Colonial**. The Hotel Italia also has a restaurant for cheaper prices. The **Tasca La Playa** on Calle Urica is unpretentious but good value, and popular with locals.

HOW TO GET THERE

Ciudad Bolívar's airport is the poorer cousin of Ciudad Guayana with regard to national flights. However, it still acts as a lifeline for the remote settlements in southern Bolívar State, served by the smaller carriers. In front of the airport, Jimmy Angel's restored airplane, brought down from the top of Auyán Tepuy by the Air Force in 1970 (see ANGEL FALLS, page 250).

From Caracas, Servivensa's flight at 11 AM, and goes via Porlamar, while **LAI** ((085) 29091 flies twice a day. **Rutaca** ((085) 22195 FAX (085) 24010, about two blocks east of the main airport building — with a desk inside the terminal — flies to Canaima, the Gran Sabana missions, and on to Santa Elena de Uairén in the morning. Rutaca restricts baggage to 10 kg (22 lb).

Ciudad Bolívar's Terminal de Pasajeros is about two kilometers (just over a mile) south of the old city center. It's located at the junction of Avenida Sucre and Avenida República. Take a bus marked "Terminal" from the Paseo. Buses to Caracas run all day but concentrate in the evenings, while they leave less regularly north to Puerto La Cruz, and west to Puerto Ayacucho. There are also numerous buses to Santa Elena de Uairén, and the closer towns such as Ciudad Guayana, Ciudad Piar and La Paragua.

CIUDAD GUAYANA (PUERTO ORDAZ)

Ciudad Guayana is a strange place. It is not particularly unpleasant, infested by crime, disease, or mountainsides of shanty dwellings. It is simply that the city has no soul, and is somehow eerie in its modernity. The city, founded in 1961, was designed by consultants and academics from the Massachusetts Institute of Technology. It formed the linchpin in the state's Corporación Venezolana de Guayana (CVG) masterplan to develop the "wild and untapped" Guayana region.

Occupying the southern bank of the Orinoco at its confluence with the Río Caroní, Ciudad Guayana incorporates the older town of San Félix, on the eastern side of Caroní, and the new-town of Puerto Ordaz on the opposite bank. It has mushroomed to encompass a population of over half a million people, many of them linked to the heavy industries that have sprung up over the years to exploit Guayana's enviable mineral and hydrographic riches.

Despite its modernity however, locals have been reluctant to adopt its new name, and you will still find the city referred to on bus or plane itineraries as "Puerto Ordaz" — residents of San Félix would never admit to living in "Ciudad Guayana." Apart from the city's parks, there is little here to waylay the traveler. However, thanks to its modern infrastructure and facilities, it arguably makes a better starting-point for exploring the wonders of the Gran Sabana, Canaima National Park and the Orinoco Delta than its more pleasant neighbor, Ciudad Bolívar, 100 km (62 miles) west.

GENERAL INFORMATION

Puerto Ordaz's **tourist office** is at the airport, while San Félix's stands on the riverfront, on the corner of Calle 1 and Carrera 1. They are open Monday to Friday, 8 AM to noon and 2 PM to 5:30 PM. You could also head to the large Edificio CVG, Calle Cuchivero, near the Plaza de Hierro in the Altavista district of Puerto Ordaz, who hand out maps of the Gran Sabana and provide information (in Spanish) about local sights around the city.

Banco Consolidado on Calle Urbana changes Amex checks, while Banco Unión lies on Avenida Principal de Castillito. Banks will not change Brazilian *reias*, so change them in Santa Elena de Uairén.

Hertz ((800) 43781 has a rental office at the airport, and some of the hotels mentioned below also have agencies. **Budget** ((086) 227170 or (086) 235094 has an office in Puerto Ordaz.

WHAT TO SEE AND DO

Cultural attractions in Ciudad Guayana are few and far between. In fact, they are nonexistent. The city's sights are either natural or industrial. To the west of the city center, at the end of Avenida Principal de Castillito, **Parque Cachamay** has great views of the roaring cataracts of the dark-stained Río Caroní. Further south, the larger **Parque Loefling** hosts a zoo with native animals including sloths and anteaters, while larger animals like tapirs and capybara roam the rest of the park's extensive grounds.

The third park worth investigating is the pretty **Parque Llovizna**, named after the spray (*llovizna*) that washes over the trees and grass from the nearby falls on the Caroní. The park occupies one of the many islands and islets in the middle of the river. On its south side, the Macagua I and II dams generate electricity without the need of a reservoir. Tours from the power company Edelca's visitors' center run until around 3 PM every day except Monday. There was also a new walkway that was nearing completion at the time of writing.

Further afield, a visit to the pharaonic **Guri Dam** (Represa Raúl Leoni) can be organized with tour operators in town. The state power company **Edelca** ((086) 603521 conducts guided tours at the dam itself. Above the dam, the huge man-made Guri Lake stretches as far as the eye can see, covering an area of 4,250 sq km (1,658 sq miles). After the dams on the Yangtse in China, and at Itaipú in Brazil, Guri is the largest in the world with a 10,000 megawatt capacity — though it rarely fulfills that promise. Its monolith concrete wall is 162 m (531 ft) high, towering above the powerhouse, part of which can be visited. Freshwater game fish, including *pavón* (peacock bass), payara and coparo teem in the lakes waters. Contact **Alpi Tour** in Caracas ((02) 283-1433 WEB SITE www.alpi-group.com, for more information.

Officially in Delta Amacuro State, the **Castillos de Guayana** are two forts built on the banks of the Orinoco to protect the original Guayanan settlement of Santo Tomás (also San Tomé) from pirates. Neither forts served their protective purpose, and Santo Tomás was eventually refounded as Angostura, where Ciudad Bolívar stands today. The forts have been well restored, and command great views over the river. To get to the forts, take a *por puesto* or a bus from the Mirador of San Félix and ask to be dropped off at "Los Castillos," the small village at the foot of the forts. The trip takes about an hour.

TOURS

Tours originating in Puerto Ordaz — for the Río Caura, Canaima, the Orinoco Delta, or to the Gran Sabana — tend to be marginally more expensive than those offered in Ciudad Bolívar. That said, there are some good, experienced operators working out of the city. Probably the most experienced, but not the cheapest is **Anaconda Tours** ((086) 223130 FAX (086) 226572, Centro Comercial Anto, Avenida Las Américas. **Keyla Tours** ((086) 231867 FAX (086) 231201, Centro Comercial Llanos, Avenida Monseñor Zabaleta, slightly cheaper, also enjoys a good reputation. Puerto Ordaz overflows with tour operators, but these two are the ones I recommend unreservedly. For a more complete list see WEB SITE http://think-venezuela.net.

WHERE TO STAY

You would have to be a masochist to stay in San Félix, to be honest. The hotels are no cheaper than

in Puerto Ordaz, and the neighborhood is not particularly salubrious, or safe. Puerto Ordaz lacks budget accommodation, but offers a range of more sophisticated hotels.

Expensive
The city's top hotel, the **Inter-Continental Guayana** ((086) 230011 FAX (086) 231914 E-MAIL guayana@interconti.com, Avenida Guayana, Parque Punta Vista, enjoys an unsurpassed location on the banks of the Caroní, just north of the Parque Cachamay. Though expensive, the hotel offers more attractive weekend rates, and also organizes river trips from its jetty. The hotel's block lacks character — fitting for the city — but its

tended gardens, pool area, tennis courts and reputable restaurant, still make it a fine option if you're passing through. I wouldn't want to spend too long there.

Moderate
Downtown, the **Hotel Rasil** ((086) 235096 FAX (086) 227703, Centro Cívico off Vía Venezuela, northwest of the main center, offers the best value and location. The comfortable hotel is split into two, with the older tower claiming the swimming pool and restaurant, while the newer, more expensive tower has a tour agency and a car rental office. More central is the **Hotel Embajador** ((086) 225511 FAX (086) 226123, corner of Avenida Principal de Castillito and Calle Urbana, with 60 comfortable rooms in its tower, and a good restaurant downstairs.

Inexpensive
On Carrera Upata, the **Hotel Tepuy** ((086) 220111 FAX (086) 233220 is popular with business people, with a decent restaurant, and large spick and span rooms. For budget level, head to **Hotel Portu's** (no phone), Avenida Principal de Castillito (west).

"Off the road" in the wilderness of the Gran Sabana.

WHERE TO EAT

With its moneyed residents, Puerto Ordaz offers a good range of restaurants, many serving international dishes as opposed to regional fare.

Expensive

Inside the Inter-Continental hotel's elegant dining room, **La Llovizna** ((086) 222244 boasts the best views of any restaurant in Ciudad Guayana, as well as an excellent international menu. **Ercole** ((086) 233356 or (086) 223319, Torre Loreto, via Colombia, is in fact a private club, but you can reserve through the Inter-Continental. The restaurant's sophisticated menu, stylish art deco decoration, and large wine list make it an excellent choice.

Moderate

Downtown, one of the most pleasant restaurants is **El Tascazo** ((086) 229851 inside the Centro Comercial El Trebol III which, along with recommended seafood dishes, includes an adjoining disco and more modest *tasca*. For some fresh pasta and Italian favorites, try **La Romanina** on Carrera Ciudad Piar, or **Marisquería La Mansión** on Carrera Palmar, for great seafood.

Inexpensive

For hearty pizzas and barbecued meats, head to good value **El Churrasco** on Carrera Upata at Calle El Callao, while **La Forchetta de Oro**, Edificio Royal on Calle Tumeremo, specializes in homemade pasta and Italian dishes, accompanied usually by live music. For a really cheap meal, there are several *pollo a la brasa* places along Avenida Principal de Castillito.

HOW TO GET THERE

Ciudad Guayana's airport, known universally as Puerto Ordaz, lies off Avenida Guayana, to the west of the city center on the way to Ciudad Bolívar. It's the busiest airport in eastern Venezuela, with flights to Caracas, Porlamar, Maturín, Barcelona and further afield. Avensa/Servivensa are the biggest carriers, but Aeropostal, Aserca and Rutaca are also represented. Avensa has a daily morning flight to Canaima (starting in Caracas) which continues on to Santa Elena de Uairén. To get to the airport from the center, look for buses marked "Sidor Directo." From the airport, ones marked "Castillito" go to the hotel district.

Puerto Ordaz's modern bus station is also on Avenida Guayana, about 20 minutes from the airport, but not all lines bound for the larger and busier terminal at **San Félix** stop here. Lots of *por puestos* link Puerto Ordaz and San Félix.

PARQUE NACIONAL CANAIMA AND LA GRAN SABANA

The praises of La Gran Sabana (The Great Savanna) have been sung ever since explorers and missionaries first began to penetrate its frontier in the eighteenth century. It leaves all its visitors enchanted, and most botanists and geologists speechless, such as the variety of its ecosystems and the age of its formations.

The Gran Sabana sits atop the ancient Guayana Shield in the southeastern corner of the country, dating back to the super continent of Gondwana in the Pre-Cambric era, nearly three billion years ago. The region is characterized by towering tabletop mountains etched with cataracts and falls, swathed in seemingly infinite yellow-green savannas and emerald forests.

Each mountain, or *tepuy* in the Pemon Indian tongue, harbors endemic species of prehistoric wonder—islands in time caught up in the clouds. The carnivorous pitcher plant *Heliamphora*; the pink, mosslike *Drosera*; or the hundreds of species of orchid — the region's flora is both weird and wonderful. Below, in montane forests and expanses of savanna, endangered mammals such giant anteaters, jaguars, ocelots and armadillos, as well as sloths, monkeys, agoutis and tapirs, hide from inquisitive eyes. It is also a fragile landscape. The topsoil throughout most of the region is barely a meter (just over three feet) deep, leaving vegetation extremely susceptible to intervention.

Officially, the Gran Sabana extends over an approximate area of 35,000 sq km (13,650 sq m), making it larger than Belgium or the state of Maryland. This area encompasses Canaima National Park. Just to confuse tourists, "La Gran Sabana" usually refers only to the eastern part of the park, crossed by Highway 10 (see EN ROUTE TO LA GRAN SABANA, and EASTERN CANAIMA NATIONAL PARK, page 251). When people refer to "Canaima" they usually mean Canaima Village and, by extension, Angel Falls (see CANAIMA VILLAGE, below).

The Gran Sabana is sparsely populated, home to Indians of Carib descent, the Pemon. They are thought to have migrated to the region around 600 years ago. The majority of Pemon still practice slash-and-burn agriculture and continue to hunt in the forests and savannas. They possess one of the most impressive oral literatures of any American indigenous people.

Much as it seems a million miles from the concrete of Caracas, the Gran Sabana isn't as isolated as it can sometimes feel. At the time of writing, environmentalists and the Pemon were fighting to prevent the construction of pylons carrying electricity to Brazil crossing Canaima National Park.

The visual impact of the pylons is already catastrophic. Mining has also had a dramatic impact on the Gran Sabana and surrounding areas. On all of Canaima Park's borders, small and medium scale mining of gold and diamonds has increased over the last two decades, causing conflicts with Indians, deforestation, disruption of important watercourses and mercury contamination.

Traveling without a car in the region is difficult. That said, if you love to walk and camp out under the stars, the possibilities are infinite. It's often best to negotiate a tour in the Orinocan towns or in Santa Elena de Uairén, the region's capital on the Brazilian border. Typical tours of the Gran Sabana take four days, and visit many of the sights listed below.

GENERAL INFORMATION

The new *Guía Ecológica de la Gran Sabana*, edited by Otto Huber (Caracas: Nature Conservancy & Chevron, 2000) makes a welcome addition to the only other guidebook on the region, Roberto Marrero's *Guide to the Gran Sabana* (Caracas: Oscar Todtman, 1999), now illustrated and available in English. Marrero also publishes maps of the whole national park and of the area — including his latest, detailing UFO phenomena. Corpoturismo also produces leaflets — one on the eastern Canaima and the whole park. You can find out more at WEB SITE www.thelostworld.org.

The region receives a high amount of precipitation: up to four meters (13 ft) a year, and in some parts more — concentrated during the rainy season from May to November. Bring waterproofs.

CANAIMA VILLAGE

The village of Canaima, gateway to Angel Falls, enjoys an impossibly idyllic setting at the northwestern edge of Canaima National Park. Ringing the southern and eastern beaches of Canaima Lagoon, the village has grown from a map-prick 20 years ago to a mini-town of about 1,000 people, most of them Kamarakoto Pemon. The brandy-colored waterfalls — collectively known as Hacha Falls — on the Río Karrao feed the *moriche* palm-fringed lagoon. Behind these, off in the distance, *tepuys* puncture the horizon with their angular shoulders.

Canaima may be touristy by many standards — the souvenir stores certainly are — and the original Hoturvensa camp's architecture somewhat disappointing, but the overall effect is magical, even to the well-traveled eye.

GENERAL INFORMATION

At the airport, you'll encounter a small Inparques hut, where you pay the entrance fee to Canaima

National Park. Ask them for directions to the main Inparques office if you want to inquire more about the area. Under the thatched "terminal," half a dozen operators organize the trip up to Angel Falls by large dugout *curiara* boats with outboard engines. These trips are restricted to the rainy season between May and December. At other times, the only way to view the falls is by plane.

If you haven't arranged a boat trip before arriving in Canaima, do so upon arrival. As well as the one-, two- or three-day river trips up to the falls, the operators also tout fly-bys and excursions to other, closer falls. In the dry season, the latter become the operators' bread and butter.

Of the operators, the most expensive is **Canaima Tours** ((086) 625560 or (086) 616981 FAX (086) 620559, the agents for the Hoturvensa camp (see below). **Tiuna Tours** ((085) 28697 at Ciudad Bolívar airport, and **Kamarakoto Tours** (/FAX in Puerto Ordaz (086) 27680 are the other larger operators.

Local Pemon families run smaller operations. Of these Nasario Rosi's **Iwana Meru** ((014) 853-2296 or (014) 884-0519, or his cousin Reynaldo's **Kaikarwa** offer the best value, but with no trimmings. Also worth mentioning is **Bernal Tours** (/FAX (086) 620443 or (014) 884-0965 WEB SITE www.worldwander.com/bernal/default.htm, run by the family of Tomás Bernal, a veteran of the Sabana who died tragically in 1998 (see below for their camp).

There are no banks in Canaima and paying with credit cards usually incurs a 10% surcharge. Arrive with cash — even dollars are acceptable for tours. You can find expensive phones and fax machines, but no cybercafés — it won't be long though.

Stores and hotels throughout Canaima sell a color map of the village and of the Auyán Tepuy region, though Corpoturismo's map is the best.

Pemon children play in the sands of Canaima Lagoon.

Be wary of swimming out too far in the lagoon since the undercurrents are strong and people have drowned. Because of the stray dogs in the village, the beach may have *niguas*, small parasites that burrow into the soft flesh under your toes, where they leave their eggs. Removing them isn't fun, so wear sandals or flip-flops.

WHAT TO SEE AND DO

Most people treat Canaima as a springboard for Angel Falls, but a boat ride across the face of the series of falls on the lagoon makes for a lovely side trip. Most of these tours head over to the impressive **Salto Sapo** (Frog Falls), and its smaller brother

the pamper-me-silly. Most are located either within the village or a short walk or jeep ride away. When booking an Angel Falls tour with a travel agent in Caracas or one of the Orinocan towns you will be offered various packages whose prices will vary according to which camp you stay in.

Most accommodation is notably cheaper if you come independently and reserve directly with the owners. Prices are high due to Canaima's remote location, where absolutely everything has to be flown in, and due to, er, greed.

Expensive

The largest development, **Campamento Canaima**, is run by Hoturvensa, part of the

Sapito. You can walk behind the deafening but surprisingly warm curtain as the water thunders down. Many tour operators include Sapo on their itineraries for Canaima.

Other nearby falls are **Yuri** and **Mayupa**. The more distant **Wareipa** cuts across on the Río Kukurital, on the western flank of Auyán Tepuy. The jeep and boat trip offers wonderful views of the savanna and surrounding tepuys.

And then of course there's just relaxing on the beach, going for a dip and feeling spoiled. A museum was under construction near the grocery-souvenir store *Quincallería Canaima* at the time of writing. You'll find telephones there.

WHERE TO STAY

Canaima has a growing list of places to stay, ranging in style from the sling-your-hammock up to

Avensa/Servivensa company ((02) 907-8054 or (02) 907-8153 FAX (02) 907-8053, Avenida Río Caura, Centro Empresarial Torre Humboldt, Piso 25, Urbanización Parque Humboldt, Caracas, enjoys pride of place on the edge of the lagoon. The camp's location is the finest in the area, but somehow its design fails to equal the majesty of the natural environment. Still, if you are looking for a hassle-free means of seeing the falls, this is it. Avensa's package includes accommodation in their comfortable cottages, all meals (buffet style), a welcome cocktail, a trip around the lagoon, and a flight over Angel Falls in an adapted DC-3 plane. The flight to and from Canaima isn't included. The package is usually sold as three days–two nights, and payment must be made in full to secure a reservation.

The other option, with far more character, charm and jungle-feel, is **Campamento Ucaima** (also known as Jungle Rudy's) (/FAX (02) 693-0618 or (086) 622359. The camp was established away from the village above the Hacha Falls in the 1950s by the pioneer "Jungle" Rudy Truffino and his wife. Their daughters now run it on the same family-basis. They offer 11 very attractive rooms, welcoming social areas, well-kept grounds and, of course, great views of *tepuys* and falls. The overall feel is far more intimate than at Campamento Canaima. Their packages can include tours to Angel Falls and all the nearby points of interest, with bilingual guides speaking English, Italian or German.

A newer option, on the road that skirts the lagoon to the north of the airstrip, **Campamento**

Parakaupa (/FAX (086) 614963 E-MAIL parakaupa @etheron.net WEB SITE www.canaima.com boasts great views of the lagoon from its hill. It accommodates up to 30 people in its neat and tidy rooms, and have three spectacular "honeymoon suite" style rooms with wraparound picture windows. They offer all-inclusive packages at competitive prices.

Inexpensive

Three places have sprung up on the same road as Parakaupa. Of these **Kaikuse** and **Tiuna Tours** are not particularly recommended, since they are disorganized, unattractive, and turn off their electricity at 11 PM. The only accommodation I thought was good value here were the rooms rented by the owners of the Quincallería Canaima, Claudio and Nohelys, **Posada Kusari** (086) 620443, which are basic but decent, with electricity all night.

In the village, local Pemon have begun to offer lodging. **Wey Tepuy** (or Wei Tüpü) ((085) 40474, or bookable through **Roymar Viajes y Turismo** (/FAX (02) 576-5655 E-MAIL roymar@cantv.net, includes 17 simple rooms with tiled floors, and is clean. They have a large restaurant next door. Close by is **Posada Churun Vena**, through Canaima Tours ((086) 625560, which rents hammock space with shared bathrooms, but also some attractive double rooms with private bathrooms which are good value. Many of the villagers will rent hammocks and space to sling them, among them Nasario Rosi of **Iwana Meru**.

Finally, the camp built by Tomás Bernal, one of Canaima's more colorful pioneers, lies over on the beach leading to the Sapo Falls, known as Isla Anatoly. The camp (/FAX (086) 620443 or (014) 884-0965 WEB SITE www.worldwander.com/bernal/ default.htm, though basic, enjoys possibly the best location of all the lodging in Canaima. Its isolated spot, just up from the pink-tinted beach, makes for a wonderful hideaway. You sleep in hammocks and the family can prepare meals with advance notice.

WHERE TO EAT

For meals, the moderate option is **Campamento Canaima**, with buffet-style service. Alternatively, reserve at **Parakaupa** for better quality meals at more economical prices, admittedly without the views or the muzak. In the village, the **Restaurant de Simón** makes for the best value in town, with a friendly atmosphere and large portions. Many of the Pemon lodgings can arrange meals for you, but don't expect anything fancy — i.e. a lot of chicken. You can also buy overpriced food at the Quincallería, or at one or two modest places in the village.

HOW TO GET THERE

Servivensa's jet leaves Caracas at 11 AM and collects passengers in Porlamar before arriving at Canaima by 1 PM. This flight is considerably cheaper if you buy their all-inclusive package, and they may even refuse to sell you tickets without one. Its cheaper DC-3 flight leaves Puerto Ordaz at 8 AM, lands at Canaima, and ends in Santa Elena de Uairén. Aerotuy flies from Porlamar in Margarita, while Rutaca's small planes leave Ciudad Bolívar in the mornings, usually providing flights out in the afternoons. Rutaca's planes essentially go to wherever there are passengers in the Gran Sabana, and are the best option for getting to Kavak and Kamarata (see below, or TOURS, page 245 under CIUDAD BOLÍVAR).

A typical Pemon village of *churuatas*, *caneys* and *malokas* in the shadow of Kusari Tepuy.

ANGEL FALLS

If there is one sight that draws travelers to Venezuela it is the highest waterfall in the world, vaulting an incredible 979 m (3,211 ft) from the vertical flanks of the Mountain of Evil, Auyán Tepuy. The falls equal 20 Niagaras piled atop one another, a sight that leaves you with few words able to describe their majesty, and, if you're standing at their foot, a sore neck.

The gothic cathedral façade of rock from where Angel Falls plunges lies up the Río Churún, deep in a canyon at the heart of heart-shaped Auyán mountain. Most trips approach the Churún

starting from the jetties above the lagoon of Canaima village, head up the Río Karrao (also Carrao), and spend a night or two in one of the camps on the Churún (see CANAIMA VILLAGE, above, and TOUCH THE ANGEL'S WINGS, page 13 in TOP SPOTS).

BACKGROUND

Perhaps it would be more poetic if the Angel Falls' name derived from a miraculous saintly figure who once appeared to an Indian, or echoed the shape of their white plume cascading down from the Heavens. The truth, however, is much more entertaining and, in a land rich in diamonds and gold, far more appropriate.

In 1921, the dour geologist and explorer, J.R. McCracken contracted a maverick bush pilot called Jimmy Angel — an ex-Canadian Air Force pilot with a penchant for redheads — to fly down to the Venezuelan outback. Jimmie followed McCracken's directions. He eventually landed his plane on top of one of the Gran Sabana's *tepuys*. "In three days," according to Angel, "we took 75 lb (34 kg) of gold out of the sand." With all that extra weight, upon takeoff, the plane plunged 1,500 m (5,000 ft) before Angel wrestled back control.

So began Angel's obsession with the "River of Gold." Over the following years, he persuaded

various backers to fund his trips into the Gran Sabana in search of "his" mountain — to no avail.

But in 1935, Angel returned to his favorite bar in Caracas, the American Club, very excited. He claimed to have sighted surely the tallest waterfall in the world. Tell us another tall story, retorted the other regulars at the bar. As B. Traven puts it in *The Treasure of the Sierra Madre*, "It was the usual gold-digger's story: true, no doubt, and yet sounding like a fairy story."

On another flight two years later, Angel attempted to land on the surface of Auyán Tepuy, the largest of the Gran Sabana's mesa mountains. His small plane stuck in a bog. He and his party were forced to find a way down off the mountain. They eventually made it to the mission of Kamarata 11 days later, somewhat slimmer. This time though, they all got a good look at the falls, and Jimmie's story didn't look so tall after all.

The year 1949 saw the falls properly measured by a National Geographic Society-funded expedition. Angel's altimeter was off by a few thousand feet, but the falls still weighed in at a colossal 979 m (3,211 ft), with an uninterrupted drop of 807 m (2,647 ft) — the Eighth Wonder of the World.

Their true name, given by the Pemon, who knew of their existence all along, is Kerepakúpai Merú. *Kerepakúpai* means "the deepest place" in Pemon, while *merú* means "falls." Following Jimmie's death in 1956, his ashes were scattered over the falls. In 1970, the Venezuela Air Force rescued his rusting plane from the top of Auyán. After restoration, the *Río Caroní* was ceremoniously placed in front of the airport in Ciudad Bolívar, where you can see it today.

GENERAL INFORMATION

No tour of the Angel Falls area is complete without insect repellent against both mosquitoes and small "no see-um" midges, waterproof and long-sleeved clothing, sun cream, sun hats, a flashlight, and twice the number of rolls of film that you thought to bring. (For information on tours, see CANAIMA VILLAGE above, or TOURS, CIUDAD BOLÍVAR page 245.)

VALLE DE KAMARATA

The area south and east of the Auyán mountain is commonly referred to as the **Kamarata Valley**. The valley's largest river, the Akanan, later becomes the Karrao (Carrao), skirts the flanks of the mountain, and eventually feeds the falls of Canaima Lagoon. Deep in the valley lies the mission of **Kamarata**. Here the Pemon José Abati and Jorge Calcaño organize trekking and river trips. Most tour operators employ their services, contacting them via radio. The mission acts as the starting point for trips downriver via Angel Falls to Canaima. But it is also the gateway for the arduous trek up Auyán Tepuy. This trek takes around 10 days, depending on how far you go on the mountain's lunarscape surface; see WEB SITE www.samexplo.org/tr56.htm.

The picturesque village of **Kavak** lies a short journey west, closer to looming Auyán Tepuy. The village consists of several traditionally built *churuata* houses at the foot of the mountain, surrounded by rolling grassland savanna. Lodging includes various houses where Pemon families offer space for hammocks or tents, with shared outside toilets. The chief attraction in Kavak, the waterfall called Tebanarempá, plunges 40 m (131 ft) within a mysterious canyon.

Uruyén lies about 10 km (six miles) southwest of Kavak, at the southern end of Auyán Tepuy. The camp presents the most sophisticated lodging in this remote area, with 10 simple but charming double and triple traditional *churuatas*, with their own bathrooms (cold water) but no electricity. Book the rooms in Uruyén through a tour operator with a radio, *not* through Aerotuy.

How to Get There

The settlements are completely isolated; small planes provide the only way in and out. They don't have phones. Rutaca ((085) 22195 FAX (085) 25955 in Ciudad Bolívar fly to them regularly (see also TOURS, CIUDAD BOLÍVAR, page 245). Make absolutely sure your pilot knows when and where you want to be picked up, and ask to confirm arrangements by radio with the Pemon in Kavak, Uruyén or Kamarata.

EN ROUTE TO LA GRAN SABANA

In a few years, Highway 10 leading south to the plateau of the Gran Sabana will doubtless be renamed *La Ruta del Oro* (The Golden Way) — or something similar — by some bright spark in an air-conditioned Caracas office. The name, though fanciful, would correctly describe the road: it passes through a region believed to covet some of the largest deposits of gold in the world. One mining company referred to the road as the "billion dollar boulevard."

Upata is the first town encountered on the highway, which shrinks to two lanes from here on. The next town is **Guasipati**, a quiet, somnolent place. The *panadería* on the corner of Plaza Bolívar, run by a family of Arabic descent, serves what is possibly the strangest cappuccino in the whole of Venezuela — it's called an *especial*.

Eighteen kilometers (11 miles) further on, **El Callao** squats on the southern bank of the Río Yuruarí. Following the discovery of a huge lode in 1849 — it was not only San Francisco — the town boomed. Venezuela is still one of the world's

largest gold producers. You can visit gold shops and jewelers around the Plaza Bolívar.

A further 108 km (67 miles) down the jungle road, you come to a sign announcing the mythical **"El Dorado"** — if only. It's a rough place, once dominated by gold miners, but now more peopled by ghosts. El Dorado's other, grimmer, claim to fame is its prison. "Las Colonias" occupies an island on the Río Cuyuní. A certain Frenchman, Henri Charrière, better known as *Papillon*, was incarcerated here in 1945.

The town actually lies seven kilometers (over four miles) off the main road. The turnoff marks km 0 of Highway 10. It stretches to the Brazilian border at km 332. All distances south from here are measured from this point. For example, San Isidro, the last town with a gas station before the rise to the Gran Sabana, is universally known as "kilometro ochenta y ocho" (km 88). Fill up with gas here, before the climb of "La Escalera" (literally "The Staircase") and the entrance to Canaima National Park.

WHERE TO STAY

At km 84, a delightful moderately priced campamento, **Barquilla de Fresa**, reservations through the Audubon at ((02) 992-3268 or (02) 992-2812 E-MAIL audubon@telcel.net.ve, includes six spotless rooms set in 35 hectares (14 acres) of forest, including a lake. Birdwatchers flock to Barquilla de Fresa, where the English-speaking owner, Henry Cleve, conducts excellent nature tours.

EASTERN CANAIMA NATIONAL PARK

The entrance to Canaima National Park lies just beyond the imposing granite rock of the **Piedra de la Virgen**, at 410 m (1,345 ft) above sea level, where the views back to the north are breathtaking at sunrise or sunset. From here, the infamous **La Escalera** climbs up the bromeliad-clad Sierra de Lema range to emerge on the plateau of the Gran Sabana.

At km 140, you cross the Aponwao river. On the southern bank, Inparques has its regional headquarters, where you should acquire camping permits, and you'll find a campsite nearby with outhouses. At km 144, an army post checks most vehicles and documents thoroughly before the turning at Luepa for Kavanayén on a dirt track.

LUEPA TO KAVANAYÉN

Kavanayén ("Place of the Cock-of-the-Rock" in Pemon) is a small missionary settlement 70 km (43 miles) from the Luepa turn, surrounded by

Canaima's greatest treasure slinkies down a rock face — Angel Falls.

imposing *tepuys*. The dirt road is pretty decent for the most part.

Two tracks split from the road to Kavanayén. The first is signposted at km 23 and leads to the lovely **Torón** waterfalls. The second veers south after 32 km (20 miles) to the hamlet of **Liwo Riwo** (also Iboribo). Here, local Pemon can put you shelter and a hammock for the night, and there is good camping as well as a humble restaurant. They take visitors to the **Chinak** waterfalls (also known as Aponwao) which thunder 100 m (328 ft) from a ledge.

The mission itself, **Santa Teresita de Kavanayén**, was established as early as 1942. In the mornings and evenings, mass is held inside the church, and some of the songs are in Pemon rather than Spanish — far more melodic. An office inside the mission includes a modest selection of local *artesanía*. Ask in the village about the beautiful **Karuay** waterfalls.

Where to Stay and Eat

The mission rents dormitory rooms and use of the shared bathrooms (with sporadic hot water) ℂ (086) 603763/625200. There was a new *posada* under construction in the village at the time of writing. Off a track from the air strip, the **Campamento Mantopai** is hidden away at the foot of Sororopan, with basic but attractive *churuatas* with double beds. The camp is usually reserved for clients of **Happy Tours** ℂ (088) 951339 or (088) 951330, but can also be reserved through Mario Lanz ℂ (086) 620800.

Inside the village, Señoras Guadalupe and Rosa serve food at a couple of small restaurants. Guadalupe's is one block back from the square's northwestern corner, and is the better and friendlier of the two.

LUEPA TO SANTA ELENA

Back on the main highway heading south, the next stop is **Rapidos de Kamoirán** ℂ (086) 512729, where many stop for coffee and to fill up at the *bomba* (gas station). By the river, local Pemon run a decent restaurant and rent out 15 rooms with bathrooms (but no hot water). Off to the east, the northern *tepuys* of the "Roraima Chain" loom in the distance. From the north: Tramen, Ilu and Karauren.

You can't see the **Kamá** waterfalls from the road at km 201, but you'll spot the bunch of *churuatas* on the right and a slip road just over the bridge. The waterfalls vault 60 m (197 ft) down into a large pool, where rainbows often form at their base. Several Pemon families now rent out basic thatched *churuatas* by the road, and two restaurants cook simple meals.

Five kilometers (three miles) further on, **Kawi** is easily missed but quite delightful. The set of

waterfalls slinky down a small river, one of my favorites on the road. Other lovely falls on this stretch include **Quebrada de Pacheco** (also Arapán), at km 238, **Balneario Suruape** at km 242, and **Yuruaní Meru** at km 250.

Over to the east from this point on the road, the twin towers of Kukenán and Roraima puncture the horizon to the southeast. If it's clear you can easily see the more northerly *tepuys* of Yuruaní and the "tree-stump" of Wadakapiapo — legend tells it was once the tree of life, laden with all the fruits in the world, until it was chopped down by the mischievous Makunaima.

San Francisco de Yuruaní is the largest Pemon settlement in Canaima National Park, and one of its most advanced. The leader of the village (*capitán*) Juvencio Gómez is also the head of the Pemon in the southeastern sector of the Gran Sabana. If you're interested in indigenous issues, seek him out here. The community phone in San Francisco is ℂ (088) 930001 or (088) 930002.

San Francisco is also the gateway for the Roraima trek, and jeeps wait around to take travelers up to the village of Paraitepui to the east. **Roraima Tours** ℂ (088) 951283 or (014) 864323, the only Pemon-run tour operator to date, offer basic accommodation. They also arrange transport and guides to Roraima at competitive rates (see RORAIMA, page 255).

The last two ports of call on this stretch, **Agua Fría** and **Quebrada de Jaspe**, are as delightful as the others. The polishing action of water turns the otherwise dull jasper (*jaspe*) stone a vivid red and orange color. The Pemon call the Quebrada, *kako paru* (fire creek) since they use jasper as a flint. The creek lies at km 273 and includes a camp site. About five kilometers (three miles) south on the highway, various tracks lead off to the left to Agua Fría.

SANTA ELENA DE UAIRÉN

Founded in 1924 by the river Uairén, Santa Elena was once one of Venezuela's most remote outposts. Its early history was more tied to British Guyana than to Venezuela. Its Capuchin mission was established in 1931, near the small Pemon community of Manakri, but it wasn't until the completion of the El Dorado–Brazil highway in the 1970s that the town merited ink on a map. It has long acted as a supply town for the mining settlements west on the road to Ikabarú, and you can still see trucks laden with machinery and men driving about the town, and stores buying and selling gold and diamonds.

Interestingly, according to the regional expert and guide Roberto Marrero, Santa Elena boasts more places of worship than virtually any other town in South America. Every Christian denomination imaginable is represented, and quite a few eastern religions too. Perhaps a mark of the Gran Sabana's beguiling magnetism?

For the tourist, however, there isn't a lot to see. The town acts more as a useful portal to the Gran Sabana than as an attraction in itself. At 900 m (2,952 ft) above sea level, it is never stiflingly hot, and evenings are pleasantly cool.

GENERAL INFORMATION

Banco del Caroní, Calle Bolívar, gives cash advances on Visa, and Banco del Orinoco changes Amex travelers' checks. To change cash, the shoe shop and store La Boutique Zapatería offers good rates, but compare them with the moneychangers

TOURS

Incredibly, Santa Elena still lacks a tourist office. Private tour operators fill this gap, and most are willing and able to help you plan your excursions, rent equipment, sell maps or aid with transportation. Joining other people to form a larger group will bring prices down.

One of the town's most experienced operators and travel agents is **La Gran Sabana Turística** (formerly Anaconda Tours) ((088) 951160 E-MAIL eduardocortez@cantv.net or gransabanaturistica @yahoo.com, Calle Bolívar, next to the popular Panadería Trigopan. Its director, the friendly

who hang around at the junction of Calle Bolívar and Calle Urdaneta, known as the Cuatro Esquinas.

Several places now offer Internet facilities, try Villa Salvaje or La Casa de Gladys (see WHERE TO STAY, page 254).

WHAT TO SEE AND DO

A Pemon crafts center over the bridge in Manakri, past the mission west of Plaza Bolívar, sells local crafts. Another store on Calle Zea also stocks Pemon wares. The hill known as Yakoo affords wonderful views of the town and Roraima, in the dry season, with some good walks further afield. Santa Elena's Carnival in February has a distinct Brazilian feel and rhythm, while its annual *fiesta patronal* takes place in the second week of August.

Eduardo Cortez, is also President of the local chamber of tourism. They can book flights for you and accept credit cards.

Other reputable, English-speaking companies include **New Frontiers** ((02) 763-5162 or (014) 927-7140 E-MAIL info@newfrontiersadventures.com WEBSITE www.newfrontiersadventures.com, Calle Urdaneta, run by the Frenchman Claude; and **Villa Salvaje** (see WHERE TO STAY, below) next to the bus terminal, run by Ivan Artal and his wife.

Arguably the ultimate tour of the Gran Sabana is offered by Raúl Arias of **Raúl's Helicopters** (also called Aerotécnica) (/FAX (088) 951157 or (088) 951049, Avenida Mariscal Sucre. The friendly and highly experienced Raúl offers tours to anywhere — literally the top of a *tepuy* if you like — in the Gran Sabana in a five-seater Bell helicopter. If your

Pemon kids in front of their simple *churuata* home, after its recent frond-cut.

group of four has around US$1,000 to spare, give him a call.

WHERE TO STAY

Moderate to Inexpensive

My two favorite *campamentos* in Santa Elena are **Yakoo** ((088) 951332 or (088) 951742 E-MAIL yakoo @telcel.net.ve, and the tour company Ruta Salvaje's **Villa Salvaje** ((088) 951134 E-MAIL ruta salvaje@cantv.net WEB SITE members.xoom.com/ RutaSalvaje. Ruta Salvaje's offices lie just next to the bus terminal, within a distinctive construction. Both command great views of the town's valley and surrounding hills, and boast equally attractive architecture set in a natural environment. The easiest way to get to them is to phone, if you are not in your vehicle, they will come and pick you up, or give you directions.

In the Urbanización Akurima, a suburb to the north of the town, the long-established **Villa Fairmont** ((088) 951022 makes another inviting option, though without the natural setting of the previous lodgings. It includes a large and recommended restaurant — serving meats and seafood, as well as oven-baked pizza — and bar area, as well as three rooms in the original grounds, and a further eight in another building. The latter rooms are larger, but they are all clean and attractively decorated, with DirecTV, large shower units, and air-conditioning.

Santa Elena's newest offer is the **Hotel Gran Sabana** ((088) 951810 or (088) 951811 FAX (088) 951813 E-MAIL servicios@hotelgransabana.com WEB SITE www.hotelgransabana.com, on the road leading out of town towards the Brazilian border. Though still being completed when I visited, this unimaginative but functional hotel will be the plushest option close to town, with its swimming pool, restaurant and small stores, along with 60 air-conditioned rooms.

Inexpensive

If you're seeking some peace and quiet with a view, consider **Campamento Temiche** ((014) 886-1675 run by Claudio Grossi and his wife Carolina Landáez, who know the Gran Sabana intimately and can organize tours. They offer 12 bright and welcoming rooms in modern-style cabins, with private bathrooms and hot water, and can arrange meals. It's best to call them to get directions to the *campamento*, which is west of town.

Of the hotels in the town center, **Hotel Lucrecia** ((088) 951130 at the beginning of Avenida Perimetral includes 15 bright and breezy rooms. **Hotel Frontera** ((088) 951095, Calle Ikabarú at Calle Zea, is clean with decent rooms around a central patio.

The favored backpacker haunt is **La Casa de Gladys** ((088) 951171 E-MAIL lacasadegladys @cantv.net, Calle Urdaneta, where Gladys Bermúdez and her family rent out simple rooms, with the newer ones around the corner the better options. She lets you use the kitchen and can rent out camping equipment. It's a great place to meet other hikers for the Roraima trek, ask advice, swap information and have a beer or a coffee.

WHERE TO EAT

For eating out, Santa Elena won't have you flying especially from Caracas, but there are still some good value places. One of the nicest is in the restaurant part of the Villa Fairmont, called **El Churuanay Akurima**, (see WHERE TO STAY for directions). Over on the other side of town, on the road to the airport (Calle Ikabarú), **El Quijote** serves up some fine *parillas* and Spanish specials. Closer to town, on Avenida Perimetral opposite Calle Urdaneta, **Pizzería Texas** is popular, as is the restaurant next door, **Parador Venezuela**.

HOW TO GET THERE

Santa Elena's diminutive "airport" is about seven kilometers (four and a half miles) southwest of town, just off the road to the border. Servivensa flies to Canaima at around 8 AM, continuing to Puerto Ordaz in the afternoon. Coming the other way, flights leave Puerto Ordaz at 8 AM, and arrive at Santa Elena at around 11 AM, via Canaima.

Rutaca is the other main company, servicing all parts of the central Gran Sabana, as well as El Pauji to the west. Their six-seater planes don't obey a schedule as such, rather the *por puesto* law of "when we're full, we fly." Check on times and costs with Gran Sabana Turística (see TOURS, page 253). Take a taxi to the airstrip.

The bus terminal might soon have moved to its plush new terminal on the northern outskirts of town, but don't hold your breath. The current terminal is at the first main junction as you enter the town. Brazilian Uniao Cascavel buses depart for Boa Vista four hours away. This bus also speeds all way to Puerto La Cruz about three times a week.

BRAZILIAN BORDER

If you're heading south to Brazil, you can acquire a visa before you get to the border, or once there. You should also carry proof of a yellow fever vaccination, or you will be given one at the border. The Brazilian Consulate is just beyond the bus terminal on Avenida Mariscal Sucre, open from 8 AM to noon.

Before leaving Venezuela, you have to pass by the DIEX for an exit stamp. The offices are near the bus station, behind the large Prefectura building, open Monday to Saturday 7:30 AM to 11:30 AM and 2 PM to 5 PM. If entering from Brazil, you *must*

pass through the DIEX for your tourist visa before heading further in to Venezuela.

RORAIMA

Roraima is the highest *tepuy* in the Gran Sabana, towering 2,800 m (9,184 ft) above the plains. Kukenán (Matawi) is its twin. They lie at the confluence of three countries — Guyana, Venezuela and Brazil — and spawn tributaries of three of the continent's greatest rivers — the Orinoco, the Amazon and the Essequibo. Pemon legend variously describes Roraima as the Mother of All Waters and the home of the Goddess Kuín, grandmother of all Men. It is also known as the "Crystal Mountain."

The incongruous-sounding pair, Everard Im Thurn and Harry Perkins completed the first ascent of the mountain in 1884 (see WEB SITE www.thelostworld.org). Their account is a clas-

sic of Victorian exploration — it makes you want to drop everything and follow in their intrepid footsteps. And follow you can.

Climbing to and exploring Roraima's surface is one of the most memorable experiences of people's lives. One small step onto a *tepuy*'s surface is one giant leap onto another planet. It's the Earth, but not as we know it. To the Pemon, *tepuys* house the mansions of the *mawariton* spirits, high up and out-of-reach. Westerners' flights of fancy regarding Roraima are no more farfetched. More recent theories claim the mountain is one of the Gran Sabana's "Invisible Pyramids" of energy.

In Arthur Conan Doyle's *The Lost World*, an expedition led by the intrepid Doctor Challenger encounters dinosaurs and prehistoric tribes running amok on the summit. The only people running amok today are day-glo clad tourists who,

The curtain falls of Salto Yuruaní, just off Highway 10.

unbelievably, continue to litter and damage the mountain's fragile ecosystem.

Tepuys are old — these were once the valleys of Gondwana and Pangea — brimming with gold and diamonds, charged with Life's current for over two billion years. The landscape is in constant motion, and yet completely static, like a giant cog in the wheel of time, slowly clunking the gears of evolution. It has witnessed every wonder of Nature, and every folly of Man.

GENERAL INFORMATION

An ascent of Roraima can be quite demanding, depending on your level of fitness and the weather

— it rains *a lot* in this part of the Gran Sabana. Don't take the hike for granted, and try to be as fit as you can before the trek. The dry season from December to April is the best time to visit — but it's no guarantee of a rain-free jaunt.

The trip usually takes six days. This allows for two nights in what are euphemistically called "hotels" — small rock overhangs in which you can pitch a tent away from the wind and rain. Weather conditions are variable and it is not uncommon for groups to turn back when paths become torrents.

Unfortunately, the impact of tourists on the mountain's environment over the last decade has been dramatic. In a cleanup operation in 1999, 360 kg (792 lb) of trash was brought down from the trekking route and summit. You should be

extremely aware of the impact you have when visiting this magical and unique place.

See WEB SITE www.thelostworld.org, for more information.

HOW TO GET THERE

Most tour operators in Venezuela, and particularly in **Ciudad Bolívar** and Santa Elena de Uairén offer trips to Roraima. If you bring your own equipment, you can also arrange an ascent directly with a Pemon guide from **San Francisco de Yuruaní**, off Highway 10 (see PARQUE NACIONAL CANAIMA AND LA GRAN SABANA, page 246), or from the village of **Paraitepui**. Some of the Pemon in San Francisco speak some English, so ask around.

All trips have to take a Pemon guide for safety reasons; they charge around US$12 a day. Do not, under any circumstances, attempt to climb the *tepuy* without a Pemon. First of all, it's illegal, and second of all, highly irresponsible. Other people will have to risk their lives to save you. It's a *long* way to the nearest hospital.

EL PAUJÍ

El Paují is a small community at the southern edge of the Gran Sabana, near the border with Brazil, 74 km (46 miles) west of Santa Elena de Uairén. Officially founded in June 1989, El Paují is one of the youngest, and possibly most singular villages in Venezuela. Over the last two decades, a potpourri of artistic and creative types have made this distant corner of Venezuela into one of its most intriguing and idiosyncratic settlements.

In only a few days, you can learn about beekeeping, carpentry, sculpture, art, dance, herbal medicine, architecture, meditation, music, and of course the flora and fauna of the Gran Sabana. Not bad for the epicenter of the middle of nowhere. Staying with the villagers for a while presents a unique opportunity to share not only the wonderful natural world which surrounds them, but also their dreams of making the village into something more than "another example of how *not* to develop a frontier."

GENERAL INFORMATION

The community lacks a telephone. Most *posadas* and *campamentos* own shortwave radios, and tour operators in Santa Elena can radio ahead for you, for example **Eduardo Cortez** ((088) 951-1160 E-MAIL eduardocortez@cantv.net or gransabana turistica@yahoo.com.

You can also leave messages for reserving accommodation, or for general inquiries, with the **Scott family** ((088) 951431 or (014) 886-1481 in Santa Elena. They also run a lovely *posada* in the village (see below). You can contact villagers via

Sidewalk pleasures in Santa Elena de Uairén.

E-MAIL elpauji@yahoo.com, which they pick up infrequently in Santa Elena. See also WEBSITE www.thelostworld.org.

WHAT TO SEE AND DO

All the *posada* owners will act as guides, or will recommend someone who can take you around the local sights for a small sum. Paulista, an ex-gold mining Brazilian with more stories than a Shakespeare anthology, knows the forests very well. Sights not to be missed in the area include the hike up to the **Abísmo**, an escarpment to the south of the village overlooking the forest; the **waterfalls** on the Río Paují and Pozo Esmeralda; the village craftspeople; and the Dance Hall called **Salón Amariba**, to the east (with lovely lodging).

WHERE TO STAY AND EAT

El Pauji's lodging offers rusticity and charm: most *campamentos* lack hot water, although some have electricity from generators at certain hours. Prices are inexpensive, but rise to moderate for all-inclusive deals with transfers to and from Santa Elena de Uairén. The village boasts over 10 places to stay.

El Pauji's main dirt road runs between the east–west Santa Elena to Ikabarú road and the small airstrip to the south — towards El Abismo. Close to the junction, the Scott family run **Chimanta** ((088) 951431 or (014) 886-1481. Luís Scott knows the area extremely well, speaks four languages, raises bees, bakes delicious bread, and meditates. Over the years he and his wife Francia have built up their *posada*, which now includes eight rooms, four of them new, all of them delightful. Solar panels provide hot water and light. They even have a small serpentarium, where Luís extracts venom for serum antidotes. The restaurant part, **La Comarca**, is separate from the lodging.

East of the village, **Weimore** ((088) 951016 E-MAIL eduardocortez@cantv.net (or in the United States ((305) 668-4703 E-MAIL mmatheus@att.net) offers the most innovative architecture in the area, the product of owner/architect Manuel Matheus' fertile imagination. His two houses, one for seven people and the other for four, both overlook the nearby waterfalls — you won't find a more unique bed for the night in the entire country. As well as the usual tours of the area, the Matheus family can organize summer camps and tailor-made excursions.

Apart from the *posadas* which prepare meals for their guests, Maripak (close to the airstrip), La Comarca and Doña Aura's restaurant offer filling meals in the village. You'll find a couple *bodega* general stores, where prices are about 20% higher than in Santa Elena and fresh food sells fast. They also sell gasoline at inflated prices. It's better to stock up on all you need before leaving Santa Elena.

HOW TO GET THERE

El Pauji lies 74 km (46 miles) west of Santa Elena along a very rough road. If you rented a jeep in Puerto Ordaz or Ciudad Bolívar, the road is a good test of its endurance. You will need to buy an extra gasoline container if you plan to stay a while, and a length of strong towrope and a shovel. Depending on when work was last carried out on it, the road can be very demanding, taking up to five hours to cover the distance.

If you haven't arranged transportation with a *posada* owner, or a tour operator in Santa Elena, jalopy taxi-jeeps run up and down the road in the early morning, leaving Santa Elena bus terminal at 6 AM. If the road sounds like too much hassle, then fly. The flight with Rutaca takes 20 wonderful minutes above the forest, and costs just US$15 one-way.

THE ORINOCO DELTA

From a rambling brook at its source in southeastern Amazonas State, to a 20 km-wide (12.5-mile) behemoth 2,140 km (1,327 miles) later, the mighty Orinoco disgorges into the Atlantic Ocean, its mouth resembling the intricate fretwork of a fan.

As the Atlantic's Equatorial Current pushes against the river's flow, the Orinoco sprouts hundreds of fingers which writhe and weave their way to the sea. The sediment they carry slowly-but-surely adds new land to the South American continent — up to 44 m (144 ft) a year, totaling a staggering 1,000 sq km (390 sq miles) over the course of the twentieth century.

Despite the impact of Man on this vast water-bound world, the diverse forest, mangrove and grassland habitats of the Orinoco Delta are still an important haven for wildlife — from mammals such as monkeys, pumas, jaguars, capybara and giant otters, to the shy and endangered manatee, or the playful sweet-water dolphin. Amphibians, reptiles and fish abound, with waters patrolled by cayman, piranhas, anaconda and stingray. Above, a huge variety of macaws, parrots, hawks, kingfishers and toucans light up dawn and dusk skies. Walter Raleigh, on his journey up the delta in 1595 described birds "of all colors, some carnation, some crimson, orange-tawny, purple, green… singing on every tree with a thousand several tunes…"

The delta is home to the Warao, the second largest indigenous group in Venezuela after the Guajiro, numbering over 20,000. They live simple lives far from the modern world, perched above the waters in their *palafitos* — wooden houses erected on stilts. Their name means "canoe people": they are masters of the labyrinthine waterways of their world. The word "Orinoco" is

thought to come from the Warao words *wiri*, to paddle, and *noko*, place. Employing their adroit hands, they fashion some of the most highly respected handicrafts in Venezuela. The men carve whole menageries of delta wildlife from the *sangrito* (Dragon's Blood) tree, while the women are expert weavers of the *moriche* palm (*Mauritia flexuosa*), their baskets and comfortable hammocks fetching high prices in Caracas.

Traveling to the delta gives the visitor the opportunity to see and buy the crafts *in situ*, but also to observe how the resourceful Warao manage to process *moriche* for breads and juices — and cultivate a source of protein to supplement their fish diet: a thumb-size beetle grub.

The southern, lower delta — the northern channel Caño Manamo was dammed in the 1960s — remains under the Orinoco's sway, with flooding occurring in the dry season as waters descend from the plains. Water levels in this part of the delta can vary up to an astonishing 15 m (49 ft). The central delta was protected in 1991 with the creation of the 2,650 sq km (1,033 sq mile) Parque Nacional Mariusa, while the boundaries of a biosphere reserve are still under discussion.

Delta Amacuro State encompasses the 25,000 sq km (9,750 sq miles) of the Orinoco Delta, and is named, somewhat misguidedly, after the small Río Amacuro to the south. The Orinoco yawns widest at Barrancas, after which it becomes the Río Grande, the main thoroughfare for shipping on its way to Ciudad Guayana. The state's capital is the unprepossessing Tucupita, the main gateway to the waterworld of the Delta, but not the only one. Increasingly, the town of San José de Buja in northwestern Delta Amacuro — close to the Caño Manamo and its attendant lodges — is treated as a springboard. Temperatures in the delta average 26°C (about 79°F), with slightly cooler nights, and the rainy season runs from April to

November, though you can expect showers year-round. Malaria is prevalent in the delta, more so during the wetter months.

Many tour operators in Venezuela now offer short trips in to the delta, traveling by motorized canoe and staying in rustic lodges built in the *palafito* style. Taking one of these tours provides a great means to get a feel for what is still a pristine, and precious, part of the country.

TUCUPITA

Tucupita squats on the banks of the Caño Manamo, where the Caño Tucupita splits from the Manamo as it flows north to the Gulf of Paria. The town's access road runs along the top of the dike, built as part of the flood control program of the 1960s and 1970s. Although two roads continue on from Tucupita, essentially that is the sum of Delta Amacuro's road network. The rest be rivers.

Though originally founded by *Margariteños* in the mid-nineteenth century, it was only the arrival of Capuchin missionaries in the 1920s that Tucupita grew to any significant size as a hub for trade in the northern delta region. The opening up of oil fields off the coast—where large companies such as British Petroleum and Amoco own concessions—and the growing tourism industry, have injected some life back in to the town. Its *paseo* along the Manamo makes for a pleasant evening stroll, but essentially travelers employ the town as a means to an end, as opposed to an end in itself.

GENERAL INFORMATION

The State's **Dirección de Turismo** ((087) 216852, Edificio San Juan, Calle Bolívar, just off Plaza Bolívar, provides some local information and, importantly, a list of registered tour companies. It's open Monday to Friday, 8 AM to noon and 3 PM to 6 PM. As a rule, everything in Tucupita shuts for a three-hour siesta at noon. Banco Unión is on Calle Petión, northeast of Plaza Bolívar, but changing cash dollars of travelers' checks is not easy. Most tour operators will accept dollars as payment, but you are better off arriving prepared. For a greater list of tour operators and places to stay, visit WEB SITE http://think-venezuela.net.

WHAT TO SEE AND DO

The **Iglesia de San José de Tucupita** has served as the Capuchin mission since its founding in 1930. It lies at the center of the Paseo Manamo. On **Plaza Bolívar**, locals sit under the shade of trees and observe the world going by without them. To the northwest, the prodigious **Catedral de la Divina Pastora** looms over the streets, having taken three decades to complete — at vast expense for such a one-horse town.

TOURS AND DELTA LODGING

Destinations in the Orinoco Delta essentially center on two areas: to the north of Tucupita towards the Golfo de Paria, and to the south on the way to the mission of San Francisco de Guayo. The northern camps make perfect brief trips. **San José de Buja**, closer to Maturín and its airport than Tucupita, provides straightforward access. Southern camps require more traveling time, though they present a better opportunity for getting to know the Delta's natural wonders and people.

Tours of the Delta are quite expensive, with prices varying according to the lodging offered by the operators. If you want to travel independently from Tucupita, inquire about passenger services

"Don't rock the boat": Warao Indians on a perilous family outing in the Delta.

north to **Pedernales**. For the eastern Delta, try your luck by taking a *por puesto* to the docks at **El Volcán**, 22 km (nearly 14 miles) south, from where services are irregular. **Barrancas**, on the northern banks of the Río Grande is another option.

Expensive

The most "luxurious" camp in the delta, **Campamento Boca de Tigre**, contact in Maturín ((091) 417084 or (091) 416566 E-MAIL bocatigr@telcel .net.ve, is also the most northerly. Aerotuy fly their guests in if the boat trip doesn't appeal. The camp boasts the best facilities in the area, with 30 comfortable rooms, private bathrooms, and a huge thatched dining and social area. The camp is the least typical of all, with little to do with the surrounding natural world, but if you want creature comforts, this is the place for you. Their packages include transfers, excursions and all meals.

In the southern part of the delta, the oldest in the area, **Campamento Maraisa**, operated by Delta Surs ((087) 216666 or (087) 210553, Calle Mariño at Calle Pativilca, Tucupita, lies on the opposite bank from the mission of San Francisco de Guayo. It comprises a range of very attractive accommodation built in traditional *palafito* style, including lovely cabins with their own bathrooms perched above the water, with walkways connecting them. The Lara family owns and operates the camp, and know the delta extremely well. Just the river trip to and from the camp from Tucupita is a joy.

Moderate

Of all the lodges in the Delta, the **Orinoco Delta Lodge** ((087) 211953 FAX (087) 21080 E-MAIL tucexpdelta@cantv.net WEB SITE www.orinoco delta.com, operated by Anthony Tahbou's Tucupita Expeditions, gets my vote for best overall value. The camp has expanded since its inception in 1993, now offering 31 individual cabins with bathrooms built in the *palafito* style, but adapted to the needs and desires of guests — without losing their traditional charm and architecture. A network of walkways above the water connect them, with the main house as the focus for eating and socializing. They recently added a further restaurant-bar *palafito* and deck over the water—perfect for watching water hyacinth (*bora*) flow back and forth throughout the day, or identifying the numerous birds found in the area. In addition to the cabins, they can also offer a more backpacker-friendly dormitory where hammocks can be slung, and two further, more rustic camps, nearby. The staff are multilingual and professional, as well as knowledgeable.

The other lodge worthy of mention in this category is **Tobé Lodge** (/FAX (087) 210709 or (087) 211146, Calle Pativilca, north side of Plaza Bolívar, run by the friendly and animal-mad French couple Arlette and Louis Carrée. The lodge is all the way over near San Francisco de Guayo and includes rustic-style beds and hammocks for guests.

Inexpensive

Of the tour operators in Tucupita, **Aventura Turística "Delta"** (/FAX (087) 210835 or (087) 212587, Calle Centurión No. 62 (by the cathedral), has two basic, rustic camps en route along the Caño Pedernales, which empties into the Golfo de Paria. The tours are well organized, led by multilingual guides and focusing on the natural world of the delta. Their two *palafito* houses provide hammock-slinging room only, with small cabins for bathrooms nearby. **Bujuna Tours** (/FAX (087) 212776, Calle Dalla Costa, run similar excursions.

WHERE TO STAY

Tucupita isn't rich in lodging, and you should call ahead to secure a reservation with these inexpensive places. In town, the best option is **Hotel Sans Souci** ((087) 210132, Calle Centurión, by the cathedral, with newish, quiet and clean rooms with either air-conditioning or fans, and its own restaurant. The friendliest budget option, **Pequeño Hotel** ((087) 210523, Calle La Paz, includes doubles with fan or rattling air-conditioning.

The unfortunately named **Hotel Saxxi** ((087) 212112 offers the best facilities in the area, with a pool, restaurant, and air-conditioned rooms, but at six kilometers (nearly four miles) south of town, it might not be worth the effort. Better is the hotel, bar, restaurant **Pequeña Venezia** ((087) 212044, Via Cierre, Urbanización San Salvador, 11 km (nearly seven miles) on the road to El Volcán.

WHERE TO EAT

No meal in Tucupita will have you watering at the mouth, but decent, hearty food can be found at **Mi Tasca**, Calle Dalla Costa, and at **Capri**, Calle Manamo. **El Rincón de Pedro**, Calle Petión, cooks up tasty chicken, while the food at **Tasca Sans Souci** will fill a gap. The best supermarket for provisions is *Supermercado Orinoco*, Calle Tucupita at Calle Mariño.

HOW TO GET THERE

Tucupita's airport has been closed since 1992, and looks unlikely to reopen. If it ever does, it's three kilometers (under two miles) north of town. Your nearest options are either Maturín or Puerto Ordaz.

The terminal for buses is a short hop southeast of the city center. Express buses leave in the evening for Caracas (about 11 hours), while other routes include Puerto Ordaz and Maturín, which are also serviced by *por puestos*. Local suburban and local traffic is served by the small terminal on Calle Tucupita, south of Plaza Bolívar.

AMAZONAS STATE

Flying over the seemingly endless Amazonian carpet of ever-green forest canopy, you enter a time-warp world. Although settlements in the north of the region have grown over the last decade, in essence the land — and its soul — belong to the Indians who have historically inhabited it. Entering this world is not unlike crossing the threshold of a cathedral. Shafts of light filter through the leaves of too-tall trees, the baroque exuberance of the vegetation overwhelms, forest paths thread like aisles, and chorister birds sing. All combine to make you tread softly and speak in hushed tones.

and even jaguars or ocelots. In the rivers, piranhas' jaws happy-snap alongside fiery peacock bass (*pavón*), freshwater dolphins (*tonino*), crocodiles (*babas*) and tortoises. On the forest floor, hairy tarantulas, marching ants, hand-length cockroaches and mighty fer-de-lance snakes turn some jungle jaunts into obstacle courses.

Although the region's protection looks impressive on a map, due to the state's remote and inaccessible nature protected areas are often little more than "paper parks." Policing them, with limited funds, is frankly impossible. Over the last two decades, thousands of gold miners have invaded the lands of the Yanomami and other groups on the Brazilian border, not only damaging rivers and

Amazonas State extends over 175,750 sq km (68,543 sq miles), of which over a third falls under protected — in theory — land. It is home to over a dozen ethnic groups, numbering over 40,000, around half the state's total population: the Guahibo (Jivi), Piaroa, Yekuana (Makiritare), Baniva, Yanomami and Sanéma. In the depths of the forest, many lead lives virtually unchanged for millennia, in houses whose basic ingenuity and aesthetic beauty is striking.

The cathedral forests also shelter immense natural riches. The Orinoco Basin, like its neighbor the Amazon, is a haven of biodiversity: an unparalleled living, breathing bank for the future. Within the protective clutches of the undulating hills and valleys, occasionally punctuated by the last mountain flings of the Guayana Highlands, you'll encounter electric blue morpho butterflies, squawking macaws, a dozen species of monkey,

contaminating the waters with mercury, but also bringing disease and vice along with them.

Opportunities to explore Amazonas independently are few. The gateway town, the state's capital, Puerto Ayacucho, lies on the eastern banks of the Orinoco, a spear's throw from Colombia. Most travelers to the region join an organized tour, either staying in hammock-slung shelters deep in the forest, or keeping to the half dozen *campamentos* that provide more comfortable accommodation.

PUERTO AYACUCHO

Originally a humble camp for workers building the detour road south to Samariapo, Puerto Ayacucho sits, sweating, on the eastern banks of the Orinoco. Its strategic position below the Atures

Pemon families sometimes travel miles to gather firewood.

and Maipures rapids — where all river travelers were, and still are, forced to take a detour overland — and the depth of the Orinoco at this point reinforced Venezuela's control of this area, long-disputed with Colombia.

The climate in Puerto Ayacucho is either hot and wet, or hot and dry. There is little in-between. As a rule, the further south you travel in the Amazonas, the wetter and more humid it gets. December to April are the driest months. Its proximity to its troubled neighbor leads to sporadic military emergencies, and also to considerable smuggling and illegal immigration. There is a strong military, naval and police presence in the town as a result, but really, it's just another frontier town with 70,000 to 80,000 inhabitants, a useful springboard for travelers, but with little to actually detain them.

GENERAL INFORMATION

Amazonas State's **Dirección de Turismo** ((048) 210033 is found inside the Palacio del Gobierno, on Plaza Bolívar. There is also a tourism booth at the airport, but don't expect to find it staffed. **Inparques** ((048) 214771 has its offices on the Avenida Principal of Barrio Unión, close to the town center.

For information about permits for traveling deep into Amazonas, contact the government agency **Sada-Amazonas** ((048) 210059, Avenida Los Lirios, vía Aeropuerto, or in Caracas ((02) 991-7853, Base Aérea Francisco Miranda (La Carlota airport). Or else ask the tourist office for advice.

The banks Unión and Venezuela are on the main drag of Avenida Orinoco. To change dollars and travelers' checks, ask tour operators or posh hotels, though they offer very low rates — come prepared. Some tour operators accept cash dollars as payment.

For e-mail, the **Biblioteca Regional** just by the cathedral was about to start offering an Internet service at the time of writing. They also have a range of books, magazines and videos (including English-language) you can explore.

Amazonas is a malaria area, so consult your doctor if you plan to visit. For an informative web site with plenty of good links, see WEB SITE www.tourismconcern.org.uk.

WHAT TO SEE AND DO

Puerto Ayacucho is by no means the cultural capital of Venezuela, but well worth a visit is the **Museo Etnológico de Amazonas**, Avenida Río Negro, by the Mercado Indígena (Indian's Market). It provides a good introduction to the indigenous world of Amazonas, with some fine models of Piaroa and other Indian structures; displays of crafts and utensils; texts explaining customs, beliefs and culture; as well as plenty of photos and historical background. The museum opens Tuesday to Friday 9 AM to noon and 2:30 PM to 6 PM, Saturday 9 AM to noon and 3:30 to 7 PM, Sunday 9 AM to 1 PM.

The **Mercado Indígena** occupies part of the large, shaded square on Avenida Río Negro. It's held every day, but best in the mornings from Thursday to Sunday when Indians from all round the region — though chiefly Piaroa and Guahibo — gather to sell their wares. These range from parrot mobiles and hardwood benches to the *katara* hot sauce (said to be an aphrodisiac) and medicinal *seje* palm oil. Come early, when you can enjoy a better selection of handmade wooden toys and wonderful baskets, for example. The market is not the "authentic" experience of tourist brochure Never-Never Land, but makes for an enjoyable stroll. If you speak Spanish, take time to have a chat with one of the Indians about their lives, problems and hopes for the future — and yours.

The **Centro CEPAI** ((048) 214956 lies in the Barrio Carinaguita on the way to the airport (ask a taxi driver to take you). It is probably the best craft shop in the country, and what's more, run as a cooperative, thus giving more profits back to the actual craftspeople. You are more likely to find crafts and products from the Yanomama people here, as well as interesting ceramics from the Curripaco.

For sunsets and views of the Orinoco rapids, head to either **Cerro Perico** or **Cerro El Zamuro** (commonly called El Mirador).

SPORTS AND OUTDOOR ACTIVITIES

Aguas Bravas de Venezuela ((048) 210541, Avenida Río Negro, between the Plaza Bolívar and the Mercado Indígena, specialize in running the Atures rapids to the south. They've been doing it for years in specially adapted craft, fitted with outboard motors. The best adrenaline rush to be found in town, by far.

Fishing is growing increasingly popular in Amazonas. The Río Casiquiare is renowned for producing more record-breaking peacock bass (*pavón*) than any other river in the world. One of the best operators organizing tours is **Alpi Tour** ((02) 283-1433 FAX (02) 283-6067 IN THE UNITED STATES FAX (520) 447-7959 E-MAIL alpitour@viptel .com WEB SITE www.alpi-group.com.

AROUND PUERTO AYACUCHO

The most popular attraction close to the town is **Parque Tobogán de la Selva**, six kilometers (nearly four miles) on a side road branching 30 km (eighteen and a half miles) south, on the highway to Samariapo. It's a fun water-slide, most impressive in the rainy season, which cascades down a steep yet smooth inclined rock.

The other sight offered by operators, **Cerro Pintado**, comprises a number of petroglyphs carved high on a rock face. They are quite hard to make out, and the light strikes them best in the early morning or late afternoon. The most impressive glyph is of a 50-m (164-ft) curving snake, thought to echo the Orinoco. The Cerro lies about 17 km (11 miles) south of Puerto Ayacucho, off a trail to the left.

TOURS

Many "freelancers" or unregistered guides and companies hang around the airport waiting for tourists. Before signing anything with anyone, ask

to see their papers, specifically their "VT" and "TTAC" documents, which allow them to carry passengers on rivers, etc. Report any bad experiences to the Dirección de Turismo and, in bad cases, insist on a partial refund. Don't sacrifice safety and quality for the sake of a few dollars.

Probably the most popular tour, the three-day river excursion up to the foot of the haunting **Cerro Autuna** *tepuy* — which the local Piaroas regard as the Tree of Life — will give you an excellent feel for the Amazonian riverine world. Autana can also be viewed from the air in one of the small planes chartered at the airport.

If you really want to absorb the jungle — with all its incumbent wonders, smells, sounds and creepy crawlies — then take a longer trip. The one touted most often, the "Ruta Humboldt," follows in the wake of the great German explorer and scientist, and takes up to 10 days.

Tour operators come and go, but Pepe Jaime's **Tobagán Tours** ((048) 214865 FAX (048) 214553, Avenida 23 de Enero, and **Turismo Yutajé** ((048) 210664, Barrio Monte Bello No. 31 (about 10 minutes' walk from the museum) have survived the years. They are among the most experienced, with all the necessary documentation, though more expensive than some. **Coyote Expediciones** (/FAX (048) 214583 E-MAIL coyotexpedtion@cantv.net, Avenida Aguerrevere No. 75, is more economical, but has received mixed reports from travelers.

For a more extensive list of tour operators, see WEB SITE http://think-venezuela.net.

WHERE TO STAY

If you are simply looking for somewhere to stay before hitting the jungle, there are many options in downtown Puerto Ayacucho, though none are particularly enticing. On the outskirts of the town, some very picturesque camps used by tour operators in Caracas usually encourage all-inclusive packages for their guests including excursions, but you can also reserve a room independently.

Expensive to Moderate

Of the out-of-town camps, my favorite is **Orinoquia**, run by Cacao Travel Group ((02) 977-1234 FAX (02) 977-0110 E-MAIL cacaotravel@cantv.net WEB SITE www.cacaotravel.com, 23 km (14 miles) south on the road of Samariapo. The camp enjoys an idyllic setting on the Orinoco facing the Atures rapids. Five thatched *churuatas* with private bathrooms below and beds in the eaves are set in lovely grounds, while Indian crafts adorn the huge "witch's hat" Piaroa-style social and dining area. There is no air-conditioning, but the breeze through the open-sided structure is sufficient, and silent. The camp, well-managed by multilingual staff, serves excellent food. Cacao can also organize specialized river trips to their other camp on the **Ventuari**, rafting, kayaking and tours of local sights as part of their package.

Just before Orinoquia, on the same split track from the main road, **Camturama Amazonas Resort** ((048) 210266, reservations through Mágico Amazonas ((02) 941-8813 FAX (02) 943-5160 E-MAIL magico@ven.net, is the "jungle camp for the urbanite" par excellence, with 46 appealing air-conditioned rooms with private bathrooms and hot water. The grounds are beautifully tended, with turtles and baby caiman paddling in a lagoon. You'll find a disco/bar social area, and even a laundry service. It is undoubtedly the plushest place you could stay in the area, often reserved for large tour groups.

Barbecue, Gran Sabana style.

Inexpensive

Of the hotels downtown, **Guácharo's Resort** ((048) 210328, Calle Evelio Roa at Avenida Amazonas, provides the best amenities, although it's a bit of a misnomer since it's nothing like a resort. Still, the hotel's rooms are comfortable enough, with air-conditioning and hot water, and there's a pool and a restaurant.

Of the budget places, by far the most friendly and attractive is **Residencias Río Siapa** ((048) 210138, on the left-hand side of Calle Carabobo, with 25 tidy rooms, with televisions and air-conditioning. Plus, quite amazing for the price, fluffy towels and bars of soap.

Out of town, a very pleasant place run by welcoming and knowledgeable people, **Nacamtur** ((048) 212763 FAX (048) 210325, lies on the road south to Samariapo, along the road at the Gavilá/ El Retiro turnoff. The rooms, large and air-conditioned with hot water, occupy an attractive compound near the forest. The owners can take you on walking and river trips, and the Cerro Pintado petroglyphs are nearby.

WHERE TO EAT

Most restaurants in Puerto Ayacucho close on Sundays, and there aren't a whole load of nice places to chose from anyway. One of the best value and attractive, **El Capi**, Avenida Evelio Roa, by the Hotel Maguarí, serves savory dishes and good salads, while the best pizzas are to be found at either **El Padrino**, Avenida Melicio Pérez No. 26-55, in Urbanización Andrés Bello, or at **Las Palmeras**, Avenida 23 de Enero, downtown.

La Estancia, Avenida Aguerrevere, serves good Venezuelan food and some regional dishes, while **Tasca El Arbolito** nearby has Spanish dishes and a convivial atmosphere for a beer in the evening. The restaurant on the first floor of the **airport** also has a decent menu with hearty portions, though the service leaves something to be desired.

HOW TO GET THERE

Puerto Ayacucho's airport lies about six kilometers (nearly four miles) southeast of the downtown, and only taxis run to and fro. The airport is not well-connected to the rest of the country, and you might have to come via Caracas if traveling from the Oriente or the west. The two airlines are Avensa ((048) 212403, with offices downtown on Avenida Rómulo Gallegos, and Air Venezuela at the terminal. Both have one flight a day to and from Caracas, departing in the morning. At the time of writing, it was still uncertain whether new routes to Mérida and Porlamar would be initiated.

The bus terminal lies six kilometers (nearly four miles) east of the city center. *Por puestos* from Avenida 23 de Enero take you there, but taxis are

also cheap. Buses leave throughout the day to Ciudad Bolívar, as well as to San Fernando de Apure, from where routes fan west. Aeroejecutivos Mary go direct, with air-conditioning, to Caracas.

COLOMBIAN BORDER

If entering Venezuela or leaving for Colombia, you need to get an exit/entry stamp at the DIEX office on Avenida Aguereverre (west). There are two ways to cross the border. The first is by taking the passenger ferry from Puerto Ayacucho's dock (*muelle*) to the northeast of the town, crossing to Casuarito. From there, a *voladora* launch leaves in the afternoon for Puerto Carreño on the Río Meta. A DAS office will give you an entry stamp there, and there is a Venezuela Consulate as well. There are a few hotels if you need to wait for the plane for Bogotá, which only leaves three times a week. In the dry season, rough road runs to Villavicencio. Alternatively, travel by road to Puerto Páez, 95 km (59 miles) north of Puerto Ayacucho. From the docks at Puerto Páez, small boats hop over to Puerto Carreño.

UP THE ORINOCO

Boats and small planes provide the only means of transportation up the Orinoco. You can only travel as far as **La Esmeralda** without a permit. Beyond that and you need a special permit from SADA-AMAZONAS.

Boats leave the embarkation port of **Samariapo**, 63 km (39 miles) south of Puerto Ayacucho, during the dry season, or **Venado** nine kilometers (five and a half miles) further south, at other times. *Por puestos* link the towns with Puerto Ayacucho. The only launch leaves at 11 AM. It takes about three hours to reach **San Fernando de Atabapo**, where the Orinoco veers east. From there you have to negotiate your way with other launches. Pack patience and mozi-guard.

San Juan de Manapiare, San Carlos de Río Negro, and San Simón de Cocuy all have landing strips for small aircraft, serviced by carriers in Puerto Ayacucho. You can always find a hammock space and someone to provide river transportation.

WHERE TO STAY AND EAT

If a hammock and a mosquito net doesn't sound like your cup of tea, a number of jungle camps cater to the traveler in search of more creature comforts. All of them are expensive, offering all-inclusive packages, though you should check carefully exactly what that includes to avoid surprises. Most will offer to organize flight charters on your behalf, but these can also be booked through Puerto Ayacucho carriers (see HOW TO GET THERE, below).

The three *campamentos* following are all found in northern Amazonas State, on tributaries of the coiling Río Ventuari. Of these, the most luxurious is **Camani** ((048) 214865 or in Porlamar ((095) 627402 FAX (095) 629859 E-MAIL camani@enlared .net WEB SITE www.enlared.net/camani, with 13 comfortable and spacious *churuatas* with two beds, ceiling fans, bathrooms and hot water, set around a welcoming pool. In addition to providing first-class catering, they offer all sorts of excursions, with great waterfalls nearby, but also horseback riding. By the time you read this, they will also be offering mountain bike riding and an observation tower in the forest. They offer to fly guests in directly from Caracas or Porlamar.

who sadly died in 1999. The camp lies in the headwaters of the Río Manapiare, close to some lovely cascading falls, and near neighboring Yekuana communities, which can be visited. Around the well-tended gardens, various thatched huts provide simple yet charming rooms for guests, which often include scientists from Cornell University in the United States. The camp has its own airstrip.

The camp in central Amazonas—the only one realistically accessible by river, unless you want to spend a week in a *"bongo"* boat — is the unpronounceable **Mawadianojodo**, in Caracas ((02) 251-0990. The camp is on the Río Cunucunuma, a tributary of the Orinoco, about three-quarters of

Junglaven, in Caracas (/FAX (02) 993-2617 E-MAIL kitti@cantv.net, more rustic than its neighbor Camani (they share the same airstrip), is more geared to the ecologically conscious tourist—they discourage the use of non-biodegradable soaps, for instance. The very enthusiastic birdwatcher, Lorenzo Rodríguez, acts as manager. At the last count, they had recorded over 400 species. In all, seven *churuata*-style cabins with private baths accommodate couples, alongside a very pleasant social and dining area. The camp is popular for fishing tours, and includes a second site for lodging anglers, with special guides.

The last of this bunch, **Yutajé** ((048) 212550 or through Alpi-Tour ((02) 283-1433 FAX (02) 283-6067 in the United States FAX (520) 447-7959 E-MAIL alpitour@viptel.com WEB SITE www.alpi-group .com, the pioneering camp in Amazonas, was established in the 1970s by the Italian José Raggi,

the way to La Esmeralda from San Fernando de Atabapo. It is the most basic of the places listed here, but charming and well-run by local Yekuana, and close to towering Cerro Duida. You sleep in hammocks under thatched *churuatas*, with only a few camp beds available.

How to Get There

Two reliable small carriers work out of Puerto Ayacucho airport. **Línea Aérea Wayumi** ((048) 210635 comes recommended by people involved in tourism. Flights leave for the interior early morning at 6 AM, Monday to Saturday, but can also be chartered. The other company is **Aguaysa** ((048) 210020 or (048) 210026. Weight allowance on these flights is restricted to 10 kg (22 lb).

A Crax Elector displays its "feather-duster" plumage.

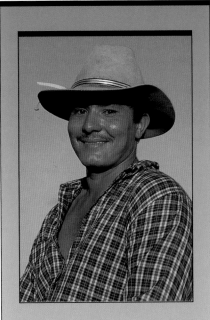

Travelers' Tips

GETTING TO VENEZUELA

BY AIR

Venezuela is the cheapest place to fly to in South America. Most major European and North American airlines have direct flights. Miami is the cheapest portal to Venezuela; contact **American Airlines** TOLL-FREE IN THE UNITED STATES (800) 624-6262, or **United Airlines** TOLL-FREE IN THE UNITED STATES (800) 538-2929.

The majority of international flights arrive at **Aeropuerto Internacional Simón Bolívar**, universally known as **Maiquetía** — for international flight information, dial ((02) 355-1225, for national ((02) 355-2307. Increasingly, charter companies fly directly to Margarita's airport, and international flights from the United States (mainly Miami) also arrive at Maracaibo, Valencia, Barcelona/Puerto La Cruz, and Maturín.

Maiquetía lies 26 km (16 miles) from central Caracas. The international and national terminals are only a short walk apart. To get to Caracas, a very economical bus leaves when full from in front of the national terminal — a five-minute walk to your left as you exit the international terminal. It stops first at Gato Negro metro station, and ends at "Parque Central," underneath Avenida Bolívar, about a 10-minute walk (two blocks east) to Bellas Artes metro. You'll find a taxi stand at the terminus. Alternatively, take a taxi from the airport. Fares are posted on the wall outside by the taxi stand, and check them before getting in the car.

Whatever you do, **do not** accept a ride from anyone offering you a taxi who isn't in the official line. Neither should you accept the "help" of a "representative of the tourist board." Ignore them. If you're arriving late in Maiquetía, stay within the terminal. If you are merely waiting for a connecting flight, and prefer not to venture into

Caracas, inquire at the tourist booth about the status of the hotels along the Litoral Central, around Macuto and Carabellada.

By International Bus Line

For overland travel to Colombia, inquire with travel agents about companies that run the Caracas–Bogotá route. The safest border crossing to Colombia is at San Antonio del Táchira in Táchira State. For the coastal route, head to Maracaibo and east to Maicao (popular with smugglers, so use caution). For travel to Brazil, the União Cascavel line runs Puerto La Cruz to Boa Vista three times a week in excellent buses. Otherwise, head to the border at Santa Elena de Uairén in Bolívar State.

By Ship

Venezuela's long Caribbean coastline and lack of hurricanes prove popular with sailors. Contact **Dockside** (/FAX (081) 677344 E-MAIL dockside@telcel.net.ve, Marina Bahía Redonda, El Morro, Sucre State, for more information about cruising. Margarita's de-facto capital Porlamar should boast an ambitious cruise port by 2002. The **Windward Islands** ferries loop via Porlamar, Trinidad, St. Vincent, Barbados to St. Lucia once a week. Contact the English-speaking travel agents **Unitravel** ((095) 617491 or (095) 630278, Calle Cedeño at Santiago Mariño, Porlamar.

By Car

Check with a Venezuela embassy in your country about bringing a car into Venezuela. The Pan-American highway connects Caracas and Bogotá, while a coastal route links Maracaibo and Santa Marta on Colombia's Caribbean. Highway 10 heads south from the Orinoco to Boa Vista in Brazil, and continues to Manaus (Highway 174).

ARRIVING (AND LEAVING)

Upon arrival at an international airport, you will be issued a tourist visa, valid for 30 to 90 days. Your passport will be stamped, but you are no longer given a tourist card (*Tarjeta de Ingreso*). You *must* carry your passport with you at all times — photocopies don't usually impress officials in Venezuela. Police checks for illegal immigrants are frequent throughout the country, and if you don't have documents on your person, you will be taken to jail. Copy all your documents upon arrival, including your airline ticket and driver's license, and carry the copies separate from your documents. Departure tax from Caracas and Porlamar's airports is around US$30. When exiting Venezuela, acquire an exit stamp from the nearest DIEX (Dirección de Identificación y Extranjería, also DEX) office. Tourist visas can be extended through the DIEX office in Caracas, or, alternatively, go to a border, and cross back in.

EMBASSIES AND CONSULATES

Venezuelan Embassies Abroad

A complete list is available online at WEB SITE www.mre.gov.ve/Misiones/dirm.htm.
Australia ((02) 6290-2900 FAX (02) 6290-2911 E-MAIL embaustralia@venezuela-emb.org.au WEB SITE www.venezuela-emb.org.au, 5 Culgoa Circuit, O'Malley, ACT 2606.
Canada ((613) 235-5151 FAX (613) 235-3205 E-MAIL embavene@travel-net.com WEB SITE www.travel-net.com/~embavene, 32 Range Road, Ottawa, Ontario, KIN 8J4.
Great Britain ((0207) 584-4206 FAX (0207) 589-8887 E-MAIL venezlon@venezlon.demon.co.uk WEB SITE www.demon.co.uk/emb-venuk, 1 Cromwell Road, London SW7 2HA.
United States ((202) 342-2214 FAX (202) 342-6820 E-MAIL despacho@embavenez-us.org WEB SITE www.embavenez-us.org, 1099 Thirtieth Street NW, Washington DC, 20007.

Foreign Embassies in Venezuela

For a full list of embassies, consult the Caracas telephone directory. All of the following are in Caracas.
Australia ((02) 263 4033 E-MAIL caracas@dfat.gov.au, Quinta Yolanda, Avenida Luís Roche, entre 6a y 7a Transversal, Altamira.
Canada ((02) 264-0833, 6 Avenida, entre 3a y 5a Transversal, Altamira.
Great Britain ((02) 993-4111 E-MAIL embcarac@ven.net, Avenida La Estancia, Torre Las Mercedes, Chuao.
United States ((02) 975-9675, Calle F con Calle Saupure, Colinas de Valle Arriba.

TOURIST INFORMATION

Corporación de Turismo, or **Corpoturismo**, Venezuela's government agency, promotes tourism and provides tourist information. It publishes a range of well-produced leaflets to some, but not all, regions and national parks (see GENERAL INFORMATION, page 72 in CARACAS). A few have been translated into English.

Outside Caracas, regional governments run their own tourist offices. These vary in quality, from Mérida's very organized offices (with half a dozen booths throughout the city) to Amazonas'

Andean color in San Rafael de Mucuchíes, Mérida State.

poor attempt. Some staff speak English, and they provide limited practical information, bar useful maps and lists of accommodation. Travel agencies and tour operators often furnish much better information.

GETTING AROUND

BY AIR

Venezuela's air network is extensive, with several carriers linking all the major cities. Smaller towns throughout the country also offer less frequent flights. In view of the country's size and comparatively cheap tickets, air travel can prove an effec-

tive way of seeing the country in a short space of time. The largest carriers in Venezuela are Avensa and Servivensa — which are in fact the same company — TOLL-FREE (800) 283672 TOLL-FREE IN THE UNITED STATES (800) 428-3672 IN THE UNITED KINGDOM (0208) 563-9779. They offer an attractive air pass, which can include domestic as well as international flights, within a period of 45 days (minimum four flights). Note that the air pass does not include Canaima and must be purchased abroad.

The other major domestic airlines include Aeropostal (also international) TOLL-FREE (800) 28466, Air Venezuela ((02) 355-2945, Aserca TOLL-FREE (800) 88356, Avior TOLL-FREE (800) 28467, Laser TOLL-FREE (800) 52737 and Zuliana de Aviación ((02) 993-9470, with even smaller regional carriers such as Rutaca ((085) 22195 in Bolívar State, Air-LAI ((094) 322186 in Sucre, and Línea Aérea Wayumi ((048) 210635 in Amazonas.

You should be in line at least an hour before departure, more on weekends and during peak periods, and reconfirm your flight through a travel agent if possible.

BY BUS

Bus services connect all the major cities in Venezuela, providing a relatively cheap and efficient means of getting about. Modern "ejecutivo" buses link large cities and run long-distance routes. These often have toilets, videos and air-conditioning. The air-conditioning can be brutal, so board with a sweater, long trousers and socks on. The videos or music played by the bus driver can also be tortuous: earplugs are a good idea. Unfortunately, though these buses are more comfortable, they usually have curtains, which they insist on keeping drawn. If they don't have curtains, most will have purple-tinted windows which don't help sightseeing much either.

On smaller, regional routes, "normal" buses are generally still decent, but have less favorable reputations. Por puestos (literally "by the seat"), a cross between a bus and a taxi, cover shorter distances. They travel fixed routes and leave when full. Small buses in Venezuela are also called carros or carritos, and sometimes micros. All towns possess a terminal de pasajeros bus terminal, usually outside the city center, linked by small buses and taxis. At some terminals you have to pay a nominal tasa de salida departure tax. Note that during vacation periods bus routes get very busy, you should buy your onward ticket on arrival, or in advance.

BY RENTAL CAR

Renting a car will allow you to explore the country at your own pace, and Venezuela offers some wonderful scenic driving (see THE OPEN ROAD, page 34 in YOUR CHOICE). Major international companies such as **Hertz** TOLL-FREE (800) 43781, **Budget** TOLL-FREE (800) 28343 and **Avis** TOLL-FREE (800) 22776 are complemented by local agencies. It's often best to stick to the big boys, since you can always seek redress in your own country. Even then, you're not guaranteed an easy ride. I've heard numerous disaster stories from travelers. It is always best to take your rental car for a test drive before signing any documents.

All major city airports have car rental agency desks, and large hotels such as the Hilton or Inter-Continental host company offices. Car rental isn't cheap in Venezuela, with rates more expensive than in the United States. Gas, on the other hand, is air-cheap.

Renting a jeep is really only necessary if you plan to go off-road in the Andes, the Llanos or in the Gran Sabana. Jeeps cost about 30% more than city cars, and the cheapest model is the Lada "Niva." Reserve jeeps in advance when possible.

To rent any vehicle, you will need a driver's license (preferably international), a credit card (Visa, MasterCard or American Express), and be aged over 21 (25 for jeeps and luxury cars) and under 65. When asking for a quote, make sure insurance is included. Also, check on mileage conditions and exclusion clauses such as flat tires, windshield damage and theft. Check your spare tire, jack, and emergency triangle and insist all marks and scratches are noted before you set off. Check they give you a *carnet de circulación*. Most companies offer "three-for-the-price-of-two-days" offers, so take advantage of these. Photocopy the documents you are given as soon as you can. If you know anything about mechanics, check under the hood for worn hoses, fluid levels and oil leaks.

If you are involved in an accident, don't move your car, even if you are blocking the highway. If you move your vehicle, your insurance might not be valid. You must wait for the transit police to arrive, or dial (167. If your accident involves injuries or fatalities, you will be routinely detained, even if you are not to blame.

of your car. Mechanics and gas stations are plentiful throughout the country. Perhaps only the Gran Sabana poses problems in this respect. Driving at night invites extra hazards from animals, maladjusted or nonexistent headlights, and security risks; it's best avoided. Though it may seem harsh, don't stop for apparently stranded people flagging you down on the side of the road. Incidents of ambush and robbery make reporting the problem to the nearest *alcabala* (National Guard stop) the best policy.

You'll encounter *alcabalas* throughout the country. Their reputation has improved greatly in the last few years, though you should always turn your stereo off, take off your sunglasses and ap-

As for driving, the best advice is not to take *anything* for granted, and not to expect anyone to obey the laws of common logic, courtesy or safety. Your attitude should be defensive.

Flashing your lights in Venezuela means "Get out of the way," not "Do please go first" as in Europe. You shouldn't shy from beeping your horn to warn other vehicles — it's not viewed as aggressive in Venezuela. Hand signals usually supercede indicator lights in many cases. Someone who waves their arm out of the window is telling you they're about to turn, stop, or do something silly. Red lights, particularly in cities, and throughout Caracas, are regarded as inconveniences, and often ignored.

Check with your rental company about what to do in the event of breakdown. If you do find yourself stuck on the side of the road, place branches *and* your hazard triangle downstream

proach them at a crawl, coming to a stop before being waved on. Always have your personal and vehicle documents ready, and be courteous. Don't be afraid of the Guardia, they're there to help you, and will often ask you to give "mi capitán" a lift to the next town.

If you wish to import a vehicle into Venezuela, or for more advice on driving, contact the **Touring y Automóvil Club de Venezuela** ((02) 781-4849, Piso 15, Torre Phelps, Plaza Venezuela, Caracas. The Audubon can reconfirm car rental bookings on your behalf. This is particularly necessary over vacation periods, and probably wise throughout the year.

OPPOSITE: Taxi top in Guanare, Los Llanos. ABOVE: A traditional air-conditioning on this truck-bus setting off from Paraguaipoa in Zulia.

HITCHHIKING

Hitchhiking is uncommon in Venezuela. In rural areas, where locals are more friendly and willing to help a stranded tourist, hitching is easier. It can be done (I once hitched from Santa Elena de Uairén to Caracas) but be prepared for long waits. Try to be dropped off at *alcabalas* where the Guardia Nacional can help you, even though they might start by telling you hitchhiking is illegal. Single women should not consider hitching.

ACCOMMODATION

Lodging in Venezuela runs the whole gamut from luxury, five-star resorts through three-star business hotels, and on to urban hotel rooms rented by the hour for couples in a hurry. In major cities, such as Caracas, Maracaibo, Valencia, and Maracay, or resort centers like Puerto La Cruz or Porlamar, large hotels provide international standards of comfort and service and can be booked in advance online, if you like. You'll find the best service in the country at the Hiltons in Caracas and Porlamar.

An alternative to hotels, which I would encourage independent travelers to investigate, are *posadas* — literally "inns" or "lodges." These can also range from the luxurious through to the bare bones. In general, *posadas* are run by local people, who often live on the premises, regarding their guests as houseguests, or part of an extended family. Personalized attention is the order of the day. Their language skills may not quite match their hospitality, but overall, *posadas* offer an excellent opportunity for the traveler to meet and interact with Venezuelans — something impossible if you're staying in a more anonymous hotel. *Posadas* in Venezuela have now reached some very high standards, where you can enjoy excellent local and

If you're staying in budget accommodation (called *hotel, residencia, hospedaje, posada* or *pensión*), always ask to see the room before committing, and check on the noise level of the air-conditioning unit — they're often very loud. These hotels will always ask for payment up-front, in cash, and might charge more for accepting a credit card.

For an exhaustive list of non-hotel accommodation in the country, acquire a copy of Elizabeth Kline's *Guide to Camps, Posadas and Cabins* (Caracas: Kline's Guides, published yearly in English and Spanish).

BOOKING HOTELS

Away from expensive and moderate accommodation, booking a hotel in Venezuela can be frustrating. Some hotels will charge you from 5% to 15% for the privilege of honoring your credit card. If they don't accept cards, you have to deposit money in their bank account and fax them the receipt to secure a reservation. It's often preferable to go through a travel agent, or better still, the Audubon (see TAKING A TOUR, page 52 in YOUR CHOICE).

HOTEL PRICES

As the bolívar has continued to devalue, accommodation in Venezuela has become evermore attractive. Combine this with weekend specials in top urban hotels, or special promotional packages in vacation resort centers, and the traveler can be pleasantly surprised by how low prices can reach.

Our categories for hotel room prices are calculated at the cost of a double room per night during normal times. Peak periods, called *temporada alta*, are regarded as Christmas and New Year, Carnival, and Easter Week. July–August school holidays are sometimes regarded as high season too, particularly in Mérida State. Prices can jump quite a bit at these popular times. Due to the sliding bolívar, most hotels list their prices in United States dollars.

Luxury	over US$150
Expensive	US$101 to US$150
Moderate	US$50 to US$100
Inexpensive	under US$50

CAMPING

Outside national parks, you will find few facilities for camping. The most popular parks often include refuges and toilets, but most of the time, you're left to your own devices. Away from large roads, in the Andes, Gran Sabana or the Llanos,

regional cooking, make the most of activities such as hiking and horseback riding on offer, and benefit from the owners' knowledge of their neck of the woods. Most *posadas* offer all-inclusive deals that include meals and activities, and can usually arrange transfers to and from major cities.

In more remote areas, such as in Amazonas or Bolívar states, you'll find *campamentos*, jungle lodges. Again, these can range from the comfortable, en-suite variety, down to basic swing-your-hammock style lodging with shared bathrooms and cold water. In this book, you'll also come across two descriptions: *churuata* and *caney*. Both these Indian words essentially mean a thatched wooden house. *Churuatas* are enclosed, usually employed for sleeping, while *caneys* are open-sided structures, often used as social and dining areas.

In Venezuela, a single room is a *habitación sencilla*, while double rooms come as *habitación doble* (twin beds) and *matrimonial* (double bed).

Tumbling hillsides, stone walls and farms: the irresistible landscapes of the Andes.

you're relatively safe, but it would be wise to ask a local landowner to camp on their land, thus providing you with added protection. Travelers do camp on beaches all along Venezuela's coast, but safety is a concern. Always try to camp near another group.

EATING OUT

When beginning a meal, it's customary to wish your fellow diners *buen provecho* (bon appetit). To toast say *salud*. For information on Venezuelan cuisine, see GALLOPING GOURMET, page 48 in YOUR CHOICE.

PRICES

Our price categories for meals are per person, without drinks, and may not include VAT.

Expensive over US$20
Moderate US$10 to US$20
Inexpensive under US$10

TIPPING

Taxi drivers don't expect tips unless they carry bags or perform an extraordinary task. Service charges (*propina*) are added to most restaurant bills. If the service was particularly good, leave a further five to ten percent. In luxury hotels, tip bellhops about US$1 for every piece of luggage, tip the concierge (*conserje*) between US$3 and US$5 depending on the task performed. Tour guides expect tips of around 10% of the tour's cost.

BANKING

In general, the least problematic way of payment in Venezuela is cash. Because the bolívar constantly devalues, if you are staying for an extended period, only change what you need at the time, rather than a lump sum upon arrival. In moderate and luxury accommodation, paying by credit card (Visa, MasterCard, American Express and Diners) is usually straightforward. However, many hotels, travel agents and tour operators pass on their bank charges to their customers, so check first. Travelers' checks are accepted as payment in many hotels and some businesses, but you might not receive favorable rates of exchange.

For changing cash or travelers checks, avoid hotels and head to exchange bureaus — *casas de cambio*. They are a better bet than banks too. *Casas* charge a set percentage commission, rather than a flat fee. Some banks now open all day from 8:30 AM to 3:30 PM, but others will work 8:30 AM to 11:30 AM, and 2 PM to 4:30 PM.

Automated Teller Machines (ATMs) in Venezuela are widely available, and personally, I find them the easiest way to get cash. Banco Unión and Banco de Venezuela are the best banks for advances on Visa and MasterCard. In case of loss of a credit card, for American Express (24 hours) call ((02) 206-0222; Diners ((02) 503-2555; MasterCard ((02) 607-7111; Visa ((02) 501-0333.

Western Union "money in minutes" wiring services are available through DHL TOLL-FREE (800) 34592.

BASICS

TIME

Venezuela is four hours behind Greenwich mean time, one hour ahead of United States Eastern Standard time.

ELECTRICITY

Venezuela operates on 110 volts (60-cycle), and outlets use standard United States flat, parallel two-prong plugs. If you're traveling from a country not compatible with this, purchase an adapter before you leave. Some *campamentos* may use their own generators, in which case you should check with the managers before plugging in an appliance.

WATER

Avoid drinking tap water in Venezuela — this includes ice. Bottled water is widely available. Three-star and up hotels provide jugs of mineral water and ice made from water that has been boiled.

WEIGHTS AND MEASURES

Venezuela operates on the metric system. Liquids are sold in liters, vegetables and fruits by the kilogram.

Distance
1 km = .625 (⅝) mile, 1 m = 3.28 ft

Weight
1 gram = .035 ounces, 1 kilogram (kilo) = 2.2 pounds

Volume
1 liter = 2.1 United States pints = 1.76 United Kingdom pints

Temperature
To convert Fahrenheit to centigrade, subtract 32 and multiply by ⅝. To convert centigrade to Fahrenheit, multiply by 1.8 and add 32.

CLIMATE

Venezuela basks in a tropical climate year-round, with an average daytime temperature of 27°C (82°F). There are only mild fluctuations throughout the year, with December to February the coolest months, and May to October the hottest. The rainy season stretches roughly from April or May to November or December. While it has little effect on some parts of the coast (for example, Falcón, Sucre and Anzoátegui states, and Isla de Margarita), the Llanos change considerably from one season to the next. South of the Orinoco, you can expect rain year-round. Altitude affects temperatures, with cold nights in the Andes all year. The average temperature in Mérida is 18°C (65°F), while Caracas enjoys a temperate climate ranging from 18°C to 21°C (65° to 70° F).

COMMUNICATION AND MEDIA

TELEPHONES

Venezuela's country code is 58. The city code for Caracas is (02), or just (2) when calling from abroad. Most numbers in Caracas are seven-digit, though you might come across some older six-digit numbers. Elsewhere, you'll find six-digit numbers and older five-digit ones. If in doubt, call ((02) 531-0333 to check a number automatically. Dial (100 for the operator in Caracas, (101 in the rest of the country, (122 for the international operator, and (113 for Directory Assistance (a very busy line).

The largest telephone company is CANTV. Upon arrival, purchase one of their *tarjeta telefónicas* prepaid phone cards for Bs2,000 or Bs5,000. Public phones have improved over the years, but head to a hotel lobby for the phones in best conditions. Some public phones carry a symbol at the top of the unit marked "International Access/Acceso Internacional" which means you can make international calls. Calling abroad is expensive in Venezuela. Have several phone cards ready if you're dialing from a street phone. When the first card runs out, press #, and insert the new one. It's easier to go to a CANTV office, called *Centros de Telecomunicaciones*, where you can also send and receive faxes.

It's cheaper to dial abroad by dialing an operator in your home country and asking them to put through a collect call. Ask your caller to return the call. To get through to an international operator dial (800-11-*your country code*-0. For the United States, dial (800-11-1-20 or 800-11-1-21, and ask for the company you wish to use (e.g. AT&T or Sprint). For Canada, dial (800-11-10-0.

You'll soon notice that Venezuelans are cell phone crazy. The country has one of the highest per capita ownership of portable phones in Latin America. There are two main companies, Movilnet prefix (016), and Telcel prefix (014). You will find many numbers in this book with these prefixes, since many *posadas* and lodges use cell phones while they await landline connections. They are expensive to call from a public phone, so avoid them if you can, or have plenty of units on your

card before you dial. To rent a cell phone, contact **Organización Rent-a-Phone** ((02) 503-4329 FAX (02) 574-6774 E-MAIL rapcb@telcel.net.ve, in the Caracas Hilton.

THE INTERNET

You'll find many hotel and tour operator listings in this book come with e-mail and web site addresses. Since the postal service is dismal, using e-mail to book rooms or trips from abroad makes a lot of sense. You'll find cybercafés in most tourist towns (a list is available at WEB SITE http://netcafeguide.com/venezuela.html), or else seek out a tour operator willing to let you use their

computers after hours. Some cafés, such as those in Mérida, are excellent, while others, mainly due to bad connections, can be frustrating for the traveler short on time.

MAIL

Postal service in Venezuela is pretty abysmal, and you should never rely on it for booking hotels or tours. Some businesses have postal boxes in Miami, but delays are still common. In general, letters to Europe or North America shouldn't take more than three weeks. Post offices are called *correos*, and are run by the state Ipostel company. Offices are usually open from 8 AM to noon and 2 PM to 6 PM, Monday to Friday. Ipostel offer national and

Encouraging conscientious tourism at the Gran Sabana's Salto Kawi. One sign reads "Hear the sound of Nature."

international express services. **DHL** TOLL-FREE (800) 34592 WEB SITE www.dhl.com, with an office in the Caracas Hilton, are reliable, but expensive.

NEWSPAPERS AND MAGAZINES

Venezuela's two largest papers are *El Nacional* WEB SITE www.el-nacional.com and *El Universal* WEB SITE www.el-universal.com. The latter is the more conservative of the two, but both offer excellent coverage of national and international news. The weekend sections of *El Nacional* are particularly good for entertainment, restaurant and travel listings and news, while *El Universal*'s Friday entertainment supplement *Brújula* is also very useful.

However, it's usually best for tourists to begin by using *usted*, changing to *tú* once the other person has begun to employ it. In general, you should always address a member of the police or armed forces, or a person in authority, as *usted*.

Such is Venezuelan informality that you might find yourself being addressed as *mi amor* (my love) when you've only just met someone. Although Venezuelans don't stand on ceremony, social graces are important. They are keen on their greetings, so always enter an office, elevator or hotel by saying "con permiso" (with permission), or by greeting "buenos días" or "buenas tardes" (good morning and good afternoon). This is usually cut short to "buenas." Venezuelans aren't shy of

The only English-language newspaper is *The Daily Journal*, primarily aimed at the expat business community. It provides listings of cinema and gallery events, with good coverage of United States sports news, and some travel articles. Look out for the Monday "Week in Review" section. You can usually find major United States newspapers at luxury hotels in Caracas, but they're rare outside the capital. *Escape*, a monthly bilingual magazine, covers world travel and many Venezuelan destinations. *Entonces* is similar and is published quarterly.

ETIQUETTE

The Venezuela character is generally laid-back and friendly. Most people employ the *"tú"* form of address (the familiar "you"), as opposed to the more polite *"usted"* used on the Spanish mainland.

confrontation or argument, but as a rule, foreign tourists should be as polite and diplomatic as possible, seeking to limit criticism, which officials often take personally. Failing to give someone due respect (*falta de respeto*) is one of the worst insults to a Venezuelan.

Topless sunbathing is rare except on some beaches on Margarita and in Mochima National Park. In general, Venezuelan men don't ever wear shorts in cities—only long pants, and you should follow their example.

HEALTH AND EMERGENCIES

EMERGENCY PHONE NUMBERS

In the case of an emergency, dial (171, nationwide. The operator will put you through to the relevant service.

Policía de Tránsito ℂ 167.
In Caracas, **police ℂ 169**, **fire ℂ 166**, **ambulance** center ℂ (02) 545-4545 or east ℂ (02) 265-0251.

HEALTH CONCERNS

Venezuela has a good reputation for health care standards. Private clinic facilities are among the best in Latin America. Before traveling however, you should check with your local doctor or travel clinic about your immunization status and their recommendations. It's a good idea to have immunizations against typhoid, tetanus, diphtheria, polio, and yellow fever. Rabies and hepatitis A are optional. If you intend to travel to the Orinoco

regions of the Delta, Guayana and Amazonas, you should follow a course of anti-malaria drugs. On the Internet, find out more at WEB SITE www.cdc.gov.

The biggest risk to the traveler unaccustomed to tropical heat is dehydration and heat stroke. Always carry plenty of water with you. Gatorade is widely available, if expensive, in Venezuela, and I suggest you drink lots of it.

If you fall foul with diarrhea, buy sachets of oral rehydration salts as soon as possible, and drink lots of clear fluids. If you can't find sachets (it's a good idea to pack them), any mixture of salt and sugar will benefit your body. If you can manage to eat, stick to a bland, carbohydrate-high diet, and avoid greasy foods.

It's wise to avoid insect bites throughout your travels, and not just for malaria. Wear loose, 100% cotton clothes, with long-sleeved shirts, and pants

you can tuck in. Carry a DEET-based repellent at all times, and either bring a permethrin-impregnated bed net with you, or a permethrin spray to apply to nets supplied. Always treat scratches and minor wounds promptly with disinfectant (strong alcohol or iodine). To avoid terrible itching from chiggers, buy some sulfur powder, place it in a sock, tie the neck, and douse your clothes with this powder every morning. Tuck pants inside your socks. For itches from mites, carry calamine lotion with you (some people swear by nail-polish remover for chigger itches), and cream such as Canesten (clotrimazole) for fungal infections. To avoid sunburn, use a high-factor sunscreen, be very wary of sun reflected off water, and snorkel with a T-shirt on. HIV and AIDS (*SIDA*) is not uncommon in Venezuela, so bring condoms with you, they're superior to the ones on sale in the country.

For serious medical problems consult your embassy about doctors and hospitals. If you have insurance, book into a private clinic. One of the best is **Clínica El Ávila ℂ** (02) 208-1001, Avenida San Juan Bosco con 6a Transversal, Altamira. Clinics can also provide vaccinations.

TOILETS

Public toilets, particularly in gas stations, leave plenty to be desired in Venezuela. I trained myself to inhale deeply *before* entering them. If you can, ask to use the toilet of a restaurant, and buy a soft drink if they put up a fuss. Always have toilet paper or tissues with you. Plumbing tubes are narrow and water pressure is often low in Venezuela. Many toilets have a wastepaper basket where you deposit your toilet paper. Flushing it often blocks the pipes. Toilets are *baños*.

SAFETY AND SECURITY

Unfortunately, with the last decade of economic strife in Venezuela, robbery of tourists is more common than ever. Though stories are often exaggerated — for example, the homicide rate in Caracas is very high, but virtually never involves tourists — you should exercise the same caution as you would in any major city, if not more. Away from Caracas, safety levels are much better.

In general, use your common sense: don't wear expensive jewelry or flash your money, and keep your money in a money belt (even better are belts which tie across the biceps or thigh). Carry enough money for taxis, etc. in your pocket, and avoid reaching into your money belt in public. Only take the money you need for that day out with you in the morning. Bypass deserted or dark streets, and always ask the advice of locals about safety. If you

OPPOSITE: A girl makes new friends. ABOVE: How much for the chicken?

are held up, don't resist. More often than not, your assailants will be young and desperate.

Photocopy all your documents, and try to keep them separate from your person. Use hotel safes where possible, insisting on a receipt for anything you hand over. Keep an emergency CANTV phone card on you. On a slip inside your passport, write "en caso de emergencia, llamar a:" and insert the details of at least one of your relatives or friends to be contacted in case of an accident. Include your blood type (*tipo de sangre*), and any allergies (*alergias*) you might have.

If traveling by car, either leave your valuables at the hotel, or stash them in the car's trunk — although that's not a guarantee. Don't leave any-

thing out. Park your car in secure off-road parking lots in cities, never on the street.

If you fancy doing drugs on your vacation, might I suggest you tour the inside of a Venezuelan prison before you decide to. About half of Venezuela's prison population haven't even been tried, and can wait *years* to be sentenced. You'll be joining them.

WHEN TO GO

Venezuela doesn't have an official international tourist high season—although you will probably see more foreign travelers during the northern hemisphere winter, or during summer vacation periods. National holidays dictate high seasons in the country. These periods (Carnival, New Year, Christmas and Easter Week) are a double-edged sword for travelers from abroad. On the upside,

you'll encounter more festivities and local color over holiday periods. On the downside, hotels get booked up, buses are crammed, road accidents soar (everyone drinks and drives), and all beaches and sights teem. If you do come at these times, it's a good idea to make your reservations as far as possible in advance.

Arguably the best time to visit for the best views and driest trails is the dry season: from November or December through to April or May. Rainfall in many coastal regions (e.g. Falcón, Margarita, Sucre and Anzoátegui) varies little between seasons, so if you're planning a beach vacation, don't worry too much about when you visit.

In other parts of the country, the seasons are more marked. In the Andes, for instance, cloud and rains affect views and walking, and make climbing or hiking more perilous. In the Llanos, arguably both seasons are just as fascinating, and totally different. The mid-dry season is probably the best time to visit for ease of access and concentration of wildlife. South of the Orinoco you will encounter rain all year-round, but less in the dry season. If you're considering traveling to Angel Falls, the season will affect how you get there. If you plan to take the river trip from Canaima village, you will need to come in the rainy season when rivers are high enough to carry boats. At other times you can only enjoy the fly-by in a small plane.

WHAT TO TAKE

You're best off coming prepared, since most goods or toiletries in Venezuela are either imported or of questionable quality. Still, whatever you do forget, you can probably buy once you arrive. Bring lightweight, preferably cotton clothing, long pants, long-sleeved shirts, shorts and skirts. Avoid scruffy or old clothes, since they're frowned upon by fashion-conscious Venezuelans. Even if you're not planning to head up to the Andes, bring a sweater for the air-conditioned buses. Bring an old pair of sneakers to avoid corals or urchins on beaches; good, waterproof walking boots; and flip-flops or sandals for jiggers (*niguas*) on beaches and unhygienic showers in cheap hotels. Don't forget your flashlight, sun hat, sunscreen, and knick-knacks or souvenirs from your country to give as gifts.

A breathable, waterproof poncho is essential if you're coming in the rainy season, or venturing south of the Orinoco. A small umbrella might also come in handy. You might also consider bringing a mask and snorkel to save on rental charges on the coast. Stock up on medical supplies, although pharmacies are ubiquitous, and you can usually find what you need. Camping gear is generally expensive, so if you intend to do a lot of camping out, come prepared. The Camping Gaz Bluet is the most popular model of gas. If you plan to do a lot of hiking, bring gaiters.

PHOTOGRAPHY

Humidity, dust, sand and water are the greatest enemies of photographic equipment. Sealable plastic bags and sachets of silica gel are your best protection. In general, avoid conspicuous camera bags that will attract attention (roll them around in the mud a bit before you come). I usually carry my camera bag inside an innocuous-looking one, and wander city streets with my camera wrapped in a magazine. You might consider bringing a disposable waterproof camera for river-trips and

widely spoken, you'll find more English-speakers in Venezuela than say, in Colombia or Ecuador. Fortunately, due to the pervasive influence of American English in day-to-day Venezuelan life, you also find many more familiar words than in other parts of the continent, e.g. *lunchería* for a modest restaurant. As in any country, locals appreciate your efforts to learn their language, and you should listen for the typical greetings and farewells they employ.

Venezuelan Spanish is fast and furious, and often omits some endings, particularly plurals. You end up with people saying *"pa' na'"* for *"para nada"* (for nothing), or *"¿ere' ingle'?"* for *"¿eres inglés?"* (are you English?). It's not the best country if you

very wet conditions, or you can buy "canoe bags" that will seal your camera completely underwater.

If you have a 35mm SLR camera, a UV filter and a polarizing filter are absolutely essential. Bring fast film (200 or 400 ASA) for low light conditions in forests, churches and dawn or dusk shots. You might also want to invest in a large zoom lens (with macro capabilities) for capturing wildlife and for more discreet portraiture. In general, film is widely available in Venezuela, but it's always best to bring your own — particularly if you take slides. For developing, I would suggest you wait until you get back home to avoid any disasters.

LANGUAGE BASICS

Your experience of Venezuela will be immeasurably enhanced if you learn some Latin American Spanish before you arrive. Although English isn't

intend to start from scratch. Only in the Andes do people slow their diction somewhat, whereas in Maracaibo you'll be lucky to catch a word.

"VENEZUELANISMS"

Venezuelan Spanish is probably the most vulgar in Latin America, peppered with swear words — a shock to many visitors accustomed to more polite countries. Not so vulgar, and often hilarious, is Venezuelans' tendency to become very familiar very quickly. Everyone is a *primo* (cousin), *pana* (buddy), *gordo* or *flaco* (fatty or skinny-ribs). From there, you can be greeted as *mi amor, mi cielo, mi rey / reina* (my love, my heaven, my king / queen).

OPPOSITE: The gruesome devil dancing masks of San Francisco de Yare. ABOVE: Musicians hit the streets for San Benito festivities in Mucuchache, Mérida State.

Nor are Venezuelans particularly politically correct, and you might have to get used to being called a *gringo/a* or *catirre/a* (light-eyed or blond). Conversely, Venezuelans are very keen on their official titles, whereby someone with just a university degree is often referred to a *licienciado/a*, and poets, artists or musicians as *maestro/a*. If you want to engage an older man or woman in conversation, and don't know their names, use *don* or *doña*.

Among unique Venezuelan words you will hear often, *chévere* means fine or great. It's the usual reply when people ask how you are. Popular greetings include *¿Qué más? ¿Qué pasó?* or *¿Qué hubó?* Another particular word is *la vaina*, meaning "the thing," and applied to just about everything you can think of. Venezuelans are also very fond of their diminutives. Sometimes it feels like all words are *-ito/a* this or *-ico/a* that. Examples include *un cafecito* (a coffee), *ahorita* (now, soon), *un carrito* (a bus) and *un ratico* (a while).

VOWELS

Vowels are pronounced very "purely" as short phonetic sounds, not the diphthong drawn out version that we mostly use in English:

a   as in apple
e   as in bet
i   as in "ee" in seek
o   as in occupy
u   as in full
y   is considered a vowel when it stands alone or appears at the end of a word. When alone it means "and" and is pronounced like our name for the letter E.

CONSONANTS

Consonants are pronounced as follows:
b and v   almost interchangeable. Both sound like an English b. In writing, b may replace what would be a v in English: like *sabana* for savanna.
c   sibilant, like the s in "sea," but hard like a k before an a, o or u
ch   plosive, as in "church."
-ción   this very common ending (as in *nación*) is pronounced "sion," not the English "shun" sound of "nation" or "station".
d   hard, as in "dog."
g   its pronunciation depends on the letters that follow. Before e and i it is guttural, like a strongly aspirated h in "hat", but is hard as in "go" before a, o or u. The exception is that when followed by ü or ua (e.g. *guava*) it becomes like the English w.
h   always silent.
j   a guttural aspirated "h" sound. *Jugo*, meaning juice, sounds like "Hoogo."
ll   pronounced like the y in "yellow."
ñ   like the "ny" of "canyon."

q   always pronounced like the English k, unless in an English or Latin word, as in *quórum*.
r   rolled, double "rr" even more so.
z   like the ss in "bass."

COMMON EXPRESSIONS

Hello   *Hola*. Hello on the phone *¿Alo?*
Pleased to meet you   *Encantado/a* or *mucho gusto*
Good morning   *Buenos días*
Good afternoon   *Buenas tardes*
Good evening   *Buenas noches*
Good-bye   *Adiós* or *ciao*
See you later   *Hasta luego*
Yes   *Sí*

No   *No*
Please   *Por favor*
Thank you   *Gracias*
You're welcome   *De nada*
Come in   *Adelante* or *Pase*
Just a minute   *Un momento*
My name is…   *Mi nombre es…* or *Me llamo…*
What is your name?   *¿Cómo se llama usted?*
How are you?   *¿Cómo está?* or *¿Qué tal?*
Fine, and you?   *Bien, ¿y usted?*
I don't understand   *No entiendo*
Do you speak English   *¿Habla usted inglés?*
I don't speak Spanish   *No hablo español*
Pardon, excuse me (apologizing)   *Perdón*
Excuse me (to pass someone)   *Con permiso*
Can you help me?   *¿Me puede ayudar?*
Where is…?   *¿Dónde está…?*
What is…?   *¿Qué es…?*
I want/need…   *Quiero…Necesito…*

I want to rent a car   *Quiero alquilar un carro*
Driver's license   *Permiso de conducir*
Do you have any…?   *¿Tiene…?*
How much is…?   *¿Cuánto cuesta…?*
The check please   *La cuenta por favor*
The restroom, please?   *¿Los baños, por favor?*
When the bus leave?   *¿A qué hora sale el bus?*
I do not feel well   *No me siento bien*
I need a doctor   *Necesito un médico*
Help!   *¡Socorro!*

far   *lejos*
left/right   *izquierda/derecha*
straight   *derecho* go straight on, *sigue derecho*
at the corner   *en la esquina*
at the back of   *al fondo*
before   *antes*
in front of   *delante de*
behind   *atrás*
between   *entre*
next   *próximo/próxima*

TIME

What time is it?   *¿Qué hora es?* or *¿Qué hora tiene?*
It's eleven o'clock   *Son las once*

PLACES

money exchange   *casa de cambio*
airport   *aeropuerto*

In the morning   *Por la mañana*
This afternoon   *esta tarde*
This evening   *esta tarde/noche* (really late)
Night   *la noche*
Today   *hoy*
Yesterday   *ayer*
Tomorrow   *mañana*
Week   *la semana*, next week *la semana que viene*
Month   *el mes*, last month *el mes pasado*
Early   *temprano*, too early *demasiado temprano*
Late   *tarde*
Before   *antes de…*
After   *después de…*

bus station   *terminal de pasajeros*
bus   *autobus* (slang for small buses: *carrito*, *micro*)
ticket office   *taquilla*
post office   *correos*
gas (petrol) station   *bomba*
hospital   *hospital*
bathroom, rest room   *baños*

AT THE HOTEL

room   *habitación*
quiet   *tranquilo*
with bathroom   *con baño*
bed   *cama*
key   *llave*

DIRECTIONS

here   *aquí*
there   *allí/allá*
near   *cerca*

Caribbean color on Adícora's main street,
Península de Paraguaná.

front desk   *recepción*
soap   *jabón*
towel   *toalla*
toilet paper   *papel higiénico*
purified water   *agua purificada*
hot   *caliente*
cold   *frío*
sheet   *sábana*
blanket   *manta*
pillow   *almohada*
what does it cost?   *¿cuánto cuesta?*
per night   *por noche*
we're leaving tomorrow   *nos vamos mañana*
bill   *la cuenta*
credit card   *tarjeta de crédito*

small   *pequeño*
soda water   *refresco*
mineral water   *agua mineral*
bill   *la cuenta*
change   *el cambio*
thanks a lot   *muchas gracias*

WEB SITES

Venezuela now boasts many good portal sites where you can search for all sorts of things and find plenty of information. Try www.auyantepui .com and www.chevere.com. At www.geocities .com/~venaventura/links.html, you'll find links to sites on Venezuelan regions. For all things to

IN THE RESTAURANT

waiter   *camarero*
waitress   *camarera*
breakfast   *desayuno*
lunch   *almuerzo*
dinner   *cena*
table   *mesa*
bread   *pan*
butter   *mantequilla*
tea   *té*
coffee   *café*
milk   *leche*
not too much   *no demasiado*
a little, please   *un poco, por favor*
ice   *hielo*
without ice   *sin hielo*
beer   *cerveza*
big/large   *grande*

do with the Gran Sabana, see www.thelostworld .org, and www.venezuelavoyage.com for images and writing. Venezuela Virtual, www.venezuela virtual.com, is also helpful.

A very good, English-language source of travel information (lodging, tour operators, car rental agencies) is Think Venezuela at www.think-venezuela.net, which includes a bulletin board. For more information on Latin American ecotravel, don't miss the excellent Planeta site, www.planeta .com, while for trip reports, books and information, see the South American Explorers site www.samexplo.org.

Recommended Reading

Books published in Venezuela listed below can be ordered online from Tecni-Cienca Libros WEB SITE www.tecnicienca.com.

CONAN DOYLE, ARTHUR. *The Lost World*. 1912; London: Puffin Books, 1995. Great adventure yarn based on Roraima Tepuy in the Gran Sabana. Essential reading for anyone heading to the region, aged eight or eighty-eight.

EWELL, JUDITH. *Venezuela, a Century of Change*. London: C Hurst & Co, 1984. Regarded as the best history of Venezuela in the twentieth century.

GALLEGOS, RÓMULO. Regarded as Venezuela's finest writer, his novel *Doña Bárbara* (New York: Continental Book Company, 1998) is set in the Llanos, and will enrich any stay in the region, while *Canaima* (Pittsburgh: University of Pittsburgh Press, 1996) makes for a fascinating account of the lives of gold miners in the Guayanas.

HUMBOLDT, ALEXANDER VON. *Personal Narrative of Travels in the Equinoctial Regions of America 1799–1801*. 1852; New York: Penguin, 1996 (paperback). Get volume two for Humboldt's marvelous descriptions of the Venezuelan regions he traveled.

KLINE, ELIZABETH. *Guide to Camps, Posadas and Cabins in Venezuela*. Published yearly in Caracas, and available widely. Kline describes every last *posada* and place to stay in every last corner of the country.

NICHOLL, CHARLES. *The Creature in the Map*. London: Jonathan Cape, 1995. Blends historical background about Sir Walter Raleigh's expedition up the Orinoco in 1595, with a modern-day expedition to the Delta and the Guayana Highlands.

GARCÍA MÁRQUEZ, GABRIEL. *The General in his Labyrinth*. 1989. London: Jonathan Cape, 1991. Remarkable account of Simón Bolívar's last days, weaving both historical fact and magical narrative as the general reminisces about his life, loves, glories and failures.

GARMENDIA, JULIO. Garmendia is my favorite Venezuelan short story writer, with numerous collections published in Spanish only, of which *Manzanita* (Caracas: Monte Ávila Editores, 1997) is perhaps the best.

GOTT, RICHARD. *In the Shadow of the Liberator*. London: Verso, 2000. The first comprehensive analysis of Hugo Chávez's first years in power, it also includes historical and political background.

HUDSON, WILLIAM HENRY. *Green Mansions*. 1904; Oxford: Oxford University Press, 1998. Evocative and romantic travelogue through the Orinoco. Great descriptions of the rainforest, and its mysteries.

O'HANLON, REDMOND. *In Trouble Again*. 1988; Penguin Books, 1989. An eloquent blend of erudition and hilarity as O'Hanlon journeys up the Orinoco in search of the Yanomami. Essential reading for any jungle trip.

USLAR PIETRI, ARTURO. *Cuarenta Ensayos*. Caracas: Monte Avila, 1990. Insightful essays on Venezuela's history, literature, culture and politics, from one of the country's foremost intellectuals.

WILSON, JASON. *South and Central America Including Mexico (Traveller's Literary Companion)*. 1993; London: Passport Books, 1995. A great collection of writing from the continent, which includes extracts from works by many Latin American and foreign writers, with a useful bibliography.

OPPOSITE: Tilled fields and white farms in the Andes. ABOVE: The striking features of Guajiro Indians from Zulia State.

Quick Reference A–Z Guide
to Places and Topics of Interest with Listed Accommodation, Restaurants and Useful Telephone Numbers

The symbols Ⓕ FAX, Ⓣ TOLL-FREE, Ⓔ E-MAIL, Ⓦ WEB-SITE refer to additional contact information found in the chapter listings.

Photo Credits

All pictures were taken by Anthony Cassidy, with the exception of the following:

Raúl Sojo: Pages 6 *left*, 12, 23, 36, 37, 40, 44, 67, 68, 92, 93, 94, 95, 97, 102, 107, 109, 111, 113, 117, 150, 160, 176, 182, 187, 193, 196, 197, 211, 214, 216, 219, 221, 230, 233, 237, 245, and 265, back cover *top*.

Dominic Hamilton: Pages 28, 39, 69, 184, 191, 195, 199, 203, 205, 207, 209, and 213, back cover *second from top*.